Religious Change and Continuity

Sociological Perspectives

Harry M. Johnson

Editor

Religious Change
and Continuity

 Jossey-Bass Publishers

San Francisco • Washington • London • 1979

RELIGIOUS CHANGE AND CONTINUITY
Sociological Perspectives
        by Harry M. Johnson

Religious Change and Continuity, edited by Harry M. Johnson, is a special double issue of *Sociological Inquiry* (Volume 49, Nos. 2–3, 1979), journal of the National Sociology Honor Society, a quarterly publication of the United Chapters of Alpha Kappa Delta.

Library of Congress Catalogue Card Number LC 79-83574

International Standard Book Number ISBN 0-87589-408-9

Manufactured in the United States of America

JACKET DESIGN BY MATHY GRAPHIC, LIÈGE

FIRST EDITION

Code 7914

*The Jossey-Bass
Social and
Behavioral Science Series*

Preface

Religious Change and Continuity offers sociologists and interested laypersons an assessment of the religious situation of American society, viewed in a temporal and a broad comparative perspective. Indeed, so many of the basic themes of the sociology of religion are discussed that the book might serve as an introduction to that discipline. Among these themes, for example, are religion as a cause of social change and as an obstacle to it, religious evolution, and secularization. Religious symbolism shapes the basic attitudes of everyone—even of people who think they have outgrown or repudiated it. This book shows the importance of religion for economic and political activity, the roles of the sexes, and the sources of self-esteem.

Part One provides theoretical perspectives. By taking Max Weber's famous essay on religious rejections of the "world" as one of his most important points of departure, Talcott Parsons, in Chapter One, analyzes the ambivalence of Christianity toward sex, the intellect, and, especially, things economic. He shows how this ambivalence has resulted in three principal manifestations: an extreme negative attitude toward the rational pursuit of economic self-interest; an exaggerated estimate of the positive significance of "selfish" economic calculation; and a qualified acceptance of economic, sexual, and intellectual activity, an acceptance in tension with recognition of the "dangers" inherent in all three. He traces the resemblances between Christian symbolism and the symbolic structure of Marxism. Finally, he places in clear religious perspective the institutionalized individualism of the West, which is the subject of a tremendous amount of distorted ideology. Not only is Parsons' analysis of the structure of Christian and Marxist symbolism more detailed than that of most other authors, but he perceives in Marxism a quasi-religious rejection of the pursuit of economic self-interest. In Marxism, however, this ambivalence takes a somewhat disguised form, as it would almost have to, considering the Reformation, which gave relative and conditional legitimation to acceptance of this world. We might say, I think, that the vision of communism pictures the ideal community as innerworldly and "materialistic" but also as noneconomic in the sense that economic "exploitation" and the "selfish" pursuit of economic interest would in principle be excluded.[1]

Louis Schneider, in Chapter Two, also deals with religious ambivalence toward the world but in a different way. He explores dialectical processes in religion, and his comments on historical examples of antinomianism help to illuminate similar phenomena today. Although his perspective is not necessarily incompatible with evolutionary theory, it does tend to focus on the perennial simultaneous presence of similar motifs in religions, motifs that may shift from one extreme to another but that virtually imply each other. Schneider's essay ties in with Parsons' in that it also shows the very common concern of religion with sex and, more generally, with the world.

Making use of his almost Weberian range of learning, Vatro Murvar, in Chapter Three, analyzes relations between religion and the state. In his estimation, religious forces have often been per-

---

[1]For an extended analysis not only of Marx's views on religion but also of others' comments and revisions, see N. Birnbaum, "Beyond Marx in the Sociology of Religion?" in *Beyond the Classics: Essays in the Scientific Study of Religion,* edited by C. Y. Glock and P. E. Hammond (New York: Harper & Row, 1973), pp. 3–70.

verted or shackled, but religion has also been able, at times, to inspire radical social change.

Eli Sagan, in Chapter Four, compares religion and magic from a psychological point of view. His chapter is similar to the first three chapters in Part One because it draws upon a broad range of historical and comparative knowledge. Sagan's analysis is somewhat unusual for its evolutionary perspective, which the reader may compare with the views of Parsons and Bellah and which I discuss briefly in the last chapter.

Part Two presents historical examples. David L. Petersen, in Chapter Five, reexamines Max Weber's sociological analysis of Judaism and ancient Hebrew society in the light of more recent Biblical scholarship. Weber holds up remarkably well. This chapter deals with one of the most profound religious changes in the history of the world: the prophetic movement and the development of genuine monotheism.

Charles L. Bosk, dealing with Hasidism in Chapter Six, provides us with an example of the fact that change is normal in the history of every religion. Whereas God in prophetic Judaism is supramundane, in Hasidism God is partly immanent in the world and partly feminine as well as masculine. Bosk shows that Weber perhaps neglected one possibility for charisma, namely, the possibility that charismatic leadership itself may become institutionalized without ceasing to be charismatic. This chapter will find a special place in the casebook of sociologists of religion.

Ronald Ye-lin Cheng's comparison of the Meiji restoration and the Chinese Revolution of 1911, in Chapter Seven, shows that religion may either help or hinder in a process of "modernization." This variance is one of the most important themes in the more recent sociology of religion. Simplifying his complex analysis, one may say that Cheng shows how religion helped in Japan and hindered in China (before Maoism).

Victor M. Lidz, in Chapter Eight, deals with another of the basic themes of the sociology of religion: the nature and importance of secularization. He shows that the Enlightenment emancipated the functional problem of legitimation from specifically religious sources without radically eliminating the need for religion. One of his points is that Enlightenment values cause less conflict in countries in which inner-worldly asceticism on an explicitly religious basis had already taken hold.

Part Three, dealing with the immediate present and the future, is necessarily the most controversial section of the book. Marie Augusta Neal, in Chapter Nine, analyzes the sexism in Judeo-Christian religious symbolism and foresees even greater turmoil for the Catholic Church and for the rest of Christianity and Judaism unless and until the sexism in both symbolism and religious organization is eliminated. Neal's essay, I believe, raises profound questions about the future.

In Chapter Ten, William C. Shepherd suggests that many people in the United States have drifted into a polymorphous kind of religiosity, a congeries of eclectic orientations, and seem not to be greatly worried about any overall pattern integrity in their varying personal portfolios. This admittedly tentative essay is lively and provocative.

Whereas Shepherd emphasizes a drift toward what he calls "inclusivism," Daniel A. Foss and Ralph W. Larkin, in Chapter Eleven, say that in the 1970s we have exactly the opposite, a tendency toward a jealous exclusivism. They review studies of four different types of religious or quasi-religious movements and maintain that all four are expressions of disillusionment, reactions to the failure of the confrontation, protest, and wide-open pleasure seeking of the hippies and activists of the 1960s. Both Shepherd and Foss and Larkin suggest in passing that there are some wily types around exploiting anxieties.

In Chapter Twelve, Steven M. Tipton presents a sympathetic analysis of a small number of American Zen Buddhists. He suggests that their religious orientation may spread undramatically into American utilitarian-Christian society, gradually transforming it into something less hectic and at once less individualistic and less "oppressive."

In Chapter Thirteen, I attempt to connect the essays more explicitly with one another and offer a few judgments on controversies. An important unifying theme is religious evolution.

Urbana, Illinois
April 1979

Harry M. Johnson

Contents

xiii

Contents

Contributors

HARRY M. JOHNSON is professor of sociology at the University of Illinois, Urbana-Champaign, and editor of *Sociological Inquiry*. He has taught at Simmons College (1942–1963) and the Massachusetts College of Art (1945–1955). In addition, he has been a visiting professor during summers at the Salzburg Seminar for American Studies (1961); the Heimvolkshochschule, Falkenstein (1962); Columbia University (1964); and the University of Munich (1970).

At Harvard University, Johnson earned his bachelor's degree (1939) in English literature, master's degree (1942) in sociology, and doctor's degree (1949) in sociology.

Johnson served as associate editor of the *American Sociological Review* (1964–1965). He has written articles on ethnic relations, religion, the mass media, and the theory of Talcott Parsons, and is the author of *Sociology: A Systematic Introduction* (1960) and editor of *Social System and Legal Process* (1978). He is currently completing a book on ethnicity and sociological theory.

CHARLES L. BOSK is assistant professor of sociology at the University of Pennsylvania. His major area of specialization is the sociology of medicine, and he is currently working on a study of the social psychology of genetic counseling. He is the author of *Forgive and Remember: Managing Medical Failure* (1977).

RONALD YE-LIN CHENG is assistant professor of sociology at the University of Colorado, Boulder. His special fields are historical-comparative sociology, social change, and the sociology of revolution. He is author of *The First Revolution in China: A Theory* (1973) and editor of *The Sociology of Revolution* (1973). Having become increasingly interested in the sociology of religion, he is completing a year as a Postdoctoral Fellow at the Fuller Theological Seminary.

DANIEL A. FOSS, formerly assistant professor of sociology at Rutgers, the State University at Newark, New Jersey, is the author of several papers in the sociology of religion and is especially concerned with new religious movements.

RALPH W. LARKIN is assistant professor of sociology at Rutgers, the State University at Newark, New Jersey. His research interests include youth, social movements, and socialization and education. He has published many articles and has a book in press on suburban youth in cultural crisis.

VICTOR M. LIDZ, assistant professor of sociology at the University of Pennsylvania, specializes in the general theory of action. He is co-editor (with Talcott Parsons) of *Readings on Premodern Societies* (1972) and (with Jan J. Loubser, Rainer C. Baum, and Andrew Effrat) of *Explorations in General Theory in Social Science* (2 volumes, 1976).

VATRO MURVAR is professor of sociology at the University of Wisconsin, Milwaukee. He has been steadily expanding Weberian sociology in a long series of articles on religious movements and, more generally, the relations between religion and government.

Marie Augusta Neal is professor of sociology at Emmanuel College, Boston. Her main interest is the sociology of religion and social change, and she is past president (1972) of the Association for the Sociology of Religion. She is the author of *Values and Interests in Social Change* (1965) and *A Sociotheology of Letting Go: A First-World Church Facing Third-World People* (1977).

Talcott Parsons, professor emeritus of sociology at Harvard University, has for many years been the dean of sociological theorists. His numerous books and articles range from *The Structure of Social Action* (1937) to *Social Systems and the Evolution of Action Theory* (1977) and *Action and the Human Condition* (1978) to a volume of essays on the human condition paradigm (in preparation).

David L. Petersen is associate professor of religious studies at the University of Illinois, Urbana-Champaign. He is the author of *Late Israelite Prophecy* (1977), and in 1977–1978 he was Fulbright senior lecturer in Hebrew Bible Studies at the University of Aarhus (Denmark).

Eli Sagan is the author of *Cannibalism: Human Aggression and Cultural Form* (1974) and *The Lust to Annihilate: Violence in Greek Culture* (in press). He is presently working on a volume tentatively titled *The Origin of Tyranny and the State: Ancient Buganda and Polynesia*.

Louis Schneider is professor of sociology at the University of Texas, Austin. He has written, coauthored, edited, and contributed to many books, among them *Popular Religion* (with S. M. Dornbusch, 1958), *The Sociological Approach to Religion* (1975), and *The Idea of Culture in the Social Sciences* (edited with C. M. Bonjean, 1977). He is currently preparing a book on Bernard Mandeville.

William C. Shepherd is associate professor of religious studies at the University of Montana and book review editor of the

Journal of the American Academy of Religion. His publications include *Man's Condition* (1969) and *Symbolical Consciousness* (1976). He was a Rockefeller Foundation Humanities Fellow in the academic year 1975–1976.

STEVEN M. TIPTON, research fellow at the Harvard Divinity School, is completing his requirements for the joint degree program in sociology and religion. He is currently preparing an article on American Zen Buddhism for a book tentatively titled *Getting Saved from the Sixties: The Transformation of Moral Meaning in American Culture.*

As this book went to press, the editor learned that Louis Schneider died suddenly on March 17, 1979.

Religious Change and Continuity

Sociological Perspectives

1 *Talcott Parsons*

Religious and Economic Symbolism in the Western World

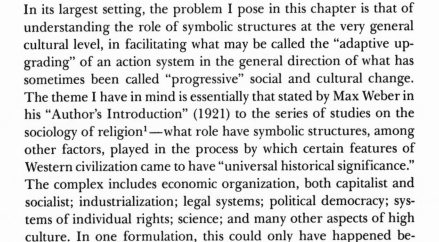

In its largest setting, the problem I pose in this chapter is that of understanding the role of symbolic structures at the very general cultural level, in facilitating what may be called the "adaptive upgrading" of an action system in the general direction of what has sometimes been called "progressive" social and cultural change. The theme I have in mind is essentially that stated by Max Weber in his "Author's Introduction" (1921) to the series of studies on the sociology of religion[1]—what role have symbolic structures, among other factors, played in the process by which certain features of Western civilization came to have "universal historical significance." The complex includes economic organization, both capitalist and socialist; industrialization; legal systems; political democracy; systems of individual rights; science; and many other aspects of high culture. In one formulation, this could only have happened because the religious conception of "Christian society" became drastically "secularized."

In this chapter, I start with a review of what we seem to know about the relevance of the framework of symbolic organization I

1

refer to as that of "age and sex" in the general religious scheme of things. In a later main section, I go on to a consideration of another framework of symbolic themes, those having to do with "things economic." My thesis is that there is both a certain parallelism in the significance of these two symbolic complexes and a set of genetic connections. However, in cultural and intellectual theory, they have tended to be treated as belonging to such radically different categories that their isomorphic features and other relations have largely escaped attention.

It will perhaps help the reader to follow my rather complex argument if I baldly state at the beginning my basic theses, ignoring subsidiary points.

1. Christianity has been conducive to the facilitation of evolutionary contributions because of its ambivalence toward "the world"; that is, essentially toward the erotic, toward the intellect, and toward wealth and things economic. Ambivalence is important as compared to simple acceptance because, although the erotic, the intellect, and the production of wealth are all indispensable, they all also involve dangers. Being ambivalent, Christianity recognized the dangers—often overplaying them—but did not simply reject or, better, did not renounce these potentials for progress. Max Weber found the perfect formula to express the post-Reformation Christian orientation: "Confucianism was a doctrine of rational *adaptation to* the world, whereas Puritanism was a doctrine of rational *mastery over* the world" (Weber, 1921, vol. 1, pp. 512–536). What this version of Christian orientation did was to provide the Archimedean "place to stand that was necessary to move 'the world.' " Given this leverage, Christianity could take advantage of the inherent set of dynamic relations among the erotic complex, with its functions in the emergence of "humanity" from "animality"; the complex of the intellect, as perhaps the most central instrumentality of "mastery over the world"; and the complex of "things economic." I shall try to show that the economic category occupies a special middle position between the erotic and the intellectual, which enables it to perform a mediating function. All three, however—erotic, economic, and intellectual—are both indispensable and dangerous, hence the objects of profoundly ambivalent attitudes.

2. Because of this ambivalence, tensions remain with regard to the erotic, the economic, and the intellectual, tensions manifested in a tendency toward "absolutism"—that is, either "all out" acceptance without regard to dangers or "all out" rejection without regard to the enormous costs of rejection.

3. Although the Reformation was central, it had to be prepared for.

4. The industrial revolution had hidden religious significance not only because it was an expression of inner-worldly discipline, with ascetic Protestantism in the background, but also because in structure it symbolically paralleled the early Christian breakaway from the particularistic Jewish ethnic community to the universalistic mission to the Gentiles.

5. Marxism, especially in the communist versions, is religious or quasi-religious and may or may not be regarded as a version of Christianity. In any case, there is considerable parallelism between Christian symbolism and Marxist ideology, although Marxism is comparatively one-sided or "absolutist."

Three earlier studies dealt with two important symbol sets: the Christian paradigm for salvation and the paradigm for human socialization.[2] Although these two are "obviously" related to each other in some sense, they deal with such disparate things (from a commonsense point of view) that they have seldom been systematically compared. Although I was the principal author of an earlier attempt at such a comparison (in the third of the studies just referred to), I was astonished to realize how close an isomorphism could be found between them.

One of the most prominent common features of the two schemes is that they are both, in a special sense, *two-level* schemes. The religious scheme taken from early and Roman Catholic Christianity is essentially the paradigm of human salvation. It constitutes, at the divine level, the essential elements in the potentiality of salvation, the three persons of the trinity, and the tradition of the divinely inspired prophets—who were not themselves divine—from Abraham through Moses and King David, who may be said to have created a "fertile" human soil in which the *word* could take root.

The human level, on the other hand, comprises in general

the holy family. The central figures are, of course, Mary, the mother of Jesus, and Jesus himself, who was both God the son and a mortal man. There is, then, a special relation between the holy spirit as a person of the trinity, and the church. In this framework, the individual's soul is conceived to be "lifted" from the merely human level to that of participation in "eternal life."

The other paradigm, which was presented in the later essay (Parsons, 1978a), concerns in the respects relevant here, the two primary levels involved in the socialization of the human individual. The upper level concerns the components of the human family at the level of adult human social organization, which are designated by the familiar terms *mother, father, son,* and *daughter.* They are arranged on the two axes of sex and generation or, in common social science "jargon," of age and sex. The constituents of the upper level are at once everyday commonsensical and problematical. They are problematical mainly with reference to whether the nuclear family is universal. Following Terence Turner (1975), we have opted for the view that, although the nuclear family as concrete structure of kinship is not universal, its structural components are. This is sufficient for our theoretical argument.

The lower level is the paradigm of the erogenous zones that was worked out by Freud in the course of his development of psychoanalytic theory. We have taken the liberty of modifying Freud's account slightly, reducing his five zones to four by consolidating the mouth and the anus into one. The resulting fourfold classification is isomorphic with that of the upper-level classification of nuclear family components. Then, on this basis, a more detailed comparison of the religious and the socialization paradigms was undertaken. The result, which it would take too much space to repeat and ground here, was the claim that there is a more detailed isomorphism than even this would suggest.

The data on which these two analyses rest are in origin about as different as they could possibly be. For the religious paradigm, they have been taken from the historic documents of Judaism and Christianity, different parts of the Bible. In their interpretation, historical knowledge from diverse sources and period contexts has been used. For the socialization paradigm, the sources are, on the one hand, common knowledge of the family, analyzed in technical sociological and anthropological terms, and, on the other hand, knowledge of human developmental psychology, some of it known but some discovered and above all systematized mainly by Freud in the course of his construction of psychoanalytic theory. All this occurred mainly in the early part of the present century.

The suggestion that these things cannot be altogether unrelated to each other rests on the fact that they both use the familiar components of the human family and their symbolic designations. After all, the trinity includes the figures God the father and God the son. Jesus was said to be "God's only begotten son." At the level of the holy family, Mary was Jesus' mother and Joseph was in some sense her husband (see Burke, 1970; Leach, 1969). Then, in the socialization paradigm, clearly Freud was attempting to understand the course of development of a child in the context of a family, especially as related to two parents, a mother and a father. This justifies designating it as the "age and sex" complex.

The problem thus arises as to whether this common involvement of familial references and symbolism can have any theoretical significance. Are there features of the social situation of members of the early Christian sect that make it more comparable than common sense would have it to the perennial situation of human families with children to bring up?

First, let me stress the symbolic aspect of the whole analytical enterprise. Above all, the erogenous zones (mouth-anus, breast, vagina, and penis) are organs of human bodies—not one but *two* types of bodies, differentiated by sex and partly by age status, in that little girls do not have breasts. It is not, however, primarily their organic characteristics and functions that are essential in the present context, but the *meanings* of these organs as symbols to human beings, meanings that have been largely "unconscious," in Freud's sense of that word.

Similarly, the use of familial role categories at the religious level is to be interpreted not literally but symbolically. The sense in which the God "which art in Heaven" is our "father" is clearly different from human fatherhood. Nor, of course, is the Catholic nun, as the "bride of Christ," to be interpreted as a literal case of human marriage.

As we have argued in the previous discussion of the eroge-

nous zones, they constitute modes of articulation of the human process of organic reproduction, involving the birth and eventual
death of the individual organism. These points of articulation—
along with others, such as the organs of sense perception—
constitute necessary conditions of the development, at what we call
the "action" level, of a human personality, able to function effectively as a member of a human society. Put very schematically, as
symbolized organic entities they provide the reference points, if
properly "utilized," for an organization of motivational energies
that is adapted to the conditions not only of the human family but
also of the participation of its members in the wider society. For the
human neonate to achieve such capacities, it is necessary not only
that it live long enough to permit organic maturation but also that
its motivational potentials, Freud's "flow of stimulation" from the
organism, be shaped and organized in relatively specific ways.[3]

In an isomorphic, although not precisely parallel way, there
is, if the position we have previously taken is correct, also a "problem" of the articulation of the human action system with reality at
what we have called the *telic* level (see Parsons, 1978a, p. 352). This,
of course, is more or less what, in common sense, we mean by the
"religious" level. At the emergence of Christianity as an historical
religious movement, the primary focus of the telic problem concerned the conditions under which the "salvation" of the individual
soul could take place. This also was conceived as a process of "ele-
vation" of the condition of the human individual, in a context
intimately related to the problem of the meaning of death (see
Parsons, 1978a, p. 264). In a sense parallel to that in which the
perpetuation of psychological infancy would be considered to be
intolerable in a society where most people are functioning adults,
the state of being "unredeemed" for the majority of those committed to Christian faith was considered unbearable. Redemption
meant "translation" from a lower to a higher order of being.

The two "paradigms," if one might call them that, meet at
the level of concrete human social organization. The family has
almost always been considered to be a crucial node of that organizational complex. It certainly has a central role everywhere in the
processes by which individual organism-persons enter into the
status of societal membership. It can be considered that, against the

background of Judaism, Christianity, with its individualizing emphases, puts special stress on the importance of the individual's leaving, through death, the status of "going" membership in the social units in which in life he or she had participated. We may thus introduce a few considerations relevant to the problem of why Christianity, by contrast with Judaism, placed a special emphasis on familial considerations and made symbolism related to the family especially prominent. By virtue of this convergence on human family and kinship organization, we may speak of this age-sex complex as a three-tier system, first moving "upward" from the organic to the human action level and then, with "redemption," up another step to the telic level, as we have called it.

Furthermore, the whole paradigm at the same time relates the human individual to the social and cultural contexts of his or her life. What social scientists call *socialization* is a process concerning the human individual, from birth on. But it takes place in a matrix of relations to other individuals. No human individual lives who is not an organism, the product of the *bi*sexual reproduction of *two* parent organisms, and the new organization belongs to a different generation from that of the parental organisms. It is *this* complex to which the symbolic meanings of the erogenous zones must refer in the organic context. But the same meaning references are carried over to the level of the components of familial role structure. It is of critical importance that both sexes and both generation figures are internalized as objects, at both levels, to become constitutive of the personality structure *of the same individual* person. This is one of the most important senses in which the so-called feral child is not human. In the religious context, then, this multiperson framework was, as it were, "projected upward" by treating the holy family as a kind of microcosm of multipersonal divinity, a step that, as has often been remarked, in certain respects undermined the stricter monotheism of Judaism.[4]

The Christian reaction to the age-sex complex, as we have called it, was a combination of acceptance and repudiation. The acceptance went so far that even the trinity itself was in a sense the family "writ large," and it was fully accepted that normal Christians, taking the holy family as model, would live in families. Indeed, in the Roman Church, marriage eventually became one of the sacraments. The negative side, however, was manifested in a variety of ways. The "ideal woman," Mary, was depicted as a virgin, although also as the archetype of motherhood (Parsons, 1969). For Paul, it was "better to marry than to burn," but until the Reformation the better life was the celibate life. Religious perfection, so far as it was attainable in this life, was confined to the segregated monastic community, protected against the temptations of "the world." There could be no doubt that marriage, with its incorporation of the sexual side of family life, was one primary focus of the life of *this* world.[5]

It is important to note that the acceptance of the conditions of life in the world that was inherent in the Christian attitude toward the family centered on the basis of the human individual's entry into the world—namely, birth. This is strongly symbolized in the figure of Jesus and in the fact that Christmas, the central festival of Christianity, celebrates the *birth*—at the human level—of Jesus. At the same time, Christianity has been a symbolic framework for the acceptance of that other equally fundamental feature of the human condition; namely, the mortality or death of the individual. Jesus' humanity is symbolized by the facts both that he was born of woman and that, like any other human being, he died. With all the emphasis on the transcendentalism of the "life everlasting" and Jesus' resurrection, the central point should not be forgotten that he *died* on the cross.

Thus, at both ends of the life cycle, Christianity was a religion of *acceptance* of the human condition, in a sense that, if not more "profound" than that in which Judaism was, certainly was much more highly *individualized*. The drama of the relation of humanity to God had been shifted from the fate of a "people" to that of the human individual. In coming to focus on the family, at all three of the levels we have discussed, the symbolism of Christianity served to accentuate what, following Shils (1975), we may call the "primordial" situation, not so much of the human species as of the individual. Its orientation to this throughout has been, as we have put it, "ambivalent." It has been accepting, in the sense just discussed, but with doubts and sharp negativity in other respects. Perhaps the best indication of the ambivalence built into the Christian age-sex complex lies, on the one hand, in the acceptance of the family built into the highest levels of religious symbolism and on the other hand, in the undoubtedly deep uneasiness about sexuality in the glorification of virginity and celibacy. But short of universal cloning, which does not seem probable in the near future, there is no possibility of a family-based society without sexuality. Of course, the Catholic Church has attempted to qualify its acceptance by confining legitimate sexuality not only to marriage but also to direct procreative intent. That this has drastically broken down in the modern world is now a commonplace.

The rather remarkable Christian ambivalence toward the erotic and even toward the family, needs some explanation. There has been much opinion, a great deal of it certainly stemming from Christian sources and hence perhaps biased, that the society of imperial Rome was peculiarly "profligate," and hence it has been common to interpret Christian anxiety about sexuality as a "healthy" reaction to this state of affairs. There may be something in this, as some of the erotic materials found in the ruins of Pompeii illustrate.

This does not, however, seem to be a sufficient basis for understanding. I suggest that the very generalized character of erotic feeling and attraction—the fact that, as Freud put it, libido is a fluid reserve that can be "invested" in a wide variety of alternative objects in varying ways—is its most important feature. In its very nature, it can readily "get out of control." For this reason, I have suggested that the patterns of institutionalized endogamy of the Jewish community constituted just such a set of controls. Indeed, Edmund Leach, in a most interesting essay (1969) on the legitimacy of Solomon (as King of Israel), reinforces this argument by his view that Solomon, as the son of Bathsheba, was, among the many progeny of a polygynous household, the one whose mother was indubitably an Israelite, unlike others of David's wives. This in turn is clearly related to the Jewish ideal of ritual purity generally. What we think of as ethnic groups have, normally at least, had a tendency to be endogamous, and from what we know of the ancient Mediterranean world this was certainly true of it. After the Babylonian exile, the Jews, as increasing proportions of them came to live in the Diaspora, elevated this to a major tenet of the law. Indeed, for orthodox Jews to this day to marry a non-Jew is one of the most serious of all offenses.

In terms of its relations to the social structure, the Christian movement introduced some major changes relative to its Israelite background, all of which are closely related to its concern with the salvation of the individual soul. I think that the most crucial step was the break with the ethnic people of Israel as the social base of the religiously significant community. The crucial point was that, to become a Christian, a convert need not adopt the Jewish law; that is, need not become an adopted member of the Jewish, as we would now say, *ethnic* community. He or she could remain an Athenian, Corinthian, Ephesian, or Roman *and* be a Christian at the same time—or could, of course, be a Jew in the ethnic sense (Nock, 1948; Moore, 1927). Although Jesus is portrayed in the Gospels as an "antinomian" charismatic leader, often saying (as Weber stresses—[1922] 1968, p. 241), "It is written [that is, it is the Law] . . . [such and such], but I say unto you [something else]," it was Paul who consolidated this break with the law, in his mission to the Gentiles.

It is sociologically important, I think, that there was a model for this new universalism of Christianity; namely, in the institution of Roman citizenship, which by that time had been considerably generalized, even extending outside Italy. Paul himself, although of course an ethnic Jew, was a Roman citizen and, we are told, was proud to be one, despite his alienation in other respects from the society of his time.

Once Christianity, however, became an interethnic body, control of the communal character of its membership in the nature of the case had to be sacrificed. Indeed, this might be interpreted as an early case of the "isolation" of the nuclear family. But the weakening of ethnic endogamous controls may well have heightened the feeling of the dangers of sexual attraction, which may flare up between any two persons of the opposite sex. The erotic component is clearly the most volatile and fluid of those involved in the normal nexus of family relationships.

As we have noted, the new universalism entailed in the mission to the Gentiles, meant that *any* human individual could become a Christian. But then how was the composition of the Christian religious community to be conceived as "bounded"? Judaism had not faced this problem because the definition of who was obligated by the law as a Jew was *given* in terms of ethnic membership by birth. But, once freed from this limitation, were there to be no boundaries short of the whole of humanity? This, as ideal, was surely an authentic strain in Christian tradition, but as a mere sociologist I am of the opinion that, without a more definite and hence necessarily narrow set of criteria for boundedness, Christianity could not have become an historic force of any high significance.

In coping with this boundary problem, it seems to me that the church was "driven" to make a pact with what many have regarded as another "devil" with strong anchorage in "the world." In this case, it was *the intellect*. The intellect was not very strongly stressed in the ancient Hebrew cultural tradition. Therefore it was a fateful circumstance that a close neighbor of Israel was the Greek world and that, well before the Christian crisis arose in Israel, the Greek cultural influence had spread widely through so-called Hellenism.

Essentially what the "fathers of the church" did, then, using the cultural resources of Hellenism, notably in the Neo-Platonic version, was to construct a system of Christian *dogma,* in the technical sense of that term. It took a long time to develop, but a major landmark was the adoption of the Athanasian Creed in 451 A.D. The decisive criterion by which a Christian as adult could be identified thereby came to be his or her subscription to the *belief* system that had been worked out and adopted by the church.

I have metaphorically labeled the intellect as a "devil" because it has potentials of generalization and hence of "getting out of control" far transcending those of the erotic complex. Indeed, a major part of the cultural history of the West since the consolidation of the Western church[6] has been preoccupied with controversies and conflicts over the status of Christian dogma, involving both its own internal divisions and its relations to "secular" intellectualism, especially in philosophy, science, and, latterly, ideology.

As background for the Reformation, the Renaissance, which came to focus in central Italy, the seat of the papacy, involved, judged by medieval standards, a considerable amount of what would usually be called "secularization." Substantial new economic development was one of its principal features, but there was also a major cultural efflorescence. There was much more or less secular literature (Petrarch), political analysis (Machiavelli), and science

(Galileo); but its cultural center of gravity surely lay in architecture and painting. Perhaps we may stress the latter. Although portraits of individuals became far more common in this time (for example, the famous "Mona Lisa") and Botticelli, for example, painted entirely secular classical scenes ("La Primavera"), the center was clearly the holy family. But here, in the central figures of Madonna and child, there was surely a marked "humanization," especially of the figure of Mary. Indeed, it would be difficult to deduce from a Madonna of Lippi or Raphael that Mary was supposed to be unequivocally a virgin and that the generation of her child had been totally dissociated from erotic pleasure. Even in the figure of Mary in the famous annunciation of Fra Angelico, there is a tone of gentle and joyful acceptance, incidentally in marked contrast to at least one painting of the annunciation by Leonardo (in the Milan Museum). Although there was at the same time a marked decline of paintings of the crucifixion, surely one of the great masterpieces of the Renaissance was Michelangelo's "Pièta," which, in its extraordinary depiction of poignant maternal grief, is very "human."

It has often been said that the Renaissance was largely a "humanistic" movement. In the context of the preceding analysis, this statement may be interpreted to the effect that, especially in art, it went far to symbolize the acceptance of at least that part of the "world" that centers on the human family and—notably, I think—on the relation of mother and infant child. Something seems clearly to have been going on here that was to have ramifications far beyond the mother-child relationship.

The Reformation erupted, not in Italy, but well north of the Alps in central Germany. It had a "grimmer" tone than the Renaissance; indeed, it was in considerable part a reaction against the "secularization" of the latter, as Luther himself testified. But it furthered the cause of what we are calling "acceptance" of the world in an extraordinary way. The crucial point was the "collapsing," if one may call it that, of the Christian dualism as between the spiritual and the temporal worlds.

The system of Roman Catholic Christianity was essentially a two-level or two-"class" system. In the religious context, the crucial difference was not between aristocracy and the common people but *between the members of the religious orders and the laity*. Within the church, the Reformation was thus in the technical sense a revolution, because in Protestant areas it overthrew the orders through the dissolution of the monasteries.

This was indeed a drastic step, led, be it remembered, by Luther, who when it began was an Augustinian monk. It could not fail to upset the delicate balance, between the Christian church and the "world," that we have attempted to characterize. The first casualty was necessarily the system of monastic celibacy and with it an organized system of religious life that had been protected against the erotic temptations of the world. Although the celibacy of the "secular" clergy was far from being identical in religious significance with that of the religious, Luther himself, who was the self-appointed leader of the Reformation movement, put the symbolic seal on this radical break by himself marrying and thereby breaking his monastic vow of celibacy. To compound the felony, his wife was a former nun.

Many interpreters, of whom Sorokin may be regarded as typical, have regarded the Reformation as a step in the line of succession of stages of "secularization" whereby the original transcendentalism of early Christianity gradually gave way to more and more concessions to "the world, the flesh, and the devil," preparing the way for the "sensate" culture of recent times.[7] Weber held very decisively, however, that the Reformation did not imply any erosion of the transcendental base of orientation. He quoted ([1904–1905] 1930) with approval Sebastian Franck's statement that the Reformation meant that "Every man was to become a monk." The important point was that now laypersons as well as "laicized" monks had "ascetic" obligations. This was the predominant background of what I have called, by contrast with the Renaissance, the "grimness" of the Reformation atmosphere.

Christian Symbolism and Things Economic

We have presented an extremely sketchy developmental outline of Judeo-Christian, Western culture. Religiously speaking, this culture has been characterized by a high tension between the transcendental foci of orientation and the "temporal" or, in Weber's formula, the "worldly" field of empirical human experience. We

have argued that the enhanced or "upgraded" transcendentalism
of Christianity, by contrast with Judaism, led to a deep ambivalence
about the sexual realm that has to do with the evolutionary transition from subhuman organic to human action levels of organization and performance. Probably "Christian" civilization has carried
the normative support of this transition further than any other
comparable civilizational form. This achievement (from a societal
and evolutionary point of view), was, as we have argued, dependent
on surmounting a "crisis of ambivalence" in the religious orientation to human sexuality. One side altogether repudiated its positive
values, as manifested in the "cult of celibacy" as the religious ideal.
Counteracting that ideal, however, was the gradual religious
legitimation of the human family, with the nonvirgin mother as the
symbolically central figure; we have argued that this was salient by
the time of the Renaissance.

The argument of this section of the chapter, then, is that the
development of industrialism, in a much later evolutionary phase,
was a phenomenon of both a significance and a structure parallel to
the mission to the Gentiles and that the situation for it came to be
defined in a symbolic system, in this case usually called an "ideology" rather than a theology, that is remarkably congruent—in a
"structural," not a concrete, symbolic sense—with that of Christianity. We return to this theme later.

The basic shift of orientation we call the Reformation was
the latent ground of a new crisis of legitimation of "worldly" concerns in the Western world, a crisis that had a predominantly Christian background. This time, the focus of moral conflict was to be,
not over "carnal concupiscence," but over "things economic," as we
have put it. As in the case of the erotic complex, the symbolic issue
did not come to a head immediately but, indeed, did so only three
centuries after the original Reformation, in the wake of the Industrial Revolution, as it has come to be called.

As in the case of the erotic complex, there was a long history
of a similar kind of moral ambivalence. One of the early manifestations of it was the fact that Aristotle (in the *Politics,* [c. 335 B. C.]
1923) attempted to establish a distinction between "natural" and
"unnatural" acquisition, using a formula that was directly taken
over by Karl Marx but that had also been highly congenial to

Thomas Aquinas. Excessive concern with wealth was a major theme of the Hebrew prophets. The Gospel admonishes, "If thou wouldst be perfect, sell all thou hast and give to the poor" (Luke 18:22) and "Take no thought for the morrow, God will provide" (Matt. 6:24); and, finally, *all* the Christian religious orders incorporated vows of poverty into their regimen. The individual monk was poor, but the orders in many cases became rich, and, indeed, some cynical interpreters of the Reformation have held that the main motives of the Reformation, perhaps particularly in England as held by Henry VIII and his ministers, lay in the plundering of this tempting wealth. But the great reduction of the monastic system certainly did not resolve the deep Christian ambivalence about the meaning of wealth, and it reappeared in other forms.

Much recent opinion seems to feel, manifesting one side of the ambivalence, that, as in the church's reaction to Roman society in the early days, it was the "profligacy" of the papal Rome in the late Renaissance that shocked Luther. There was, however, a critically important "sleeper" involved in the attack on the monasteries, for the religious had taken vows not only of chastity but of *poverty*. As in the case of celibacy, the abolition of the monasteries meant that there was no longer an *organized* religious community devoted to the protection of its members against the temptations and evils of wealth.

The other ostensibly most important innovation of the Reformation was, of course, the abolition—or at least drastic change in meaning—of the Catholic sacraments. In effect, this was the denial of the famous "power of the keys." This change eliminated the intermediary role of the priesthood between things divine and human and placed the human individual in a relation of immediacy to God. This was the foundation of the critical Lutheran formula that salvation was "by faith alone," not by "works." The sale of "indulgences" that Luther found on his visit to Rome was one of the main stimuli, at least for him personally, for his revolutionary acts (Erikson, 1958).

There was, however, an even subtler set of possible implications of the basic change. Through a great deal of Jewish and Christian history, there has been a very strong emphasis on what has often been called the "sovereignty" of God over humanity. The

introduction of the symbol "father" in place of the common Old
Testament "Lord of Hosts" greatly mitigated the "authoritarian"
connotations of the symbol lord, but still there have been innumer-
able references to humans as "children," even if God's, with the
obvious connotations of dependency (see Bellah, 1970).

My suggestion is that the Reformation, in spite of the strong
stress of both Luther and Calvin on the "absolute" characteristics of
God, at least accelerated, if it did not initiate, a very important
"democratizing" trend in the interpretation of the God-human relationship. This may be formulated as a shift from the conception
of humanity's *subjection to* God, in the direction of one of humanity's
partnership with God. Such a tendency has surely been, in Protestant
religious circles, highly hesitant and tentative, but it seems to be
implicit in the "symbolic logic" of the situation.

It seems to me that this development should be associated
with a very central pattern-conception that fully emerged in the
Calvinistic branch of the Protestant movement; namely, that the
mission of Christians had been redefined from the salvation of the
souls of individuals, to that of building the "Kingdom of God on
Earth." This conception stands, of course, in the sharpest possible
contrast to Jesus' assertion "My Kingdom is not of this world" (John
18:36). It seems to me that "logologically," to adopt the term of
Kenneth Burke (1970), this change makes God the "leader" of the
great plan of construction, no longer the "creator" and the sole
determiner of what happens in the human world. That Jesus was,
in the Gospels, portrayed as "God's only *begotten* son" seems to me
to have been a major step along this path. All this seems to be
congruent with the idea that Christianity has not been in any simple
sense "antiworldly" but has had its side of acceptance of the world,
under the formula, which Weber ([1916] 1951, pp. 226–249) formulated classically, of attempting to bring about "mastery *over* the
world," not simply rational adaptation *to* the world.

Another feature of the religious development of Protestantism is centrally important to the analysis of this paper. This feature
above all concerns its most influential branch—namely, that deriving from John Calvin. Early Calvinism presented a sharply defined
version of the Christian dualism of which we have spoken. On the
Reformation basis, of course, it could not stress the medieval con-

ception of the two "worlds" of the spiritual and the temporal. It was, rather, organized around the spiritual status of individuals on the basis of the doctrine of predestination. There were two and only two classes of such individuals, the elect and the damned, the latter often referred to by the revealing term of "reprobates." This spiritual fate had been decided by God from eternity on grounds that were in principle incomprehensible to human understanding. Weber, in *The Protestant Ethic and the Spirit of Capitalism* ([1904–1905] 1930), made a great deal of the importance of this complex. It meant that the individual's attempt to bring about his or her own salvation, either by sacramental means or by ethical conduct, became completely meaningless. What he or she could do was restricted to the attainment of the certainty or personal conviction of salvation through election. The state of being saved could be manifested in heroically intensive devotion to serving as an instrument of the divine will in building the kingdom of God on earth, through "labor" in a *calling*, a Lutheran and Puritan word of the significance of which Weber has made much. (*This* orientation to work in the world, incidentally, was the sharpest possible antithesis to the later utilitarian conception of the "rational pursuit of self-interest," although used to explain the same types of concrete action.)

Early Calvinism was the most radical version of Protestant Christianity, perhaps excepting certain sects. It combined a drastically negative evaluation of the things of this world, again in the religious sense, with at the same time a powerful injunction to act *in* the world in order to change it in conformity with Christian ideals.

Radical Calvinism, however, did not continue to dominate the Protestant scene, even in the English-speaking and Dutch worlds in which it had its strongest appeal. It gradually gave way, in the direction that may be called that of "liberal" Protestantism. Thus, the English Puritans, who constituted the movement from which the North American settlements of the seventeenth century drew, were no longer strict Calvinists of the predestinarian persuasion. As Perry Miller (1964) has so clearly shown, they held to the "half-way" covenant, which had already eroded predestination a good deal. The end result, for the majority who belonged to what Weber called "ascetic" Protestantism, was the development of a conception that the individual could not only know his or her state

of grace but also could have a major influence on it, not by acquir-
ing sacramental tokens of religious merit, but by "good works" in
the moral sense.

As Weber emphasized, the predestinarian position could be
taken seriously only with very severe psychological strain. Behind
that, however, there was also a deep cultural paradox, along the
lines of the previous discussion. This emerged from the question of
the sense in which the "world," meaning concrete human society
and the rest, could, given its history of being "sunk in sin and
death," conceivably come to be remade as the kingdom of God on
earth. Could there be criteria of progress in the task of its construction? Or were *all* human societies, as the early Christian believers
tended to assume, in their nature *equally* corrupt, in the religious
sense? The whole ascetic Protestant stance would become meaningless if this were the case. The central theological premise had to
grant that, if humanity were given the task of building the kingdom, it would be a particularly cruel "double bind" if *nothing* meaningful could be accomplished toward the fulfillment of this task in
the nature of the God-human relationship, that we are all not only
"miserable sinners" but also *equally* miserable sinners, whatever we
have done or failed to do toward building the kingdom.

Liberal Protestantism in this sense has been the religious
framework in which what now seems to have been the most influential sector of modern society has come to crystallize; namely,
that of the English-speaking societies of Great Britain and North
America and their other "offshoots"; for example, in Australia. In
my opinion, Weber was correct in saying that the framework of
religious symbolic structure in which this transition took place was
that of what he called *ascetic* Protestantism; but this included two
ambivalently conflicting components: predestinarian Calvinism
and what I have here called *liberal* Protestantism.

It is not possible in this chapter to trace the many complex
ramifications of the relevant history. I should like to focus on one
major process of structural change in the society, with the accompanying symbolic movements, in this case usually called "ideological" rather than "religious." The essential structural change I have
in mind was the complex concatenation ordinarily called the "Industrial Revolution," which began in the latter part of the eigh-

teenth century and which centered in Great Britain (Smelser, 1959).

The decisive structural process that distinguished the industrial from the preceding "commercial" revolution was the introduction of the "factory system," as it has often been called. For a strategically important sector of the population, the place and social context of residence was no longer that of work. The sector on which symbolic focus was centered was the so-called working class—persons who were "employed" in factories by the owners of the same. This meant, of course, that "workers" did not own the factory in which they worked or its equipment, nor did they own the raw materials on which they worked or the product of that work; for example, cotton cloth. This was, in one aspect, the famous "separation of the worker from the means of production"— meaning separation from ownership and control. But from another perspective it was *at the same time* the separation of the worker in the work role from those persons—namely, family and other household occupants—with whom he or she "lived" (Giele, 1977). So long as the family "living" and economically productive work had occurred in the same physical premises and were shared by the same social group, *neither* of these separations had occurred. The prototypes were the households of the peasant farmer and of the traditional craftsman.

In the transition from the Middle Ages to and through what is often called early "modernity," Western society had been undergoing a process of major structural change, the primary aspects of which I have characterized as differentiation, adaptive upgrading, inclusion, and value generalization (Parsons, 1977). The process of differentiation between the context of residence and of work affected the previous structure at a particularly sensitive point.

From one perspective, the separation of work from the social context of family and kinship living could be regarded as a derogation of the hard-won legitimation of the household context, which has been a major theme of the preceding pages. Indeed, almost ever since then recurrent Jeremiads have deplored the "decline of the family," taking it for granted that *of course* it *has* declined (see Ogburn, 1928).

From the other perspective, the problem came to the fore of

the status of the "economy," the market system that was coming to have such a prominent place, forcing whole new classes of people, not only as individuals but also as households, into the position of dependency on money wages paid by employers. Considering the readiness to greet almost any major structural change in the society with suspicion and hostility, it is not surprising that influential people readily came to believe that this was the work of an evil "monster" of some sort. This reaction was build in part on the fact that money and markets were the focus of an ancient symbolism of things that were morally dubious, as in the case of Aristotle's "chrematism" ([c. 335 B.C.] 1923); that is, the use of money (M) to acquire commodities (C) that in turn are used to get more money (M-C-M), as distinguished from "natural acquisition" or the sale of commodities for money that is spent to acquire more commodities (C-M-C). Marx took over this formula directly from Aristotle. The former was the focus of that evil thing Marx called "capitalism."

Although I do not recall ever having seen the argument put forward before, I think it is reasonable to suggest that the separation of work context from that of household was the functional equivalent, in symbolic significance, of the separation of the Christian religious community from the Jewish ethnic matrix in which it originated; Paul's mission to the Gentiles was, of course, the focus of it. The crucial common feature was that both were breakaways from a relatively particularistic *Gemeinschaft* matrix into a more universalistic environment in which basic "status," in the early Christian case, as a Christian was no longer defined in terms of "embeddedness" in the primordial community. This symbolic parallelism makes economic growth a *religiously* progressive factor—as is, at least implicitly, Weber's view.

The early modern household, as a particularistic diffuse matrix, had shrunk to much smaller proportions, being typically a unit in a small local community. But there is strong reason to believe that this decline of relative sociocultural importance had been counterbalanced by the upgrading, in the terms in which we have sketched it, of the emphasis on the concerns of the human individual, especially as personality. I think we have given some grounds for believing that the influence of the Christian religious movement had a good deal to do with this process of transformation.

Perhaps, remembering the Protestant phases we have sketched, we may put it that persons in the "main" tradition of Western Christian religious origin, having *accepted,* in the sense of the preceding discussion, the human family with its underpinning of symbolically generalized eroticism, were now confronted with the problem of what they could do about the next higher level of generalized facilities for action: the economic.

This structural change seemed to place the "worker" in a special context of "economic" forces. Workers were taken out of the kinship-dominated household and placed, in their work roles, in a context dominated by the market interests of the employer, which meant the profit system and, taking one further step of symbolic generalization, enmeshment in the "capitalist" system. Given a disposition to be morally suspicious of anything economic, even though this division was granted to be necessary and useful, it is not too surprising that it came to be the focus of two principal movements, both of which have, with varying degrees of radicality, questioned the moral legitimacy of this mode of the "setting free" of the economic complex from its previous ascription to or embeddedness in, especially, the more primordial matrix of kinship. The first of these was the socialist movement, which received a striking symbolic expression in the Marxist conception of "capitalism" in its relations to "socialism." The second was a gradually gathering focus of what has come to be called "sociological" thought, emphasizing nostalgia for the situation in which this process of structural differentiation in the society had not yet taken place. This came to a symbolic focus in the work of Ferdinand Tönnies, *Gemeinschaft und Gesellschaft* ([1887] 1963) and may be called *Gemeinschaft* romanticism.[8] It has had many repercussions.

The Triumph of "Economic" Ideology: Marxism

Since in the following discussion we shall find that the term *economic* has become highly ambiguous, it will help if we begin by defining what we mean by "economic" in a technical analytical sense.

The central theoretical problem concerns the position of the "economy," as it is often called, in the total structure of a society, particularly a modern, industrial type of society. The "economic

approach"—for example, as Becker (1976) sets it forth—draws no
theoretical boundaries within the whole field of what he calls "social
behavior," which certainly includes the whole of what we call a
"society." Transcending what I have called the "utilitarian dilemma"
(Parsons, 1937), however, leads to the discrimination of several
primary functional aspects of a society, if that entity is treated as a
social system. As Smelser and I concluded (Parsons and Smelser,
1956), it is reasonable to treat the economy, in a sufficiently differentiated society, as one of four primary functional subsystems of
the society, the other three being called the *polity,* the *societal community,* and the *fiduciary system* (Parsons and Platt, 1973). The
economy, from this point of view, is the set of structures and processes primarily concerned with the *production* (including "distribution"), to use the economists' term, of generalized resources that
can be allocated among an indefinite variety of uses for "consumption." The most generalized of all these economic resources, of
course, is money, which, as the classical economists already understood, has no "value in use" but only "value in exchange." The
availability of money income, however, enables the receiver to
choose among the goods and services available on the market without being subject to the restrictions involved in ascriptive exchange
or in a barter system.

For Marxism, the role analogous to that of Neo-Platonic
philosophy for Christianity may be attributed to the classical
economics, which was as specifically an English cultural product as
Platonism was Greek. As Dumont (1977) explicates it, it began in
the eighteenth century, growing out of the seventeenth-century
philosophies of Hobbes and Locke and certainly influenced by
Hume. Again, in Dumont's account, it took a decisively economic
turn in the eighteenth century with Mandeville, and, above all,
Adam Smith. In the nineteenth century, it came to a kind of full
maturity as *utilitarianism.* Of course, the fact that the Reformation,
particularly ascetic Protestantism, lay in the background is vital.

It is interesting that, on the whole, mainline economic
thought since those days has centered on consumption, although its
technical analysis has been neglected. In the decisive genesis period
of the economic ideology, however, the primary concern was with
production and with it the *factors* of production, as distinguished

from that other central theme of economic theorizing, the "shares of income" or the distribution of wealth.

The classical economicsts, most clearly David Ricardo ([1821] 1912), put forward a classification of three factors of production: land, labor, and capital. Skipping technicalities, including the role of "marginal" analysis, land as a central factor came to be shunted aside, largely because it was associated with agriculture and hence was not centrally relevant to the new industrial system. For the time being, this left two relevant factors—namely, labor and capital—and their relations to each other. This, in the simplest terms, is the frame of reference of the conception that there is a "capitalist" system. Marx did not invent this framework but took it over from the stockbroker-capitalist Ricardo.

Perhaps the other most central concept in the complex was that of the market. This was, of course, nothing new, although Barber (1977) has shown that its analysis has been surprisingly neglected by economists. What *was* new, however, was the development, on any such scale, of markets for the *factors of production,* whereas previously that for consumers' goods had been paramount. Furthermore, of the two factors capital and labor, the labor market became, in the decisive period, overwhelmingly salient. Within economic thought, there was a long discussion of the relations between "capital goods" (for example, materials and machinery), and "capital funds" (that is, financial resources used to finance production). More generally, however, the focus was on the combination of ownership of property, on the one hand, and employment, on the other hand, neither of which is, in the analytical sense, a strictly economic category.

What, then, was "labor?" As a symbol, a complex entity indeed! In the tradition of technical economic theory from Ricardo on, it has been in a rather strict sense a factor of production. This is to say that the concept has focused on the contribution of the action of human individuals to the production of what later came to be called the "utility" of economically valued goods and services. This conception, however, could readily be applied to the contributions both of worker, essentially defined as "employed person," and of capitalist, who not only owned and "bossed" but, especially through a complex set of decisions, made a "human" impact on the concrete

processes of production. This aspect was given a chance to emerge
theoretically, however, only well after Marx, especially in the work
of Alfred Marshall.

In the meantime, Marx had crystallized what was at the same
time both a narrower and a broader conception of labor than that
of the primarily economic analysts. It was narrower, on the one
hand, in that it confined the concept of labor to occupants of the
role of employee in the new employment system, omitting any
analysis of human action of the part of capitalists, except through
the inference that, in following their interests as defined by the
market, they were in *this* context engaged only in "exploiting" such
workers or laborers.

The concept of labor, on the other hand, came to be more
broadly defined in that it was no longer in the analytical sense an
economic category but was broadened to one of the most generalized
conceivable levels of social status. Labor was said to constitute one
of the two important social *classes,* the relations between which
would determine the whole future of human society, the two classes
being, of course, labor (or working class) and capital in one version,
proletariat and bourgeoisie in another.

This was the symbolic setting for the "radical" side of what I
think can quite properly be called the *religious* drama over the
significance of things economic, as I have called them. In the tradition of what Weber called the "religious rejection of the world," the
socialists, like the earlier Christians, conceived a symbolic view of
that world as radically evil. The theme of continuity was, in the first
although not the only place, symbolized by the fact that poverty, as
well as celibacy, became the focus of a conception of the religiously
higher life. In the case of members of the earlier religious orders, it
came to be the voluntary poverty of the monastic status. In the case
of the proletariat, it became the involuntary poverty of working-
class status, which, by Marxist definition, was one of being subject
to capitalistic "exploitation."

Marxism has frequently in recent years been referred to as a
"religion," often qualified by the adjective *secular.* More recently,
Daniel Bell (1978b) uses the adjective *political.* I think this designation is correct, if Marxism is seen in the context of the religious
history of Western civilization. It certainly belongs in Weber's

category of "religious rejections of the world." But it was a rejection that was even more sharply ambivalent than that of early Christianity. The "sinful" or, at the very least, reprehensible world was clearly the capitalist system. This is the symbolically essential aspect of the famous idea of economic determinism or historical materialism—things economic, as we have called them, in their specifically capitalist form. In a sense parallel to that in which for the early Christians the essence of the world was sin, for believing Marxists, the essence of nonsocialist industrial society is capitalism, with all its symbolic connotations.

The symbolic acceptance side of the ambivalent attitude toward this modern world centers in the concept of production, in what is at least vaguely an economic sense. The message was that production itself is a good thing. The evil lies in its control and in the *distribution* of the product. Within Ricardo's scheme of the factors of production, Marx alleged that *only* labor is truly productive. The canonical statement of this "dogma" is the labor theory of value, which, although with substantially altered meaning, was taken over from Ricardo. It was, however, parlayed to levels of generality of which the Ricardos of this world never dreamed.

There is a sense in which the "proletariat" or the "working class" was treated in Marxism as the equivalent of the "saving remnant" of some branches of Protestantism. They surely did not constitute the main population of the going society—as, indeed, Marx erroneously predicted they would—but the "working class" was the symbolically *crucial* sector. For, the proletariat was the *matrix*—note the word—from which the Communist Party as its vanguard in some sense emerged, and this was to be the agent of the salvation of this evil society from its unregenerate state, through the revolution, which has been interpreted to be the translation of the capitalist society to a "higher" state, eventually that of communism.

Let us remember that in the early Christian myth, as it perhaps had best be called, there was an enigmatically residual figure in the holy family, by specific contrast with the salient figure of Mary, the mother of Jesus. This was Joseph, whom Leach (1969) very appropriately called Jesus' "sociological father." If there is any symbolic parallel at all between Mary and Jesus, on the one hand,

and the proletariat and the Communist Party, on the other, then the Marxist mythology must be expected somewhere to provide a place for a Joseph figure.

My suggestion is that, for Marxism, this is none other than the famous "capitalist"; just as Marx had depersonalized Mary into the proletariat, so here the symbolic figure was no longer the individual person Joseph but the category capitalist. The important consideration is the ambivalence manifest in both cases. In the Christian case, in one aspect, the problem was that of the sense in which Joseph was Jesus' father. In another aspect, the problem was that of the sense in which Joseph had or had not "contributed" to the generation of the very special Jesus figure, who was both God and man at the same time. On a slightly different level of symbolic meaning, it may be said that Joseph was the symbolic Jew; that is, he represented the Jewish ethnic community from which Christianity emerged. This fits the Gospel stress on Jesus' descent from the patriarchs and kings of Israel, establishing that he was of the House of David. This genealogy, however, was, as Leach has pointed out, traced through Joseph, not Mary! Could there be a clearer expression of Christian ambivalence toward Jewishness?

Had the "capitalist"—who was partly personified—contributed to the "salvation" of the proletariat from the wicked capitalistic system? From one point of view, of course, inconceivable! Yet, Marxist doctrine held that, without the introduction of capitalist modes of production, the enormous increase of productivity that characterized the industrial revolution could not have come about. So even capitalists were not wholly without, in the relevant sense, religious merit.

There seems to have been a certain historical parallel between what the early Christians did and what the modern socialists did, including the ambiguity and partiality of their success. This is to say that, along with the rhetorically severe condemnation of the world, in its relevant aspects, they included certain "escape clauses" relative to the situation of being "lost in sin." The Christian soul was, by definition, eligible for redemption, but only on the condition of acceptance of the faith. The Marxist believer could also participate in the redemptive process by virtue of subscription to the "true" belief system. This subscription could erase the consequences of prior involvements and commitments, in the Christian case, in the "world" as defined by the Jewish ethnic community, in the socialist case, of prior involvements in the evil "capitalist" system. For the strict religion of Marxism, the only road to salvation was by way of the revolutionary party and movement. But, just as strict Calvinism gave way to what, in broad terms, we have called liberal Protestantism, so strict Marxism has been giving way to a fusion with "democratic socialism."

But this is getting somewhat ahead of the story. The congruence of symbolic structure between the two religious movements extends to their internal stratification. Thus the equivalent of "pagan," those outside the Christian community, was the "capitalist" world. Later, in Christianity, those who in a sense "ought to know better" because civilized, came to be called "heathen"; those who had "witnessed to the faith" were, however, originally members of *the* church, but after the Reformation it became *a* church. In the communist branch of Marxism, the crucial distinction has come to be that between members of *the* Communist Party, on the one hand, and ordinary socialists, on the other.

The direct meaning of the party is understandable only on the background of the Reformation. The party is most directly analogous to the Calvinistic elect, the company of the "saints" who felt that they were chosen to lead the great crusade, to build the kingdom of God on earth. Back of them, as we have outlined, lay the distinction between first, the religious of Catholicism, the members of the celibate—and poverty-bound—orders, and, second, the ordinary "lay" Christians, who lived "in the world" but who through the Church were eligible for redemption. The Marxist equivalent is clearly the ordinary worker, who is not a member of the party. The status of capitalists or, somewhat more broadly, "bourgeoisie" is again different. Although potentially contributors to the growth of productivity, they might be construed as the heathen to whom it made sense to direct missions.

If this special connection of Marxism with the background of the Reformation is correct, then it may provide a clue to the special appeal of the communist movement in predominantly Catholic areas of Europe and its offshoots, and, beyond that, in Russia. The argument is that the most advanced countries, in the

sense of industrialization, had already been through the Reformation. It was largely the Latin countries, notably France, Italy, and
Spain, that had not. It is probably no accident that the strongest
communist parties in Europe have been those of France and Italy,
and the case of Spain would probably have been similar had Franco
not won the Spanish Civil War in the 1930s. Oscillation between
communism and military dictatorships has also characterized much
of Latin America. In these countries, the communist movement
may at least be a partial functional equivalent of the Reformation.

Russia, on the other hand, has belonged to the Eastern Orthodox branch of Christianity, which is further removed from
Protestantism than is Roman Catholicism. It also came down into
the present century more economically underdeveloped than
either France or northern Italy, so we may speak of the Soviet
regime as in some ways resembling the rule of the Calvinist saints.
China, then, belongs to a quite different civilizational circle, but it
fits the pattern in a very broad way, given Mao's shift of emphasis
from the proletariat to the peasantry—over which he broke with
Stalin (Brandt, Schwartz, and Fairbank, 1952). China, of course,
was more "underdeveloped" than Russia had been in 1917.

One final characteristic of Marxism contributes to the
plausibility of this argument. Marxism, like other parts of what
Dumont has called the "economic ideology," has purported to treat
the organization of modern society, especially that developing from
the Industrial Revolution, as primarily an economic phenomenon.
Thus "labor," which originally came into the picture, notably
through Ricardo, as a "factor of production" (one of three in
Ricardo's scheme, four in Marshall's), became, in the labor theory
of value, the sole source of "value" in what was presumably the
economic sense but was clearly, in economic ideology, broader.
Then Marx took a still further step of generalization in formulating
his conception of social class. Labor as factor of production thus
came to define the essence of the working class, which was not only
the source of economic value but also the sole morally acceptable
component of modern society.

The economic category, in its historical theoretical sense,
should, I think, designate a functionally *specific* component of social
action. Most conspicuously in Marxism, however, it came to be

enormously *generalized* from this base. This generalization was not along the more familiar axis of the *universalistic* meaning of objects, which at least since Descartes has been central to the categorization of objects in our cultural tradition. On the contrary, generalization in Marxism was along the axis of *diffuseness* of motivational meaning. Diffuseness in this sense is contrasted with specificity, whereas universalism is contrasted with particularism.[9]

Unless I am grossly mistaken theoretically, the two axes of generalization, as I have called them, do not lie on the same continuum but are *orthogonal* to each other. This circumstance has been especially confusing in the modern cultural milieu, because of the latter's rationalistic bias, as it were. This is to say that universalism, being in the first instance a *cognitive* category, has tended to be contrasted with particularism, not specificity, and, conversely, the possibility of generalization on an axis other than that of universalism has tended to be ignored. It seems to me that the emergence of the *Gemeinschaft-Gesellschaft* distinction, just at the end of Marx's life, marked a new opening for a process of symbolic differentiation. As noted earlier, this related very directly to the differentiation, at the level of social structure, between the context of work and that of residence, which we have compared with that between the newly emerging Christian religious community and the Jewish ethnic community.

Generalization on the axis of *diffuseness*, as that concept is here used, refers to the "motives" of the unit of the system of action that is treated as an *actor*. Clearly, the core of this conception is the individual person. But it has been generalized to include a variety of different *collective* entities. Surely the most fundamental of these is the human family, with its involvement in socialization processes, which is the "goal attainment" equivalent of "production" in the economic sense. From the family, the gradient of generalization in diffuseness can run to wider and wider solidarity groups, notably the local community, prototypically the peasant village, then the small city. The process of generalization has historically tended to proceed to the ethnic level, which in turn has had complex relations to nationalism.

The Marxist version of this pattern of generalization, however, selected *labor*, an economic—that is, a *Gesellschaft*—reference point, not that of the residential household, a *Gemeinschaft* reference, and attempted to elevate it to the supreme reference of diffuse solidarity. No less an event than the world revolution would allegedly be organized about the "working class."

The key concept in this connection is *class solidarity*. A particularly striking relevant feature of Marxist thought in this connection is that it conspicuously neglects phenomena of social mobility. Far more than in most social science, Marxism tends to assume that an individual's class status is given at birth and remains unchanged until death. The family, which is conceived as continuous from generation to generation, rather than the individual, is thus conceived to be the essential unit of class status. A further possible implication is that this has something to do with the neglect of education in socialist literature, because education is so conspicuously a channel of mobility. The fact that the worker's *family* is implicitly taken as the unit of class perhaps helps to conceal the anomaly of treating a (narrowly defined) universalistic factor of production (labor) as the primary basis of particularistic class *solidarity*.

This concern with class solidarity presents a very deep paradox in Marxist theory. In most of modern sociology, following broadly in the tradition of Durkheim, solidarity is, analytically, treated as a category of societal *integration*. This, however, is precisely what the category of economic—for example, in the form of "interests"—is not. Thus, to derive social solidarity from the operation of economic factors as the ultimate determinants of human action is to run directly counter to main trends of thought about social action.

The way Marxist theory accomplishes the integration is to introduce a drastic dualism, which again is reminiscent of the Christian case. This is to say that economic interests are conceived to determine action only until the revolution. Then occurs the famous *Sprung in die Freiheit*, "leap into freedom," after which economic determinism allegedly ceases to operate. This surely requires the intervention of an entity that, relative to the closed system of economic determinism, is transcendental. The Marxist name for this entity is "the dialectic of history," about which economic theory in the ordinary sense has nothing to say. The state of communism that will be ushered in by the revolution, of course, closely resembles the Christian heaven; and the revolution itself resembles the day of judgment. While Marx derived his economics from the "classical" theory, adapting Ricardo especially, he derived the dialectic of history from Hegel, perhaps the most foreign of all the German idealists to English Utilitarianism. Although, as Marx said, he "stood Hegel on his head," whichever end was up, it was still Hegelian metaphysics.

Of course, because Marxism came after the Reformation, it could not very well simply reinstate the earlier Christian dualism between the things of this world and things spiritual. What it did was to separate the two levels in time, in "historical" sequence, for which there was ample Christian precedent in the conception of the millenium to follow the day of judgment. Thus even the Christian society of the medieval church could be conceived to be a temporary arrangement, pending the arrival of the millenium. Indeed, after the second coming failed to materialize, after the resurrection, and even during the lifetime of the early Christians, there had been a fixation on the year 1000 A.D. The passing of that year, without the great event taking place, probably constituted a kind of time bomb that contributed to the generation of a crisis in the society of Christendom, even though the crisis did not erupt until five centuries later. There is a sense in which the High Middle Ages lived under this shadow. This history constitutes another aspect of the ambiguity in Western culture in the relations between the ideal and the real, the spiritual and the temporal, and with it the ambivalence of orientation to the problems involved. However brave the adoption of the slogan "scientific socialism," Marxism has certainly not altogether escaped these ambiguities and ambivalences.

The Triumph of Economic Ideology: Establishment Economism

In the great cultural development that has led to the triumph of the economic ideology, as Dumont has called it, Marxism has, of course, by no means stood alone. Another branch of the movement has become associated, not with the radically dissident sociopolitical movements, but with what has come to be called the "establishment" in the Western "democratic" world. Here I think it is essential, however, to distinguish, among the professionals, the thinkers who represent a radically economic emphasis, from others in the social sciences of the present century.

By establishment economism, I have in mind the tradition that has taken for granted that economics is the "queen" of the social disciplines. There has been a variety of versions of the doctrine. It took shape largely in the England of the eighteenth century, with close relations to British empiricism in epistemology. We can follow Dumont in his stress on the contributions of Mandeville and Adam Smith. It then blossomed out in the development of the classical economics with Ricardo and John Stuart Mill. It became, however, a system of thought considerably broader than economics, most generally called *utilitarianism*. Probably the most generally philosophical of its representatives was John Stuart Mill, who wrote on many fields, not only economics but also government, ethics, logic, and various others.

It is notable that the two most distinguished analytical histories of this movement have been written by Frenchmen rather than Englishmen. The earlier was the notable book of Élie Halévy, first published in 1901. Note, too, that Halévy took the term "philosophical radicalism," which was applied to the movement in the earlier part of the nineteenth century, giving his book the title *La formation du radicalisme philosophique*. The second history is the very recently published book, to which we have already referred, by Louis Dumont (1977), *From Mandeville to Marx: The Genesis and Triumph of the Economic Ideology (Homo aequalis: Genèse et épanouissement de l'idéologie économique).*[10]

Marxism adopted essentially the cultural strategy of Western Christianity in that it set up a sharply defined system of "religious" dogma and an equally sharply defined sociopolitical organization, the Communist Party. The conservative wing of the economic religion, if we may call it that, is more difficult to identify and characterize because it lacks both of these striking characteristics. Economics remains anchored as an intellectual discipline, one of the social sciences. The transition from academic discipline to ideology is gradual, not marked by any clearly defined boundaries. Indeed, in our "liberal" society we now have a school of "radical economists" some of whom are rather orthodox Marxists, even though they may not be, politically, communists.

As the intellectual history recounted by Halévy and Dumont indicates, the most important point is whether or not the ideas in question have been organized within what, in a technical sense, I have called a *utilitarian* framework (Parsons, 1937, pp. 43–128). Indeed, utilitarianism could be characterized as a way of generalizing the economic approach, as Gary Becker (1976) calls it, to the whole field of human social behavior.[11]

The most fundamental theoretical problem that this "conservative" version of the economic ideology, and indeed the Marxist version as well, has failed to take adequately into account and to solve, is, I think, the integrative problem or that of *order*. I think it can be said that this difficulty was most fully and profoundly understood by Durkheim ([1893] 1933; also see Parsons, 1937, p. 301). (Again, it is striking that there is no reference to Durkheim in Becker's 1976 index.)

This should be familiar territory to most sociologists and should not need to be elaborated on. I may merely make two points. First, certain recent controversies (Pope and others, 1975; Burger, 1978; Warner, 1978) about my own previous work in this area have left me totally unconvinced that the position I took on this basic issue in *The Structure of Social Action* over forty years ago is erroneous. On the contrary, these controversies have served strongly to confirm me in my conviction that this position was fundamentally correct and is of great importance both to social science and to ideology in the present context. Secondly, I refer to Becker's book (1976) because he has become a leading exponent of a school of thought, centered at the University of Chicago, that has been attempting to extend the use of the "economic approach" into areas into which it has traditionally not penetrated, such as marriage and the family.

Convinced as I am of the essential correctness of the position I have taken for so long on the central theoretical issue, I do not wish to deprecate the possible importance of contributions to social science knowledge that can be made by certain of these extensions of the economic approach. Just what the limits are can be determined only by careful study of specific problem areas of social behavior with such problems clearly in mind. At the same time, I do not believe that any of the proponents of the economic approach has refuted what I think to be Durkheim's altogether crucial critique of Herbert Spencer's conception of a system of relations of contract, which he took to be the epitome of the utilitarian conception of society as a whole, to say nothing of economic relationships of the market.

However these internal discussions in the social sciences ma, turn out, I think there can be no doubt of the correctness of Dumont's judgment that there is a highly prevalent nonsocialist economic ideology in modern Western society and that it is very important to its position in the society that it can derive a large measure of cultural legitimation from the views of a prominent school at least of members of the profession of economics, that presumptive queen of the sciences of human social behavior. This is, of course, part of a culture in which the symbol "science" carries immense prestige. Many economists, well beyond the Chicago school of present reference, are convinced and proud that economics is the "most scientific" of the social sciences. This is reminiscent of Marx's adoption of the label "scientific socialism" and many other similar phenomena.[12]

Professionals in economic science are clearly highly important as legitimizers of the economic ideology but are not its principal "carriers." For this function, we must look in the first instance to what is usually called the "business community," interestingly self-labeled by a word that the economic approach would rule out of any technical vocabulary as hopelessly contaminated by sentimental associations. The economic "imperialism" involved has, of course, had a good many salient symbolic statements. Two will suffice for illustration. First, back in the 1920s Calvin Coolidge, as President, made the widely quoted statement, "The business of America is business." Then a generation later, in the 1950s, "Engine Charlie" Wilson, who had been president of General Motors but was then Secretary of Defense, made the statement, "What's good for General Motors is good for the country."

Besides such symbolic expressions, one other conspicuous recent example of this ideological salience may be cited. This is the relatively recent vogue of cost-benefit analysis. This is widely believed to be *the* universal method for achieving rational efficiency in almost any human social enterprise, far beyond the range of the "business" world. The important point for present purposes is that both costs and benefits are almost exclusively confined to those statable (and usually stated) in *money* terms.

We have compared Marxism, especially in its communist form, as the "radical" version of the economic ideology, with the early Calvinist conception of the movement to transform the world according to a divine plan. A special elite group, the party, was to bring about the revolution and, as its result, the totally ideal state called "communism." Indeed, the comparability extends to the point that membership in the "working class" was assumed to be totally ascribed, as we have noted, and thus not open to mobility, just as the distinction between the elect and the reprobates had been decided once and for all by God through predestination.

If this comparison holds, then the conservative version of the economic ideology we have just discussed tends to be associated with *liberal* Protestantism, which, in various forms, came to be dominant in the Protestant world in the later phases of its development. Liberal Protestantism, however, is by no means confined to economic determinists. In Marxism, the rough counterpart of liberal Protestantism in Christianity is perhaps democratic socialism, as we have suggested. In any case, in contrast to communism, neither liberal Protestantism nor establishment economism has ascriptive membership or a prescribed belief system. Unregenerate adherents of a non- or contraeconomic creed can still be saved if they take the proper measures, above all by renouncing the evil ways of their past. Furthermore, the critical aspect of this disposition is not their beliefs but, perhaps we may say, their "goodwill."

Surely one of the greatest merits of Dumont's study is his clear thesis that the two wings of what he calls the economic ideology have grown from the same roots, roots that, I hope the reader will be convinced, lie very deep indeed in the cultural history of the Western world. If there is a unifying theme to this chapter as a whole, I think it must be the relevance of Weber's famous conception of both the nature and the importance of what he called "religious rejections of the world" (1921, pp. 536–573). "Renunciations" might have been a better word, to suggest the ambivalence involved. The two forms of economic ideology we have considered

—Marxism and establishment economism—are opposite expressions of essentially religious ambivalence, one an absolutism rejecting as evil the rational pursuit of economic self-interest (at least in the form of profit making, which is essential to the economic in a technical sense), the other embracing the economic as the source of almost all good.

Concluding Reflections

In its original conception, this article was to be a study of certain aspects of religious symbolism. Perhaps some readers will feel they have been tricked into reading a disquisition on certain aspects of economic thought under false pretenses. It cannot be doubted, however, that these phenomena, both of Marxist socialism and of the politically conservative economic approach, are continuous with phenomena of our cultural history that no one would deny were mainly religious, such as orientations toward the erotic complex and the family in Christian history down to the Reformation and in many respects well beyond.

We have cited various symbolic indexes that there was a relation between things erotic and things economic, such as the fact that Catholic religious have for centuries had to take vows of *both* chastity and poverty, and the very telling fact that, in the English language at least, a woman in *giving* birth to a child enters into "labor," which surely fits with Marxist conceptions of the "value" of labor in "production."

In my own personal intellectual history, however, the idea of a basic connection between the religious and the economic spheres was especially aroused by my reading (first in 1925) Weber's famous study on the *Protestant Ethic and the Spirit of Capitalism* ([1904–1905] 1930). As, in the course of work leading up to *The Structure of Social Action* (1937), I gained, above all through Halévy's masterpiece, a better understanding of utilitarianism, I realized anew how radical a break with that tradition Weber had introduced; no wonder he was not cordially received by English economists and economic historians—Tawney was only a partial exception. The utilitarians had allegedly disposed of all that "nonsense" left over from the days when scholars, other than some

historians, took religion seriously; instead, they concerned themselves only with the entirely secular "given" wants of individuals
and the rational measures individuals took to satisfy them. Weber's
view, of course, was that underlying the motivation of economic
activities is a religious substratum of the most serious significance.
Weber thus threw a bomb shell into the camp of the new secular-
utilitarian understanding of the world of social behavior. The impact on me of Weber's thesis, strengthened by the experience of
translating his text, was greatly reinforced by the "discovery," as it
certainly was, of Durkheim's contributions to this problem area,
which centered on his critique of utilitarianism and his development of the idea of organic solidarity in the *Division of Labor in
Society* ([1893] 1933).

Then, the reader might reasonably ask, why did the level of
generalization, *across* the traditional lines of "things economic,"
"things religious," and "things erotic," that this chapter has attempted to present, not emerge full-blown in *The Structure of Social
Action* (1937)? At the time of writing that book, it is true, I had not
yet seriously read Freud. Perhaps that was all that was necessary! I
think not. Such a statement as this chapter would not have been
possible for me, say, in the early 1940s, because a number of necessary conditions were not yet present. One of these was further
development of the theoretical understanding of the economic
sphere, above all in its *relations* to the other sectors of the society,
and, beyond that, the understanding of the personality of the individual and the cultural system. Considered as social science rather
than ideology, it seems to me that its striking neglect of problems of
this sort is the gravest defect of the Becker type of "economic
approach," which has been briefly reviewed earlier.

Similar considerations are relevant in the sphere of the involvement of the personality of the individual, through socialization in a kinship system, in the social structure of the society, and
through it in the cultural system. It has seemed to me that such
analysis was necessary to provide an adequate analytical framework
for the interpretation of Freud's decisive contributions to the understanding of the roots of human motivation. In my own case, the
prerequisites of such understanding came rather late and certainly
were not present in the late 1930s.

Finally, a still further step in generalization has, in my opinion, contributed importantly. This is the step from consideration of the general system of action to that of what has here been called the "human condition." This, for example, has helped greatly to gain perspective on Freud's treatment of the relations between the human organism and the personality that has been emergent from it. This point is documented in *Action Theory and the Human Condition* (Parsons, 1978b, chap. 15).

All three of these courses of development have, in my opinion, helped to "relativize" the conceptions both of the "demon" eroticism and of that latter-day demon, things economic. What Dumont has called the economic ideology, however, has, in both its versions, operated to absolutize the interpretation of the economic world, as certain biologizing tendencies in modern thought have for the erotic (as well as for genetic heredity). This is *common,* on the one hand, to Marxism, with its dogma of economic determinism or historical materialism, and, on the other, to the economic approach of such contemporary writers as Gary Becker. The latter, like the liberal Protestantism to which I think it has been historically related, is conspicuously tolerant and does not attempt to draw rigid dogmatic lines, as does the communist version of Marxism or, for the Christian cases, either Roman Catholicism or old Calvinist Protestantism. This circumstance makes it difficult to treat such movements as "religious" in the usual senses. But unless our interpretation of the significance of the Reformation is wholly erroneous, I think that the relations must be said to hold up.

In conclusion, let us return briefly to the third fluid and generalized demon that has figured in our discussion, namely the intellect. On the one hand, it is a striking feature of the "radical" movements involving both the erotic and the economic complexes, that the functional problem of boundedness, as we have called it, has at least to a significant degree been met by the institutionalization of a system of *dogma*; that is, of cognitively formulated beliefs adherence to which was treated as compulsory for all members of the movement in good standing. On the other hand, what we have called liberal Protestantism has dropped the requirement of subscription to a system of dogmas. This is also broadly true of democratic socialism, as it is usually called, and of the economic approach of Becker and such other prominent figures as Milton Friedman—the "guru" of the movement, as Bell (1978a) calls him.

Is this the end of the line? Surely, many would subscribe to the view that liberal Protestantism is not "really" religious; and many Marxists would subscribe to the view that democratic socialism has equally weak claims to being "really" socialist. Indeed, some would say that the loosening of "controls" over sexual matters, which has resulted from the "sexual revolution," as it has been called, has let this ancient demon loose beyond hope of being brought under control again (see also Bell, 1978b, Tiryakian, 1978).[13]

In the tentative way in which such problems must be approached if they are to be intellectually mastered, it is my view that there is a possibility of stabilization or containment of all three of these demons alternative to that of institutionalization of a system of dogmatic beliefs. Indeed, I am strongly inclined to believe that it is too late for the latter to have any serious prospect of success in any of these sensitive fields. The experience in our time with rigid Marxist-Leninist orthodoxy seems to me to provide cogent evidence for this statement.

The direction of solution (it cannot be more) that I suggest is still predominantly cognitive. It is not the organizational enforcement of a belief system, whether by a church or a party, but the firming up of such a set of beliefs to a level that can stand on its own ground in the conviction of its adherents, rather than depending on authority.

This is the procedural aspect of the problem. There is also a substantive aspect. For the case of the erotic complex, the problem involved the acceptance, as we have put it, of certain kinship-linked aspects of the human condition, including the involvement of Christian society with the erotic grounding of motives. The ambiguity of the word *love* in our language, with both its erotic and its religious meanings, illustrates another facet of our theme. Thus its use runs all the way from the most intense and explicitly erotic relationship, through ideals of a community of persons religiously motivated to "brotherly love" (surely not in a "gay" sense) to the religious admonition, "Love thy God with all thy heart and all thy soul." At the same time, it is interesting and significant that the word *love* is not often applied to the contractual relations of buyers and sellers on the market.

I would be willing to grant that the status of the erotic complex in its relations to kinship structure, parenthood, friendship, and a variety of other themes in modern society remains problematical. Since there is not space available to enter into an adequate discussion of these problems here, let me merely state that neither of two absolutisms that have figured prominently in orientation holds out much promise of a relatively stable resolution of the attendant conflicts.

One of these, of course, is the absolutism of the negation of any positive moral or religious or even social value residing in this aspect of human experience. If total celibacy is the ideal way, there is the paradox that if everyone follows that path the human race will extinguish itself; maintenance of a population is possible only through concessions to the evils of the world. The other absolutism is some kind of paneroticism, holding that total liberation from all social control of things erotic is the only tolerable situation for free human beings.

In the development of controls, among which a particularly important part constitute definitions of what we have called "boundedness," surely cognitive understanding must play a crucial part.[14] Of course, cognitive understanding by no means stands alone. For example, especially where the economic complex is involved, a variety of legal controls is indispensable. The essential problem—balancing areas of freedom and of constraint—is central.

Reverting to the parallel between the two complexes, again in the economic case we have identified two modes of absolutism of orientation. The radical form, as we have called it, was most clearly exemplified by Marxist ideology, which is clearly identifiable, however many schools have differentiated or splintered from the original stem. For me, the core fits Weber's category of "religious rejection of the world." In Marx's case, it was the part of the concrete world of human experience that he included in what he delineated at great length under the category of the *capitalist system,* which, although it did not include everything conceivable, was surely extremely comprehensive. Just as, from the point of view especially of early monastic celibacy, the relevant part of the world was held to be dominated by "carnal concupiscence," so for orthodox Marxists the correspondingly relevant part of the world, which to them was *given*, was dominated by capitalism and the profit system. For this world, then, as in the case of the sin that underlay concupiscence, it was alleged that the *economic* factor "determined" everything. Then the revolution was not to be regarded as an economic phenomenon in any usual sense; at most, it was brought about by intolerable economic conditions. If and as it was successful, however, through its leap into freedom, it would permanently eliminate the relevance of "things economic" from the human social world.

The counterabsolutism is that of absolute acceptance as contrasted with absolute rejection. Its most conspicuous current representation is to be found in the school of social science thought of which Milton Friedman and Gary Becker are principal spokesmen. Perhaps they would not go quite so far, but it seems to me fair to suggest that what they mean is that everything that matters is in the last analysis economic and we had better accept it. At the least, they would say that the burden of proof rests on whoever claims that anything noneconomic is important. Dumont (1977), of course, has presented a broad historical account of the genesis of this movement of thought.

It would, I think, be fair to say that, however much quite different factors in the determination of human motivation have been operative at many points along the line, the great intellectual traditions of Western civilization have been of critical significance in breaking up the appeal of the absolutisms of both pairs, in each case on both sides. The case of the paired religious absolutisms we have discussed lies historically sufficiently far back so it is somewhat more difficult to discuss. The two that have arisen over the economic complex are, however, in a somewhat different situation, where we are not so dependent on "theologians." Here there has developed a notable growth in the resources of the social sciences. In this area, sociologists occupy a particularly strategic position.

With respect to burdens of proof, I would suggest that we sociologists who, within the profession, have a special concern with economic problems, should make a concerted attempt to reverse the burden of proof in our arguments with absolutists of either variety. For too long, we have been awed by the apodictic certainty with which many Marxists have expounded what to them has been the "true" doctrine and, as it were, have dared us to disagree, in the face of our imputed guilt for the evils of capitalism. Yet some of us also seem to have been awed by the air of certainty displayed by some of the proponents of the economic approach and have tended all too easily to concede the intellectual contest.

Notes

1. In German (Weber, 1921), *Vorbemerkung,* in *Gesammelte Aufsätze zur Religionssoziologie* (vol. 1, pp. 1–16), included with my English translation (Weber, [1904–1905] 1930) of Weber's *Protestant Ethic and the Spirit of Capitalism.* See also Nelson (1974) and Parsons (1978b).

2. All three of these essays on the "age-sex" complex are included, as chapters 12, 13, and part of 15, in the new book, *Action Theory and the Human Condition* (Parsons, 1978a).

3. If, however, the erotic complex that emerges in adolescence is seen in this light, it should be clear that sexual intercourse should be considered as a symbolic and hence, in an important sense, ritual recapitulation of the socialization experience. Erotic arousal usually begins with kissing, which involves the mouths of both partners. Soon after, in the course of foreplay, it is likely to involve fondling and kissing of the woman's breasts. It may or may not go on to fellatio, which may be regarded as a reversal of roles in that the woman now takes the infantile role, whereas when the man kisses her breasts he is taking the infantile role. From then, it goes on to actual genital intercourse, which is on quite a different symbolic level from these features of foreplay. I think this is enough discussion to make clear that the symbolism of intercourse is part of the more general complex of socialization symbolism.

4. Although space limits preclude analysis of it here, we should remember that another very central symbolic complex also serves to articulate the human family with socialization on the one hand and religion on the other. This is the food complex, or more accurately that of food *and* drink. The human mother, above all as symbolized by her breasts as the source of nurturance, becomes *both* the source of food and the prime object of infantile erotic attachment. The Jewish law then came to incorporate an elaborate set of

rules about food. Moreover, in the sacrificial cult of Israel, the "burnt offerings" that were so pleasing to Yahweh consisted of meat. Finally, in the central ritual of Christianity, the Eucharist, the two symbolic substances involved are bread and wine, with a ritual interpretation that has at least a suggestion of cannibalism, as respectively the "body" and "blood' of Christ, but of course not of the human Christ.

There is an important distinction between liquid and solid potentially nutritive intake. It is important that the infant's first food intake is liquid, namely milk, and that in a certain sense milk is, symbolically considered, the most "general" of foods. Moses promised the Israelites released from Egypt a land of "milk and honey." At the same time, "drink" may be regarded as more dangerous than solid food, if it has certain other properties—for example, pharmacological ones. Perhaps the concern about alcohol in modern societies involves more than meets the biomedical eye. (See also Douglas, 1973, 1975.)

5. Biological reductionism has been such a prominent feature of modern thought that I wish to stress as strongly as possible that what I have called the erotic complex is *not* only an organic phenomenon, but is the main basis of articulation of certain key features of the human organic species with the motivational structure of the human personality at the level of *action* in our technical sense. This was first worked out by Freud at a truly *theoretical* level. The erogenous zones, of course, are organs of human bodies, but they are *also* symbols that organize human personality motives. Freud above all saw that these symbols are involved not only in adult heterosexuality but also very deeply in the psychology of early childhood and thus in the socialization process as a whole. Thus Freud's discovery of the role of infantile sexuality was particularly shocking to the conservative opinion of the time. Freud's earliest extended treatment of these themes was in *Three Essays on the Theory of Sexuality* ([1905] 1962). My own fullest discussion of them is in "A Paradigm of the Human Condition" (see Parsons, 1978b, section 7, p. 352).

6. My discussion here must from now on be confined to the Western wing of Christianity, which, down to the Reformation, was Roman Catholic and subsequently was both Catholic and Protestant.

7. Indeed, it was over this issue that my sociohistorical con-

flict with Sorokin crystallized. It had a great deal to do with Sorokin's sharp repudiation of Weber's views about anything closely related to the Reformation. (See Parsons, 1963.)

8. Smelser's book (1959) presents striking evidence that this process of differentiation was far from being instantaneous and involved several stages. Whole families of the working class often moved into the factory, both parents and assorted children. A major problem created by the early Factory Acts, aimed against the employment of "child labor," was that they tended to break up families by forbidding the employment of the children—below certain ages—in the factory and left the parents with the problem of what to do with them. Smelser feels that this was a major impetus to the development of formal education, since the school could partly fulfill this function.

9. This technical terminology is taken from the so-called pattern-variable scheme. Particularly important here is the fact that whereas the universalism-particularism pair belong to what I have called the "object-modality" set, that of "diffuseness-specificity" belongs in the "orientation" set (see especially Parsons, 1967, p. 192).

10. Dumont has been a long-standing student of Indian society and culture, on which he has written a famous book entitled *Homo hierarchicus* (1970). The French title of his book on economic ideology is meant to point a sharp contrast between the West and India. I think it unfortunate that this contrast was lost in the title of the English edition.

11. A very similar position was earlier taken by George C. Homans (1961). Curiously, there is no reference to Homans in Becker's index, perhaps because Homans is identified as a sociologist, whereas Becker is an economist. On Becker's position generally, see the review articles by Duncan MacRae and by Darwin Sawyer in the March 1978 issue of the *American Journal of Sociology*.

12. That there is a symbolic linkage to psychology, at least in certain branches, is clearly indicated by Homans, who rests his case *both* on the model of economic thought and that of the behaviorism of B. F. Skinner in psychology and who has held that "in the last analysis" social science is reducible to "psychology." Needless to say, in Homans' meaning this is not psychology of Freudian persuasion.

13. This problem raises complex questions, which cannot be gone into further here. See the very interesting paper by Edward Tiryakian (1978), in which he states—correctly, I think—that the

sexual revolution, with its connection with the status of women, is one of the most important processes of social change in recent times. I hope to discuss these problems more fully on a future occasion.

14. In this particular context, surely Freud's aphorism "Where id was, there shall ego be" is classical. It is particularly important that psychoanalysis is a specifically noncoercive procedure that is organized about cognitive knowledge but that taps what are usually considered to be highly "nonrational" aspects of motivation. There is, of course, more to this case than "theory." There are also therapeutic skills but, perhaps above all, the *morality* institutionalized in a healing profession and hence the expectation that the analyst will exhibit high responsibility for the analysand's welfare.

References

Aristotle. *Politics.* (B. Jowett, Trans.) Oxford, England: Oxford University Press, 1923. (Originally written c. 335 B. C.)

Barber, B. "Absolutization of the Market: Some Notes on How We Got From There to Here." In G. Dworkin (Ed.), *Markets and Morals.* Washington, D. C.: Hemisphere, 1977.

Becker, G. *The Economic Approach to Human Behavior.* Chicago: University of Chicago Press, 1976.

Bell, D. "A Report on England: The Future That Never Was."*Public Interest,* 1978a, *51*, 35–73.

Bell, D. "The Return of the Sacred: The Argument About the Future of Religion." *Bulletin of The Academy of Arts and Sciences,* 1978b, *31*, 29–55.

Bellah, R. *Beyond Belief: Essays on Religion in a Post-Traditional World.* New York: Harper & Row, 1970.

Brandt, C., Schwartz, B., and Fairbank, J. K. *A Documentary History of Chinese Communism.* Cambridge, Mass.: Harvard University Press, 1952.

Burger, T. "Reply to Parsons." *American Journal of Sociology,* 1978, *83*, 983–986.

Burke, K. *The Rhetoric of Religion.* Berkeley: University of California Press, 1970.

Douglas, M. *Natural Symbols.* New York: Random House, 1973.

Douglas, M. "Dissection of a Meal." In *Implicit Meanings: Essays in Anthropology.* London: Routledge & Kegan Paul, 1975.

Dumont, L. *Homo Hierarchicus: The Caste System and Its Implications.* (M. Sainsbury, Trans.) Chicago: University of Chicago Press, 1970.

Dumont, L. *From Mandeville to Marx: The Genesis and Triumph of Economic Ideology.* Chicago: University of Chicago Press, 1977.

Durkheim, E. *Division of Labor in Society.* (G. Simpson, Trans.) New York: Macmillan, 1933. (Originally published 1893.)

Erikson, E. *Young Man Luther.* New York: Norton, 1958.

Freud, S. *Three Essays in the Theory of Sexuality.* (J. Strachey, Ed. and Trans.) New York: Basic Books, 1962. (Originally published 1905.)

Giele, J. "Adulthood as Transcendence of Age and Sex." Unpublished paper presented at Conference on Love and Work in Adulthood, Stanford, Calif., May 1977.

Halévy, É. *La formation du radicalisme philosophique.* Paris: Alcan, 1901.

Homans, G. C. *Social Behavior: Its Elementary Forms.* New York: Harcourt Brace Jovanovich, 1961.

Leach, E. *Genesis as Myth and Other Essays.* London: Grossman, 1969.

MacRae, D. "Review Essay: The Sociological Economics of Gary S. Becker." *American Journal of Sociology,* 1978, *83,* 1244–1258.

Miller, P. *Errand into the Wilderness.* Cambridge, Mass.: Harvard University Press, 1964.

Moore, G. F. *Judaism in the First Centuries of the Christian Era.* Cambridge, Mass.: Harvard University Press, 1927.

Nelson, B. "Max Weber's 'Author's Introduction': A Master Clue to His Main Aims." *Sociological Inquiry,* 1974, *44.*

Nock, A. D. *St. Paul.* London: Oxford University Press, 1948.

Ogburn, W. *Social Change with Respect to Culture and Original Nature.* New York: Viking, 1928.

Parsons, A. *Belief, Magic and Anomie.* New York: Free Press, 1969.

Parsons, T. *The Structure of Social Action.* New York: Free Press, 1937.

Parsons, T. "Christianity and Modern Industrial Society." In E. A. Tiryakian (Ed.), *Sociological Theory, Values, and Sociocultural*

Change: Essays in Honor of Pitirim A. Sorokin. New York: Free Press, 1963.

Parsons, T. *Sociological Theory and Modern Society.* New York: Free Press, 1967.

Parsons, T. *Social Systems and the Evolution of Action Theory.* New York: Free Press, 1977.

Parsons, T. *Action Theory and the Human Condition.* New York: Free Press, 1978a.

Parsons, T. "Letter to the Editor." *Contemporary Sociology,* 1978b, *7,* 117.

Parsons, T., and Platt, G. M. *The American University.* Cambridge, Mass.: Harvard University Press, 1973.

Parsons, T., and Smelser, N. J. *Economy and Society.* New York: Free Press, 1956.

Pope, W., and others. "De-Parsonizing Weber: A Critique of Parsons' Interpretation of Weber's Sociology." *American Journal of Sociology,* 1975, *40,* 666–669.

Ricardo, D. *Principles of Political Economy and Taxation.* New York: Dutton, 1912. (Originally published 1821.)

Sawyer, D. O. "Review Essay: Social Roles and Economic Firms: The Sociology of Human Capital." *American Journal of Sociology,* 1978, *83,* 1259–1270.

Shils, E. *Center and Periphery: Essays in Macrosociology.* Chicago: University of Chicago Press, 1975.

Smelser, N. J. *Social Change in the Industrial Revolution.* Chicago: University of Chicago Press, 1959.

Tiryakian, E. A. "The United States as a Religious Phenomena." In J. Delumeau (Ed.), *Histoire du peuple chrétien.* Toulouse: Editions Edouard Privat, 1978.

Tönnies, F. *Gemeinschaft und Gesellschaft.* (C. P. Loomis, Trans. and Ed.) New York: Harper & Row, 1963. (Originally published 1887.)

Turner, T. "Family Structure and Socialization." In J. Loubser and others (Eds.), *Explorations in General Theory in Social Science.* New York: Free Press, 1975.

Warner, R. "Toward a Redefinition of Action Theory: Paying the Cognitive Element Its Due." *American Journal of Sociology,* 1978, *83.*

Weber, M. *Gesammelte Aufsätze zur Religionssoziologie.* Tübingen: Mohr, 1921. (Originally published   .)

Weber, M. *The Protestant Ethic and the Spirit of Capitalism.* (T. Parsons, Trans.) London: Allen & Unwin, 1930. (Originally published 1904–1905.)

Weber, M. *The Religion of China.* (H. H. Gerth, Trans. and Ed.) New York: Free Press, 1951. (Originally published 1916.)

Weber, M. *Economy and Society.* (G. Roth and C. Wittich, Eds.) New York: Bedminster Press, 1968. (Originally published 1922.)

2

Louis Schneider

Dialectical Orientation
and the Sociology
of Religion

~~~~~~

The thesis of this chapter is that a dialectical orientation will guide us to important areas of religion that we might otherwise bypass too easily and will afford us a notion of how such areas may be usefully approached or studied. The term *dialectic,* itself, has been the object of much dispute and disagreement. This chapter sets out for brief exploration three meanings that the term has certainly had. In one sense, *dialectic* refers to study of the action of elements within a system, with an accent on *system* (although it may be used to refer to such action itself). In a second sense, the term refers to analysis of the play of "opposites." In a third sense, dialectic is to be understood as a kind of "language" or "grammar," which here has special application to social life. These several senses of the term are not to be taken as suggesting hard, inviolable distinctions. Rather, they suggest aspects of dialectic that one may wish to stress at one time or another. The first and second senses are very intimately connected, as will soon be evident, and the third may be constantly in the near background or on the verge of articulation when the first and second are being explored. The reality of overlap will be clearer from our account. The second sense will be explored in close association with the concept of antinomianism.

In the first sense, then, dialectic involves the idea of a system or totality in which elements—say, A and B—that demand some kind of "satisfaction" are in tension and in which "excessive" movement toward either—toward A or toward B—will tend to generate movement toward the other. Thus, Diesing (1971) writes of a certain one-sidedness in the methodology of science that is illustrated by a definition of science exclusively in terms of rigor and precision. Diesing argues that science needs a certain amount of "vagueness" and "suggestiveness" as well as rigor and precision. He finds that actual scientific traditions show a balance of precision and vagueness but that different traditions apportion the two in different ways. "The various kinds of balance serve the conflicting scientific needs of creativity and control: Vagueness and suggestiveness facilitate creativity, and precision and rigor are means of control, either empirical or logical" (Diesing, 1971, p. 221). The outcome of an exaggerated stress on rigor and precision is likely to be "theoretical stagnation and empirical preoccupation with detail," while an excess of vagueness leads to "diffuse and uncontrolled speculation." In a broad sense, then, science as a totality or system unites the "opposites" of rigor or precision *and* vagueness or suggestiveness. These opposites are never "perfectly" balanced but are in a tense interrelationship, and, as balance shifts, either may crowd out the other, to the detriment of the whole scientific enterprise. The interrelationship may also be called *dialectical*. (The reference to "opposites" already indicates the close affinity between our first and our second meanings of *dialectic*.)

The general pattern of thought—the orientation, if one will—thus suggested with regard to science is easily extended beyond science to include phenomena that are of interest in the sociology of religion. Religion can also be profitably regarded as a realm of elements in tension that are constantly productive of conflict (although also showing movement toward accommodation). But at this point we must not lose sight of system, totality, or larger context, although it is often hard to define this context with any precision in relation to religion.

Within the religious realm, we frequently discern striking swings from one "extreme" to another. Sheldon Shapiro, in an interesting article on religious reformations (1973), develops a contrast between "gnostic" and "bhaktic" strains in several religions, strains toward salvation by knowledge versus strains toward salvation by faith or by what Glasenapp (1962, p. 24) calls "believing surrender to God." But Shapiro sees more than the two strains. He also discerns a rhythm or alternation. The reaction to stress on salvation by knowledge or wisdom (or on that alone) may be noted in the popular Mahayana Buddhism, which opened a path of salvation by faith to great multitudes—or indeed in Methodism, with its reaction in favor of religious feeling against a "rationalistic," "formalistic," and "dry" religion.

We simplify Shapiro's account in the interest of presenting a sharp contrast, which, we believe with him, is basically defensible. Gnostic or cognitive has vied with bhaktic or devotional repeatedly and in religions remote from one another in space and time. But our interest in the contrast is now also connected with the notion of a religious system or totality. The swing between bhaktic and gnostic may occur over centuries. What is the time span to be allowed for a single system that can be handled in analytically useful terms by sociologists or others? And how delicately can we discriminate "elements" in which we are interested? Will a really subtle analysis show that, while the notion of alternation or rhythm has some point, it is also true that the elements or extremes between which there is movement are always still substantially *co*present? It is certainly a plausible notion, at any rate, that gnostic and bhaktic represent quite fundamental human religious orientations that are *constantly* at work within numerous religious totalities that may be fairly accurately delimited.

We are thus motivated to look for the simultaneous presence of "conflicting" or "opposite" religious impulses, not merely for alternations or rhythms (granted that we may theoretically bring even the notion of centuries-long swings within the compass of the general idea of system). This all ties in with questions about just who the adherents of a religion are, what their class affiliation is, and to whom the proselytizing endeavors of a religion, if such there are, are addressed. Particular strata may accept religious activity and thought that will not appeal to others. But religions that take in large and socially varied portions of humanity clearly appear to have a certain likelihood of catering to a variety of religious strains or impulses and of sustaining the tension of struggle among them. Conze, a close student of Buddhism, writes, perhaps somewhat testily, that "of course, if one makes up one's mind that 'original' Buddhism was a perfectly rational religion, after the heart of the 'ethical society,' without any touch of the supernatural or mysterious," then certain developments within it (say, on the lines of magic, for instance; Conze himself here refers to the Tantra, of which we shall say something later) "will become an incomprehensible 'degeneration' of that presumed original Buddhism. In actual fact, Buddhism has always been closely associated with what to rationalists would appear as superstitions" (Conze, 1959, p. 175).

Conze forthrightly criticizes a contempt for magic that may be harbored by educated people as "a serious obstacle to our historical understanding of the past." He continues, in context still of discussion of Buddhism, "In order to live, in order to keep its feet on the earth, a religion must to some extent serve the material preoccupations of the average man. It must be able to insert itself into the rhythm of communal life which in the past was everywhere permeated and dominated by magic. Then, as now, the average man was deeply absorbed in the problems of everyday life. . . . [He] expected *that same religion which was based on the renunciation of all things of the world,* to provide him with that control over the unseen magical forces all around him, which would guarantee or at least assist the secure possession of the things of the world" (Conze, 1959, p. 82, italics added).

Indeed, Conze is willing to generalize his pertinent observations and contends that "no known religion has become mature without embracing both the spiritual and the magical. . . . If . . . religion rejects the magical side of life, it cuts itself off from the living forces of the world to such an extent that it cannot even bring the spiritual side of man to maturity" (Conze, 1959, p. 84). And, referring once more to Buddhism itself, the same writer observes that "among all the paradoxes with which the history of Buddhism presents us, this combination of spiritual negation of self-interest with magical subservience to self-interest is perhaps one of the most striking. Illogical though it may seem, a great deal of the actual life of the Buddhist religion has been due to it" (Conze, p. 85). Tambiah's (1968) study of Buddhism in a Thai village, which develops such "dualities" or "paradoxes" (the language is that of the author of the study referred to) as the one in which a community of Buddhist monks renounces the world and life, while *at the same time* the monks tap powers adaptable to the life needs of laymen, constitutes in its way a brilliant confirmation of Conze's thesis.

That thesis might conceivably be more precisely stated, but there is substantial historical and comparative support for the view that religions will often at once feature "splendid heights" and accommodation even to the "grossest" inclinations. Appropriate scholarly statements may be found elsewhere than in the work of Conze. But it is an irresistible temptation to quote a pertinent statement on Tibetan Buddhist temples made by Maraini in a popular, although still substantial, work (1960, p. 162): "In a Tibetan Buddhist temple, there is darkness, mystery, magnificence, and filth; the stink of yak butter; a love of death and horror; a strange, twisted mentality; sex mingled with mystical exaltation; barbarous couplings combined with extreme asceticism; magic and gnosticism; a multiplication of arms, heads, and symbols; unbridled audacity and imagination; a continuous metaphysical shudder."

Neither yak butter nor other things Maraini mentions are present everywhere. But "magnificence and filth," "sex mingled with mystical exaltation" (even Western religious history suggests a certain affinity of these "opposites"—if that is what they are—for one another), and "barbarous couplings combined with extreme asceticism"—these must in themselves strike us strongly. A dialectical orientation in the analysis of religion will enhance our sensitivity to the tendency of religion to do some sort of "justice," to render some sort of "satisfaction," to a variety of different or conflicting or "opposite" needs, impulses, and strains. If there is no overt sign of "sex," it is what one might call a bit of dialectical sagacity, not cynicism, to obey the behest "Cherchez la femme," at least until it seems quite certain that it is profitless to do so. If God is represented as an oblong blur or the essence of all essences, it is sagacious to look for indications somewhere that he is also regarded as a

supplier of bread and meat (see Pratt, 1920, pp. 200, 207). Again, it
will be wise to be alert to the possibility of tensions, conflicts, alternations, and rhythms as the deity is passionately represented as of
one nature or another, simultaneously and over stretches of time.

But we wish to revert once more to the notion of system. It is
noteworthy that, in some of the central theoretical work that students of religion and society have at their disposal, the significance
of that notion is suggested. We have here in view, particularly, two
studies that have been very influential in the sociology of religion;
namely, James's *Varieties of Religious Experience* ([1902] 1961) and
Durkheim's *Elementary Forms of the Religious Life* ([1912] 1926). It is
well to recall each of these scholars' very mode of apprehending
religion. Religion, writes James, shall mean for him and his audi-
ence "the feelings, acts, and experiences of individual men in their
solitude, so far as they apprehend themselves to stand in relation to
whatever they may consider the divine" (James, 1961, p. 42). For
Durkheim, on the other hand, "a religion is a unified system of
beliefs and practices relative to sacred things; that is to say, things
set apart and forbidden—beliefs and practices which unite into
one single moral community called a church all those who adhere
to them" (Durkheim, [1912] 1926, p. 47).

James is interested above all in a God who is on the firing
line of human experience, as it were, a God for men and women
who are often sick and desperate, a God who is approached via
firsthand experience in a terribly compelling desire for his help.
James' book may be said to resound with the cries of sinners and
saints and mystics seeking their own distinctive encounters with a
divine existence that they must contact merely in order to live. It is
not hard to get from James the impression that "church" was for
him a rather negative symbol, connected with "ecclesiastical institutions with corporate ambitions of their own" and "the spirit of
politics and the lust of dogmatic rule" (1961, p. 267). Durkheim
had different purposes from those of James. Each man had considerable sensitivity to much in the range of religious phenomena, but
there is certainly a bias toward a different sort of appreciation of
religion in the two. Where James might well see barren dogmatisms
and uncongenially fixed religious practices or structures, Durkheim saw powerful forces indispensably strengthening group sol-

idarities, ensuring group morale, and the like. These were things from which James might consider the spirit had departed, leaving only institutional lumber.

Febrile, vibrating personal experience, we might say, is thus contrasted with the experience of social sustainment in reliable ritual and ceremony. Thus stated, the contrast is rather too simple, if only because in Durkheim's depiction of primitive Australian religion, in his *Elementary Forms,* religious ceremonies reaffirming group strength and bolstering morale could also be very quickening, "exciting" performances. But we would venture the suggestion that both "religion as living personal experience" and "religion as ritual or ceremony" are likely to be "needed" in a religious system or totality.

We may, however, catch a strong warning in these premises that we must not be satisfied too easily that we know precisely what the "opposites" within a religious system are. A dialectical orientation will be useless if it betrays us into glibness and superficiality about ostensible opposites. James was immensely interested in mind cure, in the psychotherapeutic effects of religion. He is very much concerned with persons who have "gone to pieces" emotionally and who reach out to something transcendent that they can, as it were, get on board of, transcendent yet in active contact with some portion of themselves. We might then think, on the one hand, of pressing individual needs where, for example, any considerable psychotherapeutic help, if available at all, *might* be available, let us say, only from religion, and, on the other hand, of a religion so fixed in its ritual-social orientation, so uncompromisingly churchly or ecclesiastical, that it will not be inclined to seek to provide therapeutic resources for individuals. Or, again, we might think of a contrast between the latter sort of ritual-social orientation and impulses to individual religious experience having to do not so much with psychotherapy as with cultivating novel and titillating religious adventures or "kicks," in turn connected with certain kinds of social protest or rebellion not congruous with conventional churchliness. The differences here are obvious enough, but they might hide under the common cover of what might well become *too* loose a contrast of rigid social forms and "living individual experience."

But a dialectical orientation need not betray us into foolishness or neglect of pertinent empirical realities. Its stress on system is a heuristically useful one, and when it comes to concentrate on the subtle relations of "elements in opposition" *without* particular reference to system (thereby featuring the second sense in which we deal with dialectic) it can also be most stimulating, as we shall seek to show. James Bissett Pratt makes a distinction that at once points back to our concern with dialectic in the first sense and points forward to our concern with dialectic in the second sense.

In a series of able books, Pratt worked out very shrewdly the contrast between "objective" and "subjective" worship (Pratt, 1915, 1920, 1928, 1950). The contrast is rich with implications but it may be concisely described as one between (1) a religious attitude concerned with the divine or sacred or transcendent or the like, in itself or for itself, such as one may note in ceremonies whose object is to "gratify the god," and (2) a religious attitude concerned with the effects of religion on the self or the members of a social group. In subjective worship, one seeks psychological benefit for oneself or benefit to the emotions of the members of a group. Pratt, another keen student of Buddhism, found cases, particularly in Buddhism and Jainism, where the subjective stress was very strong and where religious activity was maintained explicitly because it was psychologically beneficial. Pratt regards traditional Catholicism as relatively more oriented toward objective worship than is Protestantism.

But, thus far, we might say that Pratt is pointing to certain realities that are not at all difficult to think of in system terms. Within many religious systems or totalities, there will be tension between "worship of God for himself" (God being an appropriate symbol here that will serve also for cases where "a god" is not involved) and worship of God so that one may gain psychic benefit. (One may wonder how much Pratt's thought was affected by William James.) One might expect the usual tensions, strains toward extremes, returns to "equilibrium," and so on, but the subjective and the objective would presumably both be needed components within system or totality. However, Pratt's analysis probes the relation of subjective and objective more carefully. Another sense or aspect of dialectic is now intimated, not at all incompatible with the first but making salient the connections of the "elements in opposition." Pratt notes that where one wants and is exclusively concerned with (beneficial) subjective effects there is danger of getting no effect at all. To pray for something for one's own benefit can become exceedingly difficult when "that to which" one is somehow supposed to pray is actually believed not to exist. Pratt, as earlier stated, found a strong strain of objectivity in Catholicism but suggested that the subjective effect of Catholic religious activity was considerable *because* it was not directly aimed at. (Paradoxically, one might get more "peace of mind" by religious ventures not addressed to getting it than by ventures squarely aiming at it.) By this analysis, objectively oriented religious exercise addressed to and concerned with the divine, the sacred, the transcendent, or something cognate at least has some fair chance of bringing subjective "benefit." Subjective "benefit" has little chance of being obtained without some modicum of faith that there is "something" that is "really there," objectively existent as divine or sacred or transcendent. At the same time, one could ask how perduring any objective worship would be if it brought no subjective results. There are thus powerful connections of objective and subjective. Each depends on the other, and, because they tend markedly to come together, they may in a sense even be said to "coalesce" and exist in unity.

The coalescence or sheer closeness of opposites (or seeming opposites) is important and will engage us shortly. But we will proceed more effectively with it, and the effort to exhibit the heuristic value of dialectic will be facilitated, if we now examine the specific phenomenon of antinomianism in relative detail. (The very choice of antinomianism as a matter to attend to here is, we believe, a choice that might well be expected in anyone with a dialectical orientation toward religion.) We define antinomianism generally as either the doctrine that faith frees one from obligation to the religious or moral law or as activity that is significantly determined by such doctrine.

Adherents to antinomian views have, inevitably and repeatedly, shown "deviant" behavior, behavior that violates a variety of commonly held norms. It is a matter for astonishment that a field with so ostensibly great an interest in "deviance" as sociology has so largely neglected antinomianism, which has been intimately bound up with the emergence of sects and the occurrence of schisms. Perhaps the neglect of it is partly explained by a continuing reluctance on the part of numerous sociologists to engage seriously in historical and comparative study. In any case, antinomianism is a very salient "nay-saying" phenomenon in the framework of religions. It is by its very character oppositional, and it would be matter for surprise if some consideration of it did not allow us to develop somewhat further the sense of a dialectical orientation in the sociology of religion.

The incidence of antinomianism is so considerable that it is impossible in a short chapter to do more than refer to a relatively small number of cases of it, necessarily omitting some very important ones. But we may at least illustrate its scope. The history of medieval sects within "Christianity" is most instructive in regard to antinomianism. With foundations in Gnostic and Manichean teachings, these sects presented numerous doctrines most radically uncongenial to Roman Catholicism. There was Catharist teaching that "worldly authority and administration of justice are not admissible among true believers and constitute an alien invention not deriving from the good God and that accordingly the members of the true church are under no obligation of obedience to worldly princes and judges." Knowing this much, we are not altogether unprepared to learn that the institution of the Consolamentum among the Cathari, whereby one made a "good end" sufficient for salvation, encouraged antinomianism: One who was assured that he would receive the Consolamentum on his deathbed could, before he got there, engage in unrestrained behavior and gratify all lusts — although, certainly, not all persons did so (von Döllinger, 1971, pp. 183, 211–212, 216–217).

Barbour, in his treatment of the early Quakers, writing of the seventeenth-century Ranters, with whom the Quakers were often confused, notes that the Ranters "claimed that, since they were led by the spirit, they could do no wrong and so followed impulses into all kinds of immorality and anarchy. Some went further, saying that no man could be freed from a sin until he had committed that sin as if it were not a sin" (Barbour, 1964, p. 119). Cohn has presented documents that back the view of the Ranters thus suggested. Strong among them was the doctrine that to the pure all things are pure. (So, presumably, was that very likely concomitant of the sense of being pure: aggressive and contemptuous feeling toward the ordinary "impure.") Adultery and fornication could not defile them, nor, apparently, could incest or murder. Cohn regards it as beyond doubt that some Ranters genuinely taught total amoralism. There was some patent Ranter bias toward regarding the most "deviant" acts as identical with the act of prayer itself (Cohn, 1970, appendix).

Let us fill out the picture for English speakers a little. Gaustad, writing on the Great Awakening in New England, warns us of "the ambiguity of a word like *antinomianism*" yet does not hesitate to suggest a sufficiently clear general sense for the same word when he avers, "The antinomian could be sure that *faith without the law* was enough to save him" (Gaustad, 1957, pp. 95, 97; emphasis added). And about the existence of such people as "antinomians" in this sense in mid eighteenth-century New England there is no question. Wilbur Cross, in his study of enthusiastic religion in Western New York in the first half of the nineteenth century, pays attention to the (Adventist) Millerites, among other groups, and notes that "many of the most zealously sincere" in their ranks were led into "remarkable extravagances." There appears once more a notable and frequent tendency for those who regard themselves as especially sanctified to believe or aver that what is usually considered impure action or unconventional comportment is justifiable or even excellent for *them* because of *their* distinctive purity (Cross, 1950, pp. 314–315).

We move very briefly to the Muslim world. Hasan II, lord of Alamut near the Caspian Sea, in the twelfth century proclaimed the millennium, announcing a message of liberation from the bonds of the holy law. The word was received in Syria, and there too the faithful celebrated the law's end. Lewis writes of "the solemn and ritual violation of the law" as a (millenarian and) antinomian tendency "which is recurrent in Islam and has obvious parallels in Christendom" (Lewis, 1967, p. 73). And Grunebaum observes that Islam, too, had "had to counteract those antinomian tendencies which everywhere and at all times accompany the process of interiorization of the religious experience." It is also of interest that Grunebaum notes something of a Sufi tendency to claim or presume freedom not only from ritual but also from moral precepts (Grunebaum, 1953, pp. 136–137).

There is admitted danger in thus ranging over the world while relying on a simple rubric such as antinomianism as we have thus far described it. Moreover, we intend even to increase the danger by reference also to the extremely interesting cases of Tantrism and the antinomian activity of the seventeenth-century mystical Jewish "messiah," Sabbatai Sevi. We have noted Gaustad's saying that antinomianism is an ambiguous word, although he can also give it a rather unambiguous definition. There are differences among antinomianisms. But at least some of these various movements appear to have much in common. Let us venture some remarks bearing on common features, in the sense of dialectical orientation, before describing additional cases.

The coalescence or closeness of opposites now virtually obtrudes itself on us. The cases we have thus far reviewed suggest a remarkable coincidence of opposites: a remarkable tendency for those who strive for special, really extraordinary holiness *and* those who are by all usual standards wicked people who engage in heinous behavior, people in any case "abandoned of the Lord," to act in the same way, a way thoroughly reprehensible in the ordinary view. Thus, the religiously zealous or pious and the hopelessly abandoned come together. If anything, the religiously very zealous perhaps can exceed the wicked in the awfulness, the reprehensibility of their performances. Opposites, or ostensible opposites, meet or coalesce. (Ronald Knox, whose book *Enthusiasm* contains much that bears on our theme here, provocatively quotes Bishop Bossuet's shrewd exhortation never to believe good of those who outdo virtue itself—Knox, 1961, p. 104.)

Of course, in some few cases, it may be possible to explain such coalescence on the ground that the exceptionally zealous were fakes or hypocrites all along. In his learned treatise on the Tantric tradition, Bharati notes that Hindu and Buddhist critics of Tantric teaching and conduct "have constantly suggested that the Tantric uses religion as a mantle for sexual desire and debauchery"; but he also records the rather convincing answer of the Tantrics that the complex, elaborate, and very difficult procedures they follow "would not at all be necessary to gratify sexual desire, whose objects are much easier to obtain without any yogic trappings" (Bharati, 1965, p. 292; see also p. 284, where Bharati observes that "no one has to undergo the excessive hardships, the degree of control, the tedium of initiation, of ritualistic perfection, and of minute detail [involved in Tantrism] in order to have fun, even in Puritan India"). It is always possible that there are some few attracted to "wild" doctrines and practices for the sheer joy of the wildness, but there is far too much to suggest intense zeal and profound commitment to make plausible the notion that "wild" religious impulses are in any general way covers for mere desires to engage in crime, indulge in drink, and commit fornication, adultery, and incest. The affinities between uncommon religiousness—supererogatory religiousness, one might say—and the ways of the unqualifiedly ungodly must be sought at deeper levels.

What, then, brings together—makes "coalesce"—great holiness and flagrant wickedness? It is noteworthy that *within* sectarian contexts themselves both holiness and wickedness may make their appearance. Koch, a much more recent student of Catharism than von Döllinger, notes that by antinomian standards with a certain philosophical base one could be either ascetic or libertine on the ground that matter is utterly worthless and spirit possesses all merit. Then one could express one's contempt for the urges of the flesh (a part of matter) by refusing, ascetically, to gratify all desire; but if one indulged the flesh one was merely giving way to something entirely contemptible and one's soul would be untainted by the actions of the body (Koch, 1962, p. 107). The doctrine of the so-called dualistic Cathari, then, disdaining matter and exalting spirit, might go some way toward explaining both holiness and wickedness. (Yet it should be said that statements made about the Cathari in this chapter are not beyond controversy. Not all present-day scholars would be easy with the notion that the Cathari came to libertine conclusions from their depreciative view of the flesh.) I remarked earlier that Grunebaum noted some Sufi antinomian tendency. He connects this with a belief tendency (1953, p. 137): "The unreality of this world entails the nothingness of all its attributes. What, then, could the statutes and demands of society, what the tenets of this or that specific faith, mean to him who had seen through the meaningless mirage?" The "statutes and demands of society"—these, too, are unreal, and violation of them accordingly would mean nothing.

It is not claimed that this solves all problems that may arise in this context. It does, of course, suggest that it might be profitable for sociologists of religion to entertain the notion of particularly close affinities between ascetic and orgiastic sects. And numerous other factors may throw light on the affinity we have noted, including psychological factors such as reaction formation. A bit of wit from Bernard Mandeville, although it is perhaps rather nasty, still may have its point. Mandeville writes that to conquer his sexual desire (his "domestic enemy") St. Francis was capable of throwing himself into an ice-filled ditch or a heap of snow (or of scourging himself). Mandeville (1729, pp. 216–217) comments that "the fever of lust must be very high where such violent coolers are required." Again lust and asceticism are connected. But sociologists studying such phenomena, like historians, would be alert to the possible relevance in these matters of a variety of social circumstances, including class origins, the status of women, and the character of their opportunities in a particular social order, and level of education.

From the cases of Catharism and Sufism, we see that religions may contain components that unite "opposites" and in this sense exhibit a dialectical bias or structure. The foundations for a "unity of opposites" were apparently also present among the Ranters, by Barbour's account. The Ranters were redeemed and led by the spirit and could do no wrong; hence, anything "wrong" that they did was not really such, and "right" and "wrong" were thereby at one. (It is a particular sort of "unity" that the Ranters insisted on We do not claim that everything that might come in some sense under the rubric of "unity of opposites" would necessarily result in a sheer obliteration of distinctions.) This is actually a very common antinomian tendency, also manifested by the Millerites, for example, as we noted earlier: What the sanctified do is by the same token sanctified. For another American example, Anne Hutchinson, the seventeenth-century New England religious leader, would have found it difficult, according to Battis, "to abandon her conviction that once God's children have been sealed in His love, the seal could not be removed," which suggests that, once God's love has been sealed, if the seal cannot be removed then no matter what his children may do they will retain their sanctity (Battis, 1962, p. 16; it is of interest, however, to note Battis' opinion, p. 287, that, with Mrs. Hutchinson and her colleagues, "the deeply implanted inhibitions of Puritan morality precluded the grosser behavioral possibilities of the antinomian position"). Outside America, Knox (1961, p. 125) notes that it would appear that at least some of the medieval Beghards were antinomians, "extending the principle of perfectionism so as to hold that actions normally regarded as sinful are not sinful in the perfect."

Despite differences among antinomianisms, the literature does encourage one to think that it is worth trying out hypotheses about shared features. And a dialectical orientation may make us fruitfully curious. By now, we may be prepared to look with renewed curiosity at something that was quoted earlier from Barbour (1964), who noted the view of some Ranters that no man could be free of a sin until he had committed it as if it were not a sin. Perhaps the relations of "opposites" are more subtle than we have thus far suspected. Antinomianism might reveal not only their tendency to "come together," to "coalesce," but also other intimate relationships between them. Thus, not only may antinomian doctrine refuse to see any difference between what are called good and evil but it also might conceivably premise some sort of special connection between them.

We turn to some aspects of antinomianism in India, seeking to expand our bare survey of the phenomenon while we do not forget our suspicions about special connection just intimated. "The idea that a man is not necessarily bound by the moral law, and can reach a state that takes him beyond its precepts, is prominent in the Indian religions, particularly in the left-hand Tantric cults like those of the Saktas, Nathas, Kaulas, and Kapalikas among the Hindus, and the Vajrayanas and Kalachakrayanas among the Buddhists. The Sanskrit equivalent for the term *antinomianism* is *nirdharma*, 'unrighteousness,' which implies a lack of regard for the norms of religion and the conventions of society. Tantriks believe that the goddess Sakti is gratified by all forms of antinomian activity" (Walker, 1968, p. 51). Kenneth Ch'en writes of a Tantric Buddhist text whence it appears that a bodhisattva, dedicated as he is to the serving of all sentient beings, would find it his duty, to a woman who had fallen in love with him and was about to sacrifice her life for him, to "save her life by satisfying all her desires." The bodhisattva does not ever sin. "For this reason, it is repeatedly stated in the texts that there is nothing that the bodhisattva should not do for the salvation of others. Since the intentions and motives of the bodhisattva are noble and virtuous, whatever deeds he performs are also virtuous" (Ch'en, 1964, p. 332). This certainly has a familiar sound in the mansions of antinomianism.

Walker (1968, vol. 1, pp. 52–53) notes a widely prevalent antinomianism in Hindu sex mysticism ("unequivocally condemned by Hindus of advanced thought"), refers to "the worship of the linga of Siva and the yoni of the Mother Goddess" and writes also that "Tantrism affirms that spiritual union with god can best be attained *through sexual union* in the flesh" (emphasis added). Here we already have a significant intimation about "special connection." The "high" can be reached best *through* the "low." Further, again within the Tantric context, the ideal union is "the unconventional and perilous intimacy of a man with a woman with whom he can never unite; an antinomian adventure in defiance of the laws of society. . . . Such unions bring into play that element of awe and guilt accompanied by heightened tension so necessary in satisfying Sakti." Union with low-caste women, dancing girls, and prostitutes is yet more to be commended for its breaking of the bonds of caste; and "if this type of intercourse is accompanied by *feelings of revulsion, all the greater is its spiritual merit*" (emphasis added). Awe—and guilt: one must clearly be conscious of doing wrong, and yet this is clearly also associated with getting close to the divine or transcendent or the like. The greater the revulsion (revulsion being grounded in consciousness of "wrongdoing," of violating powerful norms), the greater the spiritual merit. Religious excellence, apparently, can be attained precisely through the "vilest" sort of behavior. (Note that "the feelings of revulsion" or the guilt alluded to are *not* simply imputed by Western scholars or observers on the basis of their own values.)

Tantrism can be rather spectacularly antinomian. There are in it elements of support for incest, best of all with one's mother. It has, further, associations with diabolism and black magic and "preoccupation with ordure and other scatological substances, with cadavers, graveyards, and cremation grounds" (Walker, 1968, vol. 2, p. 484). Since this may indeed seem extreme, it is perhaps well to add that students of Tantrism have protested that antagonistic attitudes toward it have inhibited careful examination of it. It is interesting in this connection that Walker, for all his vivid description of the "left-hand" religious activities he describes, can also say that "Tantrism contains the loftiest philosophical speculation side by side with the greatest obscenities; the most rarified metaphysics with the wildest superstition" (Walker, 1968, vol. 2, p. 484). This is undoubtedly prompted in part by the desire to be fair, but it is also a correct statement in itself. By this juncture, we might in fact be saying, "Of course! What else would one expect? In religion, it's virtually a dialectical 'law' that opposites should beget one another."

We do not pretend to give a rounded representation of Tantric religion. We do, of course, wish to stress antinomianism and the bias toward attaining "good" via "evil." The well-informed Conze, who is not in principle unfriendly to "deviant" religious forms, has made observations much like some of those made by Walker. Conze notes that the scriptures of the left-handed Tantra appear to push in the very opposite direction to that taken by Buddhist asceticism. "Just the most immoral, the most tabooed actions, seem to have a particular fascination for the followers of this doctrine ... One must feed on the flesh of elephants, horses, and dogs, and all food and drink should be mixed with ordure, urine, or meat" (Conze, 1959, p. 195). But Conze finds all this essentially quite understandable. He calls attention to the purpose of bringing the senses into contact with stimulating objects. We may come fully to realize the "vanity and relativity" of the sensual pleasures by full exposure to them. (We may add that on the same principle an extreme involvement with the world, getting one's fill of it and more, may be just the thing needed to turn from it, in the end, with utter aversion.) Overlooking nuances important in themselves but not especially to the point here, Bharati, too, appealing to the aim of "freedom from the misery of attachment," suggests that in their radical way Tantrics move toward that aim (Bharati, 1965, p. 285).

The Tantric way still is "radical" and the sort of "justification" given by Conze, say, may still strike us as far from explaining the full character of Tantrism, but it does make in some degree understandable the Tantric juxtaposition of "good" and "evil" and what would seem to be a certain disposition to reach good *through* evil. And our understanding is also aided when Blofeld (1970, p 93) writes of responding to the promptings of desire "in order to profit from the subsequent disillusion and gradually lay desire to rest." In the context of discussing Tantrism, sexual activity or the emotion and bliss that accompany it should, Blofeld (p. 227) writes, be "made to contribute to [one's] realization of not being an individual cut off by his envelope of skin from the rest of phenomena. During enjoyment, he must visualize his desire as a companion to voidness-bliss; that is to say, as an integral part of the universal play of void functioning through him but not belonging to him." It may not be reading too much into this—or too much of a simplification—to suggest that, at least where the sexual activity Blofeld thus refers to is of a highly "deviant" sort, a metaphysical or religious excellence is represented as reachable (or even best reachable) through "vileness." This hardly means that in tension between the high metaphysical or religious impulse informing antinomian activity, on the one hand, and the temptation to indulge in that activity for its own sake, on the other, the "elevated" impulse will always win out. That would be quite implausible.

One more relevant account will bring to a close our conspectus of antinomianism and allow us again a glance at how good is presumed to be advanced through evil. We draw on Gershom Scholem's monumental study (1973) of Sabbatai Sevi (1626–1676), the mystical Jewish messiah. Sabbatai was a complex character who, Scholem is quite certain, suffered from manic-depressive psychosis. But Sabbatai's doctrines and behavior require more explanation than this, and Scholem provides us with relevant theological background, particularly in kabbalism (in which Isaac Luria Ashkenazi, 1534–1572, played an important part; Gershom employs the term "Lurianic kabbalism"). Orthodox kabbalism had some notion that a messiah had in himself "something of the 'evil side.'" This became very important in Sabbatai's case. Sabbatai, the great hope and light of very many Jews in the seventeenth-century world of the Near East and Europe, became an apostate under pressure, converting to Islam. He "bought his life at the price of apostasy" (Scholem, 1973, p. 679).

This was unavoidably terribly shocking to multitudes of Jews. What worse, what more profoundly wrong, than apostasy? Faith in Sabbatai would then be (and was) taken by numbers of previous adherents as a sad illusion. One *could*, however, seek to believe in an apostate messiah, as some did. But so to believe would be "to build one's faith on foundations of paradox and absurdity, which could only lead to more paradoxes . . . The Sabbataian paradox . . . was not that of a saint who suffers and whose suffering is a mystery hidden with God, but of a saint who sins. Its dialectical premise of necessity begets conclusions that are equally marked by the dialectics of paradox" (Scholem, 1973, pp. 690–691).

Even before his apostasy, Sabbatai had engaged in various "strange," antinomian actions. But the apostasy was something that required quite special justification, and it had to be justified in terms based on traditional Judaism, even though, inevitably, the new justifying doctrine was heretical by those very terms. The complexities of kabbalism get involved here. Scholem expounds background-relevant Lurianic kabbalism, which had taught a mode of separating "holy sparks" from "the clutches of evil in which they were held." If these sparks were released and "raised," evil, by itself without power (which it obtained only from good), would simply be wiped out. And just at this point Sabbataian doctrine introduced a dialectical turn into "the Lurianic idea." Scholem notes that it was no longer enough, in the new, Sabbataian version of things, to extract the sparks of holiness from the realm of impurity. The power of holiness—as embodied in the messiah—had to go down into impurity, and good had to assume the form of evil, that holiness might carry out its mission. Sabbatai had to become a Muslim in order to fulfill his very messianic task and do ultimate, final good. He was truly a "holy sinner" (Scholem, 1973, p. 706).

In time, it even came to be contended by Sabbataian radicals that "only the complete transformation of good into evil would exhaust the full potential of the latter and thereby explode it, as it were, from within. This dialectical liquidation of evil requires not only the disguise of good in the form of evil but total identification with it" (Scholem, 1973, p. 801). Nathan of Gaza, Sabbatai's "prophet," put major emphasis on the theme of the descent of the righteous one into the realm of evil, the realm of "the other side." We find in Sabbatai the paradox of "the messiah who saves the world by himself transgressing the law" (Scholem, 1973, p. 808). Antinomianism has nourished such development elsewhere also. But what we would again especially emphasize is that aspect of Sabbataian doctrine whereby evil becomes the instrumentality of good. Despite all differences, the similarities with tendencies we have already noted in Tantrism are striking.

We must always expect a certain skill in argument on the part of significant antinomian figures. Medieval antinomians in Europe, often drawing on Gnostic or Manichean ideas, could present imaginative mythological and theological justifications for their beliefs. Nathan of Gaza, with a mind nourished on kabbalistic writings, was clearly a man of some ability in handling the theological subtleties pertinent to the vindication of Sabbatai. Even antinomians with what would appear to be relatively modest talents can present, if they do not originate, such distinctions as that between "carnal" union and "spiritual" union, the former being bad even in marriage, while the latter would be good even outside of marriage. Cross (1950, p. 243) reports that one Lucina Umphreville took up this distinction in 1835 while at about the same time one Maria Brown "decided to demonstrate that her piety could overcome lowly desires by proving that she could sleep chastely with her minister." But again and again the "dialectic" of the antinomians themselves will strike us as replete with paradox, ambiguity, and play with contradictions. This brings us to the last sense in which we wish to discuss dialectic.

Paradox, ambiguity, contradictions—up to this point, we have been concerned with the opposition of elements within a system, giving emphasis to the idea of system, precisely, and we have allowed the notion of opposition to lead us into a discussion of antinomianism, this time not stressing the idea of system but letting that fade into the background while allowing ourselves to be guided to a number of significant questions and "interesting phenomena" suggested by "opposition" itself. But it has surely been evident throughout that a dialectical orientation is markedly an orientation to the paradoxical, the ambiguous, the contradictory, the dilemmatic. There is a meaning of dialectic that now may emerge more distinctly.

Social phenomena, including phenomena of central interest in the sociology of religion, speak to us in a distinctive "language," it may be proposed—a language we are as yet far from understanding thoroughly. Dialectic can then be conceived as a striving to understand just that language—or as an effort to set out a "grammar" of that language, a conspectus of the fundamental rules by which it works or by which its expressions are controlled.

In the study of literary productions, as we know, there has long been developing a specialized and sophisticated set of terms for the description and understanding of what students encounter. This set of terms and the manner in which they are used can be very suggestive to the analyst of religion. One of the best-known terms here referred to is *synecdoche*. Kenneth Burke (1957, pp. 22–23) characterizes it as "the figure of speech wherein the part is used for the whole, the whole for the part, the container for the thing contained, the cause for the effect, the effect for the cause, etc. Simplest example: 'twenty noses' for 'twenty men.' " To this, Burke then adds these interesting words: "The more I examine both the structure of poetry *and the structure of human relations outside of poetry*, the more I am convinced that this is the basic figure of speech and that it occurs in many modes besides that of the formal trope" (emphasis added).

Given a dialectical orientation, the literary term *oxymoron* must impress us as very significant. One might almost be tempted to risk a statement just like Burke's, substituting *oxymoron* for *synecdoche* as "the basic figure of speech." Indeed, even Burke himself might sympathize with this. The view that the oxymoron is "the basic figure of speech" does not really seem very alien to him (despite what he has said about synecdoche) when we consider the interest he has had in "perspective by incongruity," an idea that strongly suggests oxymoron (see Burke, 1975, chaps. 3, 4).

It is well to remind ourselves that, as for example Webster's *Unabridged Dictionary* (second edition) indicates, an oxymoron is, etymologically, a "sharp-foolish" or, in more colloquial language, a "smart-dumb." Webster's gives the instances of "cruel kindness" and "laborious idleness." We have quoted Cross on the subject of one Maria Brown, a woman who would prove that she could "sleep chastely with her minister." The moral and lexical context in terms of which we would understand such phrasing would readily suggest oxymoron. A woman does not sleep "chastely" with a minister (of all people!) who is not her husband. Sabbatai's status as a "holy sinner" will be recalled.

Dictionaries of literary terms define the oxymoron as a figure of speech—for instance, as "a figure of speech consisting generally of two apparently contradictory terms which express a startling paradox" (Beckson and Ganz, 1960, p. 144) or as "a figure of speech which combines incongruous and apparently contradictory words and meanings for a special effect" (Cuddon, 1977, p. 462). But, to be sure, as regards our interest here much more than a figure of speech is involved. Human action in the religious sphere often takes on a kind of oxymoronic form. One "sleeps chastely" with one's minister, and the phrasing points beyond its own character as phrasing. We have a *situation* in which a woman so represents matters to herself, in virtue of some peculiar or distinctive religious construction, that to her a conventionally "unchaste" act ostensibly becomes quite pure. The Tantric adept does something abhorrently "bad" by conventional standards in the light of something, or to achieve something, that is in no way reprehensible but rather superlatively good. (Clearly, oxymoron, like synecdoche, occurs "in many modes besides that of the formal trope.") And the sociological significance of his oxymoronic comportment will presumably be more readily or immediately seen in interactions with partners, where these occur, as in the case of sexual partners. Virtually the whole of the present chapter may be allowed to suggest the salience of oxymoron in phenomena of interest to the sociology of religion.

The term *dialectic* has often been associated with the idea of irony, which is, of course, a standard item in a lexicon of literary terms and even likely to be treated at some length in such a lexicon. Irony is not all of a piece, but we refer here particularly to what is often called *dramatic irony*, which features outcomes of action incongruous with the expectations of actors involved and perceived as incongruous either by spectators of action or by actors themselves. A classic instance is afforded by Weber on the relation between certain premises of Calvinist theology and methodical this-worldly activity. Phenomena of this ironic *type* are frequently recurrent in the sphere of religion. Heimert seeks to show how, on the American religious scene, it was *orthodox* or conservative ("evangelical") religion that harbored democratic seeds and gave strength to popular activities—*not* the "liberal" religion that might, more congruously, have been expected to do so (Heimert, 1966). Here, too, there may well be material for the elaboration of a dialectical grammar in the meaning of a special sort of "grammar" of human relationships (with special reference to the sphere of religion).

The resources of literary terms and conceptions alone, for the development of such a grammar, may still not have been sufficiently tapped, despite brilliant suggestions by writers such as Burke. It would be pleasing and no doubt rewarding to set out the fundamentals of a grammar such as is proposed, in clear and very precise terms. There are severe limitations on what can now be done on such lines. If human social and cultural life "speaks" to us, in the sphere of religion as in others, a dialectical *orientation,* solely, is not enough to enable us shrewdly to compass all the speech or language thus poured out and derive a systematic grammar for it. But we abide with the heuristic value of a dialectical orientation. It can sharpen our awareness of the sheer possibility of such a grammar. It can grope for "paradigms" and illustrative matter that may be useful for the development of such a grammar. It can at least hint at the profundity such a grammar might have and constitute a provocative substitute for it until such time as we may possibly attain to a better approximation to "the real thing." We also cherish the hope that the heuristic value of a dialectical orientation has been yet more widely suggested in the earlier portions of this chapter.

References

Barbour, H. *The Quakers in Puritan England.* New Haven, Conn.: Yale University Press, 1964.

Battis, E. *Saints and Sinners: Anne Hutchinson and the Antinomian Controversy in the Massachusetts Bay Colony.* Chapel Hill: University of North Carolina Press, 1962.

Beckson, K., and Ganz, A. *A Reader's Guide to Literary Terms.* New York: Noonday Press, 1960.

Bharati, A. *The Tantric Tradition.* London: Rider, 1965.

Blofeld, J. E. C. *The Tantric Mysticism of Tibet.* New York: Dutton, 1970.

Burke, K. *The Philosophy of Literary Form.* New York: Vintage, 1957.

Burke, K. *Permanence and Change.* Indianapolis, Ind.: Bobbs-Merrill, 1975.

Ch'en, K. *Buddhism in China.* Princeton, N. J.: Princeton University Press, 1964.

Cohn, N. *The Pursuit of the Millenium.* New York: Oxford University Press, 1970.

Conze, E. *Buddhism: Its Essence and Development.* New York: Harper & Row, 1959.

Cross, W. R. *The Burned-Over District.* Ithaca, N. Y.: Cornell University Press, 1950.

Cuddon, J. A. *A Dictionary of Literary Terms.* New York: Doubleday, 1977.

Diesing, P. *Patterns of Discovery in the Social Sciences.* Chicago: Aldine, 1971.

Durkheim, E. *The Elementary Forms of the Religious Life.* London: Allen & Unwin, 1926. (Originally published 1912.)

Gaustad, E. S. *The Great Awakening in New England.* New York: Harper & Row, 1957.

Glasenapp, H. von. *Von Buddha zu Gandhi.* Wiesbaden: Harrassowitz, 1962.

Grunebaum, G. von. *Medieval Islam.* Chicago: University of Chicago Press, 1953.

Heimert, A. *Religion and the American Mind.* Cambridge, Mass.: Harvard University Press, 1966.

James, W. *The Varieties of Religious Experience.* New York: Collier, 1961. (Originally published 1902.)

Knox, R. *Enthusiasm.* New York: Oxford University Press, 1961.

Koch, G. *Frauenfrage und Ketzertum im Mittelalter.* Berlin: Akademie Verlag, 1962.

Lewis, B. *The Assassins: A Radical Sect in Islam.* London: Weidenfeld and Nicolson, 1967.

Mandeville, B. *Free Thoughts on Religion, the Church, and National Happiness.* London: Brotherton, 1729.

Maraini, F. *Meeting with Japan.* New York: Viking, 1960.

Pratt, J. B. *India and Its Faiths.* Boston: Houghton Mifflin, 1915.

Pratt, J. B. *The Religious Consciousness.* New York: Macmillan, 1920.

Pratt, J. B. *The Pilgrimage of Buddhism.* New York: Macmillan, 1928.

Pratt, J. B. *Eternal Values in Religion.* New York: Macmillan, 1950.

Scholem, G. *Sabbatai Sevi: The Mystical Messiah.* Princeton, N. J.: Princeton University Press, 1973.

Shapiro, S. "Patterns of Religious Reformations." *Comparative Studies in Society and History,* 1973, *15,* 143–157.

Tambiah, S. J. "The Ideology of Merit and the Social Correlates of Buddhism in a Thai Village." In E. R. Leach (Ed.), *Dialectic in Practical Religion.* Cambridge: Cambridge University Press, 1968.

von Döllinger, J. J. I. *Beiträge zur Sektengeschichte des Mittelalters.* Erster Teil. New York: Franklin, 1971.

Walker, B. *The Hindu World: An Encyclopedic Survey of Hinduism.* 2 vols. New York: Praeger, 1968.

3

Vatro Murvar

Integrative and
Revolutionary Capabilities
of Religion

The notion of integrative and opiate attributes of sacredness and religion originated with neither Durkheim nor Marx, but with the philosophers of the Age of Enlightenment. It is a part of the Western heritage that has dominated intellectual movements ever since. Various ambitious but unwarranted theories of universal secularization that will liberate humanity from religious legitimation of political slavery and economic exploitation are a complementary part of the same heritage. These cohesive and opiate qualities of religion were documented neither by Durkheim nor by Marx but, surprisingly enough, by Weber, who collected immense comparative evidence from numerous cultural contexts, modern and historical. But, at the same time, Weber rejected the common proposition that religion always and everywhere in any cultural context performs the "opiate" function alone. The comparative data he was able to accumulate imposed on him another, equally well-documented proposition on religion's revolutionary, challenging, and disruptive capabilities.

Through the centuries, diverse religious virtuosi, claiming supernatural visions, other-worldly messages and charismatic experiences of various kinds, have disturbed the status quo and traditional tranquility of the power structure. In the name of their unique religious experiences, they question dominant societal values or ideological principles and the ruling elite's use of power or wealth and frequently achieve a following and through it generate pressure for major social change. Since most, if not all, religious doctrines call for justice, equality of believers, and similar ethical principles, the rational arguments derived from these doctrines, as well as new interpretations of them, become increasingly powerful instruments for demanding change. This does not imply that these pressures always create a significant conflict, for sometimes they can be easily suppressed or manipulated by the power structure, but the religious virtuosi with their other-worldliness and willingness for martyrdom, and especially their frequency of appearance, are almost a continuous challenge if not a serious threat for a monistic power structure.

Today much more evidence from various cultural contexts is available, through the efforts of many historical and ecclesiological specialists. Weber's original accumulation and interpretation of facts on the relationship of sacredness to power and the religious legitimation of political power has been reinforced by this subsequent research. But unfortunately some conceptual and terminological difficulties inherent in his analysis have not been resolved.

The revolutionary and reform potentialities of sacredness and religion are clearly visible in two main streams of religious structures: *hierocracies* and various religious *movements,* sectarian or monastic. Both main streams of these religious structures of distinctive types urging change have favored and over a long period of time have heavily utilized some major revolutionary forces, two of which, charisma and *ratio,* in continuous conflict with each other, attracted Weber's lasting interest and in turn produced major theoretical propositions. Weber ([1922] 1956, pp. 142, 665–666) repeatedly stressed that *ratio* is no less a revolutionary force than charisma and that the process of rationalization is a revolutionary power of the first rank and magnitude especially in relation to traditionalist monistic rulership in general and patrimonialism in particular.

Hierocracy

To capture analytically all the religious power structures that challenge or at least attempt to differentiate themselves as *sui generis* from the power unity-identity under political rule, Weber suggested a conceptualization of hierocracy as a rationally and bureaucratically streamlined religious or priestly-elderly power. He defined it in general as the religious authority to rule supported by the sole right to administer, distribute, or withdraw sacred and religious values. This concept serves well the purposes of analyzing the contrast, the conflict, and the consensus on power supremacy between hierocratic and political rulerships. The relationship between them, Weber ([1922] 1956, p. 697) said, greatly differs when (1) the ruler is legitimated in a priestly way *(priesterlich)* as a representative of God or divine will, or (2) the high priest is the ruler and is legitimated by his sacerdotal office, or finally (3) the political ruler possesses the supreme power in religious affairs through his own political legitimation. Items 1 and 2 are cases of "hierocracy," and he added that theocracy is limited only to the second case, the high-priest's rulership. Weber labeled item 3 "caesaropapism," in spite of some obvious misgivings, as Weber was never anxious to invent new terms. He applied it to political decision making in religious affairs, in agreement with the contemporary usage of this term in Germany.

From the whole context of Weber's research including his ([1922] 1956, pp. 29ff) last revision, it seems unquestionable that the concept of hierocracy originally assumed the existence of another power structure, which is being challenged by this newly emerging or revitalized older hierocracy. This does not imply that the separation of power into religious and political spheres has definitely or permanently taken place. Frequently only ideological demands for such a separation—a far cry from the reality of actual power relationship—are put forward by the challengers, who are not always successful. Witness the struggle and failure of the

Roman bishops in the fifth to seventh centuries (Gelasius I, Gregory the Great, Martin I, Eugene I, and others) to convince the Byzantine emperors that such a separation was desirable from a religious as well as from an imperial point of view. The emperors ignored their pleading letters, and some of them were arrested, brought to Constantinople for a farcical trial, sentenced, and starved to death on an uninhabitable island. Similar failures were experienced in subsequent centuries in the papacy's struggle with the Holy Roman emperors of Frankish and German nations, but the hierocratic persistence finally exploded into what many historians have called the first major revolution, the investiture conflict in the eleventh century.

The contrast between the presence of a hierocracy independent from the coexisting political rule and the absence of such a hierocracy in various cultural and social contexts was crucial to Weber's major intellectual and scientific concerns of investigating the basic "whys" in cultural contrasts. It strictly parallels his extensive research on the presence or absence of feudalism and free cities in many cultures. Almost universally, instead of feudalism and free cities there have existed patrimonialism and the so-called oriental—or, more accurately, patrimonial—city. Taking heed of this parallelism, which is usually overlooked, is one of the fundamental prerequisites for a more accurate interpretation of Weber's unfinished opus. He frequently discussed a type of independent or autonomous hierocracy without giving it a specific typological designation.

In spite of the rarity of this type of peculiarly labile and fluctuating church-state relationship as compared to the almost universal unity-identity of power under a political or hierocratic head, Weber argued that, in the West at least, this type did gradually impose a peculiar dualism, which was the first step toward the rise of *plural* autonomous and diffused power structures. This long developmental process displayed several varieties, from the earlier structures, in which the claims for hierocratic supremacy were successfully materialized for a period of time, to later structures, in which the hierarchy was not able to avert defeat by the political rulerships. But this experience of independence and ability to struggle created ineradicable memories and strong cultural values that offered differential ideologies and a choice of loyalties. The relatively independent, successful, and durable hierocracies are interdependent with the other autonomous and autocephalous power structures, feudalism and free cities.

Since there are various sets of facts concerning hierocratic successes and failures in achieving an independent power structure and concerning the presence or absence of hierocracy in various cultural contexts, they should not be labeled with the same name. If the ambiguity is to be resolved, only one specific meaning of hierocracy should be selected out of the general meaning suggested by Weber.

The term *hierocracy* in this chapter is limited to one precise meaning, which I hope will be found attractive in future research: a relatively independent religious power structure coexistent with another (political) power structure within the same society or larger social order (such as the medieval polity in the West).

Political and Religious Varieties
of Power Unity-Identity

In order to survive, the hierocracy, if and when successfully differentiated from the original unity of power structure, must control the activities of religious virtuosi: They are the major originators of hierocratic power and subsequent challenge to the political rulership. But any political structure, if and when differentiated from the hierocratic structure, is just as vitally interested in supervising and legislating the behavior of religious virtuosi. Political rulers have universally distrusted competing priestly power and even more the hierocracy's insistence on exclusively regulating all new religious experiences.

Another, perhaps more practical source of tension is the hierocracy's wealth, accumulated through centuries, which the rulers, usually in need of money for their military projects, would periodically expropriate. Even though wealth and the style of life it produces are, in some instances at least, contradictory to the basic religious teachings, priestly assistance in matters of life and death and entrance into the next world seems inevitably to result in an unbelievable priestly accumulation of riches.   .

But above all an almost universal longing for sacred order and unity tended to produce deep tension over the issue of who is the supreme power—under the deity, of course—hierocratic or political. A resolution of this most disturbing question of who exercises the supreme rulership under the deity, whatever the source of original tension, is achieved by subordinating religious or priestly power to the political rulership or by subordinating political to hierocratic rulership:

1. The unity of power structure under a political head— political monism
2. The unity of power structure under a hierocratic head— hierocratic monism

If and when the political or the hierocratic power structure was unable to destroy or totally subordinate the other, they were forced to coexist and compromise, making various arrangements that, of course, were for most of history a far cry from separation. Various circumstances and conditions of bargaining between the two in the long run seem to favor unity instead of differentiation, with separation being even more difficult to achieve.

If the hierocracy is willing to legitimize political rule through domestication of the people by using religious, sacred, and supernatural means, the political rulers will in return extend religious uniformity over the entire country by removing dissenters and heretics and forcing other religious groups to accept the officially approved religion. Also, financial advantages for an hierocracy ready to compromise are available through various tax exemptions, privileges, gifts of land with or without peasants, and so on. This in turn binds the hierocratic leadership into a close relationship, ending of necessity in more or less total subservience to the political rule. Material means of power, prestige, and wealth are corrupting, and the rulers cleverly exploit them to subjugate all those who have less and want more of the same means, especially the church leadership. By their doctrinal commitment, they should be less vulnerable to such temptations, but historical evidence in many instances is to the contrary. The final results are an ever-increasing structural unity: one ruler, one religion, one society.

Sources of tension between the two powers thus tend to be resolved in the direction of greater unity-identity of all power in the hands of the political rulers. It is an almost inevitable development in a cultural context in which disunity or differentiation is religiously or ideologically considered evil and destructive of the harmony or natural well-being of the entire society. This image of societal unity is favorably compared with the doctrinal positions on the unity of God, the universe, the world, humanity, and even the human body.

Once the most vital question of supremacy based on the "correct," sacred, divine, just order is settled, economic and all other (educational, communicational, and so forth) issues automatically resolve themselves: Ownership, usage, control, direction, and disposition belong to the exalted supreme ruler. He is the owner of land, the people, their lives, and industry, if not always in principle, always in actuality.

Similarly, if not identically, in the monistic societal structures of the modern age, once the issues of purity and orthodoxy of the doctrine or ideology are settled, all the economic means, the entire economy of the country, are then harnessed for the achievement of the exalted ideological and political goals. This configuration in modern monistic societies certainly has most serious implications for the validity of major aspects if not the basic core of the Marxist doctrine. Also, the secularization theses, whether Marxist or not, are faulty simply because they ignore the ideological, religionlike, nontheistic system of beliefs as major sources of legitimation in modern monistic-patrimonialist societies. In those societies, liberation, from whatever moral slavery and human exploitation these secularization theses criticize so justly and eloquently, has not been achieved.

After the conflict is eliminated and the ideological supremacy "correctly" reestablished, it is only an academic question as to who are the supreme decision makers, owners of the land and people, hierocratic or political (imperial, royal, caesarist, totalitarian, dictatorial, one-party, collective) rulers. From the point of view of the value choices and life reality for the subjects there is very little difference, since the demands of the power unity-identity are always sacred, absolute, and overwhelming, and the penalty for deviation is unavoidable in this life and in afterlife. Consequently, the subjects are expected only to suffer, sacrifice, and worship gods, temporal and eternal, visible and invisible.

In addition to the relatively independent or at least autonomous hierocracy, there is clear evidence, however, of a few cases of hierocracy that absorbed the state and did not have any political (or other) power structures to contend with. Hierocratic monism, a quite distinctive type of religious rulership totally absorbing the political structure and consequently being the only power structure in the society, must be distinguished from the relatively independent hierocracy that coexists with and challenges another power structure in the same society. Weber referred to hierocratic absorption of total power in various historical instances, and his accumulation of empirical evidence is almost complete, but he neither formulated nor expressed a need for this concept. Perhaps the best examples are the universalist papal monism of Gregory VII for a fleeting moment in the history of the West in the eleventh century; the particularistic papal monism of some Roman bishops before and after him, limited to the durable but small papal states; various power structures of Calvinist monism in Geneva, Scotland, the Puritan Bible Commonwealth of Massachusetts Bay, and perhaps some structures of Dutch Afrikaners in South Africa; early structures of American Mormonism; Dalai-Lamaist monism of Tibet; some East Indian and perhaps some early Israelite hierocratic structures. Inappropriately these power structures are labeled *theocratic*. Of course, in all these instances God did not rule, but the religious officials camouflaged their rule with the deity's images. Also, unmistakably, political rulers everywhere (not only in Western and Eastern Christianity but also in Islam and Confucianism and in Inca, Khmer, and other kingdoms) have frequently claimed that their power structures were pure theocracy. To use the term *theocracy* for both sets of power structures, religious and political, is not analytically sound, because it adds confusion to abuse. For these reasons, I suggest that the term *theocracy* be abandoned.

A theory of hierocratic monism based strictly on evidence from these few case studies would ideally balance out this study; however, there is no space for it here. More significantly, hiero-

cratic monism is not a historical curiosity only, for the study of hierocratic monism can substantially help us to interpret the integrative and opiate function of the modern nontheistic systems of
belief in building, legitimizing, and maintaining modern monistic
societies.

Nonhierocratic State Churches

The term *hierocracy* should not be used when a specifically
religious autonomous power structure is absent, even though a
group of the ruler's servants, who specialize in religious matters,
are differentiated from the rest of the ruler's servants and are
formally designated as clergy. To speak of a "dependent hierocracy" is a contradiction: The power to rule ("cracy") is never dependent or subordinated. If so, it ceases to exist and is replaced by
another kind of rule.

Particularly troublesome in this area is Weber's ([1922]
1956, pp. 700 ff) attempt to link the traditional term *church* with
his newly constructed concept of hierocracy. When all the exceptions to this linking enumerated by him (late ancient Egyptian
hierocracies, Judaism, and Mahdism) and by others (Islam and
Dalai Lamaism) are accounted for, then for all pragmatic purposes
churches are limited to Christianity. The most serious objection is
that not all churches within Christianity have been able to develop
into actual hierocracies or at least to display some major hierocratic
attributes. As a matter of fact, only a few have done so. There are in
history numerous nonhierocratic patrimonial state churches, especially in Christianity, both Eastern Orthodox and Western (Protestant and Catholic, both dominated by the "enlightened des-
potism"), in which the total sum of all or any actual evidenced or
documented hierocratic qualities does not amount to any significant religious force able to make an impact on the existing power
unity.

In various segments of his opus, Weber repeatedly emphasized how crucial it is for the nascent hierocracy or for the
hierocracy's survival to appropriate a share of power for themselves: to build an independent or at least an autonomous hierarchical office structure of their own, to achieve financial indepen-

dence, and especially to create a fully developed educational system of their own, in which, without any interference from the political rulership, the most sophisticated theological training for the hierocratic elite is based on an independent theology, separated from the political (civil) as well as from canon (church) law. Only in such a total configuration, in which all hierocratic segments are supporting each other, is it possible for a successful hierocracy to perform the function of criticism, challenge, or "revolutionary" change and to force on the rulership a diffusion of political power and perhaps also a more lasting separation into at least two spheres, religious and political.

When Weber discussed substantively the numerous non-hierocratic cases in Christianity or elsewhere, he never failed to emphasize the absence of various hierocratic attributes in every one of them. Whether he analyzed evidence for or against hierocracy in Russia, Byzantium, western Europe, Islam, Inca Peru, or China, his concern with both actual and formal facts was the most persistent feature in his entire research. Strangely, then, this precious collection of factual evidence was not reflected in his attempt to link "church" and hierocracy, and perhaps this particular linking was not intended to serve as a precise definition of church. And if it did, it is plausible to argue, imitating Weber's famous refusal to define religion, that there is no pressing need in this research area to define church.

Religious Movements:
Some Traditional Dichotomies Rejected

In analyzing religious movements that have challenged both political and hierocratic monistic rule, Weber accumulated facts available at that time on Judaic prophecy, Catholic monasticism, Protestant (mostly Calvinist) sectarianism, and others. While not all religious movements have been revolutionary, it appears from more recent research (see Murvar, 1975) that religious movements performing revolutionary or challenging functions have been the most frequent, durable, and effective among them.

Most likely the church-sect dichotomy has some significance for understanding certain post-Reformation cultural contexts in

the seventeenth and eighteenth centuries on the European continent. However, it does not seem to stretch into the nineteenth and
twentieth centuries. On the contemporary scene, Berger (1958, pp.
43–44) notes that in some instances there is "a sectarian elite within
the church" and adds, "Sectarianism might then well appear as the
form of religious sociation par excellence." Martin (1965, p. 211)
points out that the history of Methodism, together with that of the
Congregationalists and to some extent the Baptists, documents a
transition from a "spiritual brotherhood" and "a holy club" to
ecclesiola to denomination, "but at no point approximates to a sect."
Littel (1967, p. 35) says that the church-sect dichotomy "is also
more confusing then clarifying. As a matter of record, Troeltsch
himself declared it inapplicable to the modern period and especially to England and America." There is a consensus that even to
Troeltsch Calvinism was neither a classical church nor a classical sect.

At the point of emergence from the catacombs, as well as
during the first three centuries of its underground existence, the
original Christian movement was neither a church nor a sect. It was
a sect neither to the believers nor to the rest of the Roman citizens.
To the believers in a purely spiritual community of love, their
religion could have appeared to be an ecclesia, but this concept of
the underground spiritual other-worldly ecclesia was obviously not
the same as the medieval ecclesia of this world or the alleged
"theocracies" of Byzantium and Russia, which, of course, were not
theocracies at all.

The chief attributes of religious sects are applicable to religious (monastic) orders as well. Hill (1971) has recently suggested
that all religious orders recognized and accepted by the mother
church are actually sects within the church, especially the Benedic-
tines, Augustinians, Cistercians, Carmelites, and Franciscans. He
emphasized the differences, of course, but these seem to fade into
relative insignificance in comparison with *nine* common attributes
shared by monks and sectarians. Similarly, Hill (1973) proposed
that Wesleyan Methodism originated as a religious order within the
Church of England. The relationship between the two, especially
the lack of appreciation of the Church of England for the legitimate challenge of the Methodist religious order, is similar if not

identical to the relationships of all other religious movements with their respective power structures.

No one has formally offered the sectarianism-monasticism dichotomy, but for all practical purposes in historical research there is a firm dividing line: If the challengers are not monks, chartered or only tolerated by the church, then they are sectarians, and vice versa. The labels *sectarianism* and *monasticism*, however, are meaningful only from the point of view of the power structure being challenged. Theologians from Augustine to the present have been quick to label any criticism, however justifiable, or any demand for reform, as sectarian or heretical doctrine. The terms *sect* and *sectarianism* still retain the pejorative value judgment of all those ecclesiastic and political decision makers who feared or disapproved of the challenge or criticism from these movements. On the basis of evidence, it seems reasonable to say that the religious movements performing the "revolutionary" function have never considered themselves as sects.

The comparative historical data Weber accumulated pointed toward a rich variety of religious revolutionary movements open to sound conceptualization, but he ([1922] 1956, p. 707) chose instead to analyze centuries-long struggles of the local, regional, national, and papal hierocracy against overpowering competition from the monks. The various religious orders seemed superior in pastoral care, in a more sympathetic attitude toward sinners, and in offering free education, while the hierocracy in practically every age drifted toward excessive enjoyment of worldly goods, participation in and identification with brutal political establishments and the general corruption that wealth and close association with political power often produce. Since the church members favor the monks, Weber concluded, every great church must arrive at a sort of unhappy and tensive compromise with the successfully challenging religious orders.

Within the concept *sect,* there is a frequent confusion: Revolutionary and integrative functions are forced into the same concept without logical reason for it. Some "sects" have performed not the revolutionary but the integrative function in the long run, in spite of an initial or potential orientation toward criticism and challenge. If successful in achieving religious dominance and ultimately controlling the society, these sects then moved toward a newly re-formulated unity of church and state, in contrast to the religious movements forcefully pushing for social change. The pattern of the nonprotesting "nonsects" becoming a part of the politicoreligious establishment, however, is identical to the pattern of monastic religious orders growing rich, politically powerful, and, of course, conservative. In this gradual process, frequently witnessed within the same monastic structure, these religious orders eventually betrayed their original function of criticism, challenge, reform, and revolt and increasingly performed the "opiate" function.

References

Berger, P. "Sectarianism and Religious Sociation." *American Journal of Sociology,* 1958, *64,* 41–44.

Hill, M. "Typologie sociologique de l'ordre religieux." *Social Compass,* 1971, *18,* 46–64.

Hill, M. "Methodism as a Religious Order." In M. Hill (Ed.), *Sociological Yearbook of Religion in Britain.* London: SCM Press, 1973.

Littel, F. H. "The Churches and the Body Politic." *Daedalus,* 1967, *96,* 22–42.

Martin, D. A. *Pacifism: An Historical and Sociological Study.* London: Routledge & Kegan Paul, 1965.

Murvar, V. "Toward a Sociological Theory of Religious Movements." *Journal for the Scientific Study of Religion,* 1975, *14,* 229–256.

Weber, M. *Wirtschaft und Gesellschaft.* 2 vols. (4th ed.) Tübingen: Mohr, 1956. (Originally published 1922.)

4

Eli Sagan

Religion and Magic:
A Developmental View

The development of the psyche is the paradigm for the development of culture. I deliberately use the word *development* in preference to the word *evolution,* which has been used by Parsons (1967) and others. If we wish to understand the direction in which culture and society have changed, we need a psychological, not a biological, paradigm. Society and culture have developed in the direction of Weber's "legal-rational," gradually liberating themselves from paleological ways of thought, because the development of the ego and the cognitive function of the psyche lie precisely in that direction. The animistic, magical, participatory, and paleological modes of cognition that are typical of early forms of human society are exhibited by *all* children in our society (Piaget, 1929). What was a stage in the development of culture is, in our society, only a stage of psychic development through which all children go.

If the development of politics within society has been from kinship forms of social cohesion to nonkinship forms of cohesion (Parsons, 1967, p. 496), that is because the human psyche in its early stages cannot imagine a world that is not family-centered; only with the development of the ego and its drives for separation and individuation (Mahler, Pine, and Bergman, 1975) does a nonfamily form of society become possible and, for the ego, desirable. The earliest form of institutionalized aggression—cannibalism—is satisfied in the mouth, because the mouth is the original source of intense sensation for the human psyche (Sagan, 1974). If early archaic forms of civilization demonstrate a development from "shame culture" to "guilt culture" (Dodds, 1957), the fact that shame is an early form of social control for the psyche and that guilt develops only after a considerable time must give us a working hypothesis as to why culture takes the same developmental direction.

If the sacred systems of early cultures are only vaguely or ambiguously moral, whereas more developed religious systems are deliberately and consciously moral, this developmental sequence cannot be unrelated to the development of the moral sense as the human psyche matures from infancy to adulthood. And, if early systems of sacred symbols and action are predominantly magical and become less and less magical as they develop, it cannot be mere coincidence that the development of the psyche presents exactly the same sequence.

Between the development of culture and the development of the psyche, I am not postulating an analogy but, rather, a parallel process. And I am not suggesting that the development of the psyche is the sole motivating force for the development of culture, although it is one such force, because clearly culture has a developmental capacity within itself. What is dictated to culture by the psyche is the *direction* development will take. Culture develops from magical to rational, not from rational to magical. The track it must take is laid down for it by the psyche.

These bald statements are in need of substantiation. It is not possible to support all these hypotheses in this chapter. I limit myself to a discussion of "religion" and "magic" and to an investigation of the cultural developmental sequence indicated by these terms and of the relationship that sequence may have with a parallel psychological developmental sequence. Such discussion will, hopefully, lend substantiation to the fundamental proposition that the development of the psyche is the paradigm for the development of culture and society.

We have no adequate theory of the development of the psyche as a whole, and therefore we lack an effective theory of cultural development. Within Freud's works, there are several developmental sequences, but the connecting links between the various sequences are never established, leaving us with no overall, coordinated theory. The most important developmental sequence in Freud's thought is the progress of the libido in oral → anal → genital stages. Related to this is the aggression sequence: oral aggression → anal sadism → genital aggression, but Freud does not speculate on how these two basic drives are related to each other, in general or in each stage.

Within the Freudian system, there are other progressive changes in the psyche: primary narcissism → secondary narcissism → object choice; pleasure principle → reality principle; a non-superego state → superego. Freud also gave some consideration to ideas that were taken up by others who were primarily interested in ego development. Included within this category of thought were notions of cognitive development, separation and individuation, and the reality principle.

Each of these notions is a part of a theory of development of the psyche as a whole. To use one of these parts in an attempt to illuminate the whole of cultural development results in reductionism. Trying to explain changes in culture by using the paradigm oral → anal → genital, for instance, not only reduces cultural phenomena to the psychological but also reduces the whole psyche to one of its parts: the libido.

As yet, we have no adequate theory that can tell us, for example, what is happening to the ego and the superego (or superego precursors) when the libido is advancing to the genital stage from the anal stage or how previous complications in the development of the ego may affect the libido as it moves into a new stage. We do not know how unsolved problems in the area of separation and individuation in the preoedipal stage will affect the psyche in the oedipal stage. We do not even know whether we should call the oedipal situation a stage in the development of the libido, or in that of the ego, or in both. We can make nothing of value from Freud's statement that "the beginnings of religion, morality, society, and art converge in the Oedipus complex" (Reik, 1946, p. 165), because the description of the Oedipus complex we have from Freud and others tells us only a fraction of what is going on in the psyche at that stage. If we possessed a complete description of the psyche in the oedipal stage, which would include the state of the ego, of the reality principle, and of narcissism, then we might be in a position to judge Freud's statement and make use of it. As yet, psychoanalytic theory is inadequate for our purposes: It can be applied to culture only with great caution.

Piaget's psychology is completely committed to the conception of development through well-defined stages, so much so that he can be fairly criticized for forcing the stage concept in some places where other ways of looking at the data might be more helpful. In regard to cultural development, Piaget has attempted to demonstrate, not merely assert, the parallel nature of cultural and psychological development. As Flavell (1963, p. 252) writes, "Piaget will take a concept from a given scientific field—for example, the concept of *force* in physics—and analyze how its scientific meaning has changed from Greek or pre-Greek times to the present. He then attempts to show crucial parallels between historical and ontogenetic evolution of this concept; for example, in both evolutions there is a progressive shedding of egocentric adherences, rooted in personal experience of bodily effort, in favor of an objective conception which is independent of the self. . . . the general strategy is to apply the constructs of his developmental theory (progressive equilibration, egocentrism, decentration, and reversibility, and so on) to the historical process, the latter construed as an evolution *across* a number of adult minds at least partially analyzable in the same terms as the evolution *within* a simple, immature one. There is thus a strong 'Ontogeny recapitulates history' strain in Piaget's thinking."

Piaget's work, however, does not result in a psychology of the whole psyche, and he did not intend that it should. His psychology lacks a dynamic quality, which is the essence of Freud's insight into human life. Piaget does not concern himself with concepts such as repression, defense, regression, sexuality, and aggression. We cannot read Piaget to discover why so many human beings lead psychologically and morally impoverished lives.

An adequate psychology of the whole psyche will be a great synthesis of the work of Freud and his followers, of Piaget and others working in the field of cognitive development, of psychoanalytic and other work in the area of ego development (particularly Margaret Mahler's work on separation and individuation), and probably of other kinds of insights that are not yet available to us. There is no question that this edifice is being built, brick by brick. One grows impatient at the pace, but there is no cure—at the moment—for that impatience.

One essential task of this chapter is to differentiate religion from magic. Traditionally, there has been a confused usage of the word *religion* when it is used in conjunction with, or in opposition to, the word *magic*. If someone writes an article on "Magical Elements in Old Testament Religion," we have no trouble intuitively knowing what the author means, and we have a reasonable expectation of what we will find in such an article. However, if we look carefully at the use of the words *magical elements* and *religion*, an intellectual confusion becomes apparent. If there are "magical elements" in "religion," what then are the other elements in "religion" that are not "magical"? Traditionally usage says that the other elements are "religious." There would be, then, "religious elements" in "religion." This absurdity is revealed when we try to imagine how we might react to an article entitled "The Religious Elements in Old Testament Religion" or another entitled "The Religious Elements in Kwakiutl Magic."

One could argue that the magical elements in religion are impurities, much as "that-which-is-not-air" exists in the air we breathe. This will not answer, however, because there has never been a religious system that did not contain a substantial mixture of magic. One cannot regard as an impurity in the system something that is integral to it.

This confusion results from using the same word, *religion*, for both the total system itself and for one element within the total system. One solution, which I shall adopt in this chapter, although there are probably other ways to rectify this, is to use for the total system a different word from that used for any element of the system. In place of *religion*, I propose to use "the sacred system of symbols and action," or simply, "the sacred system." Both of these phrases are the equivalent of what most people mean when they speak of religion or the religious system. The sacred system of symbols and action, then, consists of two essential elements: religious and magical.

It may be awkward, at first, to restrict the word *religion* to this narrow sense, but it spares us the kind of intellectual confusion we have suffered in the past, such as discovering that a course on "primitive religion" is mostly about magic. Under traditional usage, when the word *religion* served both to describe the total system and an element within it, the tendency was to undervalue the role of magic within all sacred systems, and maybe that was the hidden purpose behind the confusion. To speak of the sacred system as containing both religious and magical elements allows us to examine freely the role of magic. It also forces us to see that the crucial question to be asked of any sacred system is *to what degree* the magical (or religious) elements predominate within the system. The difference between primitive sacred systems and modern sacred systems is not that primitive systems have no religious elements and that modern sacred systems have no magical elements. The difference clearly lies in the *degree* to which magical or religious elements are important within the systems.

Both magic and religion are fundamentally concerned with power; both postulate a degree of power that does not really exist, namely omnipotence; both systems of belief have as one of their central purposes the attainment of omnipotent power for the believer. *Magic (and religion) is a system of beliefs that contends that words, gestures, feelings and thoughts are capable of achieving results in the real world that are at variance with common sense. Magical (and religious) desires result from wishes. The purpose of magical (and religious) acts is to make the believer potent enough to satisfy those wishes.*

The word *religion* appears in parentheses because this definition is too narrow to define religion, although it suffices for magic. Religion is concerned with more than power, as we shall observe later.

The term "common sense" avoids all the intellectual confusion surrounding the discussion of whether Lévy-Bruhl was correct in calling primitive mentality *pre-logical*. Some use the word *logical* to mean rational; others, to indicate commonsensical; still others refer it to certain categories of Aristotelian thought. Without defining *logical* and *prelogical,* it is difficult to determine whether the thought of any culture fits into either category. The same confusion exists within the discussion of whether primitive people are capable of "scientific thought" or not, when the word *scientific* is never adequately defined.

I prefer the term *common sense.* Common sense tells us that horses don't fly, that rocks fall down and not up, and that yams will not grow unless you put the tubers in the ground, no matter how many spells you may sing over the earth. No one has ever described a culture, no matter how primitive, that was incapable of a commonsense view of the world. We have yet to discover a people who believe that, if you hold a rock out over your foot and let go of it, you will suffer no consequences, or that magical spells without seed will produce food. Whether primitive people were capable of logical thought, or scientific notions, or not, they were all capable of common sense, and magical beliefs contradict common sense. Therefore, the belief in magical or religious power (omnipotence), in an adult in any culture, indicates a basic contradiction in thought. In their desire not to be helpless, human beings are capable of a willing suspension of belief in common sense.

All peoples have used both commonsense and magical-religious means to power. A people going to war may sing over their spears in order to make them more effective. If there ever have been people who felt they could defeat an enemy in war merely by singing and who therefore dispensed with spears, we have not heard of them; they were, undoubtedly, all dispatched in the midst of their spellbinding. Magic, Roheim (1962, p. 10) says, is "located somewhere halfway between the pure pleasure principle and the reality principle. If it were pure pleasure principle, hallucinatory wish fulfillment would be an aim in itself. If it were pure reality principle, we would set about and work to achieve a certain goal without assuming that our wish or dramatized wish is the thing that gets what we want."

Where religion and magic differ fundamentally is in the *conception* of power: where it resides, who controls it, how one gets hold of it. Magic assumes that what controls the universe is an impersonal *force;* religion assumes that persons or a person controls the universe. Frazer ([1890] 1955, pp. 58–59) saw this with great clarity:

> Are the forces which govern the world conscious and personal, or unconscious and impersonal? Religion, as a conciliation of the superhuman powers, assumes that the being conciliated is a conscious or personal agent, that his conduct is in some measure uncertain, and that he can be prevailed upon to vary it in the desired direction by a judicious appeal to his interests, his appetites, or his emotions. . . . Thus, in so far as religion assumes the world to be directed by conscious agents who may be turned from their purpose by persuasion, it stands in fundamental antagonism to magic as well as to science, both of which take for granted that the course of nature is determined, not by the passions or caprice of personal beings, but by the operation of immutable laws acting mechanically.

Frazer, after the publication of *The Golden Bough,* had the pleasure of discovering that Hegel (in Frazer, 1911, p. 424) had made the same distinction between religion and magic years before. Hegal's conception is remarkably close to Freud's conception of "omnipotence of thought."

It has become fashionable to be highly critical of Frazer, among other reasons because, making the same mistake Freud made in *Totem and Taboo,* he confused an etiological myth with a cultural reality. When Frazer announced that there had been an age of magic, followed by an age of religion, he was clearly following Hesiod and not the facts of cultural history. However, Frazer's distinction between magic and religion contained a profound psychological and cultural truth. As we shall see later, in the history of the psyche there is, indeed, an age of magic through which all children go and to which all schizophrenics return. Culture, however, is made by adults, not by children, and adults cannot live and function in a totally magical world. There has never been a culture whose sacred system was totally magical, but there has never been a sacred system that is entirely free of magic, either.

Since Durkheim's reputation is in the ascendant today, far above Frazer's, it is of interest to observe that Durkheim's attempt to distinguish religion from magic (which he accepts as two distinct categories of thought and action) yields us nothing of value. Durkheim insists that the practice of religion relates to the sense of community and that the practice of magic is a private transaction: "*There is no church of magic.* . . . The magician has a clientele and not a church" ([1912] no date, p. 44, Durkheim's italics). This leaves us totally in the dark as to what is going on when a rainmaker, in front of a large congregation, proceeds to disperse the sunshine and bring the much-needed rainfall. And when we read that "magic . . . was born of religion" (Durkheim, [1912] n.d., p. 362), we wonder how anyone so vitally concerned with the origins of things could so completely repress the recollections of his own childhood.

What Frazer, Hegel, and Freud are saying is that, in the magical view, the self is capable of omnipotence. The only difficulty in magic is to get the magical power; once attained, and assuming no one's power is in opposition and greater, one's wishes are assured of fulfillment. In the religious view, one never has that certainty, because the self cannot be omnipotent. Omnipotence, in religion, lies with others whose assistance and compliance the self must obtain. The self may be granted the use and benefits of omnipotent power that resides in ancestors or the gods. To drive a spear into the effigy of one's enemy and to know that he *must* die, is a far different thing from King David's calling on Yahweh to destroy David's enemies, because Yahweh *may* or *may not* grant such a request. To anticipate a later discussion of the stages of omnipotence, it seems clear from everything we know about the development of the child, that the first stage in the conception of omnipotence is that the self is omnipotent and that the notion that the parents are omnipotent is a later development. Magic is the first stage in the conception of power, which yields, in later stages, to different ideas of power.

The idea of stages does not preclude that earlier views of power may continue to exist, in later stages, alongside developed views. Such a mixture of magical and religious conceptions of

power occurred, for instance, in the sacred rites of the ancient
Egyptians, who put magical scrolls in the coffins of the dead in
order to *force* the gods to make a favorable moral judgment on the
life of the deceased. No matter how mixed the rite may be in a
sacred system, it is still possible to distinguish the religious from the
magical elements within the rite.

One further distinction between magic and religion that
lends weight to the idea that religion is a more developed view of
the world than magic is the fact that religion has to be taught,
whereas children will practice magical action even though no one
has instructed them to do so. Piaget describes an experiment with
his daughter when she was one year and four months old. The
child had learned to turn a matchbox over, insert her finger, and
draw out a chain contained within. Then Piaget closed the opening
of the matchbox to 3mm, so that it was now too small to allow the
chain to be pulled out. The child tried the usual procedure; it
failed; the child paused for a while, obviously perplexed, and then
"looks at the slit with great attention, then several times in succession, she opens and shuts her mouth, at first slightly, then wider
and wider!" Piaget comments, "Just as she often uses imitation to
act upon persons and make them reproduce their interesting
movements, so also it is probable that the act of opening her mouth
in front of the slit to be enlarged implies some underlying idea of
efficacy" (Piaget, in Flavell, 1963, p. 120).

When one first learns to bowl, it is necessary to be taught the
rules of the game, how to pick up and throw the ball, and so on. But
no one has to instruct us that, should we bowl a ball that creeps
slowly toward the gutter, if we twist our body toward the opposite
side the ball will certainly change direction. This belief in the efficacy of imitation seems to be a nonlearned given within the psyche.
One cannot, however, imagine any child coming up independently
with ideas of Yahweh or Allah.

Related to the idea that religion must be learned and that
magic need not be is the fact that magical practices, wherever one
finds them, are so much like each other, whereas religious practices
are as various as the cultures and societies in which they exist.
"While religious systems differ not only in different countries, but
in the same country in different ages, the system of sympathetic

magic remains everywhere and at all times substantially alike in its principles and practice" (Frazer, [1890] 1955, p. 64). Here, of course, Frazer is using "religious systems" where we would say "sacred systems." The point, however, is that the great variance that we see in sacred systems is due not to the magical elements in those systems but to the religious elements. This consistency of magical symbols and action indicates the undeveloped nature of the magical view of the world.

The religious elements within the sacred system are concerned with two crucial things that magic is incapable of dealing with: morality and meaning. Morality is a prescription for a mode of social interaction; its concern is how people are to treat other people. Magic, as we have observed, is a dialogue between one's omnipotent self and the forces that control the universe. People appear in the magical system only as objects to be used either sexually or aggressively. Religion, on the contrary, assumes that what controls the universe acts as a person. To obtain power from the gods, one has to deal with other beings; the recognition of the reality of *other* beings is the beginning of morality.

The need for meaning occurs only if one is faced with the possibility of meaninglessness. If we never felt threatened by the idea that life has no moral purpose, we would have no need of the vast edifice of meaning that sacred systems have constructed over the ages. Macbeth's great cry of desperation, that life is a "tale told by an idiot, full of sound and fury, signifying nothing," is a profound assertion of the need for meaning.

Insofar as the magical view truly believes that the self is, or can be, omnipotent, to that degree there is no threat of meaninglessness and therefore no need for meaning. The rejection of omnipotence is the first stage in the giving up of magic and the genesis of religion. It also results in the first threat of meaninglessness. Meaning is the compensation religion gives to the psyche in return for abandoning omnipotence.

At present, the psychological origins of conscience and morality are shrouded in obscurity. Taboo is a magical mode of control, and yet Freud ([1913] 1955, p. 67) writes, "Taboo conscience is probably the earliest form in which the phenomenon of conscience is met with." Here we have a clear illustration of the lack of a theory of the development of the whole psyche. We read about superego, ego ideal, taboo conscience, anal morality, and superego precursors, and the confusion mounts. The history of the development of morality from infancy to adulthood has yet to be written.

Although it is possible, analytically, to distinguish purely magical from purely religious elements within the sacred system, there has never been a sacred system that was either completely magical or completely religious. There has been some religion in the most primitive of sacred systems and some magic in the most developed. In the past, the religious elements in primitive sacred systems have been equated with the existence and importance of gods or high gods. The role of gods in some sacred systems has been minimal, but these systems are not as lacking in religion as the relative absence of gods might indicate. In many primitive sacred systems, wherein magical rites play an overwhelmingly predominant role, *ancestors* are more important than gods and provide the primary religious elements within the sacred system. The Trobriand Islanders (Malinowski, 1954) and the Arunta (Spencer and Gillen, 1938) are two such cultures. In all of traditional Africa, gods played a small part in the total sacred system, but the role of ancestors was important throughout the whole continent. In all kinship forms of social cohesion, ancestors legitimate the political order. Ancestor reverence is the "civil religion" (Bellah, 1970) of kinship societies. Clearly, also, no culture exists without meaning and a moral order. Magic, by itself, cannot create a sacred or cultural system.

It is equally true that there is no sacred system that is without magical elements. Taking the chance of contradicting the theoretical structure that has been created so far, it can be said that there is something magical in *every* religious symbol or action. To assume that the gods will take care of us, that their omnipotence will protect us, is to believe that something that does not exist can provide us with safety. All religion preserves a belief in omnipotence, although it is no longer in the self. If this belief in omnipotence (which does not exist) is the essence of magic, we then find a magical essence in the heart of religion.

An idea that will be developed later is that the child conceives of its parents as omnipotent before transferring this power onto the gods. Such a movement, from parents to gods, is at once progressive and regressive for the psyche: progressive in the sense that it allows one to symbolize one's parents and thereby to liberate oneself from their total authority; regressive in the sense that the parents, after all, do exist, although their omnipotence is merely an illusion. The omnipotence of the gods is no more real than they themselves; their power is a shadow of a shadow—a symbol—a creation of the mind—a product of thought. Thought thereby retains its capacity to create omnipotence, to be omnipotent. No matter how much magic may be transformed into religion—and the development of culture is built on that transformation—there remains a core incapable of metamorphosis.

People who have had some knowledge of the sacred rites of primitive cultures and early civilizations, on the one hand, and a close contact with compulsive neurotic and schizophrenic patients, on the other, have all been struck by what seems, on the surface, to be identical thought processes existing in these two categories of persons. In many early cultures, it is the job of a priest or the head of the political government to make sure that the sun rises each morning. "B. G., a twenty-five-year-old schizophrenic at the Worcester State Hospital, told me that it was his job to keep the sun in its place. . . . 'To make a new sun, I just have to push my hand like this. I can do things just by concentrating and thinking' " (Roheim, 1962, pp. 94–95).

The multitude of descriptions we have of love magic from early cultures are almost identical to Roheim's (1962) description of his schizophrenic patients' ideas. "A twenty-five-year-old woman, whom I analyzed many years ago, told me that she had a secret magic power. If she went through the motion of sucking, then anyone toward whom those motions of her lips were directed would inevitably fall in love with her" (p. 97). "When the patient is in love with her physician she gives him poems wrapped in many layers of paper—in the center of it all she puts her pubic hairs, menstrual blood, and occasionally a little feces" (p. 109).

Werner provides another example of the resemblance between primitive and psychotic. "When a Melanesian uses the word 'shed' instead of 'house' because the word for house, *ima*, is a constituent part of the name of the tabu daughter-in-law, Tawor-Ima, it is exactly the same as when a catatonic uses the word *ka-traver* instead of *Kleid* (clothes) in order to avoid the verbal element *Leid* (suffering) that is the constituent part of *Kleid*" (Werner, 1948, p. 373).

In traditional Australian society, there was a rare rite of sub-incision wherein an incision was made in the penis of a young man as a rite of initiation. It is remarkable to find one patient who not only wished to make an incision on his genitals but even equated the process with initiation: "One of Schilder's patients wanted to become a 'real man' by means of an incision in the form of the cross in his testicles" (Storch, 1924, p. 67).

This kind of thought is found not only among schizophrenics but also among compulsive neurotic patients. "One of these taboo patients of my acquaintance had adopted a rule against writing her own name, for fear that it might fall into the hands of someone who would then be in the possession of a portion of her personality" (Freud, [1913] 1955, p. 56).

All healthy children pass through a stage of cognitive development similar to that of sick adults in our society and healthy adults in primitive cultures. Piaget quotes a child who went out of doors with her mother after a long rain spell, saying, " 'Mamma, dry Babba's hands, so not rain any more' " (Piaget, 1929, p. 148). He also quotes one of his co-workers, who used to accompany his father to the rifle range. The father would give the child his cigar to hold, and the child decided he could control the accuracy of the father's firing by the angle at which he held the cigar (p. 137). We all remember similar experiences of our own childhood, involving stepping (or not stepping) on the cracks of the sidewalk and other magic games.

There are certain noncommonsense modes of thought—animism, nominal realism, participation—that are related to the magical view of the world, but yet may be distinguished from magic. Piaget (1929, p. 131) borrows from Lévy-Bruhl the word *participation* and defines it as "that relation which primitive thought believes to exist between two beings or two phenomena which it regards either as partially identical or as having a direct influence on one another, although there is no spatial contact nor intelligible causal connection between them." He defines animism (p. 132) as "the tendency to endow inanimate things with life and consciousness."

Both of these concepts differ from magic, because magic involves the use of these modes of thought "*to modify reality*" (Piaget, 1929, p. 131; emphasis added). Magic is not only a way of thought, it is a means to power. Mauss (1972, p. 102) supports the same contention when he observes that "sympathy [participation] is the route along which magical powers pass: It does not provide magical power itself."

One can provide a myriad of examples to demonstrate that children in our society believe in animism, participation, and nominal realism: that words have strength and not the things themselves (Piaget, 1929, p. 45); that the moon knows its own name (p. 79); that the sun follows one as one walks, by its own volition (p. 132); and that, when the conductor closes his eyes, the train goes into a tunnel (Fenichel, 1945, p. 48). What seems clear is that, in our culture, children go through an animistic-participatory stage of cognitive development out of which they subsequently grow and then move on to other stages of development. In early cultures, the animistic-participatory stage of cognitive development represents the *end product* of development. In many situations, adults as well as children use it either to explain or to act on the world. Further than this, one can postulate that the further stages of development that children achieve in our culture correspond to the stages of development in the history of culture, and this is true both for modes of thought (animism, participation, nominal realism) and for modes of power (magic and religion).

Max Weber, speaking of the Reformation, says ([1904–1905] 1958, p. 105), "That great historic process in the development of religions, the elimination of magic from the world, which began with the old Hebrew prophets and, in conjunction with Hellenistic scientific thought, had repudiated all magical means to salvation as superstition and sin, came here to its logical conclusion." If one wants to understand that process—and the stages through which it has gone—one must study the development of the psyche. And, if one would go even further and ask *why* that great historic process happened, one must look to the development of the psyche for at least a good part of the answer.

None of this is asserted to support the notion that most adults in primitive cultures are either schizophrenics, compulsive neurotics, or children. Clearly, they are not. What we have to imagine is a psychologically *healthy* child in our society around the age of five or six, a child who is not destined to become schizophrenic or even particularly neurotic. The stage of ego and cognitive development that such a child represents will be replete with modes of thought such as animism and participation and with the magical mode of power. Such a child will probably have definite religious notions of power, as well as the idea that omnipotence lies somewhere outside itself. Such a child would not lack the capacity for a great deal of commonsense activity. If we can imagine that child suddenly transported to another society where it would be subjected to no further cognitive development in the direction of rationality, a society that would reinforce rather than challenge the child's notions of animism, participation, and magic, and if we then imagine that child growing up to become an adult, biologically and psychologically, preserving its psychological health, we may then get some notion of what truly differentiates an adult in a primitive culture from an adult in a highly rational culture.

People in primitive cultures are primitive because their ego and cognitive development have been arrested. Libidinally, they are mature; they do not try to have babies in the mouth or the anus. Emotionally, they are capable of loving each other, their children, and their society and culture as much as we love. They differ from us *primarily* in the state of ego and cognitive development.

As far as it goes, this is too simplistic, because here again the theory fails us. We do not know what happens to the libido, to the moral capacity, to aggression, or to the reality principle when cognitive and ego development are cut short. In compulsive neurosis, ego and cognitive development remains fixated at an early stage; in schizophrenia, a massive regression of ego and cognitive development takes place; in previous stages of cultural development, the effect is neither of fixation nor regression, but of a failure to proceed. If we knew what effect this arrest of development has on the whole psyche, we would be much closer to understanding the process of cultural development.

Looking once again at Weber's statement about the historic process that eliminated magic from the world, it can be observed that there are several erroneous ideas expressed therein. It is a desire for omnipotence on Weber's part to think that we have succeeded in eliminating magic from the world, even in the most highly rational parts of our culture. It is also incorrect to say that the process began with the ancient Hebrews, when the reduction of the importance of magic (not its elimination) began with the creation of the first religious form within the sacred system—with the very beginnings of culture. What we observe in ancient Israel is not the beginning of the process but one culmination of the process: the triumph of religion over magic. The achievement of the ancient Hebrews was the creation of a sacred system that was *antagonistic* to magic. Such a sacred system had never existed before in Western culture; previously, the religious and magical elements within the sacred system had existed without antagonism to each other. An examination of the sacred systems of Egypt and Mesopotamia reveals how easily religious and magical elements were accommodated within one system. Magical elements, such as food taboos and blood sacrifice, were still tolerated in the Old Testament sacred system, but the process that would take the eventual elimination of magic as its goal was clearly launched.

One crucial form in the development of religion and its eventual triumph over magic was the priest and the priesthood. The priest is a development from the shaman or medicine man, his role is primarily a religious one, and the priestly role increases in importance as culture develops. The priest began to be differentiated from the shaman, and the priesthood became established as an institution at a critical time in cultural development: when kinship society was being transformed into the first primitive states. In all nonliterate state societies, such as Polynesia and early African states (Buganda, Ruanda, and so on), the priesthood played a crucial role in the sacred system and became involved in the politics of the authoritarian state. "Sometimes, as in Polynesia, priests were of special orders who resided in and were custodians of certain temples and images of gods on a full-time basis, but always these temples and gods were in the service of the authoritarian bureaucracy, supporting it at every turn. This is not to say that there was no other religion in chiefdoms. The curing shaman of egalitarian society probably continued this 'oldest profession,' as did magicians, soothsayers, witches, and other practitioners of primitive supernaturalism. But they remained largely unorganized, whereas the hierarchy of priests was an important facet of the organized hierarchial society of chiefdoms" (Service, 1975, p. 93).

We can easily observe the differentiation of the religious function of the priest and the magical function of the shaman in the rites of ancient Delphi. Delphi had organized priests of Apollo, but the function of communicating directly with the god was assigned to the Pythia, a shamanlike figure who babbled in strange noises the message from the god, which had to be translated into Greek by the priest. The mixture of magic and religion is a strange and complex one. Even in ancient Israel, the prophets—ecstatic, charismatic, possessed, magical—forced the sacred system to its most religious, most moral, most antimagical heights.

Whether or not there are nonsexual sources of power within the psyche, one fact remains true: Power is a central concept for the psychological process. Power to get what one wants, power to force or cajole others to do one's will, power to alter the real world, power to deal with inward anxieties and doubts—the health of the psyche depends on the degree to which these powers are attained.

No less important is the concept of power for all sacred systems. All such systems define and locate power and omnipotence and instruct the believer how to attain both. Morality, which is a province of religion, among other things, defines the relationship of power between people and tends to work in the direction of equalization of power. Meaning cannot exist without the notion that one is in control of oneself and the world; the sense of meaninglessness results from a loss of the power to control or organize the world or oneself.

Thirdly, society—more particularly, the political system—has power as its central subject. The Marxist analysis of society is built on the assumption that economic and political power are the sole determinants of the political system and society. One need not become that reductionist to be aware of the fundamental role of power in all social systems. Weber defines the state as the organization that has a monopoly of legitimate force within society (Weber, [1922] 1947, p. 154).

It can only be that these three conceptions of power—psychological, sacred, and political—have a definite relationship to one another. They are all three symbol systems made by people; the concept of efficacy that underlies them all is identical. For our purposes, it is crucial to emphasize that the psychological, the sacred, and the political-societal are all subject to a developmental process. The concept of power, itself, within the psychological, is subject to a development process. It would be enormously useful if we could describe the stages in the development of the concept of power—more specifically, omnipotence—within the psyche and then explore what stages of sacred systems and political-societal systems correspond with these stages of psychological omnipotence.

1. *The self is omnipotent.* "The infant does not know the limits of its power. It learns, in time, to recognize the parents as those who determine its fate, but in magic it denies their dependency" (Roheim, 1962, p. 46). Schizophrenics, in a massive state of regression, try to solve psychological problems by returning to the stage when the self was omnipotent and magic was the mode to power. Similarly, Piaget's daughter of sixteen months imagined that she could open the matchbox by opening her mouth. All of us, in stages of deep fatigue, severe anxiety, physical illness, extreme excitement or exhilaration, and in dreams, may and do *return* to the state when we were all-powerful.

Magic is the first step toward power, the first action of the psyche against dependency and passivity. "However bad this magic may look regarded in one aspect, still, in another it is higher than a condition of dependence upon nature and fear of it" (Hegel, in Frazer, 1911, p. 425). Roheim (1962, p. 3) calls magic the "counterphobic attitude, the transition from passivity to activity," and contrasts it with schizophrenic magic wherein no action follows: "Schizophrenic fantasy is generally a substitute for action."

As we have previously observed, no sacred or political system can correspond to this stage of psychological omnipotence, because there can be no completely magical sacred system. The belief that the self is omnipotent must give way to a more developed view of omnipotence before a sacred system can be constructed.

2. *The parents are omnipotent.* Ferenczi (1956, p. 194) and Piaget (1929, p. 354) concur with Fenichel's idea (1945, p. 301) that "Children who . . . have to give up their belief in their omnipotence believe instead that the grownups around them are omnipotent." This first stage in the transformation of omnipotence is of enormous importance. It means that the child is ready to give up its own sense of omnipotence, which makes the concept of reality possible. It puts the psyche into an interaction between reality and itself that leads, ultimately, to symbolism, religion, and art. It makes other people real in a way they cannot be if the self retains complete omnipotence. It makes religion possible.

We learn something of great importance in the way the psyche works when we observe this transaction. The child, in this step, does not abandon omnipotence but *transfers* it onto someone else, to a person or persons who take care of the child. Thus, helplessness does not result from the willingness to give up omnipotence. The psyche compensates itself for abandoning omnipotence by putting in its place another omnipotence that allows the psyche's safety. If the grownups are grossly inadequate for their task, the psyche will perceive that it cannot transfer its need for protection onto others and will refuse this step, keeping omnipotence to itself. This is one of the beginnings of psychosis.

Nothing leads us to believe that this first transformation of omnipotence is complete. Even the healthy psyche does not give up completely its sense of omnipotence. It keeps to itself a good proportion of the original sense and transfers only *part* of it onto the grownups. That is why the earliest sacred systems we are aware of contain such a high proportion of magical elements.

The sacred systems that correspond to this stage of omnipotence are those that are usually referred to as "primitive" or "preliterate." In those systems, magical practices and magical moral controls (taboo) abound; religion is confined primarily to the reverence of ancestors, who are the symbolic equivalent of the omnipotent parents, and gods play a very small role. The shaman, not the priest, is the primary religious figure.

The forms of political cohesion in such a society are kinship forms—the political equivalent of omnipotent parents—with non-kinship forms that lead to the development of the state playing a very minor role. All prestate societies fall into this category. None of this is to say that there is no political development from small hunting bands to large kinship societies, such as the Dinka, which could hold together nearly 1,000,000 people in one society. There has been political development *within* all the stages of omnipotence that we will be dealing with. This would indicate that the conception of power, like any other single conception, is not sufficient to explain the development of society.

3. *The gods and the king are omnipotent.* If one spent one's entire life under the shadow of omnipotent parents, it would be impossible to become a grownup oneself. Parsons (1970, pp. 45–46) observes that the solution to this is to *generalize* the conception of parents. In this way, a boy, for instance, is no longer faced with the task of replacing *his* father, but of becoming *a* father. Parsons states that the fact that the father is now a symbol and not a specific individual makes possible important further developments in the psyche. Liberation from the total domination of the parents' omnipotence is clearly one great benefit of this process. One crucial way that culture has assisted in this development is in the creation of the idea of the gods.

"Later, the quality of omnipotence is displaced from the adults to God" (Fenichel, 1945, p. 301). "Our results entirely support the thesis of M. Bovet according to which the child spontaneously attributes to his parents the perfections and attributes which he will later transfer to God if his religious education gives him the opportunity" (Piaget, 1929, p. 354).

The omnipotence of the gods is won at the expense of the parents. The perception that one's parents are not omnipotent is both a cause for anxiety and an opportunity for freedom— freedom if one can succeed in identifying with the power greater than the parents. Piaget (1929, p. 150) relates an incident in the life of Hebbel when Hebbel's father despaired over the loss of crops caused by a storm, whereupon Hebbel became aware that his father was not omnipotent. I myself remember that when I was nine or ten I realized that my father was enormously anxious about Hitler's conquering the world. At that time, I must have decided that anything that could frighten my all-powerful father must be the strongest thing in the world. Politics has remained a prime interest in my life.

The sacred systems that correspond to this stage of omnipotence are obviously those wherein the gods play an equal or greater part than impersonal magical elements. These sacred systems began in preliterate states, came to a flowering in early civilizations, and developed from there.

Monotheism has a regressive element in it that can be seen when we relate it to conceptions of omnipotence. All monotheistic gods are fathers. In polytheism, there are many gods, but only one of them is ever referred to as "father," and he receives this designation only when he is the chief or most powerful god, as "Father Zeus." Monotheism seems to be reconciling two stages of omnipotence with each other, healing the break in belief that had been caused by taking omnipotence away from the parents. God, the father, who can perform all manner of magical arts, such as raining down manna from heaven—nothing is more powerful than a symbol that can incorporate many stages of development within it.

This transference of omnipotence away from the parents has a profound political significance: The king can be as omnipotent as the gods. Nonkinship forms of social cohesion become possible. In all early, preliterate states, the conception of kingship plays a crucial role in the development of the state and the transformation of kinship values. In traditional Buganda, for instance, young men left their kinship-bound situations to go to court and become part of "the kings' men." Nonkinship forms of political cohesion were being built at the expense of kinship forms. If the potency of the king (psychologically considered) had not been greater than that of the parents or kin, no young men would ever have left home, and the political form of omnipotent kingship could not have been constructed.

We can observe the process of building the state system from weak chieftainship to strong chieftainship to kingship. As this system grows, kinship ties weaken, just as the omnipotence of the parents must be weakened if the gods and kings are to be empowered.

4. *Society is omnipotent.* The fourth, fifth, and sixth stages in the development of the concept of omnipotence I can only de-

scribe, as it were, from the outside. In the description of the first three stages, the procedure was to describe a psychological process, to infer from that a corresponding sacred and political process, and then to identify and illuminate these social forms. In the analysis of the last three stages, the procedure will be to describe a social and cultural process, from which a corresponding psychological process can be inferred. In each case, however, I lack the supporting evidence to establish the psychological dimension, and therefore the inference will have to remain merely that. This is not to say that the psychological evidence does not exist somewhere, for it may, or that it would be impossible to obtain. This reversal of approach, far from weakening the basic hypothesis of the correspondence of psychological and cultural development, actually strengthens it. If we can legitimately infer a psychological developmental step from the data obtained through social and cultural observation, then the basic hypothesis has begun to work for us.

At some point in the development of culture and society, the notion appears that no longer are the gods or the king omnipotent but that the state is omnipotent. One needs no historical sense to observe this, because we are living in the midst of such a stage and are trying desperately to contain the destructive implications of this world view. It is remarkable how unreligious the leaders of German and Italian fascism were and yet how completely committed they were to the idea of the omnipotence of the state. The belief in such omnipotence underlies Soviet and Chinese societies as well, even though both are totally antagonistic to traditional religion. The same belief in the omnipotence of economic and political relationships or of "the forces of history" underlies Marxist theory, at least in its most inflexible form. More than one person has observed that in the modern world we have stopped killing people for reasons of religion and now only kill them for reasons of state—that wars of nationalism have replaced wars of religion.

This designation of the society or the state as omnipotent is both progressive and regressive. It is progressive in the sense that it is "more real"; it is closer to the way things actually are. Unlike the gods, the state does exist; unlike the gods, society does give us our moral values; society does provide us with the food we eat; and the state, unlike the gods, really does have the power of life and death over us. Most important, society, unlike the gods, can be improved, and therefore the belief in the omnipotence of society may be a springboard for the attempt to change reality.

And yet, in a way that is more difficult to describe, there is something regressive in the idea that society and the state are omnipotent. All the elements in this belief would still be there if we felt that the state were merely powerful. It is the *omni*potence that causes one not to trust this seeming advance. The gods are a symbol of something else; the belief in them resembles the experience of art—it contains a willing suspension of disbelief. The state, however, is not only a symbol but also an actuality; it does exist. To ascribe omnipotence to it seems, in some ways, a destruction of symbolism—a regression back to the original magical conception of the world. This may help to explain why the omnipotent state has brought us so much misery.

This belief in the omnipotence of society begins only when the faith in traditional religion starts to be undermined. The first historical evidence we have of such a situation in the West is from fifth-century Athens. Alcibiades is one of the first great charismatic political leaders to scorn traditional sacred beliefs and to revere only the omnipotent state. And Thucydides is both chronicler and priest of the new sacred and political system.

Psychologically, the process seems to be one wherein the cognitive function has developed disproportionally and has outrun the rest of the psyche. This may happen because changes in the culture are forcing an increase of rationality that the psyche as a whole is unwilling to accept, although the cognitive function of the psyche may be willing and able to go along with the cultural advance toward rationality. No longer able to believe in the traditional gods because the rational function rejects them, other parts of the psyche retain the belief in omnipotence. To insist that the state is omnipotent resolves this contradiction. On the one hand, one rejects the belief in mere symbols and ascribes power only to what exists; what could be more rational? On the other, the lust for magic is preserved by making of the "real" state an omnipotent force; what could be more satisfying to the primitive drive to be all-powerful?

Within some of Max Weber's works, there are implicit ideas of development sequences, which never quite become explicit. In his discussion of the three types of legitimate authority ([1922] 1947, p. 328), he lists three such pure types: rational, traditional, and charismatic. If we reverse the order, but keep the categories, we may discover an important developmental sequence. Even in Weber's work, it is assumed that traditional modes of authority precede rational modes in the history of society. Charismatic authority, however, for Weber, is not tied into any developmental sequence.

My view is that charismatic authority is the corresponding political attitude to the magical view, that it predominates in the earliest societies and that, therefore, the sequence charismatic and traditional is the political equivalent of magical and religious. The very late historical appearance of leaders such as Mohammed, Napoleon, or Hitler would involve a return to a basic ground of authority: omnipotence and magic. Just as magical elements persist in all sacred systems no matter how developed they may become, so the original magical basis of authority persists in all political systems.

Parsons supports this last view when he writes (in Weber, [1922] 1947, p. 76), "From the second point of view, all authority has a charismatic basis in some form." And Weber himself ([1922] 1947, p. 366) lends some support to this reading when he states that charismatic authority may be transmitted from one person to another by means of ritual sanction: "The concept [of transmittal] was originally magical."

In speaking of charismatic authority, Weber had remarkable prescience into what actually happened to the United States after World War II. "For monarchies, hence, it is dangerous to lose wars, since that makes it appear that their charisma is no longer genuine. For republics, on the other hand, striking victories may be dangerous in that they put the victorious general in a favorable position of making charismatic claims" (Weber, [1922] 1947, p. 382). If we substitute the word *omnipotence* for *charismatic* in the last sentence, we do no violence to its meaning. And if we observe that the sense of omnipotence that pervaded United States foreign policy after World War II came to an end in the Vietnam War, we see how close Weber's thought about charisma is to our conceptions of magic and omnipotence. If we have a "civil religion" in our country, we are advised to recognize that we have a "civil magic" as well. Our "political sacred system" still contains the two elements of religion and magic that all sacred systems have held together.

Finally, if we examine the history of political society and go back to the very beginning of the state (Buganda, Polynesia, and so on), we find the charismatic authority of the king at the center of that state building. Only the omnipotent king had the power to break traditional kinship ties of authority. At times of great change, the psyche and the cultural system return to the roots of power for the energy necessary to radically change the social order; those roots are magical and omnipotent. This may also explain why the great prophets of Israel who brought us rationality and morality were so charismatic in their methods.

5. *No one is omnipotent: tragedy.* At some point in the development of the rational function of the psyche, when the rest of the psyche has the courage to face such a terrible insight, the idea presents itself that no one is omnipotent, that there is no real safety in the world, and that all one can strive for is a certain amount of power but all-powerfulness is unobtainable. Such a truth is unwelcome news. If we weep at a performance of tragedy, we weep, in part, for the fact that we know we must give up our desires for omnipotence. If the hero dies in most tragic plays, he dies, in part, as a symbol of the death of our narcissistic belief that omnipotence is, somehow, obtainable. The tragic view never says that life is impossible or that morality and order cannot be achieved, but all tragedy leaves us with a sense of loss, the sense that we should no longer seek something we have always wished for. The Greek view was that there was no life so happy or secure that one day and one night could not transform it into a catastrophe. Omnipotence is impossible; it is a sad day when we receive that news—tragic, in fact.

Tragedy, like the novel and unlike lyric poetry, is a culturally specific form. With possibly few exceptions, all cultures at all times have written lyric poetry. Tragedy, however, has been a characteristic form of artistic expression only at a certain few times in cultural history. We do not write tragedy today, not because it has been done before, since the novels and poetry we write have been "done before," but also because our culture is not fundamentally involved with the moral and reality questions that tragedy asks. It is a fair postulate that chronologically diverse cultures, such as fifth-century Athens and Elizabethan England, must have had certain basic similarities because they each turned to the tragic form for their highest moral statements.

The omnipotence of Yahweh made tragedy impossible in ancient Israel. The closest the Bible comes to tragedy is the book of Job, written under Greek influence, an attempt to represent the tragic view in sacred context. The attempt fails: Job ends with a paean to the omnipotence of Yahweh; and the true tragic sense is lost.

Politically, there appears to be a relationship between tragedy and democracy. It does not seem to be mere coincidence that the tragic form was born in the greatest ancient democracy and reached its second great flowering in a country that was destined to be the seed of democracy for the whole modern world. The democratic form is viable only under the assumption that no one person, no one party, is omnipotent. The reason that stable, democratic polities do not kill one another over elections is that, in this democratic view, it really doesn't make that much difference to the nation who is elected because no one is all-powerful. The Nixon view that members of the opposition were "enemies," traitors who would sell the country down the river, promoted the attitude that *anything* was permissible to defeat such an enemy; politics became warfare. This view is based on the assumption that omnipotence is possible and that one party has it.

The democratic idea is that there is no point in killing people over the difference between Liberals and Tories or Republicans and Democrats. None are traitors, and none have the omnipotent capacity to save the country in all circumstances. Democracy is the great rational system of political order. Such rationality is impossible without the abandonment of the drive to recover lost omnipotence.

6. *Power, but not omnipotence, is possible: science and rationality.* The tragic view ends neither in pessimism nor despair; it ends in action. Giving up omnipotence, we discover that real power, unencumbered by the illusion of being all-powerful, is possible. A power that is neither religious nor magical can ultimately become more

effective than either of these—the power of science and rationality. That is why, culturally, there has been an intimate link between tragedy and science.

Before the rise of classical Greek culture, the most important flowering of science in the West took place in Sumeria and Babylonia. The *Epic of Gilgamesh,* the greatest literary work of that culture, is one of the most tragic heroic poems ever written. Full of the emotions of pity and terror, it is a story about the giving up of the search for omnipotence. It closes when Gilgamesh, realizing that he cannot be all-powerful, returns to rule his city in as wise a manner as possible; he decides to do a grown-up person's work in the real world. Ancient Israel, one of the most remarkable of cultures, however, produced not one drop in the stream of scientific advance. The omnipotence of Yahweh made both tragedy and science impossible.

In Greece, the great age of tragedy was followed by an unprecedented development of the scientific view of the world. Such a growth in scientific thought was not to be seen again until the Renaissance and post-Renaissance period, the result of which was the permanent establishment of the scientific and rational views in Western culture. In this same period, great tragedies were written again, in England and in France. In the nearly two thousand years between the deaths of Sophocles and Euripides and the birth of Marlowe, no great poet took the tragic play as his form. Since the death of Racine, the writing of tragedy has, once again, become only an antiquarian pastime.

Once the scientific and rational views of reality become a permanent part of the value system of the culture, they become a part of the ego and superego of every individual psyche within the culture. Piaget's students of twelve or fourteen years of age are capable of understanding the concept of force in a way that was impossible for Aristotle. Cultural development thus changes the nature of the whole psyche through the cognitive and the moral functions. Any theory of society and the psyche that ignores this fact becomes, thereby, psychologically reductionist.

As long as we are looking at the cognitive function of the ego, by itself, there is no conflict about the progressively increasing scientific and rational views. Conflict occurs when the more primitive areas of the psyche resist the abandonment of omnipotence and insist that rationality, science, and democracy should be abandoned instead. Many of the great political struggles of this century can only be understood in terms of a great conflict, within culture and within the psyche, between reason and omnipotence.

These thoughts give us only the bare bones of a theory—a prolegomena. One serious omission is the absence of any discussion of the relationship between cognitive development and moral development. This argument concerning religion and magic is undertaken in order to demonstrate two fundamental ideas: (1) that it is impossible to understand the nature of society and culture without understanding the nature of the psyche as a whole and (2) that it is impossible to understand the psyche as a whole without comprehending the nature of culture and society. At present, we may have two fields of endeavor, but one theory will ultimately bring them both to fulfillment.

References

Bellah, R. "Civil Religion in America." In *Beyond Belief.* New York: Harper & Row, 1970.

Dodds, E. R. *The Greeks and the Irrational.* Boston: Beacon Press, 1957.

Durkheim, E. *The Elementary Forms of the Religious Life.* (J. Swain, Trans.) New York: Free Press, no date. (Originally published 1912.)

Fenichel, O. *The Psychoanalytic Theory of Neurosis.* New York: Norton, 1945.

Ferenczi, S. "Stages in the Development of the Sense of Reality." In *Sex in Psychoanalysis (Contributions to Psycho-Analysis).* (E. Jones, Trans.) New York: Dover, 1956.

Flavell, J. H. *The Developmental Psychology of Jean Piaget.* New York: D. Van Nostrand, 1963.

Frazer, J. G. *The Magic Art and the Evolution of Kings.* Vol. 1. London: Macmillan, 1911.

Frazer, J. G. *The Golden Bough.* 1 vol. (abridged ed.) New York: Macmillan, 1955. (Originally published 1890.)

Freud, S. "Totem and Taboo." In *Standard Edition of the Complete Psychological Works.* (J. Strachey, Ed. and Trans.) Vol. 13. London: Hogarth Press, 1955. (Originally published 1913.)

Mahler, M. S., Pine, F., and Bergman, A. *The Psychological Birth of the Human Infant.* New York: Basic Books, 1975.

Malinowski, B. "Baloma: The Spirits of the Dead in the Trobriand Islands." In *Magic, Science and Religion.* New York: Doubleday, 1954.

Mauss, M. *A General Theory of Magic.* (R. Brain, Trans.) London: Routledge & Kegan Paul, 1972.

Parsons, T. "Evolutionary Universals in Society." In *Sociological Theory and Modern Society.* New York: Free Press, 1967.

Parsons, T. "The Father Symbol." In *Social Structure and Personality.* New York: Free Press and Collier-Macmillan, 1970.

Piaget, J. *The Child's Conception of the World.* (J. Tomlinson and A. Tomlinson, Trans.) London: Routledge & Kegan Paul and Trench, Trubner, 1929.

Reik, T. *Ritual: Psycho-Analytic Studies.* (D. Bryan, Trans.) New York: Farrar, Straus & Giroux, 1946.

Roheim, G. *Magic and Schizophrenia.* Bloomington: Indiana University Press, 1962.

Sagan, E. *Cannibalism: Human Aggression and Cultural Form.* New York: Harper & Row, 1974.

Service, E. *Origins of the State and Civilization.* New York: Norton, 1975.

Spencer, B., and Gillen, F. J. *The Native Tribes of Central Australia.* London: Macmillan, 1938.

Storch, A. *The Primitive Archaic Forms of Inner Experiences and Thought in Schizophrenia.* New York: Nervous and Mental Disease Publishing, 1924.

Weber, M. *The Theory of Social and Economic Organization.* (A. M. Henderson and T. Parsons, Trans.) New York: Oxford University Press, 1947. (Originally published 1922.)

Weber, M. *The Protestant Ethic and the Spirit of Capitalism.* (T. Parsons, Trans.) New York: Scribner's, 1958. (Originally published 1904–1905.)

Werner, H. *Comparative Psychology of Mental Development.* New York: International University Press, 1948.

5

David L. Petersen

Max Weber and the Sociological Study of Ancient Israel

~~~~~~~~~~~~~~~~~~~~~~~~~~~~~~~~~~~

My purposes in writing this chapter are fourfold: (1) to provide an overview of the questions Weber was attempting to answer in his study of ancient Israel; (2) to articulate Weber's own theses about the nature of ancient Israelite society; (3) to assess the cogency of the ideal type "prophet" in Weber's *Ancient Judaism* ([1921] 1967) and in *Wirtschaft und Gesellschaft* ([1921] 1956), of which his *The Sociology of Religion* ([1922] 1963) is a part; and (4) to comment briefly on contemporary sociological studies of ancient Israel. This chapter should not be understood as an attempt to reconstruct the lineal heritage of Weber's work on ancient Israel, although many works of that heritage are cited in the references.[1] Furthermore, I do not intend to assess the significance of ancient Israel for the Protestant ethos or for Western society as a whole, important though these issues were for Weber. Rather, I am more concerned with Weber's attempts to exercise sociological analysis on an ancient society, a task that some have thought impossible.[2]

Weber's Contexts for the Study of Ancient Israel

Weber's purposes in writing his study of ancient Israel were at least threefold (and it should be said at the outset that Weber's predilection for many-purposed essays makes an assessment of his work all the more difficult). First, Weber felt that the existence of Judaism presented a problem: "How did the Jews become a pariah people with such highly pronounced characteristics?" Or, by way of unpacking Weber's language, why would a religious community choose to adopt a stance (and here Weber emphasizes the original voluntary character of this status) that separated them ritually from the surrounding society? In asking this question, Weber sought to understand the character of one specific religion that has continued for over a 2000-year period.

Second, Weber was concerned to ask a more universal question, one that encompassed the major cultures of both Orient and Occident. The motive that lay behind Weber's studies of China and India, as well as of Judaism and Protestant Christianity, was to distinguish between the cultural development in East and that in West. For Weber, the Occident was to be distinguished from the Orient: The former had a highly rationalized ethos of economic activity that we now label *capitalism,* and the latter had developed no similar conception. In this context, the study of Judaism was crucial for Weber's analysis, because he understood ancient Israel to have provided some of the crucial conceptions that allowed for the breakthrough we know as Western civilization.[3]

Thirdly, Weber believed, "Anyone who is an heir to the traditions of modern European civilization will approach problems of universal history with a set of questions, which to him appear both inevitable and legitimate. These questions will turn on the combination of circumstances which have brought about the cultural phenomena that are uniquely Western and that have at the same time. . . . a universal cultural significance" (Bendix, 1961, p. 212). Weber recognized that the civilization of which he was a part had been strongly influenced by the precepts of the Hebrew Bible, especially as it, the Hebrew Bible, had been conveyed by the Christian church. It was the prophetically or eschatologically conditioned Hebrew Bible with its antimagical and socioeconomic prescriptions that, Weber argued, served as important bases for later rational, scientific, and technological development in Western civilization.

From this perspective, and to a lesser degree from the perspective of the second area of Weber's concern, the study of Judaism really means the study of the Hebrew Bible, because it was the literary heritage of ancient Israel and not the Jewish religion as a continuing tradition that exercised a significant impact on Christianity and Western culture in the second millenium A.D. Or, to use Weber's words ([1921] 1967, p. 4), "The world-historical significance of Jewish religious developments rests above all in the creation of the Old Testament." This conviction about the importance of the book itself, with less emphasis on the religion that claimed it alone as its canon—Judaism—allowed Weber to focus on the detail and complexity of Hebrew Bible scholarship, a task in which he reveled, as an examination of the notes to *Ancient Judaism* quickly attests. In fact, Weber became so caught up in the intricacies of the Hebrew Bible scholarship of his time, that his own insights, his own creative interpretations of ancient Israelite society, are often difficult to perceive.

It is therefore fair to conclude that, in studying ancient Israel, Weber was, at one and the same time, studying ancient literature and the society that produced it, a living religious tradition (Judaism), the difference between Orient and Occident, and his own European civilization.

Max Weber on Ancient Israel

One leitmotif running throughout Weber's chapters on ancient Israel is the emphasis on change: from earliest times to the league, from the league to the monarchy, from the monarchy to the exile, and, more generally, from ancient Israel to Judaism.[4] By way of appreciating Weber's approach, it is instructive to place his work on early Israel's social organization alongside two other standard works: De Vaux (1965, pp. 68–90) and Pedersen ([1926] 1959, pp. 29–60). In both these books, the picture of society appears much more stable; the element of change is not emphasized. Furthermore, in the two works just cited, etymologies rather than social function tend to serve as the basis for crucial sociological distinctions.

Because Weber's essay on ancient Israel differs from his discussion of similar topics in *The Sociology of Religion* ([1922] 1963) (the former focuses on a national religious group over a period of time, whereas the latter surveys all religious performance from a "developmental" perspective) and because most readers are more familiar with his presentation of Hebrew Bible topics, for example "prophecy," as they are presented in *The Sociology of Religion* than with their treatment in *Ancient Judaism* ([1921] 1967), it seems appropriate to present Weber's basic theses as they reflect the different periods in Israel's history. I judge it most valuable to organize this summary by means of formulating four central questions that I take Weber to be addressing in his study of ancient Israel. This approach is especially valuable, because it allows us to observe that Weber was often asking questions different from those typically raised by Hebrew Bible scholars. The four central questions are (1) "What was the sociological context in Syria-Palestine out of which Yahwism developed?" (2) "What was early Yahwism?" (3) "What was the effect of the institution of monarchy in Israel on Yahwism?" and, finally, (4) "What was the effect of the defeat and end of the Judahite state on Yahwism?"

1. "What was the sociological context in Syria-Palestine out of which Yahwism developed?" Weber's answer to this question is difficult to summarize because he is doing at least three different things when he describes Late Bronze Age Syrian-Palestinian society. To be sure, he does describe Syria-Palestine, but since his source material is the Hebrew Bible and since portions of that literature do more than describe Syria-Palestinian society, Weber also treats the Israelite society of the league (the period of the judges) and, as well, the patriarchal stories, narratives that purport to describe a period earlier than the league but that, as Weber perceptively recognizes, appear to reflect the conditions of a later period.

After considering the geographic and climatic conditions of Syria-Palestine, Weber sketches the structure of Late Bronze Age society. It comprised cities, seminomadic tribal structures engaged in stockbreeding and farming, and other groups that lived in the interstices of the two previous structures. Weber understands the viability of the city to rest on land ownership. Within the city, there was an "armed patriciate," the landowners, known by various Hebrew titles: *gibbôrê ḥayil*, wealthy and militarily qualified citizens; and *zᵉkēnîm*, the elders, the only legitimately qualified political representatives. Often, one elder would achieve predominant status and would function somewhat as a prince. When a prince achieved significant power, his clan (Weber's *sib*, Hebrew *mišpāḥāh*) would outdistance the other *zᵉkēnîm* and their families in political importance. Interestingly, even in the city social organization was articulated using the language of tribal organization. The smallest grouping was the house of the father *(bêt 'ābôt);* then came the clan *(mišpāḥāh);* and finally the tribe *(šebet).* In addition to slaves, who were also part of the urban structure, Weber discerns an important plebeian stratum, especially potters, weavers, metal workers, tanners, and musicians. In sum, in Late Bronze Syria-Palestine there were fully developed cities, even though the language of tribal structure often obscures this fact.

At the opposite pole from the city, Weber notes the position of the desert Bedouin and what they represent, a tribally organized community that traces its origin back to a common ancestor. Weber, however, recognizes that there is no trace of "genuine Bedouin right" in ancient Israel. Furthermore, there seems to be an eternal hate relationship between Israelites and true Bedouins as represented by the Amalekites. Hence, while it is important to recognize what a truly nomadic society might be, it is not necessarily the case that ancient Israel was such a society.

Somewhere between the structures of the city and the desert nomad come the free peasants, farmers who could own land. As a group, they are known as "the people" *(hā'ām).* Although originally and ideally free, they could become debt slaves. Also, they could form a sort of rural militia, as they did during the time of the league (Judg. 5).

Standing somewhat outside the structures just mentioned are the *gēr* and the *nokrî,* the resident alien and the "foreigner." The former had some legal rights, whereas the latter did not. Nothing is more characteristic of the resident aliens than their variety: Israelite and non-Israelite, city dweller and herdsman, freeman and serf. Two classes of *gērîm* were of particular importance for the development of Yahwism: the stockbreeding herdsman and the Levite. "In tradition, both groups are characterized as not sharing in the land of the politically qualified army. Both, however, like all *gērîm*, had a fixed legal relationship to the settled population. In the tribal territory of Israel, no agricultural land was assigned to the two groups, but they received dwelling sites, though mostly outside the city gates. They were also granted pasture rights for their animals" (Weber, [1921] 1967, p. 36). Even though the resident alien (*gēr*) appears to be the main socio-economic stratum from which Yahwism developed, Weber is clear about the variety typical of Israel's tribal organization. "In the historical tradition, the single Israelite tribe is to be found in all stages of transition from quasi-Bedouinism to quasi-nomadic small-stock breeding and from both through the intermediary stage of occasional agriculture (Genesis 26:12 with Isaac) to urbanization as ruling sibs, as well as to settled agriculture as free and corveé-rendering peasants" (Weber, [1921] 1967, p. 42).

When he discussed the stockbreeding herdsmen, Weber of necessity had to discuss the so-called patriarchal period. According to the traditional picture, Israel became Israel during the patriarchal period, went down into Egypt, came out under Moses' leadership, conquered the land under Joshua, and so forth. Weber had begun his analysis by ignoring all these early stages and by concentrating instead on the postconquest existence of Israel. Weber defends this ploy by arguing that the patriarchal narratives are anachronistic. He observes the dissonance among the putative mode of life of the stockbreeding herdsmen and the inherent conflicts such a mode of life engenders, as well as the pacifistic character of the biblical narratives themselves. Weber contends that such pacifism could only occur in a time when the small stockbreeders lived as peaceful sojourners at the permission of a powerful urban structure and also at a time when the free herdsmen had been demilitarized, a time that Weber thinks only came with the inception of monarchy in Israel. To be sure, he discerns scattered fragments of the earlier and expected heroic stories of seminomadic conflict, for example, the story of Simeon in Genesis 34. Nevertheless, for Weber, study of Israelite society properly avoids the patriarchal texts as evidence for a seminomadic style of life and instead begins with the league, because it is only from this period that we have literature that reflects more or less accurately the socio-economic conditions of earliest Israel.[5]

In answer to the first question, we may say that the social context of Syria-Palestine was like the social character of early Israel, heterogeneous in the extreme. Or to use Weber's words ([1921] 1967, p. 56), "In pre-Solomonic times, the actual nucleus of the old confederacy consisted, on the one hand, of the numerically superior peasant mountaineers, and the slowly decreasing stock-breeders of the steppe regions on the other. To these must be added various market hamlets and rural towns in the river valleys of the mountains and the mountain passes, only secondarily—though gradually increasing—fortified cities as well." The society of Syria-Palestine was the society of earliest Israel.

2. *"What was early Yahwism?"* Given the extreme heterogeneity of social structure in Late Bronze and Early Iron Age Syria-Palestine, Weber was presented with a serious problem: What, if anything, did the term *Israel* signify in the premonarchic period? Weber's answer is "the confederacy or league"—the first important thesis of the book. Weber, not surprisingly, begins his analysis of the early Yahwistic community with an analysis of the laws, data that Weber and, more recently, Speiser (1967) have argued often provide the best index to the character and values of a society. And, in examining the laws, Weber was, as we shall see later, addressing the concept of covenant, since the laws of the Israelite community may be properly understood as the stipulations of Israel's covenant or suzerainty treaty with its god, Yahweh. Weber makes two trenchant observations on the basis of the laws. First, the earliest legal material reflects a society in which the rights of the village-dwelling peasant are the primary concern; that is, the originally free, landed peasant has now become a plebeian standing below the developing urban patriciate (Weber, [1921], 1967, p. 65). And, second, in the law codes Weber discerns "the source of the distinction between in-group and out-group morality for Jewry," one root of the pariah people concept (for example, see Exodus 22:25).

Nevertheless, it is not the law codes themselves but rather the overriding concept of covenant that Weber identified as con-

stitutive for early Yahwism. The reasons for the existence of such a
berît (covenant) are, according to Weber, twofold: (1) It depends on
the general sociopolitical conditions of the environment and (2) it
depends on "a special event in religious history" ([1921] 1967, p.
78). The general conditions were the "contractually regulated,
permanent relationships of landed warrior sibs (cities and farmers)
with guest tribes (stockbreeders) as legally protected people (the
gērîm). Contracts and more general agreements dominated the
social relationships of the larger Syria-Palestinian society." But most
of these covenants were unstable, and this instability stands in contrast with "the extraordinary stability of a religious order or cult of
a similar sort like the Rechabites" (Weber, [1921] 1967, p. 79).
Weber did not argue that the socioeconomic context produced the
ideology of covenant in Israel. Its origins are much more complex:
They include personal circumstances and vicissitudes. The real
question is why the covenant-based society survived, why it was
more stable than the other covenants and treaties around it.
Weber's answer is the solidarity that "religious fraternization" engenders. Once the covenant had forged a cultic league with a god
as partner and with charismatic "judges" as war saviors, the confederacy's stability was more or less guaranteed (Weber, [1921]
1967, p. 80).[6]

After examining the origin of the league, Weber sought to
examine its function. He holds that the confederacy had its essential function as a war league; Israel was banded together by oath to
do war and little else. Ritual circumcision is best understood as a
part of the ascetic ritual accompanying preparation for battle. The
Nazirites are likewise to be conceived as ascetically trained warrior
ecstatics. The total destruction of the enemy, the *ḥerem*, was only
part of an overarching ritual that the war had to follow. Israel, as
peasant or rural militia, was led in this ritual by war prophets, a late
example of which we may discern in Elisha.[7]

One may not overemphasize the significance of Weber's insistence on war as early Israel's essential function, because he points
to the demilitarization of the "people" during the monarchy, a time
in which Israel's kings developed a standing army, as a process of
momentous importance. Concepts of Israel both as army and
nonarmy are important for Weber's interpretations.

The war league was a confederation without well-defined political structures or officials. What was characteristic of the league's institutions was the so-called judge, a military deliverer who surfaced in times of military emergency. Actual legal decision making is not a well-attested function of the judges; this activity was more in the hands of the elders and the priests.

Although Weber understands ancient Israel to function essentially as a war confederation, he contends that the significance of the league is broader than war. The method by means of which the league was created, an elective treaty with a god, served to provide for more inclusive social relationships, relationships not only between god and people but also among the people themselves. By way of synthesizing Weber's discussion, I think he makes six basic points about Israel's god, Yahweh, and the league:

1. Israel's covenant was "unique" because it was tied to a specific historical event. The uniqueness does not depend on that event as unrepeatable, however. Rather, the crucial element for Weber is the time at which this covenant was contracted between Yahweh and Israel. The covenant was contracted before Israel "knew" Yahweh; Yahweh was an unknown quantity.

2. As an unknown god, Yahweh was understood as a god from afar. He did not enter a relationship with Israel as a familiar tribal deity. Yahweh was a god whose home was on a remote mountain. To be sure, this terrible storm god had benign features. However, he remained outside, never immanent, and always prior to the established tribal, social network.

3. As a covenant god, Yahweh was a partner and this in sharp contrast to the typical pattern in which a god served as a witness to a treaty or as one who would avenge a violation of the treaty stipulations.

4. Also peculiar to Israel's covenant with Yahweh was the character of the stipulations and pledges. There is a pronounced mutuality. Israel must obey the stipulations of the treaty, and, if the Israelites obey, Yahweh must in return give them the promised blessings. This mutuality works itself out in the future; what one does in the present affects future events. Furthermore, both covenant blessing (Weber's "salvation") and curse (Weber's "punishment") are understood to work themselves out not on individual

Israelites but rather on the entire covenant community. The mutuality of the covenant therefore extends not only between Israel and Yahweh but also within the covenant community itself and within the covenant community into the future.

5. Despite descriptions of Yahweh that associate him with the natural order—theophany in the thunderstorm, rain, or fertility god—Yahweh remained an elective god of social organization, because of his significance as war god. Yahweh was a contractual partner who instituted a series of commandments (covenant stipulations), not a god who reveals or administers permanent, pre-existing orders.[8]

6. Finally, Weber contends, "in Yahwism there were features transcending Israel and in this sense a certain universalism was inherent in the conception of Yahweh" ([1921] 1967, p. 133). The precise character of this universalism is difficult to discern. Weber is quick to point out he does not mean that Yahweh was a god of a universally valid ethic or that he was of ethical conduct himself. Rather, Yahweh's universalism centers in his function as confederate god; to the warrior he was a god in opposition to the enemies' god; to the king and urban strata, he was localized, the Jerusalem temple was his home, and the fortunes of the city were his fortunes. "The conception of Yahweh has not only undergone changes, but at any time, it varied according to different social groups" (Weber, [1921] 1967, p. 133). As god of various social groups, Yahweh was more than a city god or a god legitimating stockbreeding. Typically, Weber suggests that there were other factors contributing to Yahweh's relative universalism: his reception by Israel on the basis of his having acted on their behalf, a lack of emphasis on sacrifice (Weber overstates the evidence here), and his essentially ascetic and unmarried status. Nevertheless, Yahweh's ability to function as a god for so many different groups is the essential feature of his universalism.

The answer to the question about the character of Yahwism is that early Yahwism was a voluntary, contractual league made up of heterogeneous elements and whose primary purpose was war. Its very heterogeneous character and certain universalistic tendencies allowed this league to serve as the basis for a much broader social organization.

3. *"What was the effect of the institution of monarchy in Israel on Yahwism?"* After having examined the league and its salient features, Weber moved to almost random consideration of topics in Israelite history and religion: Sabbath, sacrifice, the relation of non-Yahwistic cults to Yahwism, priesthood, and, most especially, the Levites. One cannot overestimate the significance that Weber attributes to the Levites. It is this group, priests in direct contact with the people, who interpreted the Yahwistic religion in an oracular setting. Within the context of binary divination, they developed a "rational knowledge of Yahweh's commandments" (Weber, [1921] 1967, p. 178) that was used to allow Israelites to understand the ways in which Yahweh related to the world and, consequently, to allow them to know how to act in accordance with that will. This rational knowledge, Weber contends, helped rid Israel of magic, a development that later allowed for a naturalistic view of nature.

More important than this survey of monarchic Israel, valuable as it is, is Weber's assessment of the changes monarchy wrought. The city councils, the elders, were now less important than the central bureaucracy. The free peasants who had earlier fought as a rural militia and had beaten their Canaanite overlords were now demilitarized and socially declassed. Most importantly, the inception of monarchy and all that it meant resulted in reactions, especially writing activity. Weber contends that a unique symbiosis among "intellectuals," the Torah teachers or Levites, the declassed peasants, and especially the prophets, was responsible for the written responses to the wars of liberation, the rise of kingship, the corveé economy, metropolitan culture, and the threat of great empires and concomitant violence. This written "response" is preserved in the prophetic books and in the so-called Deuteronomistic history (Deuteronomy through 2 Kings).

Study of the prophetic response to the monarchy and its relations with the.entire ancient Near East provides the central focus for virtually the rest of the volume. Weber prefigures much recent work on prophecy by emphasizing that the prophets were not ethical innovators. Rather, they were free speakers (Weber calls them "demagogues") who forcefully propounded the tenets of the covenant that had been earlier articulated by the Levites.

Weber's interpretation of the prophets as demagogues and

pamphleteers has rankled some, but when this picture is understood in the context he intended it makes a good deal of sense. Weber was impressed by the ability of Amos and other prophets to speak freely and not to be arrested immediately by the state police. Such activity, Weber suggested, could only be allowed when the state was relatively insecure. The prophets were spokesmen for Yahweh's ideals, not spokesmen for any particular political or ideological platform—hence Weber's description of them as Utopian ([1921] 1967, pp. 271–276). One errs in describing them as populists, because the prophets regularly encountered a public that was not receptive to their words.

Although the prophets come from diverse backgrounds, numerous elements allow us to speak about them in summary fashion. There was a basic message: presentation of certain socioethical norms and judgment on the basis of those norms. Another unifying feature was the gratuitous character of the oracles (Weber, [1921] 1967, p. 278), an element that distinguished the prophets from the Levites. Also characteristic is the emphasis on audition over vision and the fact that the prophets themselves interpreted their visions and oracles in an almost cold, detached way. Finally, personal charisma, the prophets' conviction that Yahweh had spoken directly to them, was the sole source of their prophetic authority.

Weber ([1921] 1967, p. 304) identifies a "fundamental prophetic idea," "that Yahweh ordains terrible misfortunes for moral and especially social-ethical trespasses." Presupposed in this system was a sort of monism: Yahweh, not a group of competing gods or forces, was in charge of the cosmos. A corollary of the fundamental idea is a chronological factor. The classical prophets held Yahweh's action to be imminent, not off in the distant future. Yet, even though Yahweh's decisive historical action is imminent, it is also eschatological (a category of crucial importance for Weber's interpretation of prophecy and a category that for obscure reasons is rarely noted by Weber's interpreters). These eschatological beliefs were part of a larger, almost dramatic, complex. Not only were the prophets' minds saturated with war and cosmic horrors to come but they also hoped for a paradisal peace to follow. The scope and timeliness of Yahweh's cosmic action was, Weber thinks, really the decisive contribution of Israel's prophets to the Hebrew Bible. It gave their message an incontrovertible rhetorical power. "The absolute miracle is the pivot of all prophetic expectation without which its specific pathos would be lost" (Weber, [1921] 1967, p. 332). The pivot is the imminence of Yahweh's actions. "The pressing emotional timeliness of the eschatological expectation was all-decisive" ([1921] 1967, p. 334).

In answer to his question, Weber contends the institution of monarchy created fundamental changes in Israelite society. However, the most important heritage of those changes was the literrary response to them, the books attributed to the visionaries and reactionaries, Israel's classical prophets. The prophets looked back to an earlier ethos in order to critique monarchic society, and they looked forward to Yahweh's intervention against those who had violated that ethos and to a paradisal society.

4. "What was the effect of the defeat and end of the Judahite state on Yahwism?" If the inception of monarchy worked the first major change in Yahwism, the second and more decisive change was the defeat of the Judahite nation, the end of Yahwism as a state religion, and the diaspora of Yahwistic believers. What we have, beginning in the sixth century, is the development of a confessional religion deriving from an earlier national religion (Weber, [1921] 1967, p. 338). Weber argues that prophecy, together with traditional ritualism in Israel, "brought forth the elements that gave to Jewry its pariah place in the world." Unfortunately, Weber's explanation of this process is not altogether clear.

From the ritual perspective, Weber seems to be describing the breakdown of the original distinction of gēr versus full citizen, because Weber contends that by the time of the exile, gērîm were treated as full members of the Israelite community, which by that time was a ritually organized religion and not a tribally organized society. As the real political community ended, an idealized religious community replaced it. "All ritually pure adherents of Yahweh, however, whether they be Israelites or gērîm or new converts were now confessionally of equal value" (Weber, [1921] 1967, p. 338). With the homogenization of the Israelite religious community, the community began to define its identity in distinction to those outside it. Weber found this process best illustrated in the in-group versus out-group economic ethos, which prohibited usury against other Israelites (see Neufeld, 1955, for a discussion of the usury topic). Other examples of this distinction include the prohibition against mixed marriages and the dietary laws.

Weber describes the religious community resulting from this newly forged identity in the following way: It became "a ritualistically distinct confessional congregation which was recruited by birth and the reception of proselytes" ([1921] 1967, p. 362) and in so doing became "a pariah people with a cult center and a central congregation in Jerusalem and with internationally affiliated congregations" ([1921] 1967, p. 363).

Further, Weber ([1921] 1967, pp. 338, 364) insists that the formation of this pariah people would have been impossible without "the promises of prophecy." It is here that Weber attempts to explain why Israel voluntarily accepted pariah status, for it is this phenomenon—voluntary acceptance of inferior status—that Weber found unexampled in history. Weber traces the root of this paradox to the prophets. They had been proven right by the disasters of the early sixth century, when Judah and Jerusalem fell to the neo-Babylonians. Those prophets active after 587 A.D. therefore commanded serious attention. Weber thought that most post-587 prophets were engaged in theodicy, justifying the ways of Yahweh to a defeated and scattered people. Ezekiel argued that Yahweh would now deal with the individual, that each individual could expect just treatment, and that communal liability was a thing of the past. However, Weber ([1921] 1967, p. 369) contends that "the only truly serious theodicy of ancient Israel is to be found in Deutero-Isaiah (Isaiah 40–55)." For Deutero-Isaiah, "the ignominious fate of Israel is the most important means for the realization of his (Yahweh's) plan" (Weber, [1921] 1967, p. 371). Blameless suffering is valued, in sharpest contrast to preexile prophecy, in which suffering was understood as punishment. "This enthusiastic glorification of suffering as the means to serve world deliverance is for the prophet the ultimate and supreme enhancement of the promise to Abraham" ([1921] 1967, pp. 375). For Deutero-Isaiah, such suffering was coupled with eschatological promises: Better times were ahead. The ethically positive valuation of suffering, the acceptance of being ritually separate and of being thought inferior, were, along with traditional ritual practice, in Weber's opinion, the crucial elements that contributed to the pariah character of Judaism. Now that the *gēr* versus full Israelite distinction no longer existed and now that Israel was a pariah people, it is possible to contend that all Israel was understood as *gērîm,* alien residents vis-à-vis the larger society. This development stands in contrast to an earlier period in which the *gērîm* were only one part of the early Israelite social structure. The change that the defeat of Judah effected was no less than the creation of Judaism. As important as the historical developments were the positive interpretation of Israel's suffering, the theodicy of Deutero-Isaiah, and traditional ritual practice.

One may consult the literature cited in the references to discover the various reactions Weber's theses have elicited. My own general response is that most of his creative theses have stood the test of time. Perhaps the Levites play too crucial a role, but we are far from a definitive picture of their function. They were terribly important.

I should make one response to certain of Weber's commentators. Weber has come under attack for having made the covenant the central and constitutive element in early Israel. Even his most sensitive and appreciative interpreters have scored him in this regard (Fischoff, 1950). However, recent work in the field, especially in the United States, has corroborated Weber's thesis of the covenant or treaty as having overarching significance throughout Israel's history. Following the work of Mendenhall (1955), Hillers (1974), and McCarthy (1963), we can contend that the covenant was constitutive for early Israel. It was similar to, if not directly modeled on, the ancient Hittite vassal treaties. A stereotypic structure pervaded these ancient Near Eastern texts. Likewise, there was a standard ideology. The historical prologue of the treaty articulated the relationship between the contracting parties. Regularly, the suzerain had acted beneficently toward the vassal, action that was understood to obligate the latter to the former. The stipulations spelled out the nature of the obligation of the vassal to the suzerain. Such treaties were conditional. If the vassal obeyed the treaty, a blissful state was described in the blessings; conversely, if the vassal disobeyed the treaty his ruination was graphically depicted in the curses.

Much of Israel's relationship to Yahweh may be understood

within this covenant perspective: for example, the law codes as treaty stipulations. To explain the stipulations of the covenant was the sort of activity that Weber described as the work of the Levitical Torah teacher. The ethical theodicy of the prophets may be understood as reflections on and deductions from the treaty ideology. If one observes misfortunes or enacted curses in the world, one may attribute them to the suzerain Yahweh (Weber, [1921] 1967, p. 311). As for eschatology, a treaty is by its very nature eschatological. It looks to the immediate future for either the blessings or curses. This covenant ideology was a rational system. The world was not magically captive; Yahweh was in control. From the covenant perspective, Yahweh's activities were, for the prophets, Levites, priests, and wisdom writers, comprehensible, if not always palatable (here, compare with Job). Given the significance of Yahweh's covenant with Israel, one may hardly say that Weber overestimated its importance.

The Ideal Type "Prophet"

One of the consistently troubling questions that Weber's work presents is his theory of the ideal type. What are ideal types; what is their relationship to empirical evidence; and how are they to be used? These questions continue to vex scholars even today, as the work of Burger (1976), Janoska-Bendl (1965), and Rogers (1969) demonstrates. By way of contributing to that discussion of method and by way of treating a topic of considerable importance both to the Hebrew Bible specialist and to the sociologist of religion, I should like to compare Weber's own historical analysis of an ideal type—the "prophet"— to its later conceptualization with additional evidence.[9] I take my license for evaluating the ideal type "prophet" in this way from Weber himself: "[The ideal type] is a conceptual construct [*Gedankenbild*] which is neither historical reality nor even the 'true' reality. . . . It has the significance of a purely ideal *limiting* concept with which the real situation or action is *compared* and surveyed for the explication of certain of its significant components" (Weber, [1904] 1949, p. 93).

Weber's explanation of prophecy in *The Sociology of Religion* ([1922] 1963) is composed of the following. First, certain characteristics allow us to identify some religiously active persons in the social context as prophets. They are not priests, because they have a personal call; they are not magicians, because they claim revelations and proclaim doctrines or commandments; they are not legislators (although Weber thinks the border here is fluid), because the prophet need not formulate or systematize commandments; they are not social reformers, because their message is essentially religious; they are not teachers, because they express themselves in "vital, emotional preaching"; they are not religious reformers, because they claim to have revelations; and they are not mystagogues, because they do not provide sacramental action.

Second, by way of systematic statement, a prophet is "a purely individual bearer of charisma who by virtue of his mission proclaims a religious doctrine or divine commandment" (Weber [1922] 1963, p. 46). This definition is formulated on the basis of comparing a "prophet" not only with others in his society—for example, with a priest—but also with other types of religious performers from quite different societies.

Third, when one investigates the class prophet, one discovers two fundamental subtypes: the exemplary and the ethical prophet. The exemplary prophet demonstrates in his life-style the path toward salvation, whereas the ethical prophet demands obedience to his commandment as an ethical duty. Weber observes that the ethical prophet is typical of the Occident. The feature both types of prophet share is the content of the prophetic revelation: "It presents a unified view of the world derived from a consciously integrated and meaningful attitude toward life" (Weber, [1922] 1963, p. 59).

Fourth, Weber then goes on to explain the reasons for these two very different sorts of prophets. He appears to argue that prophets are a natural expression of their political and religious environments. An ethical prophet could only arise in a system in which there was a "personal, transcendental and ethical god"— personal because he had to receive his call and charisma from a personal source, transcendental because only a transcendental god required a messenger to the human domain, and ethical because the focus of the message was precisely that—ethical. Gods such as these are to be found in the ancient Near East, and the conceptions of such gods were, Weber contends, undoubtedly influenced by the imperial polity of the ancient Near Eastern states, especially Egypt and Mesopotamia ([1922] 1963, pp. 56–57). For Israel in particular, Yahweh was conceived as a king, "the real ruler of the people. Hebrew prophecy was completely oriented to a relationship with the great political powers of the time, the great kings, who as the rods of God's wrath first destroy Israel and then as a consequence of divine intervention permit Israelites to return from the exile to their own lands. . . . The distinctive character of the earliest prophecy seems to have been determined decisively by the pressure of relatively contiguous great centers of rigid social organization upon less developed neighboring peoples" (Weber, [1922] 1963, p. 58).

Now it is necessary to draw back and observe what "prophet" means up to this point in Weber's work. On the basis of *Ancient Judaism* ([1921] 1967), a prophet is a free speaker, like Amos, who had a particular message of covenant, theodicy, and eschatology. On the basis of the pages devoted exclusively to the prophet in *The Sociology of Religion* ([1922] 1963), the prophet is defined less by the content of his message than he is by his role in a given society, with special focus on the authority he claims, a personal call—and on the way in which he differs from other religious functionaries. What we have been given up to this point is a historical and a sociological definition.

Had Weber not used the word *prophet* again, the matter could rest here. Weber did, however, go on to use the term "prophet" elsewhere in *Wirtschaft und Gesellschaft* ([1921] 1956), and it is his use of the term in this context that presents problems. I should like to suggest that Weber has employed it in a third way, in an "effectual" sense.

To understand not only Weber but also Weber's interpreters, it is crucial to note what this "effectual" definition of prophet entails. Parsons, in his introduction to *The Sociology of Religion* ([1922] 1963, p. xxv), writes, "the essential criterion of prophecy for Weber is whether or not the message is a call to break with an established order." To understand that statement, it is necessary to recognize that Parsons was focusing on the "effectual" definition of prophecy and, from a wider perspective, on Weber's theory of development.

The real nub of the problem here is not the variety of the significance of "prophet" but rather the relationship between two ideal types: "prophet" and "charisma," because for Weber prophets were, by definition, individual bearers of charisma. Weber defines charisma in the following way: "The term *charisma* will be applied to a certain quality of an individual personality by virtue of which he is set apart from ordinary men and treated as endowed with supernatural, superhuman, or at least, specifically exceptional powers or qualities" (Eisenstadt, 1968, p. 48). This definition is formulated within the context of a discussion of charismatic authority and is immediately used to describe a "charismatic leader." Charismatic leadership was the concept Weber used to describe the sort of authority that could engender a breakthrough in an established social order (Weber, [1921] 1956, p. 141). Hence it was a logically natural, if not necessary, move to contend that prophets were themselves agents of change. But it is precisely at this point that the naturally logical move results in tension within Weber's own work. This is so because it is not justified to describe a "historical" prophet as a charismatic authority, in Weber's sense of that latter term. Weber writes ([1921] 1956, p. 556), "It goes without saying that the expression *charisma* is used here in a totally value-free sense . . . because what is crucial for us is only whether the charisma is valid and effective; that is, found recognition *(Anerkennung)*." In this context, Weber is using the term *charismatic* in his typology of authority. The charismatic leader is like a *Führer,* whose followers are best described as *Jünger.* One regularly expected a charismatic leader to have some sort of following in his or her own society. The charismatic leader found the necessary *Anerkennung* in the group that recognized his charismatic gifts. Such recognition was a prerequisite for the validity of the charismatic leader. When one compares the "historical" definition of prophet—with prophets in Israel, for example—with this definition of charismatic leader, real problems arise. There is precious little documentation for groups or even hangers-on around Israel's prophets that would validate their charisma or make them charismatic leaders. The single exception is the prophetic bands of the ninth century, and they are singularly atypical in the history of prophecy in Israel. Furthermore, not only is there little evidence for any sort of group that accepts the leadership of the prophets but there is likewise little evidence that the society as a whole offered the prophets *Anerkennung* in their own time. Few, if any, Israelites appear to have been impressed by the "vital, emotional preaching" of the prophets.[10]

The tension in Weber's work results from his attempt to equate charismatic authority and prophet, the results of which are discernible in the "effectual" definition of prophet.[11] Unlike products of the mass production factory, the concepts of these two handwrought systems, the typology of authority (charismatic leader) and the classification of religious performer (prophet) may not be fully interchangeable. Or put more plainly, the prophet may not be easily understood as an agent of breakthrough.[12]

If this issue seems forced, one need only turn back to *Ancient Judaism* ([1921] 1967, p. 109), to a place in which Weber noted that the prophets were to be distinguished from "the prophets," the *nᵉbî'îm*, because of the former's "solitariness." However, in that same paragraph Weber also asserted that the prophets were "intellectual leaders of the opposition against kingship." This statement and its abstract version in the form of the prophet as a charismatic leader constitute the nub of the problem.

Crucial to a proper understanding of Israel's prophets at this point is one subgenre of the class "prophet" to which Weber assigned the Israelite variety. They are "emissary prophets" ([1921] 1967, p. 299), a fundamental characteristic of whom is the lack of a congregation or venerating group. As messengers, Israel's prophets were virtually incapable of functioning as charismatic leaders because their authority was always explicitly and consciously subordinate to the one who sent them, Yahweh.

In sum, Weber's construction of the ideal type "prophet" is not without its problems. There is a tension between the historical and sociological definitions and what I have termed the "effectual" definition. The "historical" and "sociological" definitions do not justify the "effectual" definition of the prophet as charismatic authority or agent of change.

Contemporary Sociological Analysis
of Ancient Israel

Even though Weber wrote a creative study analyzing the social system of ancient Israel, few scholars have moved beyond that work. A few have accepted some of Weber's theses (I think in particular here of De Vaux (1965), although it is difficult to trace Weber's influence in his book because it lacks specific references). More frequently, however, Weber's work has been ignored by the specialists as has similar work written by "those in the field"—for example, Wallis (1912). As for the sociological approach to biblical literature in general, Hummel could write in 1966, when called to update a standard history of critical scholarship, "while it is doubtful if it is possible any longer to distinguish a special approach to the Old Testament that might be labeled 'sociological,' subsequent scholarship has by no means failed to tap the resources of this line of attack" (in Hahn, 1966, p. 275). About all Hummel could point to in this latter regard was Albright's *From the Stone Age to Christianity* (1940), a study whose focus is hardly sociological. However, since Hummel wrote those pages, a number of studies have appeared that are explicitly sociological, some only to the extent that the questions they ask allow for a sociological response, whereas others apply sociological theories to answer the stated questions. The latter studies promise to have vast importance for Hebrew Bible studies, because most current assumptions about ancient Israel rest on sociological models that these recent studies have challenged directly.

For the purposes of this chapter, I note at least three styles of work that may be deemed sociological: (1) traditional philological work used to address sociological questions, (2) the new archaeology, and (3) the application of sociological theories to the study of Israelite and other ancient Near Eastern societies.

First, I single out H. Tadmor's recent essay on political power and its relation to ancient Israelite social structure (Tadmor, 1971). Tadmor wishes to discover the role of "the people" in ancient Israel, especially during the early monarchic period. To do this, he examines biblical texts and looks particularly at the political activities of certain groups: *hā'ām* ("the people"), the people or any part of it acting on behalf of all; *hā'ēdāh* ("the congregation"), the people gathered for purposes of war and worship; an archaic term, *qāhāl* ("assembly"), which signifies the same thing as *hā'ēdāh* but is used throughout Israel's history; *hazz^{e}qēnîm* ("the elders"), the group of clan chiefs whose power was considerable before the monarchy but whose powers, under the monarchy, were curtailed; *'îš yisrā'ēl* ("the men, [literally, "man"] of Israel"), the non-professional or conscripted army. The methodological presupposition in Tadmor's work is that sociopolitical entities may be studied by examining their putative lexical equivalents. After studying the roles of these groups in two almost successful revolts against King David, Tadmor concludes that "the people," during the period of the united monarchy, remained a source of political power; they could make or almost break kings. In Israel after the dissolution of the united monarchy, the army and its commanders became the real source of authority. The military camp of Omri was now called "all Israel," a term that had earlier designated the entire free population as the source of political authority.

In Judah, the *'am hā'āres,* the people of the land, were a source of political authority only when the normal order of royal succession was threatened (2 Kings 11:14). Tadmor concludes that the institution of "the people" continues to function throughout Israel's history despite the centralization of political authority under the monarchy. Nevertheless, the function of "the people" changed radically from both premonarchic and early monarchic days.

Studies such as Tadmor's, in which word studies play a prominent role, have been and will probably continue to be the most common analyses of Israel's sociopolitical institutions in a philologically oriented field such as biblical study.

Second is the "new archaeology." I use this phrase in a general sense to refer to an integrated approach to the study of societies for which we have archaeological evidence. In particular, this phrase means the integration of stratigraphy, ceramics, paleobotany, cultural anthropology, sociology, and much more. As an example of such work, I point to a recent symposium entitled *Reconstructing Complex Societies* (Moore, 1974). Two papers of that symposium offer good examples of this new integrative work. In a paper entitled, "The Mesopotamian Social Landscape: A View from the Frontier," Adams (1974) contended that the fact of uncertainty in Mesopotamian agriculture created a fluid, rural population that could be closely related to the city when it engaged in intensive agriculture and yet could, in difficult times, specialize in what had been residual animal husbandry and move outside the urban structures and their control. Such a fluid population was organized along tribal lines. Adams adduces a model of shifting frontiers that Lattimore had developed on the basis of study of Chinese society.[13] To this extent, Adam's work is preeminently that of the cultural anthropologist. Nevertheless, it actively solicits the scholarly results of the philologian, archaeologist, and sociologist in the application of Lattimore's general hypothesis to the particular data of the ancient Near Eastern setting.

In a not dissimilar way, G. E. Wright (1974, p. 130) has argued that "the rise of complex societies in the ancient Near East cannot be separated from the emergence of the tell as their basic component." Wright proposed a typology of sociopolitical development based on the tell: the tell, the city-state, the city-state league, and the empire. This basic development is observable in both Mesopotamia and Syria-Palestine. Evidence used to construct this typology is primarily archaelogical, philological, and climatological. All are integrated to give a picture of sociopolitical development in the ancient Near East. The proper subject for study in Wright's opinion is the society that produced the tell, not just the physical tell itself.

Third, and most importantly from the perspective of this paper, there is a quite conscious sociological approach now being used in Hebrew Bible studies.[14] At present, one can point to studies focusing on two important periods in Israel's history: the period of the so-called league and the early postexile period. Although not the exclusive sponsor of these studies, the Consultation of the Social World of Ancient Israel of the Society of Biblical Literature has provided an important context for discussions of these issues.

As an example of study of the latter period, Paul Hanson has sought, in his *The Dawn of Apocalyptic* (1975) to examine the early postexile literature in ancient Israel by understanding the social tensions in the period during which this literature was written. Just as there was a fundamental bifurcation in early postexile society, a split between the hierocratic temple part, which controlled the cult, and the provincial government and the prophetic visionaries, so this bifurcation is present in the literature that society produced. The apocalyptic literature was written by the prophetic visionaries, a group that had apparently been excluded from participation in the official cult and that looked forward to an eschatological military solution and to a paradisal age. Hanson appeals explicitly to sociological theorists (Weber, Troeltsch, Mannheim) in order to justify his approach to the texts. In response to Hanson's and others' work, Kovacs, at the 1976 meeting of the previously mentioned Consultation of the Social World of Ancient Israel, presented a paper entitled "Contributions of Sociology to the Study in the Development of Apocalypticism: A Theoretical Survey," in which he examined the implications of contemporary sociological theory for work such as Hanson's. Even though Hanson's use of particular sociological theories is open to debate, it is clear that study of ancient Israelite literature has before it a new option—the combination, as in Hanson's case, of the most detailed philological work and the theoretical backing of those like Weber, Troeltsch, and Mannheim.

A more explicitly sociological approach to the study of ancient Israel has been proposed by Gottwald.[15] In a series of essays (1974, 1975a, 1975b, 1976, in press) and in a major two-volume study soon to appear, Gottwald has proposed to study the social situation of the period of the league. And, in so doing, he has asked sociological questions and has used sociological theories to achieve his results (in contrast to Hanson, who is primarily interested in the conception of apocalyptic and in the meaning of texts). Fundamental to Gottwald's thesis is his thorough-going refutation of "pastoral nomadism" as the model for understanding earliest Israel.[16] Gottwald argues that the so-called Asiatic mode of production provides a more accurate model for interpreting premonarchic society. This thesis has significant implications for reflection about Israel's origins and her "conquest" of the land. Instead of conquest and subjugation of defeated Canaanites, Gottwald describes Israel's beginnings as a retribalization movement that achieved autonomy within Canaanite society. To use Gottwald's words (1974, p. 93),

"Early Israel was a slowly converging and constellating cluster of rebellious and dissenting Canaanite peoples distinguished by an antistatist form of social organization with decentralized leadership. This Israelite 'devolution' or 'winding down' from the city-state form of social organization took the shape of a 'retribalization' movement among agriculturalists and pastoralists organized in economically self-sufficient extended families with egalitarian access to basic resources."

Although Gottwald's study will appear to be revolutionary to many specialists in the field of Hebrew Bible studies (and I do not want to suggest here that it is not a study of the first order of importance), one should note that of the five major conclusions that Gottwald identifies in the preface of his book, at least four were stated in not dissimilar form by Max Weber half a century ago.

Work on the sociology of ancient Israel is therefore at something of a "breakthrough" point. Appropriate to the rapid expansion of the work that will no doubt ensue, two remarks are in order. First, and here I echo the warnings of Kovacs, biblical scholars must beware of latching onto the most readily available theories, especially those of Weber and Durkheim, without being aware of the debates about these theories. I do not recommend paralysis in the face of methodological uncertainty, but I do propose that the implications of the theories be understood by those who opt for one theory or another. Second, dialogue between biblical scholars and sociologists will benefit both parties. That biblical scholars need to, and are beginning to, listen to their sociologist colleagues should be, at this point, abundantly clear. However, it is entirely possible that the biblical scholar will be able to contribute to study about topics such as "sect," since much of the literature with which the biblical scholar deals, both canonical and extracanonical (Qumran), no doubt derives from sectarian hands. Such dialogue was, after all, present in the work of Max Weber.

Notes

1. Some mention of the reactions to Weber's work on ancient Israel is appropriate here. Within several years of the appearance of Weber's *Ancient Judaism* ([1921] 1967), two scholars had

undertaken major responses. J. Guttmann (1925) was a philosopher who had already critiqued another sociological study of ancient Israel and Judaism, that of W. Sombart (Guttmann, 1912;
Sombart, 1911). Guttmann's essay may be characterized as an appreciative correction. Aside from summarizing what he took to be
Weber's salient points, Guttman leveled at least ten basic arguments
against Weber. Typical of these is Guttmann's insistence that
Weber had underestimated the "religious character of the covenant" and that Judaism was improperly described as a pariah religion. The latter criticism has been a repeated one, especially frequent in the response of Jewish writers to Weber; for example,
Baron (1952), Schiper (1959), Shmueli (1968). In order to comprehend Weber's attitude to and conception of Judaism, one ought
to consult Fischoff (1950), Günther (1930), Liebeschütz (1967),
Oelsner (1962), and Taubes (1966).

The second early response to Weber was that of a biblical
scholar, W. Caspari (1922), the only time a biblical scholar has devoted a major study to Weber's interpretation of ancient Israelite
society. Caspari contended, in a detailed refutation of Weber, that
Yahwism did not originate in a military covenant. To insist on such
a position, Caspari thought, was to overlook all the evidence for the
tribal (patriarchal) origin of Yahwism and also to misinterpret the
evidence of the league. To be sure, the tribes had engaged in military activity. Nevertheless, the tribes themselves were the bearers of
the earliest Yahwistic religion (Caspari, 1922, p. 207). Caspari attacked Weber in two basic areas: the character of the holy war and
the relation of the prophets to covenant ideology. As for the first,
Caspari argued that much of what Weber took to be the norms for
early military activity were in reality a late and sentimental development. War was, early on, only a pragmatic activity, more the
result of individual executive action than the result of religious
dogma or a unified league. Second, Caspari believed that prophets
were innovators. The prophets articulated something new when
they insisted that a people could leave or be left by their god (Caspari, 1922, pp. 146–147). He contended that there was nothing in
the earlier covenant ideology to suggest that Israelites conceived of
a radical break with Yahweh as possible.

Beyond Guttman and Caspari and beyond the particular
concerns about Weber's descriptions of Jews as a pariah people, the
most important summaries of and responses to Weber's *Ancient
Judaism* have been Fischoff (1950, pp. 212–264), the most detailed

assessment available; Bendix (1961), an extensive summary of *Ancient Judaism;* Hahn (1966, pp. 157–184), which discusses Weber from the perspective of Hebrew Bible scholarship; Parsons (1966, pp. 95–102), which points to Israel as a "seedbed" society; and Raphaël (1971), which accentuates the main theses of *Ancient Judaism* and relates Weber to biblical scholarship, especially the French scholars Lods (1953) and Causse (1937). See also Kimbrough (1969).

2. I have chosen to limit the scope of this chapter to Weber's work on ancient Israel and thereby to exclude the section of *Ancient Judaism* entitled "The Pharisees." Although this omission may appear arbitrary, the history of ancient Israel ends properly with the beginning of Greek rule in Syria-Palestine in the fourth century B.C. Hence the history of the Pharisees must remain the only chapter in an otherwise unwritten volume on Greco-Roman religious history, a volume that Weber did in fact hope to write.

3. For a restatement of Weber's contention that ancient Israel had a profound impact on the formation of Western culture, see Parsons (1966).

4. On the justification for the distinction between ancient Israel and Judaism, see, conveniently, M. Smith (1971, pp. 55–56).

5. Weber's doubts about the historical value of the patriarchal narratives are being echoed in contemporary scholarly circles: Thompson (1974), Van Seters (1975), Hayes (1975).

6. One searches through *Ancient Judaism* in vain to find what Weber thought to be the "historical" causes. Bendix (1961, p. 228) quite naturally pushes Moses and the events at Sinai, but this interpretation does not explain the significance of war for the league. Weber is much less specific at this point than are his interpreters.

7. For a summary of holy war ritual and concepts in ancient Israel, see Von Rad (1951) and Miller (1973).

8. Compare here the similar distinction between Israelite and Mesopotamian legal conceptions as discussed by Paul (1970).

9. Berger (1963) in a still valuable article attempted to update Weber's discussion of Israelite prophecy from the perspectives of then current biblical scholarship, which, from our vantage point today, overemphasized the "cultic" function of the prophets. Berger's essay has been criticized, in my opinion quite erroneously, by Williams (1969).

One further comment is necessary here. Since *Wirtschaft und Gesellschaft* ([1921] 1956) was written some time after *Ancient*

Judaism ([1921] 1967) and since it was written from a different perspective, one must be circumspect in comparing minor points of disagreement between the two works.

10. According to Eisenstadt (1968, p. xxii), Weber "takes for granted the nature of the appeal of the charismatic." In ancient Israel, we may have a case in which the so-called charismatic leader is not at all appealing.

11. After these pages were first written, I discovered a very similar critique of Weber's position in Emmet (1956, p. 16): "Weber, we have seen, connects charismatic authority particularly with the kind of people he calls *prophets*. But if we are to follow him and define a prophet as a person who binds his followers into personal allegiance to himself as bearer of some mission or new revelation, then we shall surely need some other name for other kinds of inspirational leadership which do not follow this pattern. Moreover, we should have to restrict the notion of prophet to a type of messianic or millenarian preacher or religious revolutionary. This would be to deny it to many of the kinds of people who are generally known as prophets—the Hebrew prophets, for instance—and this would seem unnatural."

12. A far better example of a charismatic leader in ancient Israel is the *šōpēṭ*, the so-called judge. On this topic, see the excellent article of Malamat (1976).

13. Interestingly, another of Lattimore's concepts, "enclosed nomadism," has been appropriated by an ancient Near Eastern specialist, M. Rowton. Rowton has, in a series of articles, made significant contributions to our understanding of the social structure of the ancient Near East, particularly the place of the so-called nomad (Rowton, 1973a, 1973b).

14. The same may be said for New Testament studies as well; for example, see Gager (1975).

15. Here, compare G. Mendenhall (1974) for a similar although idiosyncratic approach.

16. Gottwald comments that Weber depended too much on the biblical scholarship of his own time and to that extent overemphasized the importance of nomadism. Although to a certain extent Gottwald is correct, one ought to note that Weber perceived the difficulties of understanding ancient Israel as Bedouin nomads and that he was unwilling to treat the partriarchal narratives as sources for the reconstruction of such a society. He also observed that the ancient Israelite law codes do not reflect a nomadic style of life.

References

Adams, R. M. "The Mesopotamian Social Landscape: A View from the Frontier." In C. B. Moore (Ed.), *Reconstructing Complex Societies.* Bulletin of the American Schools of Oriental Research, Supplement No. 29. Cambridge, Mass.: American Schools of Oriental Research, 1974.

Albright, W. F. *From the Stone Age to Christianity: Monotheism and the Historical Process.* Baltimore, Md.: Johns Hopkins University Press, 1940.

Baron, S. *A Social and Religious History of the Jews.* New York: Columbia University Press, 1952.

Bendix, R. *Max Weber: An Intellectual Portrait.* New York: Doubleday, 1961.

Berger, P. "Charisma and Religious Innovation: The Social Location of Israelite Prophecy." *American Sociological Review,* 1963, *28,* 940–950.

Burger, T. *Max Weber's Theory of Concept Formation: History, Laws, and Ideal Types.* Durham, N.C.: Duke University Press, 1976.

Caspari, W. *Die Gottesgemeinde von Sinai und das Nachmalige Volk Israel: Auseinandersetzung mit Max Weber.* Beiträge zur Förderung Christlicher Theologie 27/1. Gütersloh: Bertelsmann, 1922.

Causse, A. *Du groupe ethnique à la communauté religieuse.* Paris: Alcan, 1937.

De Vaux, R. *Ancient Israel: Its Life and Institutions.* (J. McHugh, Trans.) New York: McGraw-Hill, 1965.

Eisenstadt, S. N. (Ed.). *Max Weber on Charisma and Institution Building: Selected Papers.* Chicago: University of Chicago Press, 1968.

Emmet, D. "Prophets and their Societies." *Journal of the Royal Anthropological Society,* 1956, *86,* 13–23.

Fischoff, E. *Max Weber and the Sociology of Religion with Special Reference to Judaism.* Unpublished doctoral dissertation, New School for Social Research, 1950.

Gager, J. *Kingdom and Community: The Social World of Early Christianity.* Englewood Cliffs, N.J.: Prentice-Hall, 1975.

Gottwald, N. "Were the Early Israelites Pastoral Nomads?" In J. Jackson and M. Kessler (Eds.), *Rhetorical Criticism: Essays in Honor of James Muilenburg.* Pittsburgh Theological Monograph Series No. 1. Pittsburgh: Pickwick, 1974.

Gottwald, N. "Domain Assumptions and Societal Models in the Study of Pre-Monarchic Israel." *Vetus Testamentum Supplement* No. 28. Leiden: Brill, 1975a.

Gottwald, N. "The Social World of Ancient Israel." In G. MacRae (Ed.), *Society of Biblical Literature 1975 Seminar Papers.* Missoula, Mont.: Scholars Press, 1975b.

Gottwald, N. "Early Israel and 'The Asiatic Mode of Production' in Canaan." In G. MacRae (Ed.), *Society of Biblical Literature 1976 Seminar Papers.* Missoula, Mont.: Scholars Press, 1976.

Gottwald, N. *A Sociology of the Religion of Liberated Israel, 1250–1000 B.C.* Maryknoll, N. Y.: Orbis, in press.

Günther, A. "Die Entstehung des Judentums: Die Theorien Max Webers und Siegfried Passarges." *Deutsches Volkstum. Monatschrift für das Deutsche Geistesleben,* 1930, *12,* 19–28.

Guttmann, J. "Die Juden und das Wirtschaftsleben." *Archiv für Sozialwissenschaft und Sozialpolitik,* 1912, *36,* 149–212.

Guttmann, J. "Max Webers Soziologie des Antiken Judentums." *Monatschrift für Geschichte und Wissenshaft des Judentums,* 1925, *69,* 195–223.

Hahn, H. *The Old Testament in Modern Research.* Philadelphia: Fortress, 1966.

Hanson, P. *The Dawn of Apocalyptic: The Historical and Sociological Roots of Jewish Apocalyptic Eschatology.* Philadelphia: Fortress, 1975.

Hayes, J. "The Patriarchal Age: Middle or Late Bronze?" *Trinity University Studies of Religion,* 1975, *10,* 11–21.

Hillers, D. *Covenant: The History of a Biblical Idea.* Baltimore, Md.: Johns Hopkins University Press, 1974.

Janoska-Bendl, J. *Methodologische Aspekte des Idealtypus: Max Weber und die Soziologie der Geschichte.* Berlin: Duncker & Humblot, 1965.

Kimbrough, S. "Une Conception Sociologique de la Religion d'Israël: L'Oeuvre d'Antonin Causse." *Revue d'Histoire et de Philosophie Religieuse* 1969, *49,* 313–330.

Kovacs, B. "Contributions of Sociology to the Study of the Development of Apocalypticism: A Theoretical Survey." Paper presented at the Consultation on the Social World of Ancient Israel, Society of Biblical Literature, St. Louis, Missouri, October 1976.

Liebeschütz, H. *Das Judentum im Deutschen Geschichtsbild von Hegel bis Max Weber.* Schriftenreihe Wissenschaftlicher Abhandlungen des Leo Baecks Institute No. 17. Tübingen: Mohr (Siebeck), 1967.

Lods, A. *Israel from its Beginnings to the Middle of the Eighth Century.* The History of Civilization. (S. Hooke, Trans.) London: Routledge & Kegan Paul, 1953.

McCarthy, D. *Treaty and Covenant.* Analecta Biblica No. 21. Rome: Pontifical Biblical Institute, 1963.

Malamat, A. "Charismatic Leadership in the Book of Judges." In F. Cross, W. Lemke, and P. Miller (Eds.), *Magnalia Dei: The Mighty Acts of God.* New York: Doubleday, 1976.

Mendenhall, G. *Law and Covenant in the Ancient Near East.* Pittsburgh: Biblical Colloquium, 1955.

Mendenhall, G. *The Tenth Generation: The Origins of the Biblical Tradition.* Baltimore, Md.: Johns Hopkins University Press, 1974.

Miller, P. *The Divine Warrior in Early Israel.* Harvard Semitic Monographs No. 5. Cambridge, Mass.: Harvard University Press, 1973.

Moore, C. B. (Ed.). *Reconstructing Complex Societies.* Bulletin of the American Schools of Oriental Research, Supplement No. 20. Cambridge, Mass.: American Schools of Oriental Research, 1974.

Neufeld, E. "The Prohibitions Against Loans at Interest in Ancient Hebrew Laws." *Hebrew Union College Annual,* 1955, *26,* 355–412.

Oelsner, T. "The Place of the Jews in Economic History as Viewed by German Scholars." *Leo Baeck Institute Yearbook,* 1962, *7,* 183–212.

Parsons, T. *Societies: Evolutionary and Comparative Perspectives.* Englewood Cliffs, N.J.: Prentice-Hall, 1966.

Paul, S. *Studies in the Book of the Covenant in the Light of Cuneiform and Biblical Law.* Vetus Testamentum Supplement No. 18. Leiden: Brill, 1970.

Pedersen, J. *Israel: Its Life and Culture.* Copenhagen: Branner & Korch, 1959. (Originally published 1926.)

Raphaël, F. "Max Weber et le Judaïsme antique." *Archives Européennes de Sociologie,* 1971, *11,* 297–336.

Rogers, R. *Max Weber's Ideal Type Theory.* New York: Philosophical Library, 1969.

Rowton, M. "Autonomy and Nomadism in Western Asia." *Orientalia,* 1973a, *42,* 247–258.

Rowton, M. "Urban Autonomy in a Nomadic Environment." *Journal of Near Eastern Studies,* 1973b, *32,* 201–215.

Schiper, I. "Max Weber on the Sociological Basis of the Jewish Religion." *The Jewish Journal of Sociology,* 1959, *1,* 250–260.

Shmueli, E. "The Pariah People and Its Charismatic Leadership." *American Academy for Jewish Research, Proceedings,* 1968, *36,* 167–247.

Smith, M. *Palestinian Parties and Politics That Shaped the Old Testament.* New York: Columbia University Press, 1971.

Sombart, W. *Die Juden und das Wirtschaftsleben.* Leipzig: Duncker & Humblot, 1911.

Speiser, E. "Early Law and Civilization." In J. Finkelstein and M. Greenberg (Eds.), *Oriental and Biblical Studies of E. A. Speiser.* Philadelphia: University of Pennsylvania Press, 1967.

Stammer, O. (Ed.). *Max Weber und die Soziologie Heute: Verhandlungen des 15. Soziologentages.* Tübingen: Mohr (Siebeck), 1965.

Tadmor, H. "'The People' and the Kingship in Ancient Israel: The Role of Political Institutions in the Biblical Period," In H. Ben-Sasson and S. Ettinger (Eds.), *Jewish Society Through the Ages.* New York: Schocken, 1971.

Taubes, J. "Die Entstehung des Judischen Pariavolkes." In K. Engisch and others (Eds.), *Max Weber Gedächtnisschrift der Ludwig-Maximilians-Universität München zur 100. Wiederkehr Seines Geburtstages 1964.* Berlin: Duncker & Humblot, 1966.

Thompson, T. *The History of the Patriarchal Narratives: The Quest for the Historical Abraham.* Beiheft zur Zeitschrift für die Alttestamentliche Wissenschaft, 132. Berlin: De Gruyter. 1974.

Van Seters, J. *Abraham in History and Tradition.* New Haven, Conn.: Yale University Press, 1975.

Von Rad, G. *Der Heilige Krieg im Alten Israel.* Göttingen: Vandenhoeck & Ruprecht, 1951.

Wallis, L. *A Sociological Study of the Bible.* Chicago: University of Chicago Press, 1912.

Weber, M. *The Methodology of the Social Sciences.* (E. A. Shils and H. A. Finch, Trans. and Ed.) New York: Free Press, 1949. (Originally published 1904.)

Weber, M. *Wirtschaft und Gesellschaft: Grundriss der Verstehenden Soziologie.* Tübingen: Mohr (Siebeck), 1956. (Originally published 1921.)

Weber, M. *The Sociology of Religion.* (E. Fischoff, Trans.) Boston: Beacon Press, 1963. (Originally published 1922.)

Weber, M. *Ancient Judaism.* (H. Gerth and D. Martindale, Trans.) New York: Macmillan, 1967. (Originally published 1921.)

Williams, J. "The Social Location of Israelite Prophecy." *Journal of the American Academy of Religion,* 1969, *37,* 153–165.

Wright, G. E. "The Tell: Basic Unit for Reconstructing Complex Societies of the Near East." In C. B. Moore (Ed.), *Reconstructing Complex Societies.* Bulletin of the American Schools of Oriental Research, Supplement No. 20. Cambridge, Mass.: American Schools of Oriental Research, 1974.

6

Charles L. Bosk

The Routinization of Charisma:
The Case of the Zaddik

〰〰〰〰〰〰〰〰〰〰〰〰〰〰〰〰〰〰〰

The leaders of charismatic movements face two interrelated problems: (1) how to read their message and authority into the past to forge a sense of history for their followers and (2) how to read that same message into the future to provide the promise of salvation. Seen by followers as a complexly encoded statement demonstrating how to remake the cosmos and to attain salvation, the entire person of the charismatic leader—his acts and words—becomes the text of his followers. It is the follower's interpretation of the leader that gives a religious movement its special character, its unique identity. Following Weber's *Sociology of Religion* ([1922] 1963), we may characterize movements in which followers emphasize the interpretation of the word *ethical,* in that they stress rational fulfillment of doctrine, and those the deed, "exemplary," in that they stress spiritual fulfillment of action; hence charismatic leaders are seen as ethical or exemplary prophets. If these are taken as two poles along

Note: I am grateful to Harold Bershady, Victor Lidz, and Samuel Klausner for helpful comments on an earlier draft of this chapter.

one dimension of religious organization, they may be analyzed as competing orientations. Through its emphasis on historical explanation, a Weberian sociology of religion tends to emphasize the long-run competition of these two poles and the dominance of one pole over the other through its more elaborate rationalization or articulation; for example, the role of ethical prophecy in the West (Bellah, 1970). Weber pays considerably less attention to the case where neither ethical nor exemplary action is so well rationalized as to be decisive in organizing the character of the religion.

In the history of Judaism, there is a fairly constant tension between the ethical and exemplary dimensions of action. This tension expresses itself as a tension between two alternative conceptions of God: (1) God as a transcendent lawgiver and (2) God as a spirit immanent in all creation. The religious conflict between rabbinic and Hasidic Jewry in the latter part of the eighteenth and first part of the nineteenth century is one example of this tension. The leaders of Hasidism, the Zaddiks, competed with traditional rabbis for the role of dominant religious authority. In this cultural conflict in the shtetls of Galicia, both sides won. Hasidism survives today as a vocal and vibrant segment of the Jewish religion; however, the Hasidism of today is much transformed from the original. A group that began as a fervent revival movement emphasizing personal discovery in individual experience survives today as the most traditional and ritual bound of organized groups within the Jewish religion. A role that was once a religious office earned through a demonstration of inner illumination, that of Zaddik, has become a hereditary office. Both these occurrences index the routinization of charisma within Hasidism. This routinization represents the continual accommodation of ethical and exemplary action and not the triumph of one over the other; it represents, in Weber's terms, a case of "incomplete rationalization."

First we shall examine the nature of the Zaddik's role and then the cultural legitimation for it. This analysis will make clear that at a cultural or symbolic level Hasidism is a single, unified movement, while at a social system level it is an uncoordinated group of Zaddiks and followers. In addition, we will be able to view at close range an underemphasized type of charismatic authority and leadership, "exemplary prophecy."

The Nature of the Zaddik's Authority

The Zaddik's authority is personal: It rests on the ability to generate disciples. One method for the gathering of disciples to charismatic leaders has always been working cures and performing miracles, and the Hasidic Zaddik is quite typical in this respect. When Israel Baal-Shem became Israel Baal-Shem-Tov, he is credited by Hasidic folklore as becoming the movement's first Zaddik. It is worth pointing out that Baal-Shem ("master of the Name") was an occupational title designating a magician, curer, and wanderer and that Baal-Shem-Tov ("master of the Good Name") designates a religious virtuoso. The change in Baal-Shem's name, then, signals a rather marked change in status and aspirations: An itinerant healer has become a holy man (Buber, 1947, p. 13). At the same time, the "Baal-Shem" part of the name evokes the humble occupational origins of the movement's founder.

Other Zaddiks were never very far removed from the magical soil from which the Baal-Shem sprang. In the tales of the Hasidim, it is said that the Zaddik can often travel through the dimension of space without moving through time; he knows of events in far-off places as they occur, because of the change in the heavenly vibrations; he is able to predict the future—indeed, many Zaddiks legitimated their own status by the prophecies of other Zaddiks (the Baal-Shem-Tov's coming being foretold by an angel); the Zaddik can look into a person's past and see how he or she became entangled in sin; and, most importantly, he can cleanse souls. For instance, it is told of the seer of Lublin that "Whenever a new Hasid came to him, he instantly took his soul out of him, cleansed it of all stain and rust, and put it back restored to the state it had been in the hour before it was born" (Buber, 1947, p. 307). In short, the authority of the Zaddik was legitimated by any number of proofs, often magical in nature.

Furthermore, the way of each Zaddik to salvation was unique. What Zaddiks taught their followers was not a particular scriptural message but rather an entire style of approach to life. One went to a Zaddik not so much to learn the Torah as to see how he "laced and unlaced his sandals." The Zaddik's way was his idiosyncratic method of making contact with God, who is hidden but immanent in the world. The Zaddik's way demonstrated his *devekut* (communion with God) and *kavanna* (purity of intention). Such an emphasis on everyday action sanctifies the world at the same time that it devalues activity in it. On the one hand, it provides for transforming all activity into potentially religious events. On the other hand, activity no longer has any meaning for its own sake but only takes on meaning as a pathway to God (Schatz-Uffenheimer, 1967). The saying of Zaddik Pinchas of Koretz expresses this nobly: "There are words which, in themselves, are useless. There are no actions which, in themselves, are useless. But one can make useless both actions and words by saying and doing them uselessly" (Buber, 1947, p. 122). The Maggid of Mezritch makes the same point with a concrete example and an acerbic style: "Let him love his wife only as he loves the tefillin, only because they are God's commandment; and let him not muse on her, for he is only like one who travels to the fair and he cannot travel without a horse, but should he therefore love the horse? Is there a greater foolishness? Thus in the world man needs a wife for the service of God, in order to merit the world to come" (Schatz-Uffenheimer, 1967, p. 41). Hasidic leadership rests, then, on the communication of an entire way of life to followers—a way of life that "merits the world to come." In comparison, rabbinic authority rests on learning. More clearly than others, the rabbi understands God, who is outside the world. Learned scholar, not trembling mystic, is the archetype of traditional Jewish religious authority.

So important was the "way of life" in Hasidic circles that stratification rested on a disciple's entire style of life, just as in rabbinic congregations stratification was determined primarily by the rabbi's scholarship. For Hasidim, *devekut* and *kavanna* become the principles on which the religious community is ordered: The Zaddik can achieve the highest *devekut;* his disciples are less adept and the congregation even less so. Absolute *kavanna* may be obtained by anyone, but only for a moment. In fact, a recurrent theme in the Hasidic folk culture centers on how the pure act of a humble soul redeems the actions of spiritually impure individuals, all acts being merely attempts to join man and God. However, only the Zaddik possesses both *devekut* and *kavanna;* only he is capable of a continual cleaving to the Godhead. Because of the high correlation between education and wealth in the Jewish communities of eastern Europe, the rabbinic stratification system excluded most of the community from enjoying religious rewards. Rabbinic author- ity limits religious actions and ethics to mastery of the law, which is limited by the social system to the most affluent, the study of the law being a leisurely pursuit. In Hasidism, the intent of the act itself is what matters most, and therefore the scholar and the fool enjoy equal footing before God. In fact, if anything, the folklore of the Hasidim celebrates the innocence of the unlettered. Moreover, Hasidism makes the momentary joining of man and God possible; in rabbinic circles, such contact is not possible, because scholarship is by its nature such an incremental process.

Not only were the ways to demonstrate Hasidic authority many but there were also as many personality types among Zad- dicks as there were ways to establish charismatic claims. Schneur Zalman was a rational scholar; Zusya of Hanipol, an unquestioning peasant; Elimelkh of Lizensk, an angry challenger of God; Barukh of Medziboh, a proud, arrogant, unpleasant man; Nachman of Bratzlav, a Messianic mystic. The courts of the Zaddiks were as different as their individual personalities. Israel of Rizhin's court was sumptuous, while Menachem-Mendel of Kotzk's court was desolate, and he spent his last years in seclusion.

Structural Strains, Charisma, and the Zaddik

The doctrinal looseness of the Hasidic movement combined with the emphasis on the personal qualities of the Zaddik to present serious problems to the movement's coherence, unification, and organization within the Jewish community. Two problems are espe- cially noteworthy. First, how, given the multiple ways through which the charisma of the Zaddik was documented, were genuine Zaddiks distinguished from imposters? Second, how were factional differences over what constituted a pure contact with God made manifest, and how were they limited or contained so that they did not destroy whatever unity the movement achieved? Each of these strains was built into the very concept of the Zaddik, and each deserves fuller discussion.

The charisma of the Zaddik was legitimated by his demonstration that he could establish a continual contact with the divinity immanent in the world. Usually such demonstrations involved a display of "magical" or extraordinary powers. The definition of magic here needs to be expanded beyond the manipulation of physical objects; prophecy and even unusual insight were considered evidence of magic. Whatever the grounds for believing that a Zaddik truly possessed the power, convincing proofs were for obvious reasons difficult to provide. Because of this, the legitimation of charisma had an empirically circular quality. If someone claimed to be a Zaddik and if others believed him, then indeed he possessed the requisite charisma; if he failed, of course, he lacked charisma. The problem of who is a legitimate Zaddik is made somewhat easier by the fact that certain pursuits—particularly studying with a Zaddik—were more likely to produce a Zaddik than others. However, in a movement that did not make the criteria for advancement from discipleship to Zaddikhood public, uniform, or explicit, this structural solution only isolated the problem and did not solve it. In addition, the master-disciple relationship has as its core tension the question when to allow the disciple his own mastery. So a regular avenue to Zaddikhood—discipleship—does not explain how the novice must display charisma nor does it explain to what in charisma followers respond. Nor, for that matter, does it explain why disciples sought masters in the first place. But disciples sought, and Zaddiks recruited. The Maggid of Mezritch, the movement's last undisputed leader, said he was convinced of the Baal-Shem-Tov's charisma when that Zaddik read from a text in such a way that "angels danced on the page." Exactly what a person must do to convince others that he can make "angels dance on the page" is difficult to specify in advance.

Second, the doctrinal looseness of Hasidism created great room for differences in style, tone, and practice within a single religious movement. This doctrinal looseness was managed within a framework of orthodox Jewish belief and practice; among the things introduced into that practice were dancing, ecstatic prayer, and fervent meditation. Here, the sect's primary problem was how to achieve unity in the face of different and not always compatible methods for making contact with God immanent in the world. Such unity was important to Hasidim because of pressures placed on the movement by rabbinic authority. Hasidic leaders were ridiculed, excommunicated, and exposed to mob action by protectors of established religious authority. These external pressures were intensified by the very strangeness of some Hasidic practices to those within the fold whose own Zaddik did things differently. What coherence for the movement demanded was a mode of both recognizing and making manifest similarities among Hasidim at the same time that it ordered differences.

The diversity of Hasidic faith is seen more easily if the approaches of two different Zaddiks are compared. The two Zaddiks chosen are Shneur Zalman of Liadi and Nachman of Bratzlav. Each represents a distinct approach to Hasidism: Zalman is an ethical prophet with a rabbinic style transplanted into a new setting, while Nachman as mystic with a "peasant" style is an exemplary one. Their different doctrinal positions were parallel to lines of social and geographic cleavage within the Jewish community (Dubnov, 1916). Zalman was from White Russia, where Talmudic scholarship was high and the economic situation was tolerable; Nachman was from the Carpathian Mountains, an area where scholarship was low and the economic situation intolerable. Zalman was a Zaddik in the third generation of the movement's history; Nachman, in the fifth.

Zalman carried out the rationalization of Hasidism. He insisted on being addressed, and referred to himself, as *Rabbi* and never as *Rebbe* or *Zaddik*. Zalman felt that his position was legitimated by his learning and not his inner illumination; therefore, he used the title of authority valid for members of the rabbinic school. Zalman's Hasidism is known as HaBaD, which is a Hebrew anagram for the three emanations of God: *Hakmah, Binah,* and *Deah* (wisdom, reason, and knowledge); it is through these, he felt, that God could be comprehended (Minkin, 1935). He instituted a regular program of study and viewed himself primarily as an instructor and not as a miracle worker. To emphasize his formal authority, Zalman established elaborate rules that limited visitors to him, established long waiting times for suppliants, and listed criteria for legitimate complaints. This practice established a clerical role far from the accepted Zaddik role as intermediary. Zalman further deviated from Hasidic practice by establishing *Takanoth* or ordinances that regulated the manner and conduct of daily services in HaBaD congregations. These ordinances emphasized proper decorum, congregational worship, and disciplined orderly conduct (Mindel, 1967). Many of Zalman's practices aroused much hostility from other Hasidim, as they appeared a return to *rabbinism* and a deviation from the often ecstatic, disorderly *kavanna* of prayer that was a cornerstone of Hasidic practice. In fact, the ordinances ran counter to a famous dictum of the Baal-Shem-Tov; namely, that, just as a young child who approaches his father cannot be controlled, man cannot be regulated in the manner and method of his prayer. Most of the Hasidim that survive today are linked to Zalman's Hasidism. While this is no doubt in part a consequence of the holocaust that struck eastern European Jewish culture, it is also a comment on the organizational framework Zalman provided his followers.

Nachman of Bratzlav was as ardent a mystic as Zalman was a disciplined scholar. He was a great-grandson of the Baal-Shem-Tov. Emphasizing the "magical" role of the Zaddik, he claimed for himself the ability to help men return to the original state of creation. Unlike Zalman, Nachman did not set any explicit program to find God. All ways, if performed with *kavanna* and *devekut*, will lead to God. Nachman often praised closeness to nature as one of the best ways: "When man becomes worthy to hear the song of the plants and how each plant speaks its own song to God, how beautiful and sweet it is to hear their singing! And therefore it is good indeed to serve God in their midst in solitary wanderings over the fields between the growing things and to put out one's speech before God in its truthfulness" (Buber, 1961, p. 31). Where Zalman established elaborate rules and regulations to order prayer and the assembled congregation, Nachman denigrated the communal ordering of prayer and emphasized its inspirational, individual dimensions. Nachman maintained that "It would be better for every man to pray when he feels inspired, to pray his own prayer, and in a language which is familiar to him. For in that way he will understand the words he is saying and will devote himself through them to God" (Horodenzky, 1928, p. 94). Given the place of prayer in establishing community in the shtetls of eastern Europe, it is easy to see how Nachman's style of praying undercut the organized dimensions of community.

Nachman did not articulate rules for the congregation as a guide for the future, but, then, he saw no need to do so because for a Zaddik such as Nachman there was no separation between life and death. Nachman stated (Buber, 1961, p. 31), "To him who obtains true knowledge, the knowledge of God, there is no difference between life and death, for he cleaves to God and embraces him and lives an eternal life like him." The messianic aspects of the Zaddik role are seen in Nachman's instructions to the Bratzlavers that they should always regard him as their Zaddik because even after his death he would dwell within them. And after his death Bratzlav had no new Zaddik. (This was a practice also followed in some other Hasidic congregations.) Other Hasidim criticized Nachman for his certitude in his own salvation, which they considered arrogant. The fact that Nachman appeared four generations after the Baal-Shem-Tov, and Zalman after only two, argues against simple, linear interpretations of routinization of charisma, in which it is held that over time zeal and ardor "burn out."

The Lurianic Creation Myth

A movement that could contain both Zalman and Nachman is a flexible one. Indeed, it is so flexible that one may wonder whether Hasidism was a coherent movement at all, or a series of isolated attacks on rabbinic authority, all fueled by similar religious, social, and economic discontents. Compelling as the latter interpretation may appear, it has two serious flaws. First, it views Hasidism as merely a response to external strain, and it ignores the internal logic of its development. Second, it does not pay careful attention to the way Zaddiks legitimated their authority by reference to a common cultural source, the Lurianic Kabbala. Understanding the imagery of this work and how it was manipulated by the Hasidim allows us to see the forces at work that unified Hasidim everywhere. As we stated earlier, the Zaddik's charisma depended on his convincing others that he had the power to make contact with God, who is immanent in the universe. Symbolically, this is interpreted as uniting with the *Shekhina*, the feminine element of God. It is the coital relationship of Zaddik and *Shekhina* that produces disciples.

The disciples of the Zaddik are the product of this divine coitus as surely as children are the products of the coitus of their parents. This all becomes clear when we ask what defines and differentiates the Zaddik from his disciples. To understand this, we must turn to the Lurianic myth of creation and explicate it fully. The source of much Hasidic thought, the Lurianic Kabbala, written in the first part of the sixteenth century, employs a creation myth to explain, allegorically, the suffering of Spanish Jews during the Inquisition. The Lurianic Kabbala was an extremely influential document in the Jewish mystical literature (Scholem, 1946).

The Lurianic Kabbala represents creation as a three-stage process: *Tsimtsum*, the self-exile of God; *Shevirah*, the breaking of the divine bowls; and *Tikkun*, the repair of the universe's fractured unity. The limitation of God, *Tsimtsum*, is the first stage of creation. In this divine contraction, God exiles, alienates, or withdraws a part of himself from himself in order to make room for his creation. In this explanation of creation, God was to return to himself in a perfect and orderly creation; a dialectic exists between contraction and emanation, resulting in a higher unity. However, this second stage of the plan, the orderly emanations of creation, was not successfully completed; this is known as *Shevirah*, or the breaking of the bowls. The bowls were to contain God's return from self-exile, which was to take the form of differentiated emanations flowing from a single source, as light does after it has passed through a prism—undifferentiated light broken into the bands of the spectrum is indeed a good way to conceptualize this. In the Lurianic creation myth, Adam Kadmon, the primordial man, acts as the prism receiving the undifferentiated divine light and sending it out through all his orifices in orderly emanations. These emanations were ten in number: Three belong to God alone; the other seven belong to the earthly world. Of the seven, the first six correspond to the six days of creation and are considered masculine in nature. The kabbalistic imagery is at times quite explicitly phallic; in the Lurianic Kabbala, all six emanations are considered contained in the sixth emanation, known as the *root* or *foundation* (Scholem, 1960). The seventh of the earthly emanations corresponds to the Sabbath; it is the feminine element of the divine essence. This emanation is also known as God's *Shekhina*, the divine in-dwelling presence in the world. Those seven earthly emanations and the

three divine ones were to be contained in vessels constructed ex-
pressly for this purpose. But, because of a flaw in their construction, the bowls broke, and the orderliness of divine creation was
shattered with them. The breaking of the bowls means that all
being is *Galut,* or, in exile from God. In Hasidism, one can identify
four distinct types of exile: (1) God from his emanations, (2) man
from his natural soul, (3) the nation from the land of Israel, and
(4) God from his *Shekhina* (Scholem, 1960). The Lurianic Kabbala
provides an explanation for these kinds of exiles, and the Hasidic
definition of the situation is read out of Luria's work. In this sense,
the myth serves the Hasidim as a "root metaphor," since the interre-
lationships among empirical phenomena are explained by analogy
to the parts of the myth (Ortner, 1973).

   If the first two elements of the Lurianic myth of creation
explain the present and summarize the past, the third element in
the myth, *Tikkun,* recommends for the future; it offers the key
cultural strategy, the how-to-do-it rules for mending the damage
done when the bowls were broken. Man must return those elements of the *Shekhina* dwelling in the world to God, he must lift
the other holy sparks, and he must unify his own soul. In the
Lurianic myth, two types of sparks are identified: those of God's
Shekhina and those of Adam's root soul. The Hasidim made the
differentiation between the sparks of the *Shekhina* and those of
Adam's root soul into two categories. There are general sparks and
there are particular ones. Each man has a family of sparks that
belong to him and him alone and that only he can lift. For the
individual, the goal of religious action becomes to raise those individual sparks and to join them with God. With this interpretation of
Luria, *Tikkun* is defused of its eschatological ramifications, and the
individual's relation to God becomes all-important (Scholem, 1970,
p. 186). In Hasidism, this relationship is known as *devekut,* and it
plays a critical role in the theodicy, soteriology, and cosmology of
Hasidism (Bosk, 1974).

The Zaddik and the Lurianic Creation Myth

   Whatever the magical claims to his status, the Zaddik is separated from his followers by his attainment of the highest *devekut:*

He has unified his own soul, scattered by the fall of Adam, and he is able to unite with the sparks of the *Shekhina.* The Zaddik is considered to be the perfection of the six masculine emanations in a single soul. The follower of one Zaddik explained his leader's powers as follows: "Do you know what a Zaddik is? I'll tell you. In the Jewish religion, there are 613 mitzvahs. The average person cannot do all these mitzvahs. But one who can do all these things—abide by all 613—he is known as a Zaddik" (Zborowski and Herzog, 1962, p. 160). The emphasis here is placed on the Zaddik's completeness. He is a living Torah, perfection personified, the six male potencies gathered in a single person, the root or foundation of creation. As creation restored to its original perfect state, the Zaddik is a supermasculine being. This masculine potency—the result of the fact that the Zaddik and only the Zaddik has achieved the highest *devekut*—gave the Zaddik the special power that separated him from his followers. He can unite himself with God's *Shekhina,* the feminine element of God, the seventh earthly emanation. Through this union, the upper world is joined to the lower. In and through the Zaddik, the exile of the *Shekhina* comes to an end— coitus is a means of transcending the historical situation. United with the Zaddik, the *Shekhina* ceases to symbolize the broken state of existence and stands instead for its original splendor as God conceived it. This power of the Zaddik to perform divine coitus is known as his *Yihud,* "unity," a term that further underscores the fact that the six masculine emanations are personified by Zaddik. The fecundity of the Zaddik is expressed in a saying of Abraham of Apt, the son of the Maggid of Mezritch: "The Zaddik is the basis of the world. Through him, the good and complete comes to the lower world. For no revelation is possible until it is given through the Zaddik" (Horodenzky, 1928, p. 52). The special emphasis placed on the Zaddik's coital role with the *Shekhina* is seen in the emphasis the tales of the Hasidim place on the cleaving or clinging of the Zaddik and *Shekhina.* Moreover, although potentially any Hasid might attain this special relationship with the *Shekhina,* in practice the Zaddikim usually restricted it to their own circles (Scholem, 1970, p. 192). More than a monopoly of access to religious goods is involved here, for divine coitus contained risks, and only the strongest could emerge unharmed. There are many tales in the Hasidic corpus of disaster because of a premature union with the *Shekhina.* Such tales may have functioned as moral parables in order to control subordinates at the same time that they underscored the extraordinary power necessary to consummate a coital relationship with. the *Shekhina.*

The fact that the power of the Zaddik to unite with the *Shekhina* was the core symbol that integrated various segments of Hasidism into a movement had two significant ramifications. First, it affected the transmission of authority and charisma. Second, it affected the social relations among Hasidim of different Zaddiks. As we have stated, in Hasidism divine coitus is limited to the Zaddik and the *Shekhina* and is forbidden to disciples. To establish his own claims to the masculine potency of Zaddikship, the disciple had to leave the circle of his Zaddik and gather his own circle in order to commune with the *Shekhina* in a proper fashion. There is a partial parallel between the dispersion of authority in Hasidism and the dispersion of authority analyzed in Freud's theory of the primal horde. In any Hasidic group, the Zaddik had a monopoly on relations with the *Shekhina;* to obtain his own autonomous relationship with the *Shekhina,* the disciple often had to rebel against the Zaddik, and he always had to leave the Zaddik. As a consequence, the movement grew by a fissioning process, with disciples leaving a Zaddik and establishing congregations based on their own *devekut.* One can then view the shifting centers of Hasidism after the Baal-Shem-Tov's death as a series of successful revolts against Zaddikist authority. Once again an anecdote illustrates the point: When a great Zaddik was asked why, in living as he did, he did not follow the example of his teacher, he replied, "On the contrary, I do follow his example, for I leave him as he left his teacher" (Scholem, 1946, p. 348).

This pattern of transmitting authority differs from Weber's ideal type formulation where successors are named by a laying on of the hands or some other signal by the master. In the Hasidic case, while a laying on of the hands was helpful in creating a new Zaddik's authority, a spurning of the master's gesture often had the same effect. The charisma of the Zaddik is quite personal; it rests on the ability to find and hold a congregation. Having followers was evidence of the fecundity of one's coitus with the *Shekhina.* So in the early years of the movement masters could neither name their own successor nor appoint Zaddiks to a congregation. Although Zaddiks could always make their wishes known in such matters, it was the congregations who chose. Moreover, disciples could take their case directly to the people. All this variation in patterns of succession, modes of attaining *devekut,* and general lifestyle, as well as the tensions such variations created, was managed within a routinized structure of Zaddik and disciple. Whatever variant of Hasidism a Zaddik espoused, one can be sure he was taught by an older Zaddik, that the Zaddik traced his descent from the Baal-Shem-Tov, and that all belief was grounded in the Lurianic Kabbala.

As Weber explains it, dispersion of charisma follows a pattern in which disciples from a single master fan out and spread the word. All disciples defer to the authority of the master. In the Hasidic case, there was no single pattern of appointment to leadership: Some disciples did leave the master's circle to spread the word with their master's approval, while others left after disagreements with their masters and hence without his blessing. Further, the hierarchy of Zaddiks was left undefined. All Zaddiks claim for themselves equal authority and recognize no master after the Baal-Shem-Tov or Maggid of Mezritch. All Zaddiks possess equal authority, for all possess equal power—the *devekut* capable of sustaining divine coitus.

Except at the very general level of ability to perform divine coitus, the qualities for Zaddikship must of necessity remain undefined. The lack of control built into the movement by allowing congregations to legitimate the charisma of their Zaddik presented severe problems to the movement as it spread and grew further from the original inspiration of the Baal-Shem-Tov. In the first three generations of the movement, Zaddikship was established by being in the first generation a disciple of the Baal-Shem-Tov; in the second, the Maggid of Mezritch; and, in the third, of either the seer of Lublin or Schneur Zalman of Liadi. As argued earlier, such discipleship guaranteed neither acceptance by congregation nor approval by masters; it indicated only an appropriate contact with the sacred center of Hasidism. However, by the fourth generation the movement was too dispersed for legitimacy to be controlled by the pattern of contact with the master followed by separation, as discussed earlier. Two factors explain why, as the movement grew, many would seek to become Zaddiks. First, as it was the duty of a Hasid to support his Zaddik, the role of Zaddik represented for some an easy road to riches. Also, because there were no precise educational standards that had to be maintained, the pretense of Zaddikhood was not hard to maintain. If anyone could attain *devekut,* then quite logically anyone might also be a Zaddik.

The problem of who was a legitimate Zaddik was eventually solved by making the office hereditary. The doctrinal justification for this practice was found in the Lurianic myth of creation. Given the division of Adam's sparks into the general and particular, a father and son share the same particular sparks. Hence, only the sons of the holy are capable of the same degree of *devekut.* Moreover, the Zaddik's progeny could be seen as the offspring of both his earthly marriage and his divine union. Making the role of Zaddik hereditary at the same time underscores the symbolic importance of coitus with the *Shekhina* and limits such contact to prescribed social circles. Undoubtedly, the change of Zaddik from an achieved to an ascriptive status drained the movement of vitality and inhibited the infusion of new leadership and energy. However that may be, such a change had much more immediate consequences for the structure of the movement.

The Hasidic interpretation of the Lurianic creation myth not only provided grounds for stabilizing the office of Zaddik in particular families but also provided a means for ordering similarities and differences among Hasidic groups. It provides an explanation for a characteristic of charismatic groups noted by Freud and Weber; namely, the intense bonds uniting members. Hasids who share the same Zaddik are the progeny of the Zaddik's coitus with the *Shekhina.* They are of the same metaphysical esence; they belong to a spiritual brotherhood. The naming of Hasids illustrates this familial relationship. Hasids are identified by the name of their Zaddik: a Hasid of the Bratzlaver Rebbe, or a Hasid of the Rabbi of Ger, and so on. The Zaddik's name, like our surname, establishes the substance from which the Hasid derives. This shared metaphysical substance joins Hasidim together into quasi-familiar groupings. Schechter (1916, p. 40) describes the solidarity of the Hasidic group as follows: "The Chasidim were second to no other sect in their loyalty and affection for each other. No sacrifice for a brother Chasid was too great: They knew no difference of rich or poor, old and young, wise and ignorant; for they all, with one accord, worshipped one common ideal, the Zaddik." The coitus of Zaddik and *Shekhina* also established the social distance between those groups loyal to one Zaddik and those loyal to another. Zaddiks whose concepts of *devekut* were similar were said to derive from similar root souls. The relationship among methods of divine coitus established relationship among Hasidic groups. Similar practices spoke to a closeness among groups. When *devekut* was obtained in divergent ways, root souls of the group were assumed to be divergent. There was little shared metaphysical substance. All in all, differences in methods of divine coitus ordered the social relations among the parts of the Hasidic movement. Nevertheless, all Hasids were related by the conception of *devekut,* which is a constitutive belief that they all share. Thus, the image of coitus provides a method for interpreting the shape of the Hasidic movement. Relationships among Zaddiks can be placed on a genealogical grid: Zaddiks are descended from those masters with whom they agree most closely on how *devekut* is achieved and are most distant from those with whom there is disagreement. This genealogical grid is connected by the fact that it has a single progenitor, the Baal-Shem-Tov, and a single progenetrix, the *Shekhina.* It makes clear the core task of the Zaddik: to find followers and lead them to God through his coitus with the *Shekhina* particular to his own root soul. Curiously, the notion of a particular root soul for each Zaddik alone reinforces the incest taboo at the symbolic level.

Conclusions

Each charismatic movement faces the same two core problems: how to create a sense of history and the future to followers at the same time that it radically alters routine, taken-for-granted ways of being in the world. In working out how charisma is routinized, sociologists do not always tie their analyses to the doctrinal base of a movement, however vaguely it is articulated. As a consequence, generalizations about charisma are usually of a very sweeping order, and sociological analyses of charismatic movements often terminate at the point that they should begin: The origin of a movement is assumed to follow Weber's generalizations about the routinization of charisma. However, as the argument makes clear, there are two problems in this approach. First, Weber is primarily concerned with the rise of ethical prophecy, and his generalizations fit the case of exemplary prophecy less well. Second, Weber pays little attention to the symbolic resources a movement possesses; such resources are crucial in understanding what flexibility movements have in their development. From a close analysis of a movement's symbolic structure, we can understand which developmental possibilities are open to a movement and which are closed.

This chapter utilizes the case of the Zaddik in the Hasidic movement to discuss routinization in terms of the movement's doctrinal basis and thus extends Weber's generalizations about charisma. The Zaddik was a highly personal type of leader whose authority is based on his ability to make contact with the feminine element of God, which is immanent but hidden in the world, and is demonstrated by his ability to gather disciples. Hasidic leadership was very flexible, and control over potential growth was weak. The Lurianic Kabbala's myth of creation provides a way of recognizing similarities and organizing differences among Hasidim. Interpretations of it permitted the office of the Zaddik to become an ascriptive office, legitimated the quasi-familial relations among Hasids of the same Zaddik, and explained differences among Hasids of different Zaddiks. By drawing on the internal sources of the movement's growth, we can explain changes that are puzzling if we concentrate on the external sources of strain to the movement alone. For example, why would a charismatic movement allow leadership to be hereditary? Moreover, attention to the internal and/or doctrinal development of a charismatic movement makes clear how actors defined the situation and why they acted as they did.

References

Bellah, R. *Beyond Belief*. New York: Harper & Row, 1970.

Bosk, C. "Cybernetic Hasidism: An Essay on Social and Religious Change." *Sociological Inquiry*, 1974, *44* (2), 131–144.

Buber, M. *Tales of the Hasidim: Early Masters.* New York: Schocken, 1947.

Buber, M. *Tales of Rabbi Nachman.* New York: Avon, 1961.

Dubnov, S. *History of the Jews in Russia and Poland.* Vol. 1. Philadelphia: Jewish Publication Society, 1916.

Horodenzky, S.A. *Leaders of Hasidism.* London: Hasefer Agency, 1928.

Mindel, N. *Rov Schneur Zalman of Liadi.* New York: Kehot Publication Center, 1967.

Minkin, J. *Romance of Hasidism.* New York: Wilshire, 1935.

Ortner, S. "On Key Symbols." *American Anthropologist,* 1973, *75,* 1338–1346.

Schatz-Uffenheimer, R. "Man's Relation to God and the World in Buber's rendering of Hasidic teaching." In P. Schlipp and M. Friedman (Eds.), *The Philosophy of Martin Buber.* La Salle, Ill.: Open Court, 1967.

Schechter, S. *Studies in Judaism.* Philadelphia: Jewish Publication Society, 1916.

Scholem, G. *Major Trends in Jewish Mysticism.* New York: Schocken, 1946.

Scholem, G. *On the Kabbala and Its Symbolism.* New York: Schocken, 1960.

Scholem, G. *The Messianic Idea in Judaism.* New York: Schocken, 1970.

Weber, M. *The Sociology of Religion.* (E. Fischoff, Trans.) Boston: Beacon Press, 1963. (Originally published 1922.)

Zborowski, M., and Herzog, E. *Life Is With People.* New York: International Universities Press, 1962.

7

Ronald Ye-lin Cheng

The Effect of Prerevolutionary Values, Beliefs, and Social Structures on Revolutionary Mobilization and Success

During a period of transition in a society, social changes may develop so rapidly that a new system of government is required to cope with important problems. At the same time, repeated failure of government to reform itself is perceived by various members of society as an obstacle to needed further system changes. Indeed, revolution seems to occur as a response to governments' failure to bring about change, or even resistance to change. When the ruling

Note: This chapter, substantially as it is, was presented at the meeting of the International Society for the Comparative Study of Civilizations at Bradford College, Haverhill, Massachusetts, April 14–17, 1977.

group and the system of government are perceived as stumbling blocks to change, they must be removed.

In the study of revolution, one must consider the importance of external influences. Elbaki Hermassi (1976, p. 214) states that "The world historical character of revolutions means, among other things, that they introduce new political ideals and principles of legitimacy which threaten existing power arrangements by their explosive novelty or demands for societal restructuring. They exert a demonstration effect beyond the boundaries of their country of origin, with a potential for triggering waves of revolution and counterrevolution both within and between societies." The transformation of one world system to another is what George Pettee (1966) called "systemic revolution." For instance, the French Revolution of 1789 led to the Napoleonic War and many revolutionary uprisings in Europe (Palmer, 1959). In time, monarchy was gradually replaced by constitutional government as the dominant political system in the world. Theda Skocpol (1976) also thinks that external influence is an important factor contributing to the occurrence of revolution in France, Russia, and China. The Meiji Restoration of 1868 and the Chinese Revolution of 1911 may also be considered as a part of the "systemic revolution" in the world for the establishment of a system of constitutional government. In W. G. Beasley's (1972) study of the Meiji Restoration of 1868 and R. Y. Cheng's (1973a) study of the Chinese Revolution of 1911, the importance of foreign pressure as a contributing factor has been analyzed in detail.

However, internal prerevolutionary social conditions are also important (Smelser, 1963; Cheng, 1973b). The purpose of this article is to show that, in the Meiji Restoration of 1868 and the Chinese Revolution of 1911, the prerevolutionary social conditions in Tokugawa Japan and Ch'ing China helped to determine the nature and process of conflicts, the ways of revolutionary mobilization, and the success of revolution in each society.

There are several reasons for choosing these two cases: They were both revolutions in the sense that they involved sudden fundamental discontinuity resulting in a change in the locus of political authority and in the development of a new political system. Also, during the changeover, violence or the threat of violence was used to replace one ruling group with another. In Japan, the Meiji Restoration of 1868 destroyed the Tokugawa political system and changed the locus of political authority from the shogun to a small group of Meiji leaders who ruled in the name of the emperor through a system of constitutional monarchy. During the process, violence and the threat of violence were used by Choshu and Satsuma to force Shogun Keiki to surrender. The results were both the abolition of the domains (autonomous local governments in the Tokugawa system) and the demolition of the samurai class structure. In China, the Revolution of 1911 destroyed the Ch'ing political system and changed the locus of political authority from the emperor to a president ruling through a system of republican government.

There are interesting similarities as well as interesting differences in the two cases. For instance, while both societies were dominated by Neo-Confucianism, the situations were different. Both societies were subjected to foreign pressure. The Tokugawa and Ch'ing governments were unsuccessful in their resistance to foreign encroachments, but Japan's response was much quicker and more aggressive than China's. In each case, the government was destroyed, but Japan was more successful than China in the establishment of constitutional government and in industrialization. A number of comparative studies show why Japan was more successful than China in industrialization (Levy, Jr., 1953; Lockwood, 1956; Beckmann, 1962; Reischauer, 1963). However, no comparative studies have appeared to deal with both democratization and industrialization and to analyze the effect of prerevolutionary values, beliefs, and social structures on revolutionary mobilization and success in Tokugawa Japan and Ch'ing China. Therefore, the purpose of this chapter is to fill this gap.

In both Ch'ing China and Tokugawa Japan, Neo-Confucianism occupied a dominant position in the system of values and beliefs. But there were certain differences in interpretations and practical applications in the two societies. In this chapter, the values and beliefs of Ch'ing China (Bodde, 1953; DeBary, 1953; Chai, 1964; Ch'ü, 1957; Eberhard, 1966; Hsieh, 1967; Hsu, 1926; Schwartz, 1959; A. F. Wright, 1962; Wu, 1967; Yang, 1961; and

Tokugawa Japan (Bellah, 1957; Ishida, 1964; Masaaki, 1967; Moore, 1967; Narugama, 1974; Spae, 1965; Takeyoshi, 1967; Tesshi, 1967) are analyzed in terms of seven sets of values and beliefs developed from Kluckhohn and Strodtbeck (1961, pp. 12–19) with my own additions as shown in Table 1. The seven sets of values and beliefs may be illustrated briefly with examples.[1]

Many simple societies emphasize that man is subjugated to nature and can do little or nothing to affect the working of nature. A person's prosperity and misfortune, sickness and health, are all determined by fate. In other societies, such as the Chinese, man was considered an extension and a part of nature. Therefore man should work harmoniously with and within nature. In American society, it is believed that man is the master over nature. With intelligence and scientific knowledge, we can overcome all obstacles and put natural forces to the use of human beings.

For some simple societies without written and recorded history, the past was lost and the future was too uncertain to anticipate; therefore, the present was all-important. For the Chinese, the first-order value and belief was in the "past." This showed in the Chinese preference for a return to a golden past and in the emphasis on ancestor worship and family tradition. Americans have placed emphasis on the future, which is expected to be a "bigger and better" one.

The Chinese believed in the basic goodness of human nature; it was the society that corrupted individuals. In the West, the

Table 1. Seven Sets of Values and Beliefs

Dimensions	Values and Beliefs		
Man-Nature	Subjugation to Nature	Harmony with Nature[a,b]	Master over Nature
Time	Past[a]	Present[b]	Future
Human-Nature	Basic Goodness[a,b]	Mixed Good/Evil	Evil
Activity	Being	Being in Becoming[a]	Doing[b]
Relational	Collectivism[b]	Lineality[a]	Individualism
Government	Rule of Virtue[a,b]	Rule of Law	Rule of Force
Stratification	Hierarchy[a,b]	Equality of Opportunity	Egalitarianism

[a]Ch'ing China
[b]Tokugawa Japan

Judeo-Christian tradition stressed the sinful nature of human beings; therefore there must be constant control and discipline in society. But, in modern societies, increasing numbers of people believe that human nature is a mixture of good and evil.

On the activity dimension, the value of "being" stresses the inward activity and worth of a person (for example, a yogi), while the value of "doing" stresses the outward activity and worth of a person (for example, a millionaire businessman). Traditionally the Chinese opted for the value of "being in becoming," which stressed the integration of inward and outward activities and worth of a person (for example, a Chinese mandarin, who should be a scholar as well as a government administrator).

In America, individualism has been dominant. This shows in the stress on the protection of individual rights, the right of private property, and the free enterprise system. In traditional China, the interest of the family was more important. In case of conflict between the interest of the family and the interest of the state, the family interest had primacy.[2] For instance, if a prime minister's old mother needed him to take care of her, he had to resign to serve her even if the empire very much needed his service (Ch'ü, 1965). In socialist states, collective interest overrides individual interest, and individuals should sacrifice for the good of the collective.

The Chinese believed the "rule of virtue." The state should be governed by men of superior moral virtue who set an example for the rest of the population to follow. The Americans believe in the "rule of law" not of men, and emphasize due process and rights of citizens. The Nazi Germany and Stalinist Russia governments seemed to believe in the "rule of force."

On the stratification dimension, "hierarchy" was stressed in some societies. Persons were born into their positions, and they should keep their proper stations in life. Examples are the caste system in India and the samurai class structure in Tokugawa Japan. The stratification system of Western industrialized countries stresses "equality of opportunity": individuals are supposed to have equal opportunity to achieve higher positions in society. In socialist societies, "egalitarianism" is stressed: Everybody should contribute according to ability and consume according to need in a classless society.

The similarities and differences of these seven sets of values and beliefs had important influences in the determination of the nature and process of conflicts, the ways of revolutionary mobilization, and the success of revolution in the Ch'ing and Tokugawa societies.

On the man-nature dimension, the dominant value and belief in Ch'ing China was "harmony with nature." The Chinese believed that there was a close relationship between the human and natural worlds and that a disturbance in one resulted in corresponding disturbances in the other. Therefore floods, droughts, plagues, and other abnormal phenomena were considered to be positive evidence of irregularities in society. Conversely, large-scale peasant rebellion, immorality, or tyranny of the emperor in society would lead to disturbance in the natural world. Therefore it was the responsibility of the emperor as "Son of Heaven" to maintain harmony between the human and natural worlds. If he failed to do so, his mandate of heaven would be taken away, and dynastic change could take place.

In Tokugawa Japan, the dominant value was also harmony with nature. The Japanese believed that heaven was the benevolent creative power responsible for procreation and the life of all things in the realm of nature and man. Therefore it was man's duty to assist the operation of heaven's creative will harmoniously in society.

The value and belief of "harmony with nature" had important influences on developments in both Ch'ing China and Tokugawa Japan. The effect was different, however, because on the time dimension the dominant value and belief for Ch'ing China was the "past" and for Tokugawa Japan was the "present." The Chinese believed that change in the universe followed a fixed and predictable pattern consisting either of eternal oscillation between two poles or of cyclical movement within a closed circuit, and all movement only went back to its starting point in the end. Therefore the Chinese looked toward the past, especially to the ancient days of the sage kings, as a golden age. The consequence of the combination of the two values and beliefs ("harmony with nature" and the "past") for Ch'ing China was to preserve the traditional system; to do otherwise would disturb the harmony between the human and the natural worlds. Therefore the Chinese strongly resisted any change in the traditional system.

For example, the traditional tribute system of China was a device for the manipulation of foreign countries based on the relationship of superiority and inferiority (Mancall, 1968). When the Western countries attempted to establish diplomatic relations with Ch'ing China and open the empire for foreign trade on the basis of equality, the Ch'ing government resisted strenuously. Attempts by Lord McCartney for the British government in 1793 (Fairbank and others, 1965), by Count Golovnin for the Russian government in 1805 (Liu, 1959), and by Lord Amherst for the British government in 1816 (Huang, 1964) to establish diplomatic relations and trade with China all ended in failure.

The Opium War of 1840–1842 was an armed attempt by the Western powers to open China's door for trade and diplomacy (Collis, 1968; Waley, 1968). After the Opium War, the government had to open more and more treaty ports and establish diplomatic relations with an increasing number of countries. But, from the Chinese point of view, the treaty system was an adaptation of the tribute system, which continued to operate in the second half of the nineteenth century (Fairbank, 1968). In 1861, the Ch'ing government also established a separate foreign office, called Tsungli Yamen, to set foreign affairs apart from traditional practices and to minimize the disturbances of the traditional system of government (Meng, 1962).

As foreign barbarians should not be regarded as on equal terms with the superior Chinese, the establishment of foreign legations in Peking violated the proper relationship between China and other countries, and the Chinese legations abroad were acts of submission and humiliation (Hsu, 1960). This attitude explains the Ch'ing officials' refusal to deal directly with foreign officials and representatives before the Opium War (Huang, 1964), the Ch'ing government's resistance to the residence of foreign ministers in Peking, and the reluctance of the Ch'ing government to send Chinese legations abroad (Hsu, 1960).

The two dominant values—"harmony with nature" and the "past"—in combination, had the effect of delaying fundamental social change, intensifying social conflicts in Ch'ing society, and contributing to revolutionary potential. The two dominant values in combination also affected the development of revolutionary mobilization and the success of revolution, because many people in Ch'ing society still looked toward the past for ways of restoring harmony in times of increasing conflicts and stress. For instance, the "Hundred Day" reform was attempted by the Kuang-hsu emperor in June 1898, at K'ang Yu-wei's urging, but it failed (Tang, 1960; Cameron, 1931, chaps. 1, 2). In pushing for reform, K'ang Yu-wei used the sanction of tradition, stating in his book *Confucius as a Reformer* that Confucius had created the principal classics in order to make institutional reforms (Hsiao, 1975). After the failure of the Hundred Day reform, K'ang Yu-wei and Liang Ch'i-ch'ao formed the Emperor Protection Society, which competed with Sun Yat-sen's Hsing-Chung Hui for the membership and financial support of overseas Chinese (Chi, 1966). Yuan Shih-k'ai's abortive attempt to set himself up as emperor in 1916 was the last effort in looking toward the past for solution of China's problems and the reestablishment of harmony in society (Hsu, 1970).

On the time dimension, the dominant value for Tokugawa Japan was the "present." The Japanese were worldly, realistic, and practical, and they believed that immediate experience and directness of living were of primary importance. The consequence of the combination of the two values of "harmony with nature" and the "present" for Tokugawa Japan was that harmony was to be maintained through solution to present problems and compromise rather than the reestablishment of the traditional equilibrium. Therefore the Japanese were much more willing to borrow from outside and make changes in their system if necessary.

After Commodore Perry's arrival at Uraga in 1853, both Bakufu (central government) and domain (local government) immediately initiated a series of military, industrial, and educational reforms for the purpose of meeting the challenge of the West (Beasley, 1972). Restrictions on the building of ocean-going ships were abolished. Warships and merchant vessels were purchased from abroad. Dockyards, ironworks, and other industrial plants modeled on Western lines were constructed. Envoys were sent abroad to study foreign conditions. A translation bureau founded by the Bakufu in 1856 quickly became a major center for the study of Dutch, English, French, and German, together with military science and metallurgy.

By the time of the Meiji Restoration, according to one estimate, sixty domain schools teaching Western subjects had been established. The case of Shimazu Nariakira, daimyo (feudal lord) of Satsuma, is interesting. He did not see any contradiction among his liberal foreign policy, conservative politics, and technological innovation. The three elements could be harmoniously combined to strengthen Japan in dealing with problems of the Western challenge.

In Tokugawa Japan, military reform came in the 1840s, but in Ch'ing China it did not start until the 1860s (M. C. Wright, 1962; Mow, 1956), more than twenty years after the Opium War of 1840. Thus the two dominant value orientations: "Harmony with nature" and the "present," in combination, had the effect of speeding up fundamental social change in Tokugawa society.

On the human-nature dimension, the dominant value and belief for both Ch'ing China and Tokugawa Japan was the "basic goodness" of human nature. For both Chinese and Japanese, the universe was harmonious, and its basic principle was goodness. Since man and the nonhuman universe were one and human nature was what Heaven had given, humans must by nature be good. Evil arose from imperfections in society, and the universal perfectibility of all men was firmly believed in. Thus both the Chinese and the Japanese put great stress on the importance of education, especially on the moral integrity and conduct of individuals.

The Chinese believed in the superiority of mental workers over manual workers, thinking the former should rule the latter. The Chinese literati's right to rule was based on the mastering of the Chinese classics and was demonstrated through achievements in the examination system (Ho, 1964). The Japanese believed that moral and intellectual accomplishment in education was a means to an ethical end, therefore virtuousness in conduct, respect for superiors, loyalty to the lord, and filial piety were qualities held up for praise (Dore, 1968). Because the traditional education in Ch'ing China and Tokugawa Japan was of little use in training the type of talent and ability needed to meet the Western challenge, the traditional system of education was a liability rather than an asset in the promotion of fundamental changes in both societies. Those who responded to the Western challenge and promoted reform or revolution were largely people who had some acquaintance with Western education in one way or another.[3] For instance, the Chinese students who returned from Japan played an important part in the Chinese Revolution of 1911 (Hackett, 1949). Most of the leaders of the Meiji Restoration had knowledge of Western language and education. Many of these leaders moved further upward after the establishment of the Meiji governments, while those without knowledge of Western language and education were gradually dropped (Choi, 1956; Silberman, 1964).

On the activity dimension, the dominant value for Ch'ing China was "being in becoming." The Chinese believed in the doctrine of the unity of activity and quiescence. A superior man must carry out self-cultivation leading to personal self-realization as well as the ordering and harmonizing of the world. Indeed, a superior man could achieve complete self-realization only in his public vocation; conversely, society could be harmonized and set in order only when men who had approached the ideal of self-realization were in public office. In Ch'ing China, the effect of this value was that the Chinese mandarin was usually a generalist who often spent more time on scholarly and cultural activities than on the administration of government; the work of government itself was carried out under the principle of "government by inaction." Consequently, the Chinese officials were rather unresponsive to demands for change and development both before and after the Revolution of 1911.

On the activity dimension, the dominant value of Tokugawa Japan was "doing." Japanese believed that man's sacred duty was to carry out heaven's ways according to one's status and profession. For the Japanese samurai, the value of "doing" was associated with the martial spirit. Therefore, the Japanese response to the Western challenge was much more aggressive and immediate than was the Chinese response, and the Japanese were much more willing to go into various Western professions. In fact, their main emphasis was to put "men of talent" in positions of responsibility, so changes could be made to meet the Western challenge (Harooturnian, 1970). For example, in response to Perry's visit in 1853 and 1854, a naval school was established in Nagasaki. By 1860, without help from foreign experts, the school produced a ship's company capable of taking a vessel to San Francisco (Beasley, 1972). Substantial changes were also carried out in political, military, economic, and educational systems shortly after the restoration (Beasley, 1972). In China, Western-style education developed slowly because of the opposition from the literati. A new department of mathematics and astronomy was established in Peking T'ung-wen Kuan in 1867. Because of the influence of conservative anti-Westerners, none of the desired type of young scholars applied for admission (Biggerstaff, 1961), and the plan failed. In Japan, the value of "doing" had the effect of promoting more rapid social change and development both before and after the Meiji Restoration.

On the relational dimension, the dominant value for Ch'ing China was "lineality" and for Tokugawa Japan, "collectivism." In Ch'ing China, the primary loyalty was to the family, while in Tokugawa Japan the primary loyalty was to the overlord. As the Ch'ing dynasty declined during the second half of the nineteenth century and the beginning of the twentieth century, corruption and nepotism became widespread and contributed further to the undermining of the Ch'ing governmental administration. The attempt of Yuan Shih-k'ai to set himself up as emperor in 1916 was another indication that his primary loyalty was to himself and his family, not to the country.

In Tokugawa Japan, the primary loyalty to the immediate overlord was transferred to the state; thus the value of "collectivism" facilitated the unification of the people in the service of the state. For instance, there was evidence of strong desire in many quarters, including the Bakufu government, to avoid full-scale civil war because of the fear of possible foreign intervention (Beasley, 1972). Shogun Keiki was willing to submit when Choshu and Satsuma confronted his government with troops, and his opponents were also willing to pardon him and his followers for the sake of the unity of the country. This is in strong contrast to the disunity of China's leaders after the Revolution of 1911 and the breakdown into warlordism soon afterward. The value of "lineality" in Ch'ing China undermined the Ch'ing government's ability to cope with social change and increased the difficulty of unifying the country after the Revolution of 1911. Conversely, the value of "collectivism" in Tokugawa Japan, together with "harmony with nature," helped to unite the people to serve the country both before and after the Meiji Restoration.

On the governmental dimension, the dominant value and belief of both Ch'ing China and Tokugawa Japan was the "rule of virtue." On the stratification dimension, the dominant value and belief for both Ch'ing China and Tokugawa Japan was "hierarchy." Both Chinese and Japanese believed that human beings differ in social intelligence, ability, and morality; therefore society was necessarily hierarchical, and people must have unequal rights and obligations according to their status. People with lower status were to obey people with higher status, who had the right to rule through their cultivation of perfect virtue and universal love. People with lower status were to submit to people with higher status who possessed the knowledge and moral virtue to rule. Neither the Ch'ing nor Tokugawa political systems had significant legal mechanisms for the lower classes to redress grievances. People were largely dependent on the benevolent rule of their government.

The value of "lineality" further contributed to the subjugation of the people to the ruler as children were subjugated to their parents in Ch'ing China. The value of "collectivism" further contributed to the subjugation of individuals' interests to those of the state in Tokugawa Japan. In times of increasing change and conflict, people with grievances will turn to illegal means to redress their grievances if there are no legal channels available. Therefore the value and belief of "rule of virtue" and "hierarchy" had the effect of increasing revolutionary potential in both Ch'ing China and Tokugawa Japan.

Certain prerevolutionary social structures also had significant effect on the nature and process of conflicts that developed, on the way revolutionary mobilization was carried out, and on the degree of success in the Chinese Revolution of 1911 and the Meiji Restoration of 1868.

The Ch'ing system of stratification was not very rigid, and it was possible for a commoner to become an official and rise to the highest office in the land. There was quite a lot of vertical mobility in Ch'ing China. For instance, Ping-ti Ho (1964) found that, for the

entire Ming and Ch'ing period (1368–1911), 42.3 percent of the
Chih-shih (holders of the highest degree) and *Chu-jen* (holders of the
second highest degree) were commoners. During the entire Ch'ing
period (1644–1911), virtually as large a proportion of commoners'
sons reached high-rank posts after entering the civil service as did
sons of officials and degree holders (Marsh, 1964). The considerable vertical mobility in Ch'ing China had the effect of maintaining
support for and prolonging the life of the Ch'ing dynasty, because
many people still aspired to become mandarin officials, and the
examination system made the prospect possible.

The Tokugawa system of stratification was rather rigid.
There was very little vertical social mobility within the samurai class
and between the samurai and commoners (Beasley, 1972). It is
likely that proportionally more people in Tokugawa Japan than in
Ch'ing China were discontented and welcomed radical change
(Strayer, 1968). So the rigidity of the Tokugawa stratification sys-
tem may have lessened support and hastened the downfall of the
Tokugawa government.

After the Meiji Restoration of 1868, employment had to be
found for the samurai in order to integrate them into the economic
system and solve their long-term problem of livelihood. They
numbered approximately 1,800,000 samurai, or 400,000 families,
and their discontent greatly increased the instability of the newly
established Meiji government (Harooturnian, 1960). Therefore,
from 1868 to 1889, a specific program for the rehabilitation of
samurai, called *shizoku jusan,* was carried out to encourage emigra-
tion and reclamation of new areas, to establish branches of the
national bank as a safeguard for samurai investments, and to set up
machinery for loaning rehabilitation money for the development
of agriculture, industry, and commerce. The programs were successful to a certain extent, and by the late 1880s the serious threat
of class discontent had been largely, but not entirely, removed.

In terms of political structure, the Ch'ing authority was
much more unified than the Tokugawa authority. The Ch'ing Emperor was the Son of Heaven, with a mandate to rule and maintain
harmony in society. Theoretically, all legislative, executive, and ju-
dicial power belonged to him (Hsieh, 1966). Therefore, legitimacy
and power were vested in the Ch'ing emperor. In Tokugawa gov-

ernment, legitimacy and power were divided. The emperor, as the descendant of the Sun Goddess, Amaterasu Omikami, had the undisputed legitimacy to reign for more than a thousand years, but the shogun of the Tokugawa House, the greatest of the feudal lords, had the undisputed power to rule in the name of the emperor (Webb, 1968; Totman, 1967). This difference in the authority structures of Ch'ing China and Tokugawa Japan had significant influences on the processes and outcomes of the Chinese Revolution of 1911 and the Meiji Restoration of 1868.

The increasing attack on the Ch'ing government had led to a decline in both the legitimacy and the power of the emperor, so the legitimacy of the emperor could not be borrowed by the revolutionaries. As a result, the revolutionaries appropriated a foreign source of legitimacy in the name "sovereignty of the people," which did not have traditional roots in China. Partly for this reason, constitutional democracy did not work in China after the revolution of 1911.

When Yuan Shih-k'ai attempted to borrow the emperor's source of legitimacy by setting himself up as emperor, he failed miserably because the emperor's source of legitimacy had been destroyed in the Ch'ing dynasty and could not be revived. The lack of a clear source of legitimacy that could be readily understood and accepted by the Chinese people may be an important reason why it was so difficult for the Chinese people to unite under a centralized government after the Revolution of 1911.

In Japan, the increasing attack on the Tokugawa government weakened the power of the shogun, but left the emperor's legitimacy intact. Therefore, Choshu and Satsuma could attack the shogun and his government in the name of the emperor (Beasley, 1972). After the Meiji Restoration, the government was able to use the emperor's legitimacy to unify the country and centralize the political system (Beasley, 1972).

The governmental administration was much more centralized in Ch'ing China than in Tokugawa Japan. The Ch'ing emperor appointed or approved all civil and military officials; there were no hereditary governmental positions. The armies were under the centralized command of the emperor. The taxation system was centralized under the board of revenues; provincial governments were responsible for the collection and delivery of taxes to the central government, after retaining a portion for their own use. Decision making was also centralized in the hands of the emperor and the central government, and provincial government could not make important decisions without approval of the central government (Hsieh, 1966).

In Tokugawa Japan, the daimyo had considerable independence (Totman, 1967; Beasley, 1972). Each daimyo had his own territory in which to carry out his administration, to collect his taxes, and to establish his army. The daimyo's position was hereditary, and he did not have to pay taxes to the shogun's government. Therefore, Tokugawa Japan had, not one government, but many, each exercising authority within its own territory. The shogun had no direct and simple means of asserting his authority on the daimyo's government short of using force. In the last resort, the shogun had to choose between ineffectiveness and civil war.

As the Ch'ing political system was more centralized than the Tokugawa political system, the Ch'ing government seemed to have more staying power than the Tokugawa government. The Ch'ing government withstood a series of shocks: the Opium War of 1840; the repeated defeats in the foreign wars of 1856, 1884, 1895, and 1900; and the large-scale internal rebellions such as the Taiping Rebellion from 1851 to 1868, the Nein Rebellion from 1853 to 1868, and the Moslem Rebellion from 1855 to 1873. The Ch'ing government did not collapse until 1912, lasting for a period of ninety-two years. But the Tokugawa government survived only fifteen years after Perry's arrival at Uraga in 1853. It collapsed in 1868 under the challenge of Choshu and Satsuma.

The speedy collapse of the Tokugawa government was related not only to the decentralized nature of its political system, which enabled the daimyo to challenge the shogun's position, but also to the working of the Sankin Kotai system, which was originally designed to keep the daimyo in check by requiring their residence in Edo in alternate years and by holding their wives and families as political hostages (Tsukahira, 1966). The Sankin Kotai system unexpectedly created a public forum in Edo, a network of communication and transportation for the daimyo to contact their domains and to travel back and forth to Edo, and the development of a competitive spirit among the daimyo (Choi, 1956). The Sankin Kotai system provided Japan with a sensitive nervous system. Any events of a political nature, even unfavorable news, such as the weakening of the shogun's government or the arrival of Perry, was quickly communicated. Therefore the Sankin Kotai system played an important role, increasing challenges and multiplying revolutionaries.

In the case of Ch'ing China, the huge size of the country and difficulties of travel and communication tended to slow down the dissemination of news and information. Foot-post stations and horse-post stations existed, but these were under the control and use of the central government (Chou, 1957). The metropolitan examination occurred every four years in Peking and did provide a public forum for the dissemination of news and information, but it was a sporadic, not a permanent, system of communication. A system of communication of news and Western ideas did develop in the treaty ports along the coastal areas and Christian missionary stations all over China, but these came later and were not a part of the preexisting social conditions in Ch'ing society (Cheng, 1973a).

Another factor contributing to the greater resistance of the Ch'ing ruling elite to fundamental social change in comparison with Tokugawa was the different basis of their positions (Beasley, 1972). The Ch'ing mandarin officals held office by virtue of being Confucian. The Western challenge to Neo-Confucianism undermined both their legitimacy and power to rule. In contrast, although the samurai in Tokugawa Japan had accepted Neo-Confucianism they did not depend on it. The positions of Japanese feudal lords and retainers were based on their birth and inheritable status, received as a reward for their past military contributions. Therefore it is understandable that there was less resistance to fundamental change in the case of the Tokugawa ruling elite in comparison with the Ch'ing ruling elite.

In summary, the prerevolutionary values, beliefs, and social structures in Ch'ing China and Tokugawa Japan were very important to the revolutionary mobilization and success of the Chinese Revolution of 1911 and the Meiji Restoration of 1868. In the case of Ch'ing China, the values and beliefs of "harmony with nature" and "past" contributed to the intensification of social conflicts and increase of revolutionary potential. In addition, the values and beliefs of "rule of virtue" and "hierarchy" limited legal channels for the redress of grievances and turned discontented people in the population to revolution, while the value of "lineality," which reduced the possibility of reform as an alternative, fostered corruption and nepotism. Because they were generalists with belief in the "past" and because they based their rule on Confucianism, which was challenged by the West, the mandarins and gentry were less willing to change and more inclined to look toward the past for solutions. Furthermore, with substantial vertical social mobility, large proportions of persons with traditional Confucian education continued to support the Ch'ing dynasty. The centralized nature of the Ch'ing government, the difficulty of communication, and the huge size of the country also helped to prolong the life of the Ch'ing Dynasty. After the Revolution of 1911, the traditional values of "past" and "lineality" contributed to Yuan Shih-k'ai's attempt to set himself up as the emperor at the expense of the Republic, and the Republican government had problems unifying the country because they could not find a new source of legitimacy acceptable to the people after the destruction of both the power as well as the legitimacy of the emperor.

In the case of Tokugawa Japan, the values and beliefs of "harmony with nature" and "present" helped in promoting social change to a certain extent, but the values and beliefs of "rule of virtue" and "hierarchy" limited legal channels for the redress of grievances and turned discontented people in the population to overthrow the Tokugawa government. Being "doers" with orientation toward solving "present" problems and basing their rule on their past military contributions, which the West did not threaten, the feudal lords and retainers were more willing to change and were less inclined to look toward the past for solutions. However, the substantial rigidity of the stratification system had reduced support for the Tokugawa government. The decentralized nature of the government, the availability of communication, and the small size of the country also helped to shorten the life of the Tokugawa rule. After the Meiji Restoration of 1868, the value of "collectivism" helped to transfer loyalty from overlord to the state, and the emperor's source of legitimacy, being intact, assisted in the unification of the country.

Thus, prerevolutionary values, beliefs, and social structures contributed to crisis in both societies, although to a lesser extent in Tokugawa Japan. These conditions delayed revolution in Ch'ing China but hastened it in Tokugawa Japan, led to growing disunity in Republican China but contributed to increasing integration in Meiji Japan, after revolution.

The purpose of this chapter is not to show that other factors are unimportant in revolution; the purpose is to point out that prerevolutionary social conditions in a society do play an important part. The study of the effect of prerevolutionary social conditions on revolution helps us to increase our power of explanation and prediction, because revolutionary potential may be indicated by prerevolutionary social conditions long before the occurrence of revolution.

Notes

1. These high-level generalizations sacrifice details and complexity for the sake of bringing out fundamental differences of values and beliefs among different societies. For the purpose of illustration, examples from other societies besides Ch'ing China and Tokugawa Japan were also used to cover the full range of differences in values and beliefs, although these examples may or may not have anything to do with Ch'ing China and Tokugawa Japan, which are under study here.

2. It is true that there was always conflict of interest between state and family in traditional China. When serious conflict arose, the state would use its power (for example, executing an official and his family members for serious corruption) but not its legitimacy. Out of the "five social relationships" (those between ruler and minister, father and son, husband and wife, elder and younger brothers, and friend and friend), three are family relationships. Not only was the ruler and minister relationship not considered to have primacy over the father and son relationship, but the ruler and minister relationship was modeled on the father and son relationship and borrowed its legitimacy from it.

3. It is here used in the sense of science and constitutional democracy, which were perceived by the Chinese and Japanese at that time as the source of wealth and power.

References

Beasley, W. G. *The Meiji Restoration.* Stanford, Calif.: Stanford University Press, 1972.

Beckmann, G. W. *The Modernization of China and Japan.* New York: Harper & Row, 1962.

Bellah, R. N. *Tokugawa Religion.* New York: Free Press, 1957.

Biggerstaff, K. *The Earliest Modern Government School in China.* Ithaca, N.Y.: Cornell University Press, 1961.

Bodde, D. "Harmony and Conflict in Chinese Philosophy." In A. F. Wright (Ed.), *Studies in Chinese Thought.* Chicago: University of Chicago Press, 1953.

Cameron, M. E. *The Reform Movement in China, 1898–1912.* Stanford, Calif.: Stanford University Press, 1931.

Chai, C. "The Spirit of Chinese Philosophy." In China Institute in America (Ed.), *A Symposium on Chinese Culture.* New York: Paragon Book Gallery, 1964.

Cheng, R. Y. *The First Revolution in China: A Theory.* New York: Vantage Press, 1973a.

Cheng, R. Y. *The Sociology of Revolution.* Chicago: Regnery, 1973b.

Chi, P. *Controversy Between the Revolutionaries and the Constitutional Monarchists in the Late Ch'ing Period.* Taipei: Academia Sinica, 1966. (In Chinese.)

Choi, K. "Tokugawa Feudalism and the Emergence of the New Leaders of Early Modern Japan." *Explorations in Entrepreneurial History,* 1956, *9,* 72–90.

Chou, I. *The History of Public Roads in China.* Taipei: Public Road Press, 1957. (In Chinese.)

Ch'ü, T. "Chinese Class Structure and Its Ideology." In J. K. Fairbank (Ed.), *Chinese Thought and Institutions.* Chicago: University of Chicago Press, 1957.

Ch'ü, T. *Law and Society in Traditional China.* The Hague: Mouton, 1965.

Collis, M. *Foreign Mud.* New York: Norton, 1968.

DeBary, W. T. "A Reappraisal of Neo-Confucianism." In A. F. Wright (Ed.), *Studies in Chinese Thought*. Chicago: University of Chicago Press, 1953.

Dore, R. P. "Talent and the Social Order in Tokugawa Japan." In J. W. Hall and M. B. Jansen (Eds.), *Studies in the Institutional History of Early Japan*. Princeton, N.J.: Princeton University Press, 1968.

Eberhard, W. "Fate in the Life of the Common Man in Non-Communist China." *Anthropological Quarterly*, 1966, *39*, 148–160.

Fairbank, J. K. "The Early Treaty System in the Chinese World Order." In J. K. Fairbank (Ed.), *The Chinese World Today*. Cambridge, Mass.: Harvard University Press, 1968.

Fairbank, J. K., and others. *East Asia: The Modern Transformation*. Boston: Houghton Mifflin, 1965.

Hackett, R. F. "Chinese Students in Japan, 1900–1910." *Papers on China*, 1949, *3*, 134–169.

Harooturnian, H. D. "The Economic Rehabilitation of the Samurai in the Early Meiji Period." *Journal of Asian Studies*, 1960, *19*, 433–444.

Harooturnian, H. D. *Toward Restoration*. Berkeley: University of California Press, 1970.

Hermassi, E. "Toward a Comparative Study of Revolutions." *Comparative Studies in Society and History*, 1976, *18*, 211–235.

Ho, P. *The Ladder of Success in Imperial China*. New York: Wiley, 1964.

Hsiao, K. *A Modern China and a New World: K'ang Yu-Wei, Reformer and Utopian, 1858–1927*. Seattle: University of Washington Press, 1975.

Hsieh, P. *The Government of China (1644–1911)*. New York: Octagon Books, 1966.

Hsieh, Y. "Filial Piety and Chinese Society." In Charles A. Moore (Ed.), *The Chinese Mind: Essentials of Chinese Philosophy and Culture*. Honolulu: East-West Center Press, 1967.

Hsu, C. Y. *The Philosophy of Confucius*. London: Student Christian Movement, 1926.

Hsu, I. C. Y. *China's Entrance into the Family of Nations: The Diplomatic Phase, 1858–1880*. Cambridge, Mass.: Harvard University Press, 1960.

Hsu, I. C. Y. *The Rise of Modern China.* New York: Oxford University Press, 1970.

Huang, C. *Diplomatic History of China.* (3rd ed.) Taipei: National University of Political Science, 1964. (In Chinese.)

Ishida, I. "Tokugawa Feudal Society and Neo-Confucian Thought." *Philosophical Studies of Japan,* 1964, *5,* 1–37.

Kluckhohn, F. R., and Strodtbeck, F. L. *Variations in Value Orientations.* New York: Harper & Row, 1961.

Levy, M. J., Jr. "Contrasting Factors in the Modernization of China and Japan." *Economic Development and Cultural Change,* 1953, *11,* 161–197.

Liu, H. "Investigation of Early Trade Between China and Russia." In T. Pao and others (Eds.), *Collection of Essays on Modern Chinese History.* Set 1, No. 3. Taipei: Cheng Chung Bookshop, 1959. (In Chinese.)

Lockwood, W. W. "Japan's Response to the West: The Contrast with China." *World Politics,* 1956, *9,* 37–54.

Mancall, M. "The Ch'ing Tribute System." In J. K. Fairbank (Ed.), *The Chinese World Order.* Cambridge, Mass.: Harvard University Press, 1968.

Marsh, R. N. "Formal Organization and Promotion in Chinese Society." In W. J. Cuhnman and A. Boskoff (Eds.), *Sociology and History: Theory and Research.* New York: Free Press, 1964.

Masaaki, K. "The Status and the Role of the Individual in Japanese Society." In C. A. Moore (Ed.), *The Japanese Mind.* Honolulu: East-West Center Press, 1967.

Meng, S. M. *The Tsungli Yamen: Its Organization and Functions.* Cambridge, Mass.: Harvard University Press, 1962.

Moore C. A. "Editor's Supplement: The Enigmatic Japanese Mind." In C. A. Moore (Ed.), *The Japanese Mind.* Honolulu: East-West Center Press, 1967.

Mow, A. *The Movement to Imitate the Western Affairs.* Shanghai: Shanghai People's Publisher, 1956. (In Chinese.)

Narugama, M. *Studies in the Intellectual History of Tokugawa Japan.* Princeton, N.J.: Princeton University Press, 1974.

Palmer, R. R. *The Age of the Democratic Revolution.* Vols. 1, 2. Princeton, N.J.: Princeton University Press, 1959.

Pettee, G. "Revolution—Typology and Process." In C. J. Friedrich (Ed.), *Revolution: Nomos VIII*. New York: Atherton, 1966.

Reischauer, E. O. "Modernization in Nineteenth-Century China and Japan." *Japan Quarterly*, 1963, *10*, 298–307.

Schwartz, B. "Some Polarities in Confucian Thought." In D. S. Nivision and A. F. Wright (Eds.), *Confucianism in Action*. Stanford, Calif.: Stanford University Press, 1959.

Silberman, B. *Ministers of Modernization*. Tucson: University of Arizona Press, 1964.

Skocpol, T. "France, Russia, China: A Structural Analysis of Social Revolutions." *Comparative Studies in Society and History*, 1976, *18*, 175–210.

Smelser, N. J. *Theory of Collective Behavior*. New York: Free Press, 1963.

Spae, J. J. "The Japanese Concept of Sin." *Japan Christian Quarterly*, 1965, *31*, 262–271.

Strayer, J. R. "The Tokugawa Period and Japanese Feudalism." In J. W. Hall and M. B. Jansen (Eds.), *Studies in the Institutional History of Early Modern Japan*. Princeton, N.J.: Princeton University Press, 1968.

Takeyoshi, K. "The Status of the Individual in the Notion of Law, Right, and Social Order in Japan." In C. A. Moore (Ed.), *The Japanese Mind*. Honolulu: East-West Center Press, 1967.

Tang, C. *Short History of the Hundred-Day Reform*. Peking: Chung Hua Bookshop, 1960. (In Chinese.)

Tesshi, F. "The Individual in Japanese Ethics." In C. A. Moore (Ed.), *The Japanese Mind*. Honolulu: East-West Center Press, 1967.

Totman, C. D. *Politics in the Tokugawa Bakufu, 1600–1843*. Cambridge, Mass.: Harvard University Press, 1967.

Tsukahira, T. G. *Feudal Control in Tokugawa Japan: The Sankin Kotai System*. Cambridge, Mass.: Harvard University Press, 1966.

Waley, A. *The Opium War Through Chinese Eyes*. Stanford, Calif.: Stanford University Press, 1968.

Webb, H. *The Japanese Imperial Institution in the Tokugawa Period*. New York: Columbia University Press, 1968.

Wright, A. F. "Values, Roles and Personalities." In A. F. Wright and D. Twichett (Eds.), *Confucian Personalities.* Stanford, Calif.: Stanford University Press, 1962.

Wright, M. C. *The Last Stand of Chinese Conservatism: The T'ung-Chih Restoration, 1862–1874.* Stanford, Calif.: Stanford University Press, 1962.

Wu, J. C. H. "Chinese Legal and Political Philosophy." In C. A. Moore (Ed.), *The Chinese Mind: Essentials of Chinese Philosophy and Culture.* Honolulu: East-West Center Press, 1967.

Yang, C. K. *Religion in Chinese Society.* Berkeley: University of California Press, 1961.

8

Victor M. Lidz

Secularization, Ethical Life, and Religion in Modern Societies

An enduring intellectual concern of the sociology of religion has been to gain understanding of the distinctive qualities of religious life in modern societies. The concern was passed on to sociology from Enlightenment philosophers such as Locke, Hume, Rousseau, and Kant. It was incorporated into the discipline by such founding fathers as Comte, Marx, Durkheim, and Weber. It has been sustained to the present by such contemporary contributors as Bellah, Berger, and Luckmann, to cite only some of the more widely read and discussed figures. This chapter will not presume to offer a new general interpretation of the religious situation within contemporary civilization. However, it will sketch out a view of the modern religious situation that may provide an essential component of a new interpretation.

Note: I should like to acknowledge the helpful comments I received from Harold J. Bershady, Donald N. Levine, Talcott Parsons, and Jackson Toby. That I have not been able to respond to all their points of criticism does not lessen my appreciation.

The discipline of sociology has arisen out of an acute self-consciousness, albeit one expressed quite variously by different theorists, of the distinctive nature of modern civilization. The writings of Tocqueville, Comte, Spencer, Marx, Tönnies, Weber, Simmel, Pareto, Durkheim, and others, although diverse in intellectual background, strategy of analysis, and empirical focus, nevertheless gain a degree of unity from the sense in which they share an animation to understand the social transformations that have produced the modern type of society. Some features of the modernizing transformation have been widely agreed on and taken up as foci for elaborating technical means of sociological analysis, however divergent the subsequent conceptual frameworks may have become. Thus, the processes of extension of the market, industrialization, formation of bureaucracies, democratization, rationalization of the law, leveling of formal class distinctions, narrowing of kinship networks, and development of formal education (Parsons, 1971b), to cite only some principal cases, have been analyzed intensively within almost all schools of thought as major aspects of modernization. The usual and often justified, sensitivities of sociologists to the immense intellectual gaps among the various schools of thought tend not to do justice to this evidence of broad continuity in research and agreement in understanding.

I wish to focus, by contrast, on an aspect of modernization for which there has not been a comparable degree of continuity of research. The classical sociologists regarded a new order of degree of secularization as one of the principal sources of the qualities of modern social life. Some, for example, Marx, Comte, and Durkheim, were passionate proponents of secularization. Others, notably Weber in aspects of his writings on rationalization, marked out a major domain in comparative sociology for the study of secularization despite a deep-seated ambivalence toward the complex phenomenon. Nevertheless, contemporary sociology has not developed a technical field focusing on the analysis of the secularization process. There appears to be widespread agreement, although not unanimity, on the empirical generalization that the modern era must be characterized as distinctively thorough in its secularity. Yet a serious, sustained, and conceptually refined effort to grasp the nature of secularization has not emerged.

A few remarks may be ventured on the question of why the secularization process has been accorded relatively little theoretical attention. Perhaps only in the tradition of French positivism, from Saint-Simon through Comte to Durkheim, was there a sustained effort to analyze secularization closely. At its height, from the 1880s to World War I, it enjoyed not only the political sponsorship of the avowedly secularist leadership of the Third Republic (Clark, 1973) but also a philosophical patronage based on a reception of Kantian concerns for moral rationality into the post-Comtean interest in the "religion of humanity" (Tiryakian, 1978). With the change in the political and philosophical-ideological setting after World War I and with the loss of Durkheim's passionate involvement in moral sociology, the topic of secularization seems to have lost its attractions as an autonomous focus of research. It became embedded in more diffuse concerns with the possibilities of socialist transformations of society and with study of the social foundations of ideologies and ideological movements.

Anglo-American social science, in a sense handicapped by its emergence in settings where intense and sustained conflicts between religion and secular ideologies were rarely prominent, did not construct a penetrating appreciation of the importance of secularization. Its own underpinnings were so firmly positivistic that it took secularity of outlook quite for granted. Paradoxically, it could not conceive of the importance of secularization for modern social life, because it did not grasp the continuing importance of religious orientation. To be sure, the historical and comparative study of religion thrived, especially in British anthropology, but not in close engagement to the sociological understanding of the distinctive characteristics of modern society. The general British rejection of Weber's analysis of the ascetic Protestant sources of modern economic ethics perhaps indicates deep-seated limitations in the intellectual framework.

The German idealistic tradition, with its Romantic underpinnings, adhered firmly to the view that the sources of true meaning and truly civilized patterns of life were essentially religious. Scholars specializing in the study of law, administration, economic institutions, and the forms of community could appreciate the enhancement of practical functioning brought about by secularizing rationality in particular social domains. Indeed, Weber could synthesize an encompassing view of the transformations wrought by rationalization with an understanding of the importance of secularization within the rationalizing processes (Weber, [1922] 1968). Yet, the predominant view, as indexed by the popularity of Tönnies, but shared in large measure even by Weber, was that secularization necessarily involved the loss of meaning, rootedness in tradition, and communal loyalty. The debasement of human feeling and moral discipline was the expected outcome of worship of the ideals of impersonal reason. Enlightenment of society, as a general project, was to be distrusted or at least regarded with wary ambivalence, although perhaps acceded to on various specifics out of considerations of practical rationality. Hence, the ultimate moral legitimacy of secularizing transformations was questioned so profoundly that secularization itself tended to fall from view as an object—integral, although multifaceted—of intensive scholarly examination.

However widespread the agreement that modern civilization must be characterized as especially secular, then, hindrances to the sustained study of secularization have arisen on diverse intellectual grounds within the traditions of sociological thought. Perhaps only Durkheim set up a strong framework for sustained, penetrating, holistic understanding of the secularizing transformation (Durkheim, [1950] 1957, [1925] 1961, 1973). Durkheim brought to the subject matter more than generalized political and philosophical sponsorship, however. He managed to combine a sensitivity to and respect for the religious dimensions of social life with an interest in the possibilities for transforming institutional arrangements through the invocation of secular principles of reason (Lidz, 1976b; Tiryakian, 1978). Moreover, Durkheim became quite perceptive of the latent effects of religious orientations on doctrines that proclaim their own secularity, effects that are essential not only to the efficacy of many complexes of secular belief but also to the continued vitality of religion in modern life. The loss of Durkheim's balanced overview of the relations between religious and secular orientations—or its failure even to appear, as in Anglo-American social science and, with the important but partial exception of Weber, in the German social and historical disciplines—left sociology without the conceptual means for analyzing with appropriate objectivity the manifold of possible combinations that can emerge among religious and secular elements of moral orientation. Parenthetically, this specific conceptual poverty has been especially prevalent among Marxist and materialist theories, which have tended not only to be insensitive to the institutional effects of religious orientations but also to reify the legitimacy of secular principles of moral belief.

Given the partiality and imbalance of the conceptual schemes that sociology has brought to the study of secularization, it is hardly surprising that the phenomena under examination have not been well synthesized. The field has produced a wide variety of particularized ideas about the nature of secularization, but, aside from an empirically problematic notion of a generalized decline of religiosity, it has produced no broad conception of a fundamental sociocultural transformation. Hence, there have been many discrepancies as to what exactly is under discussion, which have in turn heightened disagreements about the consequences of secularization.

A number of the more common particularized conceptions of secularization may be noted. For some, the separation of church and state, regarded as a narrowing of the scope of legitimate public concerns on the part of the churches, has been a crucial secularizing process. Others refer more narrowly to judgments of a decline in church attendance, of more casual attitudes toward religious rituals, and of lessened discipline in the maintenance of certain religious norms, such as "keeping the Sabbath holy" (Wilson, 1966). Many have stressed a generalized weakening of the prerogative of the priesthood, ministry, or other religious leadership to supervise the moral lives of individuals and the moral qualities of social institutions. Some have emphasized an alleged cultural decline of religious beliefs such that the field of moral judgment appears to have been abandoned to the unregulated play of self-interest, placing the integrity of all normative order in jeopardy (MacIntyre, 1967).

To be sure, secularization has not always been viewed as necessarily a harmful process. Some scholars have seen the decline of religious orientations as hastening an expansion of individual and collective freedoms. Various positivists and rationalists, often naively inattentive to the requisites of moral order, have treated secularization as simply a decline of irrational magic, arbitrary superstition, and parochial traditionalism. The moral authority it undermines is understood, then, as merely particularistic and repressive, and often as narrowly subservient to interests of privileged groups as well. Secularization appears in consequence to bring a liberation of human capacities to be naturally reasonable in social life; that is, to find orientation in science, other rational doctrines, or the "lessons" of practical experience, once the encrustations of tradition have been shattered. If the more "positive" views of secularization seem at first to present a more unified analysis of the process, however, it is also the case that they are less penetrating sociologically. As they do not capture the complexity or intensity of the moral dilemmas involved in secularization, they remain partial and selective.

A new stance may be taken up "in between" the others in that it may view the moral qualities of secularized civilization without either a generalized, principled pessimism over the decline of religion or a lack of self-critical reflection about the grounding of secular morality. The new stance must be independent of the other perspectives in that it cannot accept their common feature, the treatment of secularization as simply a loss of some aspect or another of religiosity.

I will argue that secularization especially in the modern era, must be regarded as more than the displacement of religious factors from the moral or normative regulation of social life. Attention must be given not only to the stripping away of regulation anchored in concern for the sacred but also to a complementary process, the building up of new elements of secular moral doctrine, belief, or culture. The moral aspects of modern civilization may then be seen not simply as functioning in the absence of crucial ethical resources (or repressive constraints) but, and as importantly, as operating on the basis of new kinds of ethical resources and moral constraints.

The process of secularization that has transformed modern civilization began with the Enlightenment. That cultural movement was carried forth with elan and vitality. It originated in an age still intensely religious and in societies still profoundly under the sway of religious forms of moral authority (Becker, 1932). Yet it became a strong counterforce to the moral dominance of religious orientations, delimiting them profoundly where it did not challenge or undermine them (Gay, 1966). The vitality of the Enlightenment derived above all from the moral principles and ideals that it came to pronounce. The conceptions of reason, natural law, progress, humanity, freedom, universal rights, and so forth captured the moral imagination of the age. They gained sufficient control over moral consciences to bring about a certain constriction in the scope of the moral authority of religious orientations. Whatever decline of religious beliefs was brought about occurred largely because of the capacity of secular ideals, with their own vitality, to gain greater, if more specialized, moral respect.

All sociocultural systems contain elements of secular morality. In the broadest comparative perspective, secularization appears not as emerging with the beginnings of the modern era but as an evolving aspect of social life reaching back to the earliest societies. Even the most "primitive" human societies sustain substantial elements of their normative orders on a profane basis. Among the great premodern civilizations, Greece, Rome, and China may be cited as having incorporated secularized components in the universalistic moral orientations with which they broke through older, archaic institutional orders. Late medieval and Renaissance Europe was perhaps distinctive, among the civilizations legitimated by one of the world religions, in the degree to which it tolerated not just secular thought but also secular thought rationally and systematically articulated with basic theology (Troeltsch, 1960). Yet the secularization developed through the Enlightenment has been qualitatively different from that of any previous epoch in human history. The Enlightenment built foundations of a new type for secular moral thought, ones that encompassed a direct transcendence of their own and established a new degree of autonomy from religious culture (Cassirer, 1955). The *philosophes* construed natural law neither as divine nor as subordinate to divine law (as it had been in Aquinas' vision of what Troeltsch called "Christian society"), but as an order intrinsic to human nature and the moral requisites of human social life, very abstractly and universally conceived. The dictates of natural law were to be apprehended sheerly by the exercise of reason, held to be the quintessential human capacity. The moral authority of particular traditions, doctrines, dogmas, or churches was undermined, as man was properly to take his guidance from what was universally and transcendentally reasonable. God continued to be acknowledged by many *philosophes* as the "author" of natural law, but reason could no longer be acknowledged properly to submit to revelation in the effort to envision the ethical or moral bases of human society (Gay, 1966). Reason and natural law together could dictate ultimate moral truths and necessary moral standards to all men in all social conditions. They were universal sources of moral authority beyond which men had no need to appeal in order rightly to found and regulate their societies.

The speculation about the transcendent groundings of moral culture profoundly affected practical thought on social issues. That secular frameworks of moral belief could be set forth in transcendent terms provided a new seriousness, a new level of cultural justification, to judgments about the institutional ordering of society (Palmer, 1959–1964). Secular doctrines addressing the moral responsibilities of conscientious men to undertake the ethical transformation of their societies—that is, ideologies in the modern sense—began to proliferate (Bendix, 1970). Ideologies arose out of ethical concern over the shortcomings, as indicated by transcendent moral standards, of institutions in practically all spheres of society. New energy and especially new autonomy from a "religious ethic" were accorded to disputations over the moral qualities of economic markets and credit transactions, the purposes of the state, authority, and political obligation, the nature of law, constitutions, and the "social contract," the justifications for estates, classes, and social inequalities in general, and the rights and responsibilities accruing to conscientious individuals as members of secular society. Through such ideological debate, the moral foundations of practically all social institutions were newly subjected to thorough, intensive, and continuous examination. Moreover, the rationalistic cast of the transcendent principles of moral judgment predisposed the outcomes of ideological disputations to evolve, albeit unevenly, toward higher levels of rationality. The moral authority to resolve disagreements about the nature of secular institutions came increasingly to be controlled by technically rationalized and largely disenchanted complexes of belief.

Through the cultural workings of the Enlightenment, then, a newly autonomous, thoroughly reconstructed domain of moral belief gained primary control over the problems of the legitimation of social institutions. The new domain of moral culture has become firmly established—in many variations, to be sure—throughout "modern" civilization because of its capacity to provide transcendentally grounded but specialized and intensively elaborated orientations for resolving the moral dilemmas of institutional order. Secularization has encompassed the processes in cultural evolution by which the new kind of moral culture has come to intervene in the relationship of legitimation between patterns of religious belief and the institutional structures of society.[1] The vitality and rationalistic proficiency of secular moral culture has tended to place religious culture in a position of some remove from the ongoing, routine processes of legitimation in modern societies. Of course, it should not be concluded that religious action has thereby been made inconsequential in the ethical and conscientious life of modern civilization. However, it does seem that the nature of modern religious life cannot be fully grasped without understanding of the respects in which issues of institutional legitimation have been largely desacralized or disenchanted and subjected to moral principles that are as profanely practical as they are transcendent.

Commentary on *The Protestant Ethic and the Spirit of Capitalism* (Weber, [1904–1905] 1930) has appropriately concentrated on Weber's analysis of the ways in which ascetic Protestantism evolved toward ethical support of the early growth of modern economic enterprise. Weber himself, however, also emphasized an analytic theme important to our concern with secularization. He maintained that the complex institutions of modern capitalism require ethical regulation framed independently of any directly religious ethic. The term "spirit of capitalism" was introduced to stand for a differentiated, specifically economic body of ethical orientations (Weber, [1904–1950] 1930, chap. 11).

Weber shies away from close analysis of the ethical substance of the twentieth-century spirit of capitalism, especially from treatment of the elements bound up with moral legitimation of market structures and freedom of enterprise. He focuses instead on the historical emergence of the first forms of a pure spirit of capitalism. He concentrates on the prototypical figure of Benjamin Franklin.

Franklin is in several respects a convenient figure for Weber's analytical concerns. He was a self-made man and took great pride in having risen to prominence from a humble background by means of his individual energies, wit, and self-discipline.[2] Franklin himself was aware that his achievements had been fostered to no small extent by his stern, demanding Puritan (Presbyterian) upbringing and by the extraordinary care taken by his father to assure that he would use his talents productively. As profoundly as a Puritan tenaciousness of discipline and devotion to self-improvement remained at the center of his conscience, however, Franklin became more diffusely, essentially, and comfortably engaged "in the world" than a proper ascetic Protestantism could tolerate. He became not a Puritan but a secular figure. If he may properly be regarded as an "epitome of a rising people" (Bercovitch, 1975), he was the representative American, not only for the Puritanism of his background, but also for the flexible, practical creativity he gained by leaving many Puritan restrictions behind him.

Weber's account of the spirit of capitalism, as found in Frankin's writings, stresses that it "has the advantage of being free from all direct relationship to religion" (Weber, [1904–1905] 1930, p. 48). It enjoins hard work, disciplined use of time, systematic exploitation of capital and credit, honesty, concern for one's personal and business reputation, quality of work, strict performance of contractual obligations, and creativity in entrepreneurship, but to no "ultimate" end. Duty in one's calling, hard, systematic work for the sake of sheer productivity, and the earning of money just to control capital become self-standing obligations. The valuation of economic productivity is intrinsic, no more a derivative of higher ends than it is a matter to be questioned. Specific ethical injunctions are established entirely on notions of how they support the productive process. The legitimacy of broadly capitalistic institutions and of work carried out within them is profoundly presumed.

Yet we should not suppose that Franklin or his extraordinary career can be understood simply as the creature of the spirit of capitalism. Franklin's secularity was much more broadly based. From early in his career, Franklin sustained interests quite independent of his concerns for hard work at his craft and success in business. Once he had secured a comfortable wealth, he was content to live off of investments and of partnerships in which he played relatively inactive roles. His energies turned primarily to a complex welter of activities in scientific study and research, civic and political leadership, philanthropy, and what might loosely be called "moral philosophy." He developed a notable public career, for example, as agent for Pennsylvania and other colonies in London, as a leader in intercolonial affairs, as a diplomat, and as an elder statesman, by adhering to a strict ethic of fairness, tact, selflessness, discretion, and utter scrupulousness. In times of severe crises of trust, he managed to project a strong sense of fiduciary responsibility to the public interest by embodying virtues that, although related, did not coincide with qualities enjoined by the spirit of capitalism. Thus, Franklin's ethical views, those realized across the whole range of his creative activities, must be seen as very broadly pragmatic and progressive, not as narrowly utilitarian.[3]

Franklin must be accounted a *philosophe,* an adherent of, contributor to, and publicist for a broad spectrum of the ideals of the Enlightenment. He favored the practical betterment of many dimensions of human society under the guidance of principles and standards of reason. He held to a confident optimism in human capacity for reasoned self-betterment and looked forward to a future of meaningful social progress. Progress certainly involved the material, economic well-being of men but also encompassed political structures devoted to the common welfare, social stratification responsive to the achievements of talent, rationally and justly ordered law, higher levels of popular education, the advancement of knowledge and the practical arts, moral and ethical improvement, and even heightening of the spiritual sensitivities of members of society (Franklin, 1945). The range of Franklin's own practical activities is testimony to the scope and intensity of his secular optimism, to the vitality of his hopes for the pragmatic improvement of society. Yet the central, most profoundly animating concern of his moral outlook, characteristically American, was for the autonomy in conscience and judgment of the individual member of society. The priority he accorded to material well-being and to the gaining of wealth rested on a conviction that economic independence had to be secured before the citizen could assert his autonomy over a meaningful range of his practical affairs. The rationalizing social changes he envisioned as progress in the spheres of politics, stratification, law, and education all heightened the freedom of action of the achieving, conscientious individual.

Franklin's secular moral orientation arose in complex relation to his religious background and to continuing religious sensitivities. His *Autobiography* tells us that Franklin set concern for details of Christian dogma thoroughly behind him in his adolescence. In his mature years, he seems to have given up attending church on the ascetic grounds that he gained more knowledge and moral edification from his personal studies than from sermons that were generally devoted to matters of sectarian dogma. Yet he always remained a contributing member of the Presbyterian Church. He remained capable of enjoining church attendance on members of his family, in part to deny political opponents a possible point of attack on him, but also out of a belief in the benefits of proper attention to wise and pious prayers for "amending the heart" (Franklin, 1945, p. 237). He made it a practice to contribute to the building funds of all new churches in Philadelphia out of a conviction that a thriving spiritual competition would better the moral qualities of the community. It is also apparent that he retained a lively interest in the religious beliefs and practices of the various sects and denominations that he encountered among the diverse people of Pennsylvania. Indeed, it is clear that in his view of religious diversity as "not properly *dividing* but *multiplying*" spiritual energies (p. 233) and in his scruple always to "let others enjoy their religious sentiments, without reflecting on them for those that appeared to me unsupportable and even absurd" (p. 245), he had genuinely arrived at a First Amendment position of toleration. Religious activity was positively valued for its contributions to the moral qualities of the community as well as to the conscientiousness of individuals, yet the community was denied the prerogative of regulating the conduct of its religious subgroups.

In personal religious belief, Franklin is properly considered to have been, in the sense of his own time, a deist. He affirmed a belief, "in one God, creator of the universe," who "governs it by his providence" and "ought to be worshipped" (Franklin, 1945, p. 244). He believed that "the soul of man is immortal, and will be treated with justice in another life respecting its conduct in this [life]." These beliefs he regarded as "the fundamental principles of all sound religion" and in that sense as transcending matters of dogma not founded on reason. Jesus' "system of morals and his religion" he regarded as "the best the world ever saw or is likely to see," yet he doubted Jesus' divinity and perceived "various corrupting changes" of Christian ethics in the church doctrines of his day. On some points, a continuing influence of the Puritan beliefs with which he had been reared is evident, if latent. Thus, he denied that "good works" can "merit heaven" with the observation that one who, "for giving a draught of water to a thirsty person, should expect to be paid with a good plantation, would be modest in his demands, compared with those who think they deserve heaven for the little good they do on earth" (p. 235). Yet the central theme of his ethic is the importance of performing good works. Since God "is infinitely above being benefitted by our services," men can repay the manifold "mercies from God by a readiness to help his other children" (pp. 234–235). The proper service to God consists in "works of kindness, charity, mercy, and public spirit, not holiday keeping, sermon reading or hearing, performing church ceremonies, or making long prayers, filled with flatteries." His dissatisfaction, indeed partial alienation, relative to the churches was that they seemed to distract their adherents from undertaking practical good works that would benefit themselves and other men. The concern of the churches with matters of doctrine, ceremony, and devotion seemed to turn them away from the more important matter of the moral character of their members' public conduct. It was in large part by subordinating the structure of concerns of the churches that Franklin gained the personal conscientious freedom to pursue the range of moral interests in practical secular matters that became constitutive of his career.

For Franklin, a religious conception of good works, emptied of most doctrinal detail and church-related obligation, became the foundation of a wide-ranging concern with secular ethics. The spirit of capitalism in Weber's sense was one principal manifestation of Franklin's zeal for secular good works. His systematic philanthropy, his fiduciary style of political leadership, his devotion to scientific experimentation, and his involvement with the philosophy and belles lettres of the day likewise derived meaning from his very open notion of good works while also resting on thoroughly secular and "enlightened" standards of achievement. The underlying significance of Franklin's career, the element of coherence beneath the dazzling variety of his creative powers, is simply the breadth of his optimistic conviction that social affairs are susceptible to improvement through dedicated use of human reason. His spirit, economic, political, scientific, philanthropic, strove to specify in secular terms details of standards by which men could realize progressive improvements in their respective contributions to social life.

If Franklin has appeared since his own times as the prototype of the American, that is less because of his achievements per se than because of the spirit or ethic they represented.[4] The elaboration of an open-ended, multifaceted, progressive optimism for secular institutions on a foundation of a simple but intense Puritan sense of self-discipline has proved enduringly paradigmatic for American moral culture. It has provided the model for the ways in which Americans have striven to articulate their personal energies into general patterns of institutional cooperation. However, the paradigmatic status of Franklin's ethic has been the result not only of the strength of its component formulations but also of its relations to other developments in American moral culture. That culture passed through a crucial formative stage during Franklin's time. Indeed, the length of his active career made him practically unique in having participated in so many phases of its formative process.

The years reaching from the aftermath of the Great Awakening in the 1740s to the establishment of the institutional framework of the Republic in the 1790s and the early 1800s comprised the fateful era of the foundation of American secular moral culture. The era encompassed, politically, the rise of intense constitutional disputes with Britain, the American Revolution and the founding of the unified Republic, the adoption of the Constitution, the establishment of a newly complex legal order, and the first emergence of legitimation for competitive mass politics. Beneath these tumultuous political events, and in important degree animating them, arose a new moral vision of the nature of society (May, 1976). The ascetic Protestant traditions of most of the American peoples, accentuated by the enthusiasms of the Great Awakening (Heimert, 1966), provided a major source of the new vision. Protestant moralism underpinned the intensity of the dissatisfactions with continued dependence on Britain, viewed as a corrupt "Babylon" (Bailyn, 1967); set forth crucial ideals concerning the nature of societal association, as in the symbolically central notion of "convenant" (Bellah, 1975); and framed the serious innerworldliness that stimulated a newly systematic examination of the possibilities of secular social life (Commager, 1977). However, the major content of the new vision of society derived from a wide-ranging, if selective, delimited, and not entirely trusting, reception of the Enlightenment. Ideas were taken most comfortably from sources that had already combined radical Protestantism with "enlightened" rationalism—for example, the English Commonwealthmen and the Scottish moralists—but also from sources that dealt more directly with problems of the overall design of sociopolitical order, such as Locke and Montesquieu (Bailyn, 1967). Reason and the law of nature were firmly established as the ultimate, transcendent arbiters on issues of how social institutions might best be arranged (Corwin, 1957). Matters such as the separation of powers among the branches of government, the legitimate sources of legal obligations, and the rights and freedoms properly reserved to individuals came to be discussed universalistically within the rationalistic frameworks of enlightened philosophy (Eidelberg, 1968). The law, embodying potential for formally, procedurally rational resolution of normative differences and social disputes, became vastly accentuated as a cultural and institutional matrix for sustaining and developing social order (Pound, 1938). In short, American society had come to be envisioned not only as embodying a special spiritual mission but also as taking shape under the technical guidance of the best of rational philosophy. It was to be a society in which all basic institutions conformed to the reasonable dictates of natural law.

Franklin's ethic[5] addressed the issue of how the individual ought to contribute to the construction of such a progressive society. It spoke to the qualities of self-discipline, hopeful striving, creativity, and civility that were requisites for meaningful participation in a liberally covenanted social order. The ethic cannot be fully understood without some grasp of the many respects in which it enjoins a multidimensional rationalization of society quite in line with the more pragmatic strains of the Enlightenment. The general content of the American Enlightenment cannot all be seen in Franklin's ethic, however. In an age when the primary issues of legitimation concerned the overall design of political institutions and of legal order (Wood, 1969), Franklin was neither lawyer nor political philosopher of the first rank. The works of figures such as Adams, Jefferson, and Madison must be examined, for they deal with the macrosocial issues and were more direct sources of revolutionary and constitutional ideals, if the full secularizing impact of Franklin's ethic is to be judged.

American moral culture has evolved a long way since the era of the founding fathers. One index of the extent of the change is the intellectual embarrassment that generally accompanies any contemporary appeal to principles of natural law. The erosion of belief in natural law under the critiques of Romantic and then relativistic thought (Arieli, 1964) may indeed be a major cause of the relative transparency or invisibility of secular moral culture in our own time. The systematic foundations of our moral beliefs now often go unobserved, and their putative absence is often much lamented. Many observers find not an organized system of moral culture but only a hodgepodge of ideological biases, traditional prejudices, and self-serving interests. Indeed, secularization is frequently understood to imply the complete loss of moral foundations. Yet many who disparage all belief in systematizing principles of natural law as thoroughly naive carry deep convictions about the "inalienability" of certain fundamental rights of all men. Indeed, individualism, progressive optimism, rationalism, the encouragement of achievement, belief in civil freedoms, and other elements of what Hartz termed the "liberal tradition" (Hartz, 1955) have proved massively persistent in the functioning of American moral culture. The continuities of belief—most importantly of philosophical foundations of belief—have been real and important in the moral domain, however transparent.

The core of the American liberal tradition, and a chief factor in its persistence, has been a pattern of accommodative integration between differentiated systems of religious culture and of secular moral culture. The secular morality has sustained a pragmatic, rationalistic, technical manner of orientation. Its focus has remained on the provision of morally authoritative judgment on problems concerning the legitimacy of secular institutions. Its ultimate, transcendent terms have been ones appropriate to stabilizing a system of belief operating in such a specialized fashion. Insofar as problems of justice have assumed aspects of genuine theodicy, the profane traditions of liberal moral thought have tended pragmatically, often rather legalistically, not to attend to them. Yet, liberal morality has also proved able—some delimited, largely fundamentalist episodes aside—to defend its functional autonomy against intrusions of particularistic religious standards. The preservation of the subtle First Amendment safeguards against "establishment," but also maintenance, of secularized ideals of rationality, notably in the law, has been its primary bulwark against resacralization. However, more positive integration between the secular and religious spheres has also been present and has been an important factor in religious toleration of the autonomy of secular moral culture. American secular morality has operated as a major mode of realization of religious interest in the "world," as we have seen for the formative era in connection with Franklin's notion of "good works." Hence, it need neither stand up to widespread, principled religious opposition to its basic frameworks nor strive to sanctify its own transcendent principles in order to find stable grounding in a true theodicy.

The comfortable accommodation between religion and secular morality in America has enabled the liberal tradition to bring the intensity of the ascetic Protestant concern for transformation and perfection into the domain of systematic, rational thought about profane institutions. The secular moral culture has become thoroughly and flexibly oriented to progressive social betterment without becoming impassioned or strident on the issue of secularization itself. Elsewhere in the modern world, however, the Enlightenment and its aftermaths have not always resulted in comparably well-integrated relations between ongoing religious traditions and secular ideologies. A few other types of outcome may be noted in order to indicate how profoundly modern societies have been affected by the relations they have established between the religious and secular domains of culture.

A first type is characterized by deeply seated, enduring tension between an institutionalized secular morality and an institutionalized religious tradition. Modern France, oriented partly in terms of the secularism of the revolutionary tradition and partly in terms of Roman Catholicism, may be taken as a prototype. Neither orientation has been able fully to supplant the either—that is, not in a stable way, over a long period—and, historically, neither orientation has accepted more than grudgingly and partially the basic legitimacy of the other. Moral judgments developed in terms of one moral system have tended to generate principled opposition from judgments made in terms of the other. The resulting weakness in the moral authority of both belief systems has prevented the society from finding a culturally unified and socially unifying basis of legitimation. Over the long run, France has tended to oscillate substantially between the religious and secular orientations in developing its grounds of legitimation.[6] It appears that the range of the oscillation has been dampened somewhat in recent generations, at least as compared with the nineteenth century. The difference in orientation between the Fifth Republic and the Fourth Republic does not seem so great as the obverse difference between the Third Republic and the Empire of Louis Bonaparte, for example. Perhaps common evaluation themes lying deep within Western traditions have gradually been accentuated through the competitive relations between religious and secular orientations as partially unifying and stabilizing grounds of accommodation.

Many other nations, perhaps especially on the fringes of the European system and in the "underdeveloped" areas, must confront the problem of establishing patterns of legitimation out of cultural materials that are still more fundamentally divergent. Almost everywhere in the contemporary world, impetus toward "modernization" has been bound up, albeit often complexly and ambivalently, with reception of one strain or another of Enlightenment rationalism (Lidz, 1976a, 1976b). A problem of legitimation then typically crystallizes over the issue of the relations between "enlightened" moral orientations and the indigenous moral traditions, which are at least predominantly religious. Forthright and uncompromising attachment to modernizing Enlightenment rationalism tends to breed profound and disturbing alienation from the indigenous traditions and generally from the nonelite masses (Bellah, 1965). Thorough attachment to the sustenance of the national traditions often carries the cost of a loss of moral leverage for progressive, rationalizing social change. Hence there is a structured possibility for oscillation somewhat in the French mold. Western enlightened rationalism is affirmed until the discontents of alienation breed a reaffirmation of indigenous tradition. Then traditionalism is maintained until the discontents of social stagnation, or at least of an absence of an ideal, universalistic program of change, breed a new "fashion" for rationalistic orientations. However, there are alternatives to the oscillatory pattern. The "meaningless" oscillation may be eschewed for a systematically antirationalistic traditionalism (or less extremely what Bellah (1965) has called a neotraditionalism providing a limited scope, but no more, to secular rationalism) or, quite the opposite, an ardent secularism basically intolerant of religion.

A second type, then, consists in just such an ardent secularism, perhaps best exemplified in the intolerant Marxism established in Soviet Russia and, somewhat differently, in China. The secular morality, for example, Marxist doctrine, is accorded a formal monopoly over matters of legitimation. Some freedoms may be granted to individuals and social groups of limited size and scope of activity to preserve traditional orientations, perhaps especially religious ones that do not challenge the established doctrine with ideological claims to "rational" status. However, the formal legitimation of the law and of all social structures having public importance rests entirely on the system of secular moral belief. Stringent repression may be undertaken to prevent public challenge to the moral doctrines of the legitimating ideology. A great deal of energy may be devoted to sustaining clear, direct, and public consistency in the ideology itself and, secondarily, among the ways in which it is invoked to legitimate practical policies on public matters (Schurmann, 1966). Indeed, the efforts to demonstrate doctrinal consistency before the public may impart a "fundamentalistic" simplicity and rigidity to the ideology. Moreover, the secular belief system tends to come under pressure to provide meaningful orientation across ever broader ranges of morally problematic activities, pressure it generally cannot resist without giving up its claim to a formal monopoly of the grounds of legitimate judgment. Hence, its secular specialization and its organization specifically on standards of rationality tend to be lost. A process of sacralization may set in. The central principles and ideals of the ideology may be placed above the possibility of rational criticism, and they may be viewed as sources not just of practical legitimation but of truly ultimate resolution of problems of meaning. Thus the secular moral doctrine tends to become engaged in a religious dimension of action and is thereby transformed into a secular or political religion. It may take on much of the dogmatic rigidity of the more systematized premodern belief systems but tends to retain a thoroughly modern activism and innerworldliness. It continues to accord an importance to matters of the secular organization of society unknown before the Enlightenment.

A third type emerges where an antirationalistic traditionalism—or, at least a neotraditionalism quite distrustful of universalistic rationalism—becomes predominant. In the extreme cases, a xenophobic fascism may arise out of the search for orientational stability within indigenous traditions. Milder efforts to affirm a traditional religious ethic in a diffuse fashion that restricts greatly the autonomous functioning of Enlightenment or secularized moral culture have been more common. They have provided perhaps the principal ethical foundation for conservatism in the parts of the developing world that have had established traditions grounded in one of the world religions (Lidz, 1976a, 1976b). Latin American societies in relation to Roman Catholicism, Middle Eastern and Asian societies in relation to Islam, and Theravada Buddhist societies have perhaps been most prone to sustaining traditionalism in this mode. Black African societies have for the most part lacked religious traditions that can provide sufficiently inclusive integration and sufficiently flexible legitimation to make such an exclusive, principled traditionalism viable. The societies that have attempted to institutionalize a thorough-going traditionalism have generally sacrificed the capacity of rational secular culture to absorb flexibly the changes induced by international social and cultural forces. Societies that have formulated a more qualified and adaptable neotraditionalism, perhaps notably Japan in the years since World War II, have managed to accommodate substantial components of universalistic secular moral culture. They differ from the liberal societies—for example, the "Anglo-Saxon democracies" or even India—principally in that the articulations between religion and secular morality are substantially more rigid.

I have discussed secularization as an "evolutionary universal" (Parsons, 1964) of modern societies. I have tried to show that a view of secularization as simply the decline of religion and the loss of ethical foundations fails to account for the empirical complexities of the phenomenon. Secularization has everywhere in the modern world engaged fundamental moral issues and has in many societies resulted in actual enhancement of capacities to resolve ethical issues in an orderly way. To be sure, secularization may bring a certain shallowness in addressing problems of meaning. That aspect of the phenomenon may be regarded as a phase of the disenchantment of the social world (Weber, [1922] 1963). If it appears to be a profanation, we should also note that it is a condition of rationalization, which may bring diverse human benefits.

As I have indicated, societies have responded to the issue of rational secularization posed by Enlightenment culture in varied ways. I have discussed the liberal response of mutual accommodation between religious and secular complexes of culture most fully because it seems to embody the most complete realization of the evolutionary universal. It appears to impart the greatest capacity for stability and continuity, on the one hand, and for rationality and flexibility, on the other hand. Yet, we may ask, in conclusion, "What is the future of religion in societies firmly secularized in the liberal sense?"

Much as modern religion has had to adapt to the rise of scientific culture, it has had also to adapt to the establishment of secular moral culture. In both cases, it has had to acknowledge the primacy of other complexes or subsystems of culture, differently specialized, whenever certain kinds of practical problems are raised. We can expect that there will be repeated outbreaks of "warfare" between religion and secular ideologies, even liberal ideologies, as there have been recurrent "wars" between science and religion. However, we may expect the "warfare" to be limited, because of the extensive integration that has been established between religion and secular morality. Indeed, it may be suggested that the liberal pattern of cultural specialization, with the practical problems of legitimation being alienated to secular moral culture, may hold out some opportunities for religion.

The rise of secular morality as culture specialized around the provision of rational orientation toward issues of legitimation need not involve a removal of religious concerns from the social world. It need only imply their withdrawal from routine engagement in matters of legitimation. Hence it may open up new possibilities for selective incursion into issues of legitimation guided by judgments about when spiritually critical contributions may be made most effectively. The practical entanglements of religious ethics in public matters may be reserved for occasions when problems of genuine theodicy have become truly acute.

The routine functioning of religion may then turn toward the more purely spiritual. It has been noted that modern religion has apparently been evolving toward greater self-consciousness of the symbolic multidimensionality of belief, toward greater concentration on "existential" problems, and toward greater personalization of ultimate commitments (Bellah, 1970; Lidz, 1972). It may be that these aspects of spiritualization are responses to reduced needs for codified dogma and uniform belief now that issues of the social and moral order can be resolved in the secular domain. If participation in overtly religious activities is tending to concentrate more sharply on life transitions, life crises, and times of personal difficulty or ethical challenge, a proper interpretation might well acknowledge that religious traditions still provide active meaning when meaning is most sorely needed.

In sum, secularization has vastly affected the sociocultural environment of religious action. It has not necessarily affected the inner vitality of our diverse religious traditions. Manifold opportunities remain for the religious spirit to animate social life, and it may be finding ways of doing so with renewed concentration.

Notes

1. It may be helpful to the reader if I outline the relations among key terms introduced to this point in the analysis somewhat more systematically. I am arguing that, through the effects of the Enlightenment as a cultural movement, secular moral thought gained a new grounding in a transcendent modality. By this, I mean that secular moral thought came to be derived from free-standing or autonomous principles and premises that were not formally derived from religious beliefs, although a variety of meaningful symbolic interconnections obviously remained. Moreover, the principles and premises were applied to a wide, indefinite range of substantive moral domains and were accorded moral authority independent of their particular implications in any domain or under any specific practical circumstances. Their transcendent status was itself sustained through a special moral respect that they came to be granted, a special seriousness of belief devoted to them. Yet they were not treated as sacred in the sense of religious belief. They have been regarded—except when resacralized as in such cases as Marxist doctrine, where it provides a formally exclusive foundation of belief and legitimation—as themselves parts of the profane world. Most importantly, they have been treated as subject to rational criticism—indeed, even principles and standards of reason have generally been regarded as profane by this crucial criterion in the liberal traditions of moral thought. For this understanding of the nature of secularization, see Durkheim ([1925] 1961, 1973) and Lidz (1976a, 1976b). Note that there are important parallels between the transcendent terms of secular morality and the special status of the rational premises of methodology in scientific culture. Scientific premises also transcend particular bodies of scientific knowledge while yet remaining profane and subject to rational criticism (Whitehead, 1947).

The transcendent grounding of secular moral belief enabled it to develop as a subsystem of culture with a new degree of systematic differentiation and practical autonomy from religious culture. In the analytical terms of Parson's action theory, secular moral beliefs have the formal standing of the integrative sector of culture while religious beliefs are treated as the pattern maintenance subsystem of culture. The consequences of the enhancement of this specific differentiation within the cultural system are discussed more fully in Lidz (1976b).

Parsons himself has addressed some of the problems of secularization in recent essays (1971a, 1974). He has stressed the importance of the Reformation as a source of modern secularization and has highlighted many features of the ethically serious inner-worldliness of modern value orientations. He has also emphasized the basic compatibility between values of serious engagement in worldly institutions and certain genuinely religious patterns of belief, notably in the tradition of Protestantism. The present discussion differs from his analysis chiefly in stressing the importance of the Enlightenment as a watershed of cultural change between the Reformation and the contemporary era and in suggesting that greater differentiation between the pattern maintenance and integrative subsystems of culture arose from effects of the Enlightenment.

2. This theme first appears in the opening paragraph of the *Autobiography* and reappears many times.

3. Weber actually speaks of Franklin as a utilitarian or, at least, says that "all Franklin's moral attitudes are colored with utilitarianism" (Weber, [1904–1905] 1930, p. 52). Aside from a few brief, unsystematic passages in early writings, I find nothing that appears to me utilitarian in a technical sense; that is, views human action and social relations systematically through the perspective of utilitarian categories of understanding. Moreover, it seems to me that the principal moral thrust of Franklin's ethic approaches a comprehensive pragmatism, with an economic stress, more closely than the utilitarian outlook of, say, Bentham.

4. On the status of Franklin's ethic as a prototype of the American ethic and on its practical impact on socialization in America, see Mark Twain (1875, p. 211). He writes, "The subject of this memoir was of a vicious disposition and early prostituted his talents to the invention of maxims and aphorisms calculated to inflict suffering on the rising generation of all subsequent ages. His simplest acts, also, were contrived with a view to their being held up for the emulation of boys who might otherwise have been happy."

5. The secularity of Franklin's ethic can be noted in the system of moral bookkeeping that he adopted and Weber especially noted. The virtues on which Franklin scored his daily conduct for a period in his early adulthood were temperance, silence, order, resolution, frugality, industry, sincerity, justice, moderation, cleanliness, tranquility, chastity, and humility. As Franklin discusses them in his *Autobiography* (1945, pp. 119–122), only the last listed virtue seems to have been treated in a directly religious fashion, although it is true that their meanings in each case have symbolic connection with centuries of Christian thought.

6. I have taken the notion of oscillation from Pitts (1963) and Clark (1973), although I believe that the analysis of the secular and religious basis of the oscillation is my own formulation.

References

Arieli, Y. *Individualism and Nationalism in American Ideology.* Cambridge, Mass.: Harvard University Press, 1964.

Bailyn, B. *The Ideological Origins of the American Revolution.* Cambridge, Mass.: Harvard University Press, 1967.

Becker, C. L. *The Heavenly City of the Eighteenth Century Philosophers.* New Haven, Conn.: Yale University Press, 1932.

Bellah, R. N. *Religion and Progress in Modern Asia.* New York: Free Press, 1965.

Bellah, R. N. *Beyond Belief.* New York: Harper & Row, 1970.

Bellah, R. N. *The Broken Covenant.* New York: Seabury Press, 1975.

Bendix, R. *Embattled Reason: Essays on Social Knowledge.* New York: Oxford University Press, 1970.

Bercovitch, S. *The Puritan Origins of the American Self.* New Haven, Conn.: Yale University Press, 1975.

Cassirer, E. *The Philosophy of the Enlightenment.* Boston: Beacon Press, 1955.

Clark, T. N. *Prophets and Patrons: The French University and the Emergence of the Social Sciences.* Cambridge, Mass.: Harvard University Press, 1973.

Commager, H. S. *The Empire of Reason.* New York: Doubleday, 1977.

Corwin, E. S. *The "Higher Law" Background of American Constitutional Law.* Ithaca, N.Y.: Cornell University Press, 1957.

Durkheim, E. *Professional Ethics and Civic Morals.* London: Routledge & Kegan Paul, 1957. (Originally published 1950.)

Durkheim, E. *Moral Education.* New York: Free Press, 1961. (Originally published 1925.)

Durkheim, E. *On Morality and Society.* (R. N. Bellah, Ed.). Chicago: University of Chicago Press, 1973.

Eidelberg, P. *The Philosophy of the American Constitution.* New York: Free Press, 1968.

Franklin, B. *A Benjamin Franklin Reader.* (N. G. Goodman, Ed.). New York: Crowell, 1945.

Gay, P. *The Enlightenment: An Interpretation; The Rise of Modern Paganism.* New York: Knopf, 1966.

Hartz, L. *The Liberal Tradition in America.* New York: Harcourt Brace Jovanovich, 1955.

Heimert, A. *Religion and the American Mind: From the Great Awakening to the Revolution.* Cambridge, Mass.: Harvard University Press, 1966.

Lidz, V. "Comments on the Religiosity of Contemporary Cultural Movements." *Sociological Inquiry, 42* (2), 1972, 161–168.

Lidz, V. *The Functioning of Secular Moral Culture: Steps Toward A Systematic Analysis.* Unpublished doctoral dissertation, Harvard University, 1976a.

Lidz, V. "Secular Moral Culture and the Intercivilizational Foundations of Contemporary Societies." *Bulletin of the International Society for Comparative Study of Civilizations,* 1976b, Spring.

MacIntyre, A. *Secularization and Moral Change.* London: Oxford University Press, 1967.

May, H. F. *The Enlightenment in America.* New York: Oxford University Press, 1976.

Palmer, R. R. *The Age of Democratic Revolution.* 2 vols. Princeton, N. J.: Princeton University Press, 1959–1964.

Parsons, T. "Evolutionary Universals in Society." *American Sociological Review,* 1964, *29*(3), 339–357.

Parsons, T. "Belief, Unbelief, and Disbelief." In R. Caporale and A. Grumelli (Eds.), *The Culture of Unbelief.* Berkeley: University of California Press, 1971a.

Parsons, T. *The System of Modern Societies.* Englewood Cliffs, N.J.: Prentice-Hall, 1971b.

Parsons, T. "Religion in Postindustrial America: The Problem of Secularization." *Social Research*, 1974, *41* (2), 193–225.

Pitts, J. "Continuity and Change in Bourgeois France." In S. Hoffman and others (Eds.), *In Search of France.* Cambridge, Mass.: Harvard University Press, 1963.

Pound, R. *The Formative Era of American Law.* Boston: Little, Brown, 1938.

Schurmann, F. *Ideology and Organization in Communist China.* Berkeley: University of California Press, 1966.

Tiryakian, E. A. "Emile Durkheim." In T. Bottomore and R. A. Nisbet (Eds.), *History of Sociological Analysis.* New York: Basic Books, 1978.

Troeltsch, E., *The Social Teachings of the Christian Churches.* New York: Harper & Row, 1960.

Twain, M. "The Late Benjamin Franklin." In *Sketches New and Old.* New York: Harper and Brothers, 1875.

Weber, M. *The Protestant Ethic and the Spirit of Capitalism.* New York: Scribner's, 1930. (Originally published 1904–1905.)

Weber, M. *The Sociology of Religion.* Boston: Beacon Press, 1963. (Originally published 1922.)

Weber, M. *Economy and Society.* 3 vols. New York: Bedminster Press, 1968. (Originally published 1922.)

Whitehead, A. N. *Science and the Modern World.* New York: Pocket Books, 1947.

Wilson, B. R. *Religion in Secular Society.* London: Watts, 1966.

Wood, G. S. *The Creation of the American Republic.* Chapel Hill: University of North Carolina Press, 1969.

Women in Religious Symbolism and Organization

Religions bind people in groups sharing certain moral perspectives that constitute their ultimate standards of evaluation and interpretation. Implicit or explicit in the religious interpretations of life and death (origin and destiny, success and failure, good and evil) is some notion of human nature and of the relationship of the sexes. Such notions, in historically changing ways, influence the social order. This chapter will focus on part of that process: on how people, gathered in religious solidarity, have used women as symbols, treated women because of existing symbols, and allocated women to roles both within the religious system and in the wider society. It will further explore the question of what the emancipation of women in general has to do with the status of women in religion.

At the present time in Western and Middle Eastern societies, and to a growing degree in Asiatic and African societies, women are expressing a growing and shared awareness that their subordination to men in top decision-making roles in the state and the economy is strikingly similar to their position in the household and religious organization and that in fact the different role sets vary together. This connection needs to be examined, explained, and challenged.

Women have always worked, and some have worked very hard. This is true also of men. Today, over half the women in America work outside the home, three quarters of these working full time. This is a continuing pattern, not a response to an emergency as it was during World War II. The image of the non-working mother, created in the nineteenth century as the main symbol of the new upward mobility and conspicuous consumption (Veblen, [1899] 1934), lost its power in 1963 with the publication of Betty Friedan's *The Feminine Mystique*. This monograph marked a turning point. It exposed the propaganda base idealizing the American woman as a suburban housewife who does not have to work. And it gave impetus to the third American feminist movement.[1] Even when women work full time outside the home, however, it is apparent that housekeeping, child care, and the children's education remain their primary responsibilities. Men continue to manage the state, production, and service systems even when the productive force is made up predominantly of women. As professional workers, women specialize in the service industry, but even here top management is held by men. Even the socialist states, despite their good intentions to divide the labor differently, have only succeeded better in incorporating women into the labor force. They have not yet achieved effective partnership in sharing domestic chores in such a way that married women cease to be doubly burdened. As a result, there are no more women ruling in the Soviet Union or China than there are in the West. Top management remains intentionally male. Evidence from thoughtful review of anthropological materials (Gough, 1972), as well as from such modern experiments as the kibbutz (Talmon, 1972), lead serious thinkers to conclude that, as long as the measure of excellence is quantity of production for gain, this division of labor will continue and, with it, the effective claim to male dominance.

Such a goal and relationship, to persist, need celebration and reinforcement. Religion provides these. Given its goals and the roles it expects people to play in achieving them, a management system also needs to incorporate affirming beliefs and symbols.

What managers want to achieve is related to what people believe they can achieve. It is necessary, then, that management goals be associated with supporting definitions of human nature and destiny. This is why those in power control the operative images of God. As long as only men are in power, the symbols of God will reflect their dominance. Recent decisions rejecting the ordination of women to the priesthood rest on the rationale that women are not made in God's image (O'Faolain and Martines, 1973). That rationale is more generally accepted than many realize (relatively few reflecting much today on images of God), and its influence is felt on many decisions besides the ordination of women (Morgan, 1977).

What religion celebrates, however, it celebrates for its relevance to ultimate survival. When a given role appears on reflection to be irrelevant to survival, religious commitment to it dies; when a given relationship appears finally irrelevant, the religious symbols embodying it become meaningless. As the current feminist movement brings people in increasing numbers into the process of reflection, this reevaluation of role and symbol is taking place. Like the previous movements, the present movement includes a significant component of religiously committed advocates and participants. However, although dependent on the previous movements, many factors make the current women's movement different from them: (1) the large size of the world population base; (2) the increasing availability of professional education for women; (3) the immediacy of international media coverage; (4) the breakdown in the universality of traditional religious symbol systems; (5) the availability and effectiveness of methods of birth control, as well as the political and ethical debate about their uses; (6) the changing structures and functions of Catholic religious congregations of women internationally; (7) the shift of youth potential to the Third World nations; (8) exposure, through educational systems, of the use of power by production and distribution interests through national governments; (9) the potential for leisure for men and women alike, in view of the technological advances in production systems; (10) women's manifest and felt need for a new division of domestic, communal, and societal labor, independent of sexual definitions of human capacity; (11) the United Nations' recognition of human rights as rights independent of pay scales and civil rights, and (12) the current ideological and religious implications of ordination and marriage.

In sociological perspective, the issue today is not whether earlier periods of history or different cultures allowed the free access of women to the role of leadership in religious worship, the evidence for which is not persuasive (O'Faolain and Martines, 1973). Rather, these are the issues: What basic trends, if any, in the current struggle around changing roles of women in society indicate a shift from the patriarchal family model as the basis of public life? What shift, if any, is observable in religious symbolization that would legitimate the equalizing of women's and men's roles in public life? What relationship, if any, exists between the popularity of sociobiology—with its affirmation of patriarchy on the basis of animal sociology—and the theological debates about the ordination of women in the churches? Finally, what relationship holds among images of God, role relationships of power in religious and other social systems, and the interpersonal division of labor in procreation systems?

In the following section, I will present the function of symbols from several different but related perspectives—those of Clifford Geertz, Emile Durkheim, Sigmund Freud, Paul Ricoeur, and Mary Douglas—in order to examine the subtle functions of symbols and to point out a difference between men's and women's perspectives on them.

The Function of Symbols

The interrelationship of the cultural, political, and economic order is fragile at any time. In times of crisis—always times both of danger and opportunity—the old ideologies and their symbols do not have the power to hold that order together in a way that can guarantee its continuing to operate as expected. In his novel, *Things Fall Apart* (1959), Achebe demonstrates persuasively that the collapse of one societal system by no means guarantees the development of one to replace it; but collective symbols are needed to inspire people to solidarity in action. Symbols stand for conceptions of the desirable, the feared and the inevitable that for a substantial segment of the population are morally compelling and economically and politically feasible. They are a part of reality that people can use as a frame for action (Berger and Luckmann, 1967). Loss of symbols means loss of affective meaning, and loss of affective meaning generates anxiety. Symbols legitimate a certain definition of the situation influencing the way people are treated, and the way people are treated in turn reinforces the definition and the symbols. Treatment and symbol borrow authority from each other (Geertz, 1966).

In his effort to explain why the suicide rate remains constant over a period of time in modern industrial societies, Durkheim ([1895] 1951) postulated that even modern societies, bonded as they are by functional interdependence, have a collective conscience or consciousness. He meant that, despite greater personal freedom and relative independence of traditional values, modern societies as much as traditional ones are bound together by some common symbols expressing affective beliefs about right order. Because they are created by the members of a society in interaction with one another, symbol systems are passed along by them and are reflective of the social order. Symbols remain constitutive both of personal consciousness and of society. In making this observation, Durkheim (p. 312) is affirming the essential role of religion, as of the arts, in social systems: "Religion is, in a word, the set of symbols by which society becomes conscious of itself; it is the characteristic way of thinking of collective existence." This does not mean that the existing symbolic representations are pleasing to the members or that they bind them to joyful consensus. They may bind some in joy and others in angry but powerless submission.

Symbols represent concepts, the concepts being the meanings of the symbols. As distinct from other symbols, religious symbols define the cosmic order. All religions affirm something about the general order of existence. For the Navajo, nature is enormously powerful and terribly dangerous. For the Calvinist, it was a challenge to be overcome by human initiative. Depending on the idea of nature it represents, the symbol induces corresponding moods and motivations. Reinforced by songs and rhythms in religious ceremony and guided by authority, idea and symbol encourage action. The very enactment of the ritual reinforces for religious people acceptance of the uniquely realistic dimensions of belief. While their persuasive power increases and declines according to social conditions and their meanings can change with time, the traditional symbols nevertheless retain a powerful hold on collective and individual behavior.

The most basic symbol is the symbol of God. In the West, God is still usually symbolized as the father of a family. Across many societies, and across classes of the same society, woman is a symbol of servant. In finding the oedipal myth central to his culture, Freud discovered a way of thinking that made sense of the social order of his day. It entered into socialization as a basic anxiety because it was, and still is, a myth for preserving that societal structure (Freud, [1928] 1959). Freud treated neurotic women by helping them adapt to their servant role. This is social reality, but a reality providing models for and models of what women now experience as oppression (Geertz, 1966). Those not represented in the symbols of a society or those represented as servants (even respected servants) will be treated as nonpersons in that society. Women cannot see their destiny in this setting today. Just as Mary Daly (1973) asks what is beyond God the father, many women are looking beyond institutionalized myths such as the Oedipus story that, in explaining their humanity, reserve to men the right to make decisions.

What the bases of symbols are, what the God symbol stands for, and who manipulates the meaning of symbols are questions that remain after a review of the analytic literature, because anthropologists and sociologists are in disagreement on these issues. Lévy-Bruhl claims that symbols have no referent but themselves; for Marx, social class is the basis; for Durkheim, it is society; for Eliade, varieties of cosmic rhythms (Eliade, 1976). The fourteenth international conference on the sociology of religion, held in 1977 in Strasbourg, addressed the topic of symbol and social class. In a paper entitled "The Symbolic Structure of Action" (1977), Paul Ricoeur argued for a distinction between constituent symbolism, which is necessary for action, and representative symbolism, which is independent of action. Representative symbolism enables a social group to represent itself as a group and so has its place in that imaginary collective entity called *ideology*; it is the symbolism characteristic of religion. In supplying an image of the social order, religious ideology performs an integrating social function; in concealing other ways in which the social order might be represented, it also performs a masking function. The masking function is easily exploited by the powers that be, Ricoeur explains, in which case religion becomes Marx's opium of the people. But, unlike Marx, he argues that the masking function is not religion's only function. It is a prop of collective identity, a necessary principle of affirmation, although it must be prevented from becoming, in the hands of the powerful, a principle of deceit and enslavement. Ricoeur claimed that we do not yet know why a social group feels the necessity to represent itself by means of symbolism on the ideological level.

Mary Douglas adds another element to the analysis of symbols; namely, their rootedness in the natural. The process of social interaction, she claims, constructs the typifications and recipes that make up social reality. Dimensions of time and space are socially constructed; in fact, the whole of physical nature must be endowed with its reality in this way. The same applies to the symbols by which we interpret the roles of women. Certain social interactions lead to certain definitions of reality. "Human thought serves human interests and therefore carries in itself at any given moment the social configurations of that time and place," Douglas (1973b, p. 11) points out, adding that "taxonomic systems bear heavy loads, even ones with so few categories as male and female." In *Natural Symbols* (1973a, p. 18), she argues convincingly that "the dimensions of social life govern the fundamental attitudes to spirit and matter," distinct cosmologies sustaining distinct social organizations. Inevitably, a shift in social organization entails a shift in cosmology:

> Anyone who finds himself living in a new social condition must, by the logic of what we have seen, find that the cosmology he used in his old habitat no longer works. We should try to think of cosmology as a set of categories that are in use. It is like a lens which brings into focus and makes bearable the manifold challenge of experience. It is not a hard carapace which the tortoise has to carry forever, but something very flexible and easily disjointed. Spare parts can be fitted and adjustments made without much trouble. Occasionally a major overhaul is necessary to bring

the obsolete set of views into focus with new times and
new company. This is conversion. But most of the
time adjustments are made so smoothly that one is
hardly aware of the shifts of angle until they have
developed an obvious disharmony between past and
present. Then a gradual conversion that has been
slowly taking place has to be recognized. Inevitably, this recognition of a new viewpoint produces a revulsion against dead ritual [Douglas, 1973a, pp.
179–180].

We have examined five perspectives on symbol, all five those
of social scientists. Of the five, Douglas alone recognizes the shape
that the new symbolic forms must sacralize. Of the five, Douglas
alone is a woman.

Women in Religious Symbolism

Rosemary Ruether (1977) has produced a little study providing a panoramic view of the idealized women in religious worship—images ranging from the fertile mother goddess of pre-
biblical times, producing the world egg that fertilizes itself, to the
Greek virgin goddess Athena, pure wisdom emerging from the
head of Zeus; from the Canaanite goddesses of nature to an Israel
portrayed as the bride of her male god of history; from Isis, the
Egyptian goddess of wisdom, to the idealized virgin of the biblical
wisdom literature; from Mary as mother of Christ, mother of God,
madonna, mother goddess and provider of the harvest, to Mary as
virgin, wisdom, pure nature, immaculately conceived, assumed
into heaven, protectress of the monastery. Increasingly, it is not the
actual woman who is celebrated, not the married woman, but the
virgin; not the material provider, but the spiritual ideal. The
former becomes more human, the latter more divine.

This idealizing of the virgin, already developing in Christianity at the time of the Reformation, was a factor in the reformers'
total rejection of celibate life. Although both Calvin and Luther
accepted the doctrine of Mary as mother of God, mariology declined in the Protestant nations of their day. In Protestantism, no
woman symbol would be revered. Moreover, since the recent Sec-

ond Vatican Council, Roman Catholicism has seen the same decline in mariology. In each case, Protestant and Catholic, the decline in the symbolic uses of the feminine in religion is associated with an enhancement of women's actual role and with increased interest in communal models of holiness outside of formal religious institutions. And in each case it occurs as part of a wider social movement—the movement, in the sixteenth century, from monarchy to democracy and, in the twentieth century, from monopoly capitalism to socialism.

Religion's idealized women are available to men "as the nurturers and servants of a selfhood that can actively appear only in males" (Ruether, 1977, p. 79). As a religious symbol, Ruether argues, woman has connoted passivity, dependence, subordination, and self-negation, a symbolization that effectively rules out any relationship calling for independence and self-esteem. While the symbols idealizing women were being fashioned, making it possible for men to realize attractive aspirations, theologians were systematically dissociating real women from their own spiritual aspirations by finding in religion legitimation for the subordination of women to men.

In their documentary collection of Western theological treatises on the subject, O'Faolain and Martines (1973) could find none that portrayed women in God's image. Some examples follow of what they and others have found. In the fourth century, Augustine deliberated the meaning of the Hebrew record of creation in Genesis. "We must notice," he wrote, "how that which the apostle says, that not the woman but the man is the image of God, is not contrary to that which is written in Genesis, 'God created man; in the image of God created He him; male and female created He them.' . . . For this text says that human nature itself, which is complete (only) in both sexes, was made in the image of God, and it does not separate the woman from the image of God which it signifies. . . . The woman together with her husband is the image of God, so that the whole substance may be one image. But when she is referred to separately in her quality of helpmate, which regards the woman herself alone, then she is not the image of God. But as regards the man alone, he is the image of God as fully and completely as when the woman too is joined with him" (quoted in

O'Faolain and Martines, p. 130). Eight centuries previously, Aristotle had described procreation in this way: "The male provides the 'form' and 'principle' of the movement, the female provides the body, in other words, the material" (quoted in O'Faolain and Martines, p. 19). An excerpt from the Koran, written three centuries after Augustine, illustrates a normative application of these analytical principles: "With regard to her children, God commands you to give the male the portion of two females. . . . Half of what your wife leaves shall be yours, if they have not issue . . . and your wives shall have a fourth part of what you leave, if you have no issue" (quoted in O'Faolain and Martines, p. 114).

Aquinas discusses the distinction in the thirteenth century: "The image of God in its principal signification, namely, the intellectual nature, is found both in man and in woman. Hence after the words, 'To the image of God He created him,' it is added, 'Male and female He created them' (Genesis 1:27). Moreover, it is said 'them' in the plural. . . . lest it should be thought that both sexes were united in one individual. But, in a secondary sense, the image of God is found in man and not in woman: For man is the beginning and end of woman, as God is the beginning and end of every creature" (quoted in O'Faolain and Martines, 1973, p. 131).

Luther, although affirming women in many ways, still believed that they existed to keep house and to bear children (O'Faolain and Martines, 1973, p. 197). Calvin, objecting strongly to women as ministers, wrote, in the *Institutes* (quoted in O'Faolain and Martines, p. 202), "The custom of the church, before St. Augustine was born, may be elicited first of all from Tertullian, who held that no woman in church is allowed to speak, baptize or make offerings; this in order that she may not usurp the functions of men, let alone those of priests. It is a mockery to allow women to baptize. Even the Virgin Mary was not allowed this."

This image of women as the servants of men, as men are the servants of God, continues into modern times and is taken up by the philosophers, as in this excerpt from Rousseau's *Emile* (quoted in O'Faolain and Martines, 1973, p. 247), where the critical question of education for women is being considered: "Men and women are made for each other, but their mutual dependence is not equal. . . . We could survive without them better than they could without us. In order for them to have what they need . . . we must give it to them, we must want to give it to them, we must consider them deserving of it. They are dependent on our feelings, on the price we put on their merits, on the value we set on their attractions and on their virtues. . . . Thus women's entire education should be planned in relation to men. To please men, to be useful to them, to win their love and respect, to raise their children and care for them as adults, counsel and console them, make their lives sweet and pleasant. These are women's duties in all ages and these are what they should be taught from childhood."

These distinctions do not decline with modern writers. Writing in the early twentieth century and recognized by many as the most important Protestant thinker since Schleiermacher, Karl Barth sees it as part of the Christian vocation to affirm the differences between masculinity and femininity. Clark and Richardson (1977, p. 242) note that Barth "criticizes sharply all attempts to overcome the border between maleness and femaleness; in fact, he sees in such efforts blasphemous attempts to aspire to divinity." Thus, in discussing the creation story of Genesis, Barth writes (quoted in Clark and Richardson, p. 242) that the text means that the woman "in her being and existence belongs to the man. She is ordained to be his helpmeet. She would not be woman if she had even a single possibility apart from being man's helpmeet." And, pressing the distinction, he adds (p. 242), "Accepting one's maleness or femaleness is only the first step in maintaining a correct sexual ethic. Even within the relation which God has ordained and from which neither male nor female must flee, a further command is given: man is to be superordinate, woman subordinate. Man is A and woman is B, man is the initiator, woman the follower." This pattern, Barth thinks, has the sanction of the New Testament. To be fair to him, Clark and Richardson advise (p. 242), "We must note his own emphasis; the woman is not subordinating herself to the man so much as she is to the order God has established, an order to which man also subordinates himself." The same theology, as we shall see, was affirmed in 1977 by the Vatican declaration on the ordination of women.

There have been breaks in this tradition. In 1898, Elizabeth Cady Stanton challenged it with the *Woman's Bible* (Stanton,

([1898] 1972). Mary Daly's *Beyond God the Father* (1973), building both on the liberal theology of Paul Tillich and the philosophy of Alfred Whitehead, makes the best-known current challenge. Both documents have been defined by contemporary theologians as sacrilegious. Daly's book challenged modern systematic theology for several reasons: (1) Many women took it very seriously and acted in an organized way within divinity schools to challenge the basic tenets of formal theology as it was being presented to them (Hageman, 1974); (2) male theologians found it difficult to take seriously what Daly said, but they had to cope with her effect on the women they were teaching; (3) her content challenged the sexual assumptions on which theologizing was done, especially that of the fatherhood of God. With her focal attack on the structure of patriarchy itself, all doctrines of God that remained alive after the death-of-God criticism of the early 1960s were again subject to serious review. She has challenged the teaching of the clergy, not only regarding the status of women but also regarding the status of God. She has moved such theologians as Gordon Kaufman to review their whole system of theology in order to respond to her. Kaufman's conclusion (1972) is that systematic theology cannot move beyond God the father.

Daly's cause had to be espoused by liberal schools of theology because her university was in the process of rejecting her bid for tenure on the basis of inadequate performance, and this at a time when—as is evidenced by her presenting at Tübingen in 1975 a paper at the international meeting on unbelief sponsored jointly by the Vatican Commission on Unbelief and the University of California Department of Sociology at Berkeley (Daly, 1977)—she was having a major influence on theology internationally. She had a thorough traditional theological education, which few women have been able to achieve. She has taken a radical stance regarding the obedience and deference accorded to men in the church. She has been an iconoclast. At a chapel service at Harvard's Memorial Church in 1971, in the first Sunday sermon preached by a woman at the church since its founding 336 years before, Daly invited all women to symbolize their becoming an exodus community from the Christian churches by standing together and leaving the church, never to enter again until the symbols change. Many women did just this. The purpose was to refuse "to give our energies and support to the structures and ideologies of patriarchy" (Clark and Richardson, 1977, p. 263). What happens to Daly and her teachings is directly affecting the role of women in the church (see Daly, 1979).

Women's Roles in the Church

The history of religion reveals specific roles for women. We get glimpses of Egyptian sacred queens, Greek priestesses and oracles (Pomeroy, 1975), Roman vestal virgins (O'Faolain and Martines, 1973), African mediums (Mbiti, 1970), medieval congregations of Beguines, nuns, mystics, and witches (Richardson, 1971; Tavard, 1973; Morris, 1973). In early modern times, women have been Quaker preachers and ministers' wives (Culver, 1967). In the nineteenth century, increasing numbers of women missionaries established medical centers, schools, and churches in colonial wildernesses (Culver, 1967). Sisters of Charity have taken foundlings and prostitutes into their homes and subsequently founded huge enterprises such as schools, hospitals, and orphanages (Code, 1929). Out of religious commitment in the nineteenth century emerged founders of churches, such as Mary Baker Eddy; founders of religious orders, such as Elizabeth Seton; and leaders of social reform movements, such as the Grimke sisters of the abolition movement, Lucy Stone, Elizabeth Cady Stanton, Susan B. Anthony, and Lucretia Coffin Mott of the suffrage movement, and Frances Willard of the temperance movement (Flexner, 1973; Clark and Richardson, 1977; Gilman, [1898] 1966; Ruether and McLaughlin, 1979). Among the evangelicals, faith healing and gospel preaching provided yet other roles for women (Clark and Richardson, 1977).

In the twentieth century, the main new role is that of administering formal organizations of active churchwomen. By 1966, the Catholic sisterhoods alone in the United States had 181,000 members in over 500 different congregations (Muckenhirn, 1965; Grollmes, 1967). Each Protestant church had its own women's national organization (Bliss, 1952). The Jewish sisterhoods were organized. Church Women United, having differentiated women's interests from the general interests of the World Council of

Churches, dissociated itself from the Council but developed a liaison with it. Heads of the Catholic religious orders were organized as the Leadership Conference of Women Religious. A grass-roots initiative, across the religious orders, organized as the National Association of Women Religious (Kennedy, 1972). Nuns involved in direct political work for the poor formed a group called Network. Each of these groups has its own headquarters, news journal, and social service agenda, with a strong orientation toward human rights and liberation. A link has developed between them and secular organizations of the women's movement, with whom they now share a considerable overlapping membership (Colgan, 1975; Ruether and McLaughlin, 1979; Goldenberg, 1972). Of these roles, I will treat here only those necessary to put the current situation into a perspective—namely, those of witch, nun and sister, social movement leader, missionary, administrator, and ordained minister, for which last there is a current and growing demand in the Catholic churches, Episcopal and Roman (Hewitt and Hiatt, 1973; Gardiner, 1976; Swidler and Swidler, 1977).

Today's renewed examination of the medieval phenomenon of witch burning yields further evidence that this was another effort to repress nonconformity (Daly, 1979; Clark and Richardson, 1977; Trevor-Roper, 1967; O'Faolain and Martines, 1973; Culver, 1967). The practice continued for 500 years. Some men were also condemned for wizardry, but by far the larger attack was directed against women. From 1300 to 1700, women were imprisoned and burned at the stake or otherwise killed, ostensibly for bringing down the wrath of evil spirits on communities. The best known of the witch trials is that of Joan of Arc, called by her voices to help put the Dauphin of France onto the throne as Charles VII. Tried as a witch and burned at the stake in 1431, retried and exonerated in 1456, canonized in 1920, and made patroness of France in 1922, she is a prototype of women as a symbol going through several reinterpretations.

Rules for identifying people as witches were actually drawn up by two Inquisition appointees, Dominican monks, and published as the now notorious *Malleus Maleficarum* (see Clark and Richardson, 1977). Its authors had the permission of Pope Innocent VIII, who authorized them in 1484 to extirpate witches.

Preoccupied with sexual functions, the *Malleus* is a vicious attack on women in general. In one section, entitled "Concerning Witches Who Copulate with Devils: Why It Is That Women Are Chiefly Addicted to Evil Superstition," the following statement occurs: "Since women are feebler both in mind and body, it is not surprising that they should come under the spell of witchcraft. For, as regards intellect or the understanding of spiritual things, they seem to be of a different nature than man, a fact which is vouched for by the logic of the authorities, backed by various examples from the Scriptures" (quoted in Clark and Richardson, 1977, p. 122). Equally powerful statements adduced as evidence for attacking women include the following (p. 122): "For as she [any woman] is a liar by nature, so in her speech she stings while she delights us" and "The natural reason is that she is more carnal than man." The book was a best-seller in its day, going through several editions. Because of it, several thousand women were tried, found guilty, and burned to death. They included many whose fault was that they tried to preach a new perspective.

The contemplative vocation, familiar from the eleventh century on and frequently described in tales of the cloister (Conwell, 1968), gave way as the primary religious calling for women in the Catholic Church to what became, by the twentieth century, a distinct vocation to apostolic works in the wider society. The contemplative orders continued to attract those who intended a secluded life of prayer, singing the Psalms and praying the hours of the office of the church, but with the rise of the city and foreign missions a new calling developed: to provide homes for orphans, bring food to the elderly, to instruct children and young girls, and to staff hospitals and clinics. The first attempts to combine a celibate life vowed to obedience and poverty in convents with a daily emergence into the city to feed the poor attracted a number of women but were severely condemned by church authorities. The Visitation sisters who attempted it in 1610 were required after five years either to give up their apostolic work and return to the cloister or to disband. They chose the cloister. Twenty years later, the Daughters of Charity—now, with a membership of about 36,000, the largest organization of religious women in the world—tried to do the same work by defining themselves not as cloistered nuns with permanent vows but as sisters with vows renewable each year. They were allowed to continue. By the mid twentieth century, the one million sisters in the world were predominantly engaged in this kind of work.

The Second Vatican Council, an international gathering of bishops held between 1961 and 1964, mandated an updating of all church structures, including the religious orders of women still structured in life-styles fashioned after the late medieval cloister. Beginning in 1965, a year after this mandate was promulgated, members of religious orders of women in the United States initiated changes in the structure of their life and work that will significantly affect the church and society in ways just coming to be understood. For some 50,000, this meant their leaving the cloister altogether (Ebaugh, 1977). For the vast majority, 130,000, it meant a new initiative toward social reform (Muckenhirn, 1965; Grollmes, 1967; Neal, 1975).

Several Protestant women with active denominational affiliation felt called in the nineteenth century to initiate or to further specific social movements (Stanton, [1898] 1971; Gilman, [1898] 1966; Lerner, 1971). They were moved to do so by the restrictive laws that gave the husband rights over the wife that prevented her from being a free person. These rights included the husband's custody over the wife's person, use of her real property, right to her wages, inequality in inheritance settlements, "the whole system in which legal existence of the wife is suspended during marriage, so that she had no legal choice of residence, right to make a will, to be sued in her own name or inherit property" (Culver, 1967, p. 173). These were the issues that Lucy Stone espoused and carried into the public forum for redress. She and women like her recognized support of the causes of the women's rights movement as the rightful task of their churches. Churchwomen initiated the movement and played a considerable role in other social movements as well. The temperance movement, which originated to address the problems of the migrants adapting to American culture in the 1840s, was advanced through the quiet work of Frances Willard as well as the direct hatchet approach of Carrie Nation. Dorothea Dix advanced prison and hospital reform efforts. Harriet Tubman led slaves to freedom. Elizabeth Blackwell's attempt to get into medical school considerably advanced the cause of professional education for women (Culver, 1967).

While some of the most ardent support for these movement leaders came from individual fellow clergy, their churches were generally reluctant to support them. Established churches were structured to celebrate the existing order, not to challenge it, and, when themselves challenged, the churches resisted. Their ministers expressed genuine fear of the action for social reform that these women espoused, using arguments about God's intended role for women and condemning the movements as not according to God's intention. Cardinal Gibbons, the leading American Catholic bishop in the early twentieth century, who had himself expressed support for movements toward the elimination of some of the more glaring inequities in the treatment of immigrants, had this to say about the vote for women (Gibbons, 1916): "Equal rights do not imply that both sexes should engage promiscuously in the same pursuit but that each should discharge those duties which are adapted to its physical constitution. The insistence on a right to participation in active political life is undoubtedly calculated to rob women of all that is amiable and gentle, tender and attractive; to rob her of her grace of character and give her nothing in return but masculine boldness and effrontery. Its advocates are habitually preaching about women's rights and prerogatives and have not a word to say about her duties and responsibilities. They withdraw her from those obligations which properly belong to her sex and fill her with ambition to usurp positions for which neither God nor nature ever intended her." Churchmen continue to resist churchwomen's participation in leadership roles in social movements into the late twentieth century, although they support acceptance of changes effected by these movements—revised laws, enhanced civil rights, and access to education—once these changes become established (Jacquet, 1973; Swidler, 1972; Gibson, 1970; Ahlstrom, 1972; Neal and Clasby, 1968).

Some of the denominations saw the call for ordination of women, which became part of the movement demands a century ago, as a logical outcome of the demands in justice for representation in civil, social, and other bodies. Some who experienced the religious quality manifest in the felt call of women to preach, especially in the evangelical churches, adapted the ministerial role for women to her familiar role as mother (see Ann Lee in Clark and Richardson, 1977, pp. 161–172). The current pressure to ordain women in the Episcopal and Roman Catholic churches represents a unique challenge to ancient institutional structures (Meer, 1976). The celebration of the Eucharist is a stumbling block. It is an issue entwined with that of the relationship between men and women. It is an issue of power and social form. The schism that followed the decision of the Episcopal Church regarding the ordination of women in 1977, like that of the Lutheran Church in 1961, indicates how deeply rooted is the conviction that priesthood is a male role. To understand the institutional bases for this conviction, we need to look at the pressures to change currently facing the priesthood, the family, and the religious order. The need to change the shape of governance from hierarchy to community, from pyramid to circle, is not merely symbolic; it is a survival process (Neal, 1975).

In the more congregational Christian churches, in which the Eucharist is more a memorial of an event than an event in itself, ordination has been allowed to women sooner than it has in the episcopal churches, although even in these cases it has not always meant for women full participation in the ministerial roles or in ecclesial decision making (Jacquet, 1973; Hewett and Hiatt, 1973; Norberg and Wallace, 1973). Only among the Quakers, among whom there is no sacred meal, has participation for women come relatively easily. They have allowed full ministerial functions to women since the nineteenth century but with some limitations (Culver, 1967, p. 178). As late as 1973, the Unitarians, while claiming for women the full right to ordination, gave to the few ordained women in the church pastoral roles only in problematic settings, including places where salary was low or duties were doubled.

Anna Oliver, the first Methodist woman attending theology school at Boston University, registered under an alias rather than disgrace her family (Culver, 1967, p. 214). Methodists ordained women but would not allow them to be members of the conference responsible for the appointment of ministers (Culver, 1967, pp. 215–216). The Presbyterian Church allowed full ordination of women only in 1956; southern Presbyterians, not until 1964. Jewish women were seeking ordination by 1961, with only the non-Orthodox assenting, and this in the middle 1970s (Rabbi S. E. Sasso, personal communication, 1975).

The Church of England approved ordination of women in principle, and the Episcopal Church, its counterpart in the United States, did likewise, following the illicit ordination of eleven women in Philadelphia in 1974. Since then, while the English church remains hesitant, the American church has ordained ninety women to the priesthood. Because of the sacred character of the Eucharist in the Catholic belief system, this action has critical significance for Anglican–Roman Catholic relations. The symbolic significance of the Eucharist as nourishing life is raised in the more political and social question of who can legitimately provide food for the family.

The Roman Catholic case is the critical one at present. St. Joan's International Alliance, organized since 1911 to further women's rights, has taken the ordination of women as its current project. They were joined by the Catholic sisters and laywomen in a national call to priesthood at a Detroit conference on ordination in October 1975 (Gardiner, 1976). The momentum for this meeting, which was attended by 1,300 people, came from women in divinity schools. The increase in Christian and Jewish women attending seminaries to train for ministry is a phenomenon of the past ten years. Presently, some of the leading divinity schools, which had no women students in 1960, have enrollments over a quarter female (Taylor, 1977). Harvard Divinity School and Union Theological Seminary are cases in point. Catholic women, still excluded from diocesan seminaries, are attending multidenominational schools in increasing numbers. In 1977–78, twenty of the women at Harvard Divinity School were Roman Catholic, and this at a time of decline in membership and new applications to the Catholic sisterhoods. There has been no special drive to attract these women. Although welcome because of declining attendance of men, the increase of women students has been unsolicited. Clearly, many women, married and single, are seeking ministerial roles in the churches. There is a growing solidarity among them and strong support for the efforts of Catholic women to achieve the right to ordination in their church (Swidler and Swidler, 1977). In October 1978, Roman Catholic women joined by ordained women of other denominations met at the Civic Center in Baltimore for three days of strategy conferences entitled "New Women, New Church, New Priestly Ministry."

On February 3, 1977, a formal Vatican declaration rejected ordination for women. The reasoning recalled the negative judgment of Aquinas in the thirteenth century: "The whole sacramental economy is in fact based upon natural signs, on symbols imprinted upon human psychology. 'Sacramental signs,' says St. Thomas, 'represent what they signify by natural resemblance.' The same natural resemblance is required for persons as for things: when Christ's role in the Eucharist is to be expressed sacramentally, there would not be this 'natural resemblance' which must exist between Christ and his minister if the role of Christ were not taken by a man: in such a case it would be difficult to see in the minister the image of Christ. For Christ himself was and remains a man" (Vatican Congregation for the Doctrine of the Faith, 1977; compare with Aquinas as quoted by Clark and Richardson, 1977, p. 96). Of the text in Galatians 3:28 regarding nondiscrimination between Jew and Greek, slave and free, male and female, since all are one in Christ Jesus, the Vatican document (1977, p. 522) offers this explanation: "Nevertheless, the incarnation of the Word took place according to the male sex: this is indeed a question of fact and this fact, while not implying an alleged natural superiority of man over woman, cannot be dissociated from the economy of salvation: it is, indeed, in harmony with the entirety of God's plan as God himself has revealed it, and of which the mystery of the covenant is the nucleus." And finally, there is the question of power. Speaking about the church as a society, the document states (Vatican, 1977, p. 523; emphasis added), "The pastoral charge of the church is normally limited to the sacrament of order; it is not a simple government comparable to the modes of authority found in the states. It is not granted by people's spontaneous choice: Even when it involves designation through election, it is the laying on of hands and the prayer of the successors of the apostles which guarantee God's choice: and it is the holy spirit, given by ordination, who *grants participation in the ruling power* of the supreme pastor, Christ."

In 1966, Krister Stendahl observed of the Anglican Church

that it still has "a prior question to ordination; namely, whether women ought to be permitted to vote in ecclesiastical affairs." "This," he added (p. viii), "is the most basic question." Obviously, for the Roman Church, too, this is the basic issue. Underlying the exclusion of women from officiating at the celebration of the Eucharist is the exclusion of women from decision making. Entangled with this most sacred of services, the mystical transformation and distribution of food, is an issue about production of food for life. Symbolically it has to do with power. The struggle basically is with social relations around the mode of future production and distribution of what is needed for human survival. Food stands for survival.

Despite the formal papal proclamation, the movement of Catholic women toward priesthood may be the prophetic action for social change that Weber analyzes in his treatment of charisma (Weber, [1922] 1963, chap. 4). Far from putting an end to the discussion, the papal document has elicited a flood of responses from theologians (Connor, 1977), bishops (Quinn and others, 1977; Murphy, 1977), and scholars (Swidler and Swidler, 1977).[2] The general trend of the debate indicates that a movement is afoot that cannot be stopped. And it is not going in one single direction. As in the women's movement in general, some of the advocates are interested only in liberal reforms, the opening up of the job market, and the fairer distribution of resources for the membership as colleagues (Rossi, 1973). Some are genuinely and personally concerned about a felt experience of a call to priesthood to which they want to respond. Others are aware of the social structural factors involved in the debate on ordination and in the reaction of church dignitaries and protectors of the maleness of the priestly role (Gardiner, 1976). Changes in the old status relation of men over women affect the whole structure of society. To experiment with a new division of labor is to generate a new division of power. One has to have reasons for wanting that. These reasons will eventually be embodied in a new symbol system (Daly, 1979; Engels, [1884] 1943; Bebel, [1883] 1971; Bruns, 1973; Janeway, 1971; Hays, 1972; Russell, 1974; Ermarth, 1970).

The rationale for the church's rejecting women as priests is closely related to its interpretation of the marriage relationship, which rests on St. Paul's New Testament directive, "Women, be subject to your husbands as the church is to Christ" (Ephesians 5:23), and on the creation story of Genesis. Grounded in the Roman law of Paul's day and codified in the sixth century as the Code of Justinian, this role relation between husband and wife has become sacralized in Christian education, coming in the course of time to legitimate control over a women's property and over women as property.

In his 1931 encyclical letter "On Christian Marriage" (*Casti Connubii*), Pope Pius XI specified the role relations expected of husband and wife: "Domestic society being confirmed, therefore, by this bond of love, there should flourish in it that 'order of love,' as St. Augustine calls it. This order includes both the primacy of the husband with regard to the wife and children, the ready subjection of the wife and her willing obedience, which the Apostle commends in these words: 'Let women be subject to their husbands as to the Lord, because the husband is the head of the wife, as Christ is the head of the church'" (Pius XI, 1931, p. 11).

According to Boston canonist Richard Cunningham, *Casti Connubii* itself represented something of a breakthrough in Vatican thinking in that, unlike previous magisterial documents, it acknowledged conjugal love as an end of marriage. The Second Vatican Council document "Gaudium et Spes (Vatican Council II) and the changing practice of the Roman Rota,[3] the church's highest marriage tribunal, also reflect an increasing recognition by the church of marriage as "a community of love" (Cunningham, 1976, p. 615). But none of this, according to Cunningham, adds up to a "new theology" of marriage. Marriage remains a relationship of obedience, one of superordinate man and subordinate woman.

Yet John Finnegan, another canonist and a former president of the Canon Law Society of America, argues that there is a new theology of marriage, one informed by the evidence provided by the behavioral sciences—in their analyses of language as symbol—of greater equality and respect in the relationship of the sexes. In responding to a question of mine early in 1978, Finnegan (personal communication) confirms the hypothesis of this chapter; namely, that a new perception of a common human nature is operative in social relations between men and women because women, educated and active, experience themselves in a way that does not accord with the traditional, limited definitions imposed on them. Older norms of superordination and subordination, no matter how finely nuanced in exegeses, do not describe people's experience and self-understanding today. In Eastern and Western society alike, the marriage relationship is redefined in more egalitarian forms at the ideological level and, as a result of the efforts of the nineteenth- and twentieth-century women's movements, as well as of popula- tion increase (Neal, 1976), the newer forms are now grounded in normative practice recognized by civil law. This is evidenced by changes in the textbooks on the sociology of the family and mar- riage counseling (Glazer-Malbin and Waehrer, 1972; Coser, 1974). Changes in civil law give leverage to the role demands of women in the churches, a dramatic factor in Catholic Church decision making on such issues as divorce, birth control, abortion, and rape (Swid- ler, 1978). The unequal treatment in law and custom that limits access to critical power centers, and hence limits the perspective of decisions emanating from such centers, is experienced today for what it is—conscious and unconscious exploitation of some human beings by others, made legitimate by established law and custom buttressed by built-in myths and symbols that are no longer suffi- ciently credible to be effectively binding. The desacralization of the exploiting symbols can destroy the credibility of the structures in which they inhere if the decision-making role players are unaware of the changed understanding of what they are saying and doing (Baum, 1975; Beauvoir, 1961; Boston Women's Health Book Col- lective, 1971; Callahan, 1969; Cuneen, 1968; Greer, 1971; Lakoff, 1975; Noonan, 1967; Raming, 1976; Soelle, 1977; Weitz, 1977).

An examination of the Second Vatican Council documents on marriage provides evidence of the change in language noted by Finnegan. In the *Pastoral Constitution on the Church in the Modern World* (Abbott, 1966), there are numerous references to the mutual- ity of the love relationship in Christian marriage but no reference to the hierarchical relationship enjoined by St. Paul and still clearly specified in the 1931 document. The Vatican Council document explains marriage as a mutual relationship of love and equality: "Just as He [sic] (God) loved the Church and handed Himself over on her [sic] behalf, the spouses must love each other with perpetual fidelity through mutual self-bestowal." Marriage is "a mutual self-gift of two persons." And, "firmly established by the Lord, the unity of marriage will radiate from the equal dignity of wife and husband, a dignity acknowledged by mutual and total love" (in Abbott, 1966, p. 250, 253). In response to a shift in practice among church members, the official church is apparently deemphasizing the subordinate role of women in favor of a peer relationship.[4]

Peter Berger and others have claimed that this new emphasis on mutual affection is caused only by the privatization of religion characteristic of church practice since the separation of church and state rendered less functional the monarchical model of the family (Berger, 1969, p. 134). Berger's explanation not only deflects attention from women's growing consciousness of their rightful place, however, but also provides an interpretation functional for the preservation of male-dominated, Western-type political states, just as the repudiation of all religions is functional for recurrent male domination in Soviet and Chinese systems. The Western state, beginning with Hegel ([1837] 1953), domesticates religions: the Eastern replaces them.

It seems relatively certain that the emerging socialist states of the southern hemisphere—that is, Latin America, southern Africa, and Southeast Asia—will not affirm either of the northern hemisphere styles of religious institutional structures. Because their models of power sharing will necessarily be more circular than pyramidal, their theologies will express this experienced participation in decision making, and their liturgies will celebrate communality. The symbol of circularity is present in the theological method and discourse emerging from both continents (Miguez-Bonino, 1975; Moore, 1974; Cardenal, 1976). The same quality is evident in liberation theology as discussed by women (Ruether, 1972). The task of continuing the rationale for the subordinate, private role for women has recently been adopted by social scientists (Wilson, 1975, p. 554), a circumstance that leaves the religious calling freer to develop the symbols for equality. Latin American theology is leading the way in this direction (Guttierez, 1973). There is evidence that theological reflection within the Protestant tradition has been preparing for substantially more egalitarian relationships between men and women in the public sector for some

time, even before those engaged in the reflection can let go their
assumptions about the service roles of women in the household setting. There is little evidence, however, of the intentional sacralization
of a fundamentally new distribution of power relations in the public
domain.

The ritual impurity associated with menstruation bore the
burden of evidence for female inferiority for centuries (Leviticus
12:1–5) and still does today to some extent (Shulman, in Hageman,
1974). The nineteenth-century Protestant woman's access to the
church buildings as a place for gathering for social action movements, the early twentieth-century Jewish women's experimentation with status change in family and work roles in kibbutz living
(Talmon, 1972), and the Catholic nuns' late twentieth-century initiative in restructuring their mission and life-styles culminated in an
assurance that ordained ministry for women was needed in the
churches, not only to lead the community in prayer and worship
but also to generate models for the now powerless to participate
fully in the decisions that affect the lives of the world's people. The
development of human solutions to the issues of divorce, abortion,
and population control will not be achieved before women participate as full members in making major policy decisions concerning
production, work, ownership, and armament. A protest group demanding their rights as outsiders is only the first step toward
structural change. Social movements for structural change call for
representation of the oppressed in the decision-making gathering
before those who gather can, in interaction, provide one another
with the new social consciousness necessary if they are to arrive at
just solutions.

Church doctrine is now incapable of legitimating subordinate roles for women, even though belief in this relationship is still
quite strong in evangelical preaching and in some traditional
societies unaware of new experiences won through education and
reflective action. There is no further functional need of the greater
privacy of domestic life for women. All people need a protected
private life and a public life as well in order to make wise decisions
and to have the psychic strength to realize them. Segregated
domestic life for women was functionally necessary when the population size threatened extinction of peoples. The current large size

of the world population base eliminates that source of basic anxiety. Public decisions about the destiny of whole populations are the new source of anxiety (Neal, 1975). The biblical mandate to increase and multiply and fill the earth has been fulfilled. The mandates of social justice have not been so well addressed or protected (United Nations, 1976). It remains to be seen what sacred symbols will emerge to legitimate equal status and what moral solidarities will socialize to this norm and celebrate the related social structures, energizing people to attempt their realization. The old symbols, which separately celebrated mother and virgin and singularly celebrated father and God, no longer "act to establish powerful and long-lasting moods and motivations" necessary for their implementation (Geertz, 1966, p. 4). They can, therefore, no longer provide effective socialization to roles for women essential for men to rule alone with faithful domestic partners.

Notes

1. For the first movement, see the account of the trial of the Quaker Anne Hutchinson by the Church of Boston in 1638 (Dexter, [1638] 1888). For the second, see Elizabeth Cady Stanton's call to American housewives at Seneca Falls in 1848 (Culver, 1967, p. 178).

2. *Origins* is the National Catholic (NC) News Service, which operates out of 1312 Massachusetts Avenue, N. W., Washington, D. C. 20005. This is the central office building of the United States Catholic Conference of Bishops. The NC News Service, however, is an independent organization.

3. The Roman Rota is the body analogous to the U. S. Supreme Court. Its decisions are not subject to review except for a few cases that may be referred to the Apostolic Signatura. It differs from the U. S. Supreme Court, however, in one major respect: Its decisions are advisory to other courts, and do not establish a new binding norm as do Supreme Court decisions. Thus, they function far less as agents of change. Because the Rota is established on Roman law, the jurists sitting on it are drawn mainly from countries whose law has the same base; namely, France, Spain, Portugal, Italy, and some Latin American countries, including Brazil, Argentina, and Paraguay. The United States and England have little influence

on the court. This is why the insightful interpretations of the Canon Law Society of America seldom influence international policy in the Roman Catholic Church.

    4. Clearly, the two sexed pronouns in this quotation belie the changed relationship expressed in the reference. Their use highlights the centrality of sexed language about God as a problem when trying to develop an understanding of a human nature common to men and women.

References

Abbott, W. *The Documents of Vatican II.* New York: Guild Press, 1966.

Achebe, C. *Things Fall Apart.* Greenwich, Conn.: Fawcett, 1959.

Ahlstrom, S. E. *A Religious History of the American People.* New Haven, Conn.: Yale University Press, 1972.

Baum, G. *Religion and Alienation.* New York: Paulist Press, 1975.

Beauvoir, S. *The Second Sex.* New York: Bantam Books, 1961.

Bebel, A. *Woman Under Socialism.* New York: Schocken, 1971. (Originally published 1883.)

Berger, P. *The Sacred Canopy: Elements of a Sociological Theory of Religion.* New York: Doubleday, 1969.

Berger, P., and Luckman, T. *The Social Construction of Reality.* New York: Doubleday, 1967.

Bliss, K. *The Service and Status of Women in the Churches.* London: SCM Press, 1952.

Boston Women's Health Book Collective. *Our Bodies, Ourselves.* New York: Simon & Schuster, 1971.

Bruns, J. E. *God as Woman, Woman as God.* New York: Paulist Press, 1973.

Callahan, S. (Ed.). *The Catholic Case for Contraception.* New York: Macmillan, 1969.

Cardenal, E. *The Gospel in Solentiname.* Maryknoll, N. Y.: Orbis, 1976.

Clark, E., and Richardson, H. *Women and Religion: A Feminist Sourcebook of Christian Thought.* New York: Harper & Row, 1977.

Code, J. *Great American Foundresses.* New York: Macmillan, 1929.

Colgan, M. "Nuns and the Women's Movement." *Origins,* 1975, *4* (38), 593–598.

Connor, J. "Jesuits' Letter to the Apostolic Delegate." *Origins,* 1977, 6 (421), 661–665.

Conwell, J. F. "Contemplative Life." In *New Catholic Encyclopedia.* Vol. 4. New York: McGraw-Hill, 1968.

Coser, R. *The Family: Its Structures and Functions.* (Rev. ed.) New York: St. Martin's Press, 1974.

Culver, E. T. *Women in the World of Religions.* New York: Doubleday, 1967.

Cuneen, S. *Sex, Female; Religion, Catholic.* New York: Holt, Rinehart and Winston, 1968.

Cunningham, R. "Is There a New Theology of Marriage? *Origins,* 1976, 5, 300–304.

Daly, M. *Beyond God the Father.* Boston: Beacon Press, 1973.

Daly, M. *The Church and the Second Sex.* (Rev. ed.) New York: Harper & Row, 1975.

Daly, M. "Radical Feminism, a Qualitative Leap Beyond Patriarchal Religion." In Rocco Caporale (Ed.), *Vecchi e Nuove Dei.* Torino, Italy: Editoriale Valentino, 1977.

Daly, M. *Gyn-Ecology: Metaethics of Radical Feminism.* Boston: Beacon Press, 1979.

Dexter, F. B. "A Report of Anne Hutchinson Before the Church of Boston." March, 1638. Transcribed from the original by Ezra Stiles, September 3, 1771. Boston: Massachusetts Historical Society, 1888.

Douglas, M. *Natural Symbols.* New York: Vintage Books, Random House, 1973a.

Douglas, M. (Ed.). *Rules and Meaning.* London: Penguin, 1973b.

Durkheim, E. *Suicide.* New York: Free Press, 1951. (Originally published 1895).

Eastern Sociological Society, Section on Women in the Sociology of Religion. "Women in Ministry." Panel discussion, New York, April 20, 1975.

Ebaugh, H. R. F. *Out of the Cloister.* Austin: University of Texas Press, 1977.

Eliade, M. *Occultism, Witchcraft, and Cultural Fashions.* Chicago: University of Chicago Press, 1976.

Engels, E. *The Origin of the Family, Private Property and the State.* New

York: International Publishers, 1943. (Originally published 1884).

Ermarth, M. *Adam's Fractured Rib: Observations on Women in the Church.* Philadelphia: Fortress, 1970.

Firth, R. *Symbols Public and Private.* Ithaca, N. Y.: Cornell University Press, 1975.

Flexner, E. *Century of Struggle: The Women's Rights Movement in the United States.* New York: Atheneum, 1973.

Freud, S. *Beyond the Pleasure Principle.* New York: Bantam, 1959. (Originally published 1928.)

Friedan, B. *The Feminine Mystique.* New York: Dell, 1963.

Fustel de Coulanges, N. D. *The Ancient City: A Classic Study of the Religious and Civil Institutions of Ancient Greece and Rome.* New York: Doubleday, no date.

Gardiner, A. M. *Woman and Catholic Priesthood: An Expanded Vision.* New York: Paulist Press, 1976.

Geertz, C. "Religion as a Cultural System." In M. Banton (Ed.), *Anthropological Approaches to the Study of Religion.* London: Tavistock, 1966.

Gibbons, J. "Message to the National Association Opposed to Women's Suffrage." Paper presented at the National Anti-Suffrage Convention, Washington, D. C., December 7, 1916.

Gibson, E. *When the Minister Is a Woman.* New York: Holt, Rinehart and Winston, 1970.

Gilman, C. P. *Women and Economics.* (C. Degler, Ed.). New York: Harper & Row, 1966. (Originally published in 1898.)

Glazer-Malbin, N. H., and Waehrer, Y. *Women in a Man-Made World: A Socioeconomic Handbook.* Chicago: Rand McNally, 1972.

Glock, C. Y., and Bellah, R. N. *The New Religious Consciousness.* Berkeley: University of California, 1976.

Goldenberg, J. P. (Ed.). *Women in Religion.* Montana: American Academy of Religion, University of Montana Press, 1972.

Gough, K. "An Anthropologist Looks at Engels." In N. Glazer-Malbin and H. Y. Waehrer (Eds.), *Women in a Man-Made World.* Chiago: Rand McNally, 1972.

Greeley, A. M. *The Mary Myth: On the Femininity of God.* New York: Seabury Press, 1977.

Greer, G. *The Female Eunuch.* New York: Bantam Books, 1971.

Grollmes, E. *Vows But No Walls: An Analysis of Religious Life*. Missouri: Herder, 1967.

Guttierrez, G. *A Theology of Liberation*. Maryknoll, New York: Orbis, 1973.

Hageman, A. L. *Sexist Religion and Women in the Church: No More Silence*. New York: Association Press, 1974.

Hays, H. R. *The Dangerous Sex: The Myth of Feminine Evil*. New York: Pocket Books, 1972.

Hegel, G. W. F. *Reason in History: General Introduction to the Philosophy of History*. Indianapolis: Bobbs-Merrill, 1953. (Originally published in 1837.)

Hewett, E., and Hiatt, S. *Women Priests: Yes or No?* New York: Seabury Press, 1973.

Howell, M. K. *Women and the Kingdom: Fifty Years of Kingdom Building by Women of the Methodist Episcopal Church*, 1878–1928. No date.

Jacquet, C. H. *The Status of Women in Various Constitutional Bodies of the National Council of Churches: Result of an Inquiry*. New York: Office of Research Evaluation, National Council of Churches, 1973.

Janeway, E. *Man's World, Woman's Place: A Study of Social Mythology*. New York: Dell, 1971.

Jesuit School of Theology. "Women's Ordination: Letter to the Apostolic Delegate." *Origins*, 1977, *6*, (42), 661–665.

Kaufman, G. D. *God the Problem*. Cambridge, Mass.: Harvard University Press, 1972.

Kennedy, E. *Women in Ministry: A Sister's View*. Chicago: NAWR Publications, 1972.

Lakoff, R. *Language and Women's Place*. New York: Harper & Row, 1975.

Legrand, H. "Views on the Ordination of Women." *Origins*, 1977, *6* (29), 459–468.

Lerner, G. *The Grimke Sisters from South Carolina: Pioneers for Woman's Rights and Abolition*. New York: Schocken, 1971.

McGoldrick, R., and Yuhaus, G. J. (Eds.). *Facts of the Future: Religious Life USA*. Huntington, Ind.: Our Sunday Visitor, 1976.

McGrath, A. M. *What a Modern Catholic Believes About Women*. Chicago: Thomas More Press, 1972.

Mbiti, J. *African Religions and Philosophies.* New York: Doubleday, 1970.

Meer, H. van der. *Women Priests in the Catholic Church. A Theological-Historical Investigation.* Philadelphia: Temple University Press, 1976.

Miguez-Bonino, B. J. *Doing Theology in a Revolutionary Situation.* Philadelphia: Fortress, 1975.

Millett, K. *Sexual Politics.* New York: Avon Books, 1969.

Moore, B. *Challenge of Black Theology in South Africa.* Atlanta, Ga.: John Knox Press, 1974.

Morgan, M. *Total Woman.* Old Pappen, N. J.: Revell, 1977.

Morgan, R. (Ed.). *Sisterhood Is Powerful: An Anthology of Writings from the Women's Movement.* New York: Vintage Books, 1970.

Morris, J. *The Lady Was a Bishop.* New York: Macmillan, 1973.

Muckenhirn, M. E. *The Changing Sister.* Notre Dame, Ind.: Fides, 1965.

Murphy, P. F. "Women in Ministry." *Origins,* 1977, 7 (17), 257–260.

Neal, M. A. "Cultural Patterns and Behavioral Outcomes: A Study of Religious Orders of Women in the USA." In *Religion and Social Change.* Lille, France: CISR, 1975.

Neal, M. A. "A Sociological Perspective on the Moral Issue of Sexuality Today." In F. Böckle and J. Pohier (Eds.), *Sexuality in Contemporary Catholicism.* New York: Seabury Press, 1976.

Neal, M. A., and Clasby, M. "Priests' Attitudes Toward Women." In W. C. Bier (Ed.), *Women in Modern Life.* New York: Fordham University Press, 1968.

Noonan, J. *Contraception: A History of Its Treatment by Catholic Theologians and Canonists.* New York: New American Library, 1967.

Norberg, T. A., and Wallace, L. M. "Report of the Task Force on Women in Church and Society." Paper presented at the 4th General Synod of the United Church of Christ, Denver, Colorado, July 1973.

O'Faolain, J., and Martines, L. (Eds.). *Not in God's Image.* New York; Harper & Row, 1973.

Paul VI. "Defending the Stability of Marriage." *Origins,* 1976, 5 (39), 614–616.

Pius XI. *On Christian Marriage.* Washington, D.C.: National Catholic Welfare Conference, 1931.

Pomeroy, S. *Goddesses, Whores, Wives, and Slaves: Women in Classical Antiquity.* New York: Schocken, 1975.

Quinn, J., and others. "Declaration on Women in Ministerial Priesthood." *Origins,* 1977, *6* (34), 545–548.

Raming, I. *The Exclusion of Women from the Priesthood: Divine Law or Sex Discrimination?* Metuchen, N.J.: Scarecrow Press, 1976.

Richardson, H. W. *Nun, Witch and Playmate: The Americanization of Sex.* New York: Harper & Row, 1971.

Ricoeur, P. "La Structure Symbolique de L'Action." In *Symbolism: Religious, Secular and Social Classes.* Lille, France: CISR, 1977.

Rossi, A. S. (Ed.). *The Feminist Papers.* New York: Columbia University Press, 1973.

Ruether, R. R. *Liberation Theology.* New York: Paulist Press, 1972.

Ruether, R. R. (Ed.). *Religion and Sexism: Images of Woman in Jewish and Christian Traditions.* New York: Simon & Schuster, 1974.

Ruether, R. R. *Mary—The Feminine Face of the Church.* Philadelphia: Westminster Press, 1977.

Ruether, R. R., and McLaughlin, E. (Eds.). *Women of Spirit.* New York: Simon & Schuster, 1979.

Russell, L. M. *Human Liberation in Feminist Perspective: A Theology.* Philadelphia: Westminister Press, 1974.

Soelle, D. *Revolutionary Patience.* Maryknoll, N.Y.: Orbis, 1977.

Stanton, E. C. *Eighty Years and More: Reminiscences 1815–1897.* New York: Schocken, 1971. (Originally published 1898.)

Stanton, E. C. *The Women's Bible.* New York: Arno Press, 1972. (Originally published 1895.)

Stendahl, K. *The Bible and the Role Of Women.* Philadelphia: Fortress, 1966.

Swidler, A. *Women in a Man's Church.* New York: Paulist Press, 1972.

Swidler, A. "Some Thoughts on Rape." *Commonweal,* 1978, *105* (3), 75–78.

Swidler, L., and Swidler, A. *Women Priests: A Catholic Commentary on the Vatican Declaration.* New York: Paulist Press, 1977.

Talmon, Y. "Sex Role Differentiation in an Equalitarian Society." In N. Glazer-Malbin and H. Y. Waehrer (Eds.), *Woman in a Man-Made World.* Chicago: Rand McNally, 1972.

Tavard, G. *Women in Christian Tradition.* Notre Dame, Ind.: Notre Dame University Press, 1973.

Taylor, M. J. (Ed.). *Fact Book on Theological Education.* Vandalia, Ohio: American Association of Theological Schools of the United States and Canada, 1977.

Trevor-Roper, H. "Witches and Witchcraft." I and II. *Encounter,* 1967, *28* (5, 6).

United Nations. *International Covenants of Human Rights and Optional Protocol.* New York: United Nations Public Information Office, 1976.

Vatican Congregation for the Doctrine of the Faith. "Vatican Declaration: Women in the Ministerial Priesthood." *Origins,* 1977, *6* (33), 519–524.

Vatican Council II. "Gaudium et Spes." In W. Abbott, *The Documents of Vatican II.* New York: Guild Press, 1966.

Veblen, T. *Theory of the Leisure Class.* New York: Modern Library, 1934. (Originally published 1899.)

Vidulich, D. *Peace Pays a Price: A Study of Margaret Anna Cusack, The Nun of Kenmare, Foundress of the Sisters of St. Joseph of Peace.* Teaneck, N.J.: Garden State Press, 1975.

Weber, M. *Sociology of Religion.* Boston: Beacon Press, 1963. (Originally published 1922.)

Weitz, S. *Sex Roles: Biological, Psychological and Social Foundations.* New York: Oxford University Press, 1977.

Wilson, E. O. *Sociobiology: A New Synthesis.* Cambridge, Mass.: Harvard University Press, 1975.

10 *William C. Shepherd*

Conversion and Adhesion

~~~~~~

Of the many scholars who have emphasized the pronounced analogy between the religious situation in the Hellenistic world and our own, Hans Jonas' work (1963) still stands as the clearest example. The basic contours of his argument are well known. Jonas says that in philosophical stratagems Sartre, early Heidegger, and modern existentialists in general precisely parallel gnostic religious systems of the first three centuries of the common era. The account that the modern existentialists and the ancient gnostics give of the primordial human situation is the same. Human beings are thrown like frightened animals into a world that is strange, foreign, and alienating. It is the opposite of the cozy home and multiple fences provided by the agency-based cosmologies of tribal religions and, for that matter, of subsequent medieval Catholicism in the West. Home, if there be home at all, is elsewhere; this world is the product at best of a bungler deity, at worst of a bestial deity. The body is a prison; its environment merely a larger one. Escape from both is devoutly to be wished. All nomos or order in the cosmos is subverted, and cosmic fate is experienced as deeply oppressive. Humans are brutally placed in a situation totally disruptive from nature in both gnosticism and existentialism, although of course the latter is far more radical than the former because it envisages no divine origin for the soul and no eternal repose for it in the realm

251

of light. Rather, the realm of darkness is all we have, and the universe is fundamentally uncaring. There is no power struggle going on between the battalions of good and evil. God—or, indeed, any supersensible agent containing the explanatory principles for the world in which we live—is truly dead. The meager human project of self-creation is all that is left.

This argument fails if pressed to an analogy between religious situations and not just particular systems of thought. It fails for two reasons. It is too static, for one reason—systems of thought do not just hover in thin disembodied air; they are profoundly embedded in cultures and linked both to institutions and to other kinds of modes of thought. And it fails because it does not see diversity and pluralism of religious options as the keynote of the analogy. In other words, by singling out only the nihilistic strains of thought in both Hellenistic and contemporary philosophy, a much more fundamental node of comparison is overlooked. Colorful and even cheerful religious alternatives existed in late Hellenistic cosmopolitanism, and competition among them for the allegiance of human hopes and hearts was intense. Sparklingly packaged and managed religious wares were hawked then by the same sort of public relations experts who today in America hawk products ranging alphabetically from Arica to Zen Buddhism. It is a mistake to concentrate solely on the pessimistic strands, although of course they are indeed a part of both pictures. More glaring and obvious as social phenomena, however, is the boggling array of religious *answers*. Jonas (1963) emphasizes the question of human homelessness in the Hellenistic world and ours. I would shift the focus of attention to the wild variety of makeshift homes available to psychically deprived and fanatical religious seekers. In the light of these two objections to Jonas' formulations, a closer scrutiny of the analogy between the religious context of late antiquity and our own cultural situation is required.

All analogies exhibit both similarities and distinctions. Given our question, the distinction between the Hellenistic world and ours is not just that modern existentialism is radically extreme compared to gnosticism. It is more basically that the entire religious dynamics of the one context are diametrically opposed to the other. To understand the analogy at all, we have to take a close look not just at static systems of thought but also at the historical dynamics of the cultural situations in which all intellectual accounts are rooted and to some extent shaped. Religiously, the Hellenistic age was driving toward exclusivism, the obligatory religious monopoly of the Middle Ages. After Diocletian, the short-lived Julian was the only emperor who had both the will and enough traditional Roman piety to try to stem that enveloping tide of Christianity. His program of dusting off and refurbishing the latinized Olympians died with him. Our religious movements in contemporary America, on the other hand, are driving toward greater and greater inclusivism—new cults are springing up everywhere overnight, and new prophets and new hawkers are not slow to take advantage of the billowing market for religious vendibles to help us make it through the night.

The difference between exclusivism and inclusivism can be more clearly perceived by pressing into service the terms that form the title of this chapter, Arthur Darby Nock's distinction between *conversion* and *adhesion*. Generally stated, Nock, in his classic book *Conversion* (1933), argues that until Christianity and Judaism arrived at the lists adhesion had been the keynote of Hellenistic religious thought and behavior. Cults flowing into Mediterranean cosmopolitanism had been matters of choice available to those living within the empire. And the range of cults involved matters of taste that either appealed in doctrine, rite, and ceremonial or did not. Adherence to one or another new cult meant *adding it on* to one's already *engagé* religious life. It did not mean turning from one deep commitment to another; it was more like taking on another activity in an already crowded schedule. One could be cheerfully syncretistic and eclectic about religious choices, adding decorations on to heavily interpreted traditional piety regarding the Roman gods. Taking on Orphism, for example, meant taking on participation in rites that "were actions efficient in themselves as rites and not as the expression of a theology and of a world order sharply contrasted with those in which the neophyte had previously moved" (Nock, 1933, p.13). Adhesion was indeed very easy; no conflict was involved with one's earlier religious commitments, which may even have been deepened by being perceived in a more synoptic perspective. Cults were nonauthoritarian and nondogmatic. Communal activities organized around rites and ceremonials were what counted. Nonexclusivism is the essence of the religious picture prior to the late first century of the common era. One could simultaneously be a devotee of both Mithra and Isis without experiencing either schizophrenia or pathology. Deep exclusivistic metanoia, a total change of life and a total turn away from previous religious allegiances, was not required by stock Hellenistic cults.

With the appearance of the ethical as opposed to exemplary prophecy characterizing both Christianity and Judaism, the possibilities dim for eclectic polysymbolism in religious adherence. Adhesion, in Nock's lukewarm sense, begins to decline. Christianity and Judaism radicalize the options: "Stake everything on Jesus the Christ" or "Turn away from all idolatry and become a naturalized member of God's Chosen People" (Nock, 1933, p. 13). Christianity and Judaism demand wholesale change, an extreme break with the past religiously, and a totalistic entrance into the new times—indeed, that is the meaning of the term *gospel*. Exclusivistic conversion stands in sharp contrast to easygoing inclusivistic adhesion or eclectic, multiple religious polysymbolism. The rewards, however, are great as well, and the rewards of eternal life appealed deeply to minds newly distrusting of philosophy and newly participating in a greatly expanded political order far from those who called the shots. Christianity appealed to psychic deprivation, to deep feelings of homelessness and alienation, particularly among the rapidly growing urban proletariat. On the religious marketplace of the Roman Empire, Christianity was hugely successful and in a very short period of time. Its very success created a new kind of competition. Mere adhesion in the face of what Christianity in particular both demanded and offered came to look not terribly attractive and indeed quite shallow in its appeal to the deep, affective life of the self. So the cults began offering up a new image, requiring exclusivism, dogma, and revealed knowledge: In short, the cults were forced by the powerful success of Christianity (and to a lesser extent of Judaism) toward mandating conversion rather than adhesion. The religious dynamics of the Hellenistic world began their fateful move in the direction of religious exclusivism. Constantine simply put the seal of approval on a process already well under way, and Julian could do not a whit to undo historical dynamics far beyond his control. His modest aim was to reintroduce pluralistic adhesion, making Christianity into a cult marked by adhesion among its members rather than conversion. Even that goal turned out to be quite unattainable.

If we are to be serious about drawing a parallel between that religious situation and our own, we need to be quite clear that, whatever the similarities, the dynamics of contemporary religious thought and behavior are exactly the opposite of those characterizing the Hellenistic age. William Irwin Thompson (1971, 1974, 1976) seems to think that we are now simply repeating history and are living at the dawn of a new global "Dark Age" precisely analogous in macroscope to early medieval times in the West. Statically or synchronically his analysis and my own of contemporary religiosity converge: "Yoga, Sufism, Tibetan and Zen Buddhism, Yaqui shamanism, and Celtic animism: The planet has become a Ptolemaic Egypt of syncretistic religious movements, and the Alexandria of it all is America" (Thompson, 1976, p. 14). Thompson, however, sees all this diversity and fragmentation moving in the direction of global or planetary religious consolidation on the model of the exclusivistic Middle Ages that came on the heels of Hellenistic inclusivistic pluralism. I think that his judgment on this point is premature. It may be that the *form* of religiously eclectic syncretism is becoming increasingly shared on a global scale, but the *content* of religious thought and behavior is still splintering, fragmenting, becoming more and more diverse in the presence of both more and more religious alternatives and possibilities for combinations of religious symbols as well. So Thompson is right about modern religious polysymbolism and, I believe, wrong about the direction in which it is moving historically. I see polysymbolism pressing toward an even more florescent, inclusivistic, individualistic, privately chosen mix of religious symbols. Again, as Kafka said, sects are reduced to one, and religious fragmentation is being taken in America about as far as it can go.

Taking a look at that "Alexandrian center of it all," America, it is also strikingly clear that American religious polysymbolism is characterized by increasing adhesion and not, as in Hellenistic days, increasing conversion. Swinging from one cosmic palm tree to another (Horton, 1967) is quite easy, and the changing, changeable pattern of religious behavior not only goes on all the time but is, indeed, on the increase. There are even indigenous roots for this phenomenon in America too. When the old Oglala Sioux medicine man Black Elk converted to Catholicism in the early 1930s, he did not really convert; he simply *added* Catholicism to an already flourishing and extraordinarily profound traditional religious life. The same pattern continued in his family and among many Oglala on the Pine Ridge Reservation in South Dakota. On the occasion of the recent death of Benjamin Black Elk, son of Black Elk, the basic funerary rites consisted of two back-to-back all-night-long ceremonials in which traditional Sioux death songs and funereal drumming went on simultaneously with recitation of the Catholic rosary! Or take the Flatheads, who "converted" to Catholicism in order to reap the power of the "Black Robes" and gain military supremacy over the Blackfeet. But when Father de Smet made the mistake of proceeding to allure the Blackfeet as well, the Flatheads immediately felt betrayed and promptly "deconverted" (Harrod, 1971). I should, of course, say "de-adhered," but that's not a word. By definition, here we have illustrations of adhesion and precisely not of conversion.

Something like this pattern of religious adhesion also is evident in contemporary polysymbolism, which is inclusivistic, syncretistic, eclectic, and individually tailored according to private voluntaristic choice. This kind of religious thinking is not like scientific thinking. When paradox and incongruity in a scientific theory begin to occur with some regularity, it becomes necessary, however difficult, to seek out a replacement, another first-order theory. In religious matters, however, especially in polysymbolism, paradox and flat-out logical contradiction abound, yet no effort is made to get it all together. Indeed, as David Miller says (1974, p. 81), the point is the opposite; namely, to keep it all apart. To the extent that polysymbolism as a unifying label gives coherence to this religious flux, it does so only in a second-order manner, in sociological shorthand of a descriptive sort. It does not pretend to unravel the individual mysteries of how so many contradictory religious options can be managed simultaneously in the same mind. In the case of that unsurpassable example of imaginative polysymbolism in action, Norman O. Brown's *Love's Body* (1966), the managing act is handled by basing psychoanalytic and Christian and Buddhist and primitive symbolism on body symbolism, so that there is a potential source of structure and order (Shepherd, 1976). I suspect that such an ordering principle need not, and in fact is not, the case in most varieties of American religious polysymbolism.

Instances of apparently exclusivistic cults, such as the UFOers or the Krishna Consciousness people who decorate our airports and streetcorners, seem to provide prima facie evidence against the case I am making here about the prevalence of adhesion and polysymbolism in American religious life. Admittedly my argument is mostly limited to the generation born in the 1950s and early 1960s, rather than to older folk, although among middle agers the fanatical quest for self-improvement of one sort or another at the hands of Esalen group groping or those piquant programs devoted to assertiveness training has, from my perspective, a distinctively religious (and polysymbolic) tinge. As Thomas Robbins remarks (1977, p. 310), "Countercultural styles are adopted by the larger culture because they can be *adapted* in ways which reinforce existing cultural patterns and do not pose a threat to dominant institutions. If you spend the weekend in the ashram, perhaps you can better tolerate working in the bureaucracy all week."

That caveat about the age spectrum aside, however, the most extreme apparent counterexample that would seem to disprove my case about polysymbolism is the cult of Jesus. Many of its disparate forms seem still to be successful in modern American life, particularly among the young. An initial point to note is that the Jesus movement *is* a cult in the precise technical, sociological sense, not either a sect or a denomination. Why? Because it is not only novel and indigenous but also because, unlike a sect, it bears little resemblance to the Christian tradition and does not even claim to be a reinterpretation of it. In fact, the cult of Jesus is grossly heretical from the point of view of traditional Christianity, so different that one would be hard pressed to see in it a mere reinterpretation or divergent set of emphases. For one thing, the image of Jesus has been transformed from an ethical prophet speaking duty in the name of God the father, to an emissary prophet the imitation of whom is the religious end in itself. This is a religious monolatry of the second person far more radical, and far less nuanced, than Karl Barth's or Karl Rahner's Christocentrism. An extreme rejection of history in favor of immediate ecstatic "highs" also undercuts traditional Christianity's reliance on linear salvation history as the redemptive events that give shape and meaning to the whole of history. Decidedly nonintellectual, really the only content of faith among the Jesus cult is intense devotion to the human figure of Jesus. A more dramatic usurpation of the father's place by the son is unimaginable.

Second, like members of all modern American cults, the Jesus people with their T-shirts stressing that there's only One Way are utterly constrained to *sound* exclusivistic. They literally *must* sound thus. While they are not exactly persecuted, many peers with whom Jesus people have to coexist look on the latter with faintly jaundiced eyes. Exclusivistic-sounding slogans are products among Jesus people of quite deeply embedded needs for mutual and continuing reassurance. For much the same reason, one can be sure that a report of a new sighting boosts the spirits of any hard-core UFOer. Furthermore, the Jesus people were born out of a specific set of historical circumstances that led to a fairly profound sense of psychic deprivation, which in turn led to a widely experienced psychological need for an undemanding and simple way out. As Robert Ellwood puts it (1973, p. 121), "The Jesus Movement has taken such a hold because it has provided an alternative community for a class which had already experienced alienation. These people sensed a difference between themselves and the norms of society. They were possessed by a new vision and a new kind of self-identity, which no one else, it seemed, understood. The drug experience, the new occultism, and radical politics gave them a feeling of being the firstborn of a new and mystic age. But the new age was crucified by the dark side of the psychedelic world and the apparent defeat of their political causes. The new age community had to find another identity in which crucifixion and dark powers had a place as real as that of 'highs.' "

We should not be fooled by the apparent exclusivism that has resulted among Jesus people as among members of other cults. Commitments made to cults in modern America are extremely precarious. Things are changing very fast, and the circumstances under which one makes such a commitment alter dramatically overnight, sometimes perhaps making a person wonder why in the world he or she got involved in the first place. Also there is considerable overlap between Jesus people and groups like the Unification Church of Reverend Moon, and the lines of demarcation among them are not sharp and clear-cut (Sontag, 1977). Lines dividing other cult and occult groups are even less vivid and meaningful.

The upshot of these considerations is that from a diachronic or time-related point of view, polysymbolism can take the form of *serial adhesion,* of people fairly readily moving from one set of religious commitments to another. Allegiances in this context cannot be really deep; these are not genuine conversions to the extent that they are so easily changeable and transformable into new mutants.

Polysymbolism and serial adhesion are notable marks of our religious situation just as they were of Hellenistic religiosity prior to Christianity's triumph in the fourth century. The analogy is surely there, and it is a more telling one than that between ancient gnosticism and modern existentialism. But, rather than heading toward increasing doctrinal specificity and more exclusivistic fences, our historical dynamics are faced in the opposite direction. Cosmetically deep slogans to the contrary, religious wares stripped of doctrinal exclusivism are riding atop the impulse toward the future. To see where conversion as opposed to adhesion still reigns in America, we must look to the evangelical Protestants, to sects and denominations that are hangovers of institutional religion in our society. Institutionalized Pentacostalism among some Protestant (and even Catholic) groups is still growing, and it is the only phenomenon on the American denominational or sectarian fronts that can boast of an increasing enrollment. There may be an element of genuine conversion experience involved in these religions, but even among evangelicals doctrinal specificity is not overly stressed, and, just as for the cults, a certain quality and intensity of religious experience are what count. The variation from one denomination to another in belief in God is considerable. For example, 99 percent of the Southern Baptists, but only 41 percent of the Congregationalists, could say, "I know God really exists and I have no doubts about it." Similar variation exists with respect to other traditional beliefs, for example, belief in life beyond death. We should add, however, that traditionalists with respect to one such belief are likely to be traditionalists with respect to others and that the percentages go up considerably if we include among believers those who admit to having some doubt. For example, in addition to the 41 percent of Congregationalists who have no doubts about the existence of God, 34 percent could say, "While I have doubts, I feel that I do believe in God." (For details, see Glock and Stark, 1965.)

The overall conclusion from these considerations is reasonably clear. A prevalent religious need in America is for religion in a generic sense, whether it take the form of private polysymbolism, serial adhesion, or conversion to an established sect or denomination. While the picture is no doubt confusing, I believe that it is amenable at least to a weak form of sociological explanation.

What do the Healthy-Happy-Holy Organization of Yogi Bhajan, the Unification Church, Erhard Seminars Training (est), Transcendental Meditation, and Scientology have in common? And what do they have in common with older, well-established denominations that emphasize religious experience and being "born again" or, still further, with older sectarian movements such as Jehovah's Witnesses and Christian Science? One thing that all the religious movements in America have in common is of course a shared context. The people making up that social context for the most part cherish individualism as a value, and they are a practically oriented people who feel that whatever works is worthy and that problems, even ones caused by technology, can be solved by more technology. But still deeper problems began to surface in the last half of the twentieth century. Social disruption in America, while it is surely not new, took on real intensity for the first time in a fully modernized situation—its manifestations were the civil rights movement, protest against the Vietnam War, and various kinds of experimentation with differing styles of belief and life among the young. Only the last has survived with much power in American life, and now its form is often a religious one.

Politics and most other social organizations have returned to business as usual in the 1970s, but experimentation with novel ways to mold inner personal experience has mushroomed. "The religious and quasi-religious movements of the seventies are 'successor movements' to the general spiritual crisis of the sixties" (Robbins, 1977, p. 312), and they are meeting deeply felt needs in the general American populace for solace and meaning in an increasingly secularized, bureaucratic, and impersonal world in which the threat of nuclear warfare has not just gone away. All the roles that the modern American plays out in relation to the corporation, to government, or even to the family no longer can add up to a coherent identity. That is a private matter, which Americans often simply *continue* to address religiously—the difference now is that religious and surrogate religious wares have multiplied, so that the scope of available choices for experimentation has never been paralleled in human history.

Americans have always valued almost any variety of religious belief, as indicated by Dwight Eisenhower's famous remark to the effect that everybody ought to believe in something, but exactly *what* is more or less immaterial. We are witnessing now simply a proliferation of religious forms, coupled with a burgeoning self-improvement industry. Ever-increasing amounts of leisure time and apparently unrelenting problems, which are clearly felt sincerely, about personal meaning and identity, combine to form the perfect capitalist symbiosis of high demand for salable productions.

Emphasis on the specific intellectual content of a religious preference is less and less significant in most contemporary religious movements. A kind of deliberate vagueness characterizes institutional Christianity, while deliberate flux and interweaving are the marks of polysymbolic religiosity. Both indicate a continuing press toward religious inclusivism, and to foresee, as Thompson and others do, a totalistic unification and a new religious monopoly in the immediate future seems quite contrary to all the evidence we have at hand. A new "Dark Age" may indeed be on us, but there is not much reason to think that it will be shaped by an obligatory ecclesiastical authority.

Religious symbolism is more and more being taken in a presentational rather than a discursive sense, to use Susanne Langer's distinction (1942). Discursive symbolism is literal and is, like mathematical notations, to be taken in only one way. Presentational symbolism has to do with drama, myth, ritual; it opens up possibilities, and its meanings are multiple, complex, open-ended.

Music offers the chief parallel (Shepherd, 1972). Religious polysymbolism is esthetic, and it yields the same sort of promiscuity that is evident in the person who feels no contradiction whatsoever in loving Palestrina, Beethoven, Dizzy Gillespie, and Carly Simon and Dolly Parton as well. Bearing in mind once again that all analogies exhibit both a similarity and a distinction, however, the difference between musical preferences and religious polysymbolism is that the latter is entertained at a single simultaneous hearing, while presumably it would be less than esthetically pleasing for our music lover to run all of his or her tapes at the same time. That is not a bad image, though, for what I have in mind by the term *polysymbolic religiosity*. All the tapes are indeed being run simultaneously, and the cacophony of voices is extreme. If there is continuity and stability in the identities of polysymbolically religious persons, it lies solely in the very self-consciousness itself of fluidity and flux. This self-consciousness not only acknowledges that the center is gone and irretrievable but also positively revels in that freedom from literalism and univocal dogma. "Meaning," as Norman O. Brown (1966, p. 248) has it, "is new, or not at all; a new creation, or not at all; poetry or not at all. The newness is the metaphor, or nonsense—saying one thing and meaning another. It is the legal fiction, which liberates from the letter of the law and from the tyranny of literal meaning."

References

Brown, N. O. *Love's Body.* New York: Vintage, 1966.

Ellwood, R. S., Jr. *One Way: The Jesus Movement and Its Meaning.* Englewood Cliffs, N. J.: Prentice-Hall, 1973.

Glock, C. Y., and Stark, R. "Is There an American Protestantism?" *Transaction,* 1965, *3* (1), 8–49. Reprinted in R. D. Knudten (Ed.), *The Sociology of Religion: An Anthology.* New York: Appleton-Century-Crofts, 1967.

Harrod, H. L. *Mission Among the Blackfeet.* Norman: University of Oklahoma Press, 1971.

Horton, R. "African Traditional Thought and Western Science." *Africa,* 1967, *37* (1), 50–71; *37* (2), 155–187.

Jonas, H. *The Gnostic Religion.* Boston: Beacon Press, 1963.

Langer, S. K. *Philosophy in a New Key*. New York: Mentor Books, 1942.

Miller, D. L. *The New Polytheism*. New York: Harper & Row, 1974.

Nock, A. D. *Conversion*. New York: Oxford University Press, 1933.

Robbins, T. "Old Wine in Exotic New Bottles." *Journal for the Scientific Study of Religion*, 1977, *16*, 310–313.

Shepherd, W. C. "Religion and the Counter Culture–A New Religiosity?" *Sociological Inquiry*, 1972, *42* (1), 3–9. Reprinted in P. H. McNamara (Ed.), *Religion American Style*. New York: Harper & Row, 1974.

Shepherd, W. C. *Symbolical Consciousness: A Commentary on "Love's Body."* Missoula, Mont.: Scholars Press for the American Academy of Religion, 1976.

Sontag, F. *Sun Myung Moon and the Unification Church*. Nashville, Tenn.: Abingdon, 1977.

Thompson, W. I. *At the Edge of History*. New York: Harper & Row, 1971.

Thompson, W. I. *Passages About Earth*. New York: Harper & Row, 1974.

Thompson, W. I. *Evil and the World Order*. New York: Harper & Row, 1976.

11

Daniel A. Foss
Ralph W. Larkin

The Roar of the Lemming:
Youth, Postmovement Groups, and the Life Construction Crisis

~~~~~~~~~~~~~~~~~~~~~~~~~~~~~~~~~~~

Following the movement of the 1960s, youth culture in the early 1970s was characterized by mass psychic depression[1] and some extremely bizarre phenomena: youthful ex-acidheads shaving their heads, swearing off drugs, sex, and hedonism and donning the saffron robes of the Hari Krishnas; the trial of mass murderer Charley Manson and his family; the rise of various Marxist sectarian groups out of the ashes of the New Left, such as the National Caucus of Labor Committees, Weather Underground, New American Movement, Revolutionary Union, October League, Communist League, and, on the West Coast, the Symbionese Liberation Army; the emergence of fundamentalist Christian sects such as the Children of God, the Alamo Foundation, and the World Christian Liberation Front among ex-movement participants; the development of the Divine Light Mission, headed by the teen-age "Perfect Master and Lord of the Universe," Guru Maharaj Ji; and, more recently, the mass suicide of over 900 members of the socialist People's Temple in Guyana.

The sociology profession has treated these phenomena

under such rubrics as the "new religions" (Needleman, 1971); the "new morality" (Yankelovich, 1974); or "social movements," even though they are not engaged in overt conflict with dominant institutions (Foss and Larkin, 1976). More importantly, sociological researchers have not adequately explained the rise of these religious, communal, and political organizations and their phenomenal success in the early 1970s. Almost all researchers have noted that these religious groups received an influx of ex-movement participants in the period between 1969 and 1973. Hashimoto and McPherson (1976) and Oh (1973), in their studies of Nichiren Shoshu, indicate that it appealed to "hippies" and young, educated, and disaffected youth in the early 1970s. Jesus Freaks and Hari Krishnas were almost exclusively recruited from these ranks. Judah (1974, p. 183) demonstrates that the Krishna organization (ISKON) emerged out of the counterculture and experienced its major growth spurt between 1970 and the middle of 1972, stabilizing in 1973 and 1974. This corresponds quite closely with observations of the Jesus Freaks (Enroth, Ericson, and Peters, 1972; Simmonds, Richardson, and Harder, 1974; Balswick, 1974; Adams and Fox, 1972). Curiously, there is no sociological research on the rise and development of left sectarianism at the same time. The closest we have to an analysis of these groups is O'Brien (1978). However, O'Brien focuses mainly on doctrinal disputes between Leninist parties.

A serious problem of the research in this area is that, in attempting to explain the popularity of these organizations to ex-movement participants, the researchers either debunk or take the newly converted members' explanations at face value. Thus Enroth, Ericson, and Peters (1972), who are pleased and relieved to see unwashed hippies become responsible Christians, view the young as resurrecting the spirit of early Christianity. Balswick (1974) claims they synthesize countercultural ideals with religious fundamentalism. Adams and Fox (1972) and Kopkind (1973) view Jesus Freaking as a form of copping out and privatization, a critique that has been made of the various religious organizations in the early 1970s by the left. None of the approaches lead us to a sufficient explanation as to why the phenomenon has occurred in the first place.

The closest sociologists have come to explanations as to why these groups arose and attracted ex-movement participants are found in Robbins, Anthony, and Curtis (1975), Mauss and Petersen (1974), Petersen and Mauss (1973), and Gordon (1974). Robbins, Anthony, and Curtis and Mauss and Petersen agree that the Christian groups operate as way stations to conventional lives for ex-freaks and countercultural types by enforcing rigorous discipline on their members. Mauss and Petersen also suggest that Jesus Freaking is a response to psychic and social deprivation. Gordon, however, focuses on what he calls *identity synthesis;* that is, adopting a third identity that subsumes two earlier ones. While these hypotheses are true, they ignore the really difficult questions, such as why ex-movement participants needed a road back to conventionality, why they needed to assume new identities, why this occurred primarily among formerly dissident youth, and why it occurred in the early 1970s.

In an earlier paper, we characterized these new organizations as "postmovement groups" and demonstrated their relationship with the youth movement of the 1960s (Foss and Larkin, 1976). It is our purpose in this chapter to sketch the structure of such postmovement groups and analyze why they arose when they did, why they tended to manifest exotic forms and bizarre behaviors, and most importantly, why these groups appealed to former movement participants.

The research reported here is based on (1) a three-and-a-half year participant observation study of the Divine Light Mission; (2) observation and reading of the documents of the following Marxist organizations: the National Caucus of Labor Committees (NCLC, now the U.S. Labor Party), Revolutionary Union, Attica Brigade, October League, and Youth Against War and Fascism; (3) personal experiences with co-counseling, the Sullivanians, and the Hari Krishnas (International Society for KRSNA Consciousness [ISKON]); and (4) an examination of journalistic and sociological literature in the field. Some difficulty arose from the fact that some groups were overtly violent (for example, the Manson Family, the Lyman Family, and the Symbionese Liberation Army), thus precluding investigation; others were extremely circumspect about their internal workings and required infiltration (for example, the

Tony and Susan Alamo Foundation and Scientology); and most are extremely suspicious of sociological investigation. For example, even though the authors received the secret knowledge of Guru Maharaj Ji at their initiation into the Divine Light Mission and were active in it over a three-and-a-half year period, devotees regarded our sociological probing as a deviation from pursuit of the experience of the absolute and rebuked us accordingly. In their terms, we were too "mindy." However, one compensating factor was that most groups were highly media conscious, because they wanted to propagate the faith to the larger public.

Postmovement Groups

Postmovement groups are organizations that emerged in the wake of the youth movement of the 1960s. Each group attempted to reconcile the freak vision of an anarchist communard post-scarcity society[2] generated by the 1960s movement with the re-ascendance of dominant institutions and the attenuation of the movement. On some level, formerly dissident youth had to make peace with the dominant structure or die.[3] Because of the contradiction between the movement "vision" and the declining possibilities of its fulfillment, youth who were highly committed to the movement were left in the difficult position of reconciling the irreconcilable. We call this the "life construction crisis," which the postmovement groups attempted to resolve and which we will explicate in detail later.

It is obvious that only a small percentage of activist youth actually joined postmovement groups. Nevertheless, their cultural importance far outstripped their numbers. Postmovement groups were "indicative minorities" (see Foss and Larkin, 1976) and as such tended to draw the trends in youth culture to their logical (and often absurd) conclusions. In the same way that hippies were an indicative minority during the period between 1965 and 1967, the postmovement groups occupied the same position between 1971 and 1975.[4] Indeed, the variety observed among the postmovement groups and groups that share some postmovement characteristics serves to underscore the pervasiveness and depth of the cultural syndrome we are analyzing.

Postmovement groups can be classified according to their historical and cultural relationship to the white middle-class youth movement of the 1960s. Some groups evolved organically out of the decomposing youth culture at the end of the 1960s or later. In this category, we can place the Divine Light Mission of Guru Maharaj Ji, the Children of God, the Alamo Foundation, the More Houses, and many of the psychotherapies under the aegis of the "Human Potential Movement." Other groups were formed at least in part in order to repudiate some or all of the characteristic cultural manifestations of the 1960s either during the movement period or afterward. Such groups are the Hari Krishnas (see Judah, 1974), NCLC, and the Progressive Labor Party. Still other groups antedated the existence of the movement, sometimes by decades; did not appeal to freak youth during the movement period; and, after the movement's demise, received an influx of former movement participants and still younger people, all cast adrift as atomized individuals and demoralized by the prospects of the 1970s. These groups include Scientology, United Pentecostal Churches, various Trotskyist sects, and Nichiren Shoshu (Oh, 1973).

Postmovement groups took four forms: (1) Authoritarian communes such as the Metelica Aquarian Foundation ("Spirit in Flesh" Commune) in western Massachusetts, the Lyman Family in Boston, the Manson Family in California, and the More Houses in Oakland, California. Each of these communes was formed around a charismatic leader who was, more or less, deified by the followers and allowed to exercise almost absolute power over their lives (Foss, 1974; Feldon, 1972). (2) Mechanistic Marxist parties such as the October League, Revolutionary Union (which successively became the Attica Brigade and the Revolutionary Student Brigade), the National Caucus of Labor Committees (now known as the U.S. Labor Party), and the Symbionese Liberation Army (which combined the Marxist and commune forms). All these parties claim to be revolutionary vanguards, enforce on their members rigorous discipline, and demand strict obedience (O'Brien, 1978). (3) Oriental sects such as Nichiren Shoshu, the Hari Krishnas (ISKON), and the Divine Light Mission of the "Teen-age Perfect Master," Guru Maharaj Ji. All believed that, when the world learned of their mystic experiences generated through meditation or chanting, the millennium would come about, and people would live together in peace, sharing a common level of elevated consciousness (Levine, 1974; Oh, 1973; Foss and Larkin, 1975). (4) Various Christian sects such as the Children of God, the Tony and Susan Alamo Foundation in Southern California, and various "Jesus Freak" collectives throughout the country. Their doctrine was similar to that of the Oriental sects, except that the central mystery was "allowing Jesus into your heart," which was the prerequisite for personal and world peace (Enroth, Ericson, and Peters, 1972; Gordon, 1974).

In our study of postmovement groups, we found that they cater to similar motivational syndromes and conform, more or less, to the following characteristics: (1) an authoritarian structure, (2) appropriation of a fragment of the vision articulated in the youth culture of the 1960s (peace, love, revolution, ego transcendence, and so on), (3) a nonconflictual stance toward society at large, (4) denigration of sensual indulgence, (5) minute regulation of the lives of their membership, (6) maintenance of a fierce exclusivity based on doctrines claiming a monopoly of the truth, and (7) the claim to be solutions to the meaninglessness of life.

1. Postmovement groups, regardless of whether their manifest goal was to transform the social order through the development of a revolutionary vanguard, as in the case of the Marxist sectarians, or through propagation of the faith, as in the case of the religious sects, developed an authoritarian structure, formally articulated with sharp boundary definition. Each of these groups developed a cult of personality around a single leader who served as an embodiment of the vision of the membership and whom they revered. In the religious groups, the leader became deified and was worshipped. Prabhupada, the spiritual master of the Hari Krishnas, Guru Maharaj Ji of the Divine Light Mission,[5] and Moses David of the Children of God are all examples of such deified leaders. Even when postmovement groups were established on nonreligious grounds, such deification occurred. Mel Lyman, the founder of "The Family," a Boston-area freak[6] commune, had proclaimed himself God by 1970. Victor Barranco, the originator of the More Houses in Oakland, California, became the spiritual father of the "marks" (his term) he exploits in a profit-making

scheme to rebuild old houses (Feldon, 1972). According to Feldon, Barranco induced young ex-freaks to rebuild houses without compensation and, when they were finished, charged them $200 a month to live in them. He also ran the Institute of Human Abilities, which amounted to having his devotees pay up to $65 for an hour in his presence. As for the Marxist sectarians, Lyndon Marcus (now La Rouche) of the National Caucus of Labor Committees (NCLC) has been credited with the ability to foretell the precise development of world capitalism for the next five years, down to a worldwide depression, culminating in the mass strike, in the midst of which the Labor Committee, knowing exactly what to do, will seize power (Foss, 1974).

Each of these groups was pyramidal in structure with line of authority highly articulated from the top down. The NCLC, directed by ex-efficiency expert Marcus, operated a tightly knit bureaucracy that measured its progress *by the hour* (Foss, 1974). The Divine Light Mission was rampant with "titleism" and had developed a centralized bureaucratic structure that spent most of its effort printing, filling out, filing, and data-processing forms that monitor organizational activity. Maharaj Ji himself held the title of "Supreme Chief Executive of the Mission" in addition to that of "Perfect Master and Lord of the Universe" (Foss and Larkin, 1975). Other, perhaps smaller, groups did not manifest bureaucratic structures. In these cases, as in the Lyman Family or the Alamo Foundation, the authority was patriarchal and came directly from the leader (Feldon, 1972; Cahill, 1973; Enroth, Ericson, and Peters, 1972).

2. Each group appropriated a fragment of the freak vision, often using it as the basis of legitimation of the authoritarian structure. The servility of the members was used as evidence of spirituality, ego transcendence, or manifestations of peace and love (Levine, 1974; Foss and Larkin, 1975). When members allowed themselves to be subject to hierarchical authority, such personal subjugation was *prima facie* evidence of commitment to the propagation of love and peace or the historical necessity of the revolution.[7]

3. Postmovement groups developed nonconflictual stances toward society at large. Like their predecessors, youth of the 1970s believed in the inevitability of radical change; however, unlike

youth of the 1960s, they believed that social transformation could not be achieved by immediate action on and conflict with objective social reality but must be brought about by the attainment of spiritual perfection by the members and the diffusion of spiritual perfection to the population.[8] Where conflict did occur, it was not with the larger society but among postmovement groups competing with each other for constituencies or contending over minute differences in doctrine. For example, in mid 1973, the NCLC began "Operation Mop-Up," a campaign to destroy the Communist Party by beating up its members. At Millennium '73, a Divine Light Mission festival, thirty Hari Krishnas were arrested while protesting Guru Maharaj Ji's claim to Perfect Mastership.

4. All postmovement groups broke sharply with the notion, widely disseminated in the late 1960s among white middle-class youth, that removal of limitations on immediate gratification and rediscovery of the body was a necessary aspect of the transformation of the entire social order. Instead, they stood for an earlier cultural syndrome: They advocated self-discipline, self-sacrifice, hard work, systematic and orderly living, and renunciation of the pleasures of the flesh. All or nearly all of these groups discouraged uninhibited sexuality, and many encouraged sexual abstinence. Among the Jesus Freaks and the Eastern sects, renunciation of sexuality tended to show that one had attained spiritual perfection and that one was relying on the source of ultimate satisfaction, which lies within: on the holy spirit; Krishna, the Reservoir of Pleasure; Theta waves (in Scientology); the universal energy source (Divine Light Mission) (see Robbins and Anthony, 1972; Judah, 1974; Adams and Fox, 1972; Malko, 1970; Cameron, 1973; Levine, 1974). Among the Marxist sects, sexual restraint seemed to be taken as a sign that one is "serious." A member of the NCLC once boasted to one of the authors, "I've got no time for girls. I'm too busy doing class organizing." O'Brien (1978) has also noted the cultural conservatism of Marxist-Leninist parties, which often led them to take reactionary positions on women's and gay rights issues. Some groups, such as the Children of God and the Hari Krishnas, have not discouraged marriage but have insisted that marital sex be intended exclusively for procreation.

5. These groups minutely regulate the everyday lives of

their membership. Short hair, conventional dress for men, and modest dress for women have been the norms in several groups. Most prohibited the use of substances defined by the conventional culture as drugs, and many banned alcohol as well.

In our study of the Divine Light Mission (DLM), we found they maintained a rule book called "The Ashram Manual," which listed page after page of rules, regulations, and injunctions concerning the behavior and demeanor of the *premies* (a Hindi word meaning "lover"), as devotees of Guru Maharaj Ji call themselves. It contained dress codes for male and female *premies,* daily schedules, and even advice on how to act toward parents; and it advised against hitchhiking—one of the main sources of mobility for many *premies* a few years before (Foss and Larkin, 1975).

6. All postmovement groups maintain a fierce exclusivity based on the claims of their doctrines and leaders to embody a monopoly of the truth. The fragmentation of the youth culture was most dramatically demonstrated in such claims of exclusivity. During the 1960s, as the vision developed, it was able to incorporate greater varieties of orientations and, because of its subjectivist and existentialist core, became more or less universally accepted, because it raised personal experience as the ultimate criterion of validity (Foss, 1972). Although postmovement groups gave lip service to the criterion of personal experience, those experiences that were the exclusive domain of the group became the basis of the arbitration of truth. For example, devotees of Guru Maharaj Ji could not seem to complete a sentence without including the word *experience.* However, to them "experience" meant experience *in the knowledge,* which those who had not been initiated into the secret meditative techniques of the Divine Light Mission could not possibly comprehend unless they too become devotees. Because the sole purpose of the organization was the propagation of the one and only truth, the organization became the embodiment of that truth, and membership in the organization was the only means by which one could have access to the truth.

7. In line with the freaks' characterization of conventional society as meaningless, postmovement groups offer themselves as remedies for the meaninglessness endured by average middle-class citizens and drug-soaked hedonistic hippies alike (and those that

did not make overt promises also seemed to attract members who joined at least in part out of a desire for a more "meaningful existence"). Whereas freaks of the 1960s found meaning in maintaining a position of defiance and opposition to the "plastic world," postmovement groups found meaning in escape from the complexities and incongruities of the material world (or the world of the mind) into a more transcendent, simplified view of the cosmos independent of material reality. Jesus Freaks recruited among "long-hairs" by denouncing the pointlessness of conflict or the hedonistic life and by claiming that the true Christian can stay permanently high on Jesus and obtain greater joy than can be derived from drugs or sex: "Try Jesus—God's eternal Trip!" (Adams and Fox, 1972; Cahill, 1973; Petersen and Mauss, 1973; Enroth, Ericson, and Peters, 1972). They promised the end of all earthly mental anguish, which was said to be derived from being caught up in the toils of a society dominated by Satan. The Eastern cults promised the same thing, using different words: The material world is illusion, and a life committed solely to activity in the material world was bound to be meaningless and incapable of sustaining true happiness (Petersen and Mauss, 1973; Judah, 1974). Marxist sectarians promised a meaningful life by indicating that the individual could choose to swim either with the inexorable tides of history or against them (Foss, 1974).

Postmovement Groups and the
Life Construction Crisis

The "life construction crisis" is not a part of the "identity crisis" that neo-Freudians such as Erikson (1950) state is necessary for adolescents to survive if they are to be autonomous adults. The focus of such "identity crises" is the paternalistic family, which is diminishing rapidly in contemporary society (see Kenniston, 1968; Friedenberg, 1959; Gillis, 1974; Kohn, 1969). Nor is it the kind of "cognitive dissonance" that occurs as a result of the failure of prophecy (Festinger, Reichen, and Schacter, 1956). Although closer to Kenniston's notion of the problem of the integration of the individual self into the social order experienced by youth (Kenniston, 1970), the life construction crisis is, on the one hand, more historically determined, and on the other, much more acute in terms of the contradictions experienced.

Postmovement groups emerged in the early and mid 1970s to help youth resolve the contradictions and alleviate the psychic pain[9] resulting from the clash of two incompatible interpretations of social reality: one derived from the dominant ideology of bureaucratic rationality (as they perceive it) that pervaded the society of their formative years and the other derived from experiences of the 1960s that had given rise to the subjectivist "movement" ideology. The ideology of bureaucratic rationality gave heavy emphasis to the maintenance of the reality principle, centering on the importance of getting ahead, future orientation, cognition, deferred gratification, deference to authority, sexual inhibition, punctuality, blandness, and getting along and going along (Freud [1931], 1962). The "movement" attacked all such notions and, although it never had a really coherent ideology, gave greater emphasis to the pleasure principle relative to the reality principle. The "movement" ideology centered around joy, immediate gratification of impulses, creativity, open sexuality, sensuality, love, living in the present, ego transcendence, mysticism, and suspicion of *all* hierarchy.

With the ebbing of the movement in the early 1970s, the prospects for social transformation were visibly diminished, and formerly dissident youth were forced to accommodate themselves to the newly emerging reality and the reassertion of the authority of dominant institutions. There was no returning to the *status quo ante*. The vision of the 1960s had generated aspirations that were impossible to fulfill.[10] Caught between lives they despised and lives they could not possibly live, youthful dissidents of the 1960s experienced acute personal crises in the wake of the movement in the early 1970s.[11] The life construction crisis was subjectively experienced as a crisis in meaning. Activities previously experienced as revolutionary, antiestablishment, or intrinsically satisfying—such as the taking of psychedelic drugs, marching in protests, or participating in sex—were drained of their meaning as the movement subsided, leaving the movement participant with a feeling of senselessness and emptiness. What was previously pregnant with meaning and purpose had become mechanical, disembodied, and a source of acute despair. Judah (1974, p. 164; emphasis in original) quotes a devotee on her reasons for joining the Krishnas:

> I was getting crazier and crazier each year, and more and more frustrated ... *so what brought me to Krishna Consciousness was complete, overwhelming, undeniable, and irrevocable distress.* There was nothing I could do. I was even considering going through psychotherapy ... I can't begin to describe how empty I was feeling. I had no association; I was seventy or eighty pounds overweight. I had no money. I considered myself completely mad. I had no education, no skills, no friends—I had nothing.

Members both of Christian sects and the Divine Light Mission made the claim that their saviors "filled them up." No longer were they empty containers.

Our research indicates that postmovement groups offered themselves as alternatives to the meaningless participation in a dying movement and to the meaninglessness of middle-class existence. In the first phase of their development, from about 1971 until early 1974, they tended to attract ex-movement participants who were forced to reconcile themselves to the end of the movement. This was a period of rapid expansion, and postmovement groups proliferated (see Note 4). However, beginning in about 1973, postmovement groups began to attract younger members who had not been participants in the youth movement but who tended to come from more traditional bourgeois culture and who, when faced with the more "liberated" youth of the 1970s, dropped out of the highly competitive sexual marketplace where they felt they had low exchange value. For the older members, the life construction crisis was more historically generated, while for the younger, more inhibited members, it was more developmental, arising more from the problems of the life cycle.[12] Following the postmovement period, which ended in 1975, groups that have been able to survive into the latter half of the decade cater primarily to this stratum of youth, with the Unification Church of Sun Myung Moon being the prime example.

Because the life construction crisis was generated by the collision of two incompatible realities, the postmovement groups resolved the contradiction through the determination of a fixed absolute point of reference that stood apart from, repudiated, or subsumed both of the rival interpretations of social reality.[13] The Marxist vanguard parties tended to adopt ideologies that repudiated both the dominant and movement interpretations of reality by imposing defiantly obsolete interpretations of reality based on Marx's description of mid-nineteenth-century capitalist society (O'Brien, 1978). Some fundamentalist Christian sects did the same thing, using a literal interpretation of the Bible (Enroth, Ericson, and Peters, 1972; Petersen and Mauss, 1973). The more gnostic Christian sects and the Oriental sects subsumed rival interpretations by focusing on more "ultimate" questions than those dealt with by either bureaucratic rationality or the subjectivist ideology of the youth culture. That is, the phenomenal world and sense data became merely illusory and changeable surface phenomena, which only lead to idle speculation about a reality that by virtue of its mutability was manifestly false. Behind and beyond these illusions of the mind was the "true and absolute" reality of God realization, which transcended mere mental speculation, was infinite, eternal, and unchanging (Judah, 1974; Levine, 1974; Foss and Larkin, 1975). This truth was represented as entirely external to the individual, as was the case with the Marxist sects that taught different versions of the comprehensive theory of dialectical and historical materialism and simultaneously offered a "vanguard" organization whose ultimate mission was to accomplish the consummation of the historical process (Foss, 1974). More commonly, however, the absolute truth was located partly "inside" and partly "outside" the individual. The group promised the individual a subjective experience more "fulfilling," "transcendental," "pure," or "divine" than may be derived from either the chemical and sexual indulgences of the youth culture or the pursuit of a conventional middle-class life pattern. ("Guru Maharaj Ji gives you the knowledge you can't get in college!" was a common aphorism in the Divine Light Mission— Foss and Larkin, 1975.) At the same time, the truth was manifested in the leader or spiritual master who revealed it and in the hierarchy he had established and to which he had delegated the task of propagating it.

The ideologies and subcultures of postmovement groups as a rule scrambled elements of both conventional and freak interpretations of social reality. But people attracted to these groups were in search of a reality so ultimate that contradictory interpretations of *social* reality could be shrugged off as minor quibbles. They therefore compulsively searched for some form of the ultimate. The postmovement group accordingly obliged by doing the following: First, it furnished an interpretation of reality centered around absolute truth. Second, it systematically manipulated fears and anxieties about straying from concentration on the ultimate (Richardson, Harder, and Simmonds, 1972) and furnished a system of rewards, punishments, and peer-group pressures to ensure that the individual at least try to appear to other members to be firmly concentrated on the goal. Third, it relieved the believer of the necessity of becoming an individual by condemning the rival ideals of middle-class individualism, "doing your own thing" in pointless revolt, and pecuniary accumulation in the corrupt outside world (Judah, 1974; Enroth, Ericson, and Peters, 1972). Fourth, it systematically attacked the concepts and assumptions about social causality, social organization, and the legitimacy of hierarchy that the individual had derived from the "outside world" and did so most rigorously when such concepts and assumptions were applied to the organizational structure (or patriarchal hierarchy) itself (Foss and Larkin, 1978).

Concepts and assumptions about social behavior and social relations were most commonly attacked by dissociating from all unauthorized mentations. Especially for lower-ranking members, the group norms prescribed that all verbal expression be accompanied by evidence of concern with the ultimate. There was a consistent tendency for these groups to prohibit "thinking" as spiritually dangerous, conducive to animalistic behavior, or symptomatic of mental illness (Cahill, 1973; Feldon, 1972; Adams and Fox, 1972; Levine, 1974). The struggle against the ego made possible the perfect subordination of the believer to the leader and the proper performance of one's duties in the leader's scheme of things. The simultaneous liquidation of both ego and thinking was therefore closely linked in postmovement ideology.

The Hari Krishnas were strictly enjoined against "mental speculation" and were taught that vain "philosophies" were part and parcel of the decline of civilization. Levine (1974, p. 98) cited one of Prabhupada's maxims: "If you begin a sentence with 'I think,' you better end it in the closet." Hari Krishnas spoke of "the tongue" in exactly the same way that DLM *premies* spoke of "the mind": as uncontrollable, treacherous, endowed with a malicious life of its own (Foss and Larkin, 1975). Levine (1974, p. 163) quoted a devotee: "The tongue is an uncontrollable clown, a juggler, a spy in the house of God." To avert subversion by the tongue, it was best to keep it occupied by chanting the names of God.

To DLM *premies,* the "mind" was a tormentor that "keeps jumping around from place to place." The knowledge "stills the mind" and brings it to a "center point." To "the mind" was attributed a malevolent will of its own; "the mind" sought to preserve its own existence against the threat represented by the knowledge. DLM attitudes toward "the mind" were partially revealed in a skit performed at Guru Maharaj Ji's birthday party on December 10, 1973, where it was portrayed in Devil costume. The *premies* took seriously Guru Maharaj Ji's Third Commandment, "Leave no room in your mind for doubt." They gave *satsang* (literally, "company of truth," applied to testimonials given by *premies*) to each other as much as possible in the course of conversation such that only a few standard themes could be expressed (stories of the holy family and mahatmas—Mission "Holy Men"; praise of the holy family and Guru Maharaj Ji in particular; the knowledge—mystical teachings of Guru Maharaj Ji; how I received knowledge; love; peace; how soon it will be before everyone has this knowledge; and so on). An individual who failed to give sufficient *satsang* in the course of conversation, using the proper inflections and gushes, even if he or she had received knowledge, was not to be trusted (Foss and Larkin, 1975). Researchers of the Jesus Freaks found similar syndromes that included fearing and loathing of the mind. Adams and Fox (1972) found that Jesus Freaks used gnostic experiences to avoid thinking about problems. Richardson, Harder, and Simmonds (1972) claim that the Jesus Freaks learn a language of "nonthought."

The pain generated by the life construction crisis could be characterized by postmovement groups as *needless* pain self-inflicted by deviation from the absolute truth. Yet the path to the realization of the infinite was also fraught with difficulty and pain, as many initiates of postmovement groups who were originally promised instant enlightenment found out. Yet the pain generated by the quest for the absolute was legitimated in postmovement groups as the pain of *growth* as opposed to the pain of nothingness and despair (Judah, 1974). Thus, members of postmovement groups would undergo what an outsider might consider suffering without admitting it except as a process leading to greater joy. NCLC members claim they have transcended the bourgeois ego and have become true beings. Among the religious sects, there was a celebration of surrender and a fierce pride in having overcome the difficulties of the spiritual path. A Hari Krishna devotee said, "The personal battle is the story, the defeat of *maya* [a Hindi word that, roughly translated, means "illusion" and refers to the world of sense data], the vanquishment of *maya's* ego. And the death of sex, daughter of *maya's* ego, is only a subplot" (Levine, 1974, p. 163).

Whether the goal is to be a true revolutionary or a seeker of God, within the crucible of the postmovement group, former definitions of selfhood and former notions of social reality are burned away as the "new person" is forged with his or her eyes focused only on the "ultimate goal." Lapses that create pain are in turn lessons for future behavior, in which the postmovement member attempts to purify him- or herself in preparation for the apocalypse (Enroth, Ericson, and Peters, 1972; Richardson, Harder, and Simmonds, 1972). This state of continual preparedness and vigilance for deviations in oneself and one's fellows not only allows the postmovement group member to negate both conventional and movement interpretations of reality but also helps him or her to shut them out of the mind, because *any* considerations of alternate interpretations of reality are *prima facie* evidence that the individual has lost sight of the ultimate goal and is needlessly causing him- or herself grievous pain.

Thus the pain of the life construction crisis was alleviated through circumvention. The world that generated it was trivialized: The vision of the 1960s was simultaneously effaced and transformed into a "new consciousness" in which various fragments of the vision were incorporated into more "ultimate" concerns, competitive struggles that created much fear and anguish were avoided, and, because postmovement groups maintained ideological opposition to conventional existence and some mode of "alternative life-styles," their members were able to support the belief that they were building a new society that fulfilled the (revised) vision of the 1960s.

Notes

1. The psychic depression was noted by *Newsweek* Magazine in June 1970. They stated that college students saw Kent State not only as the expression of a corrupt system but also as a defeat for dissident youth. Since Woodstock in August of 1969, the "counter-culture" was showing unmistakable signs of degeneration: the defeat of People's Park in September, the Altamont fiasco in December, the uncovering of the Manson Family in early 1970, and, finally, the Kent and Jackson State killings. To top it off, there was no end in sight of the Vietnam War. Other commentators on the onset of psychic depression among youth in 1970 are Mehnert (1976) and Hendin (1975).

2. Probably Abbie Hoffman (1968, 1969) was the best formulator of the freak vision of the 1960s. He emphasizes the anarchist-communard postscarcity view in his writings. More academic views of the 1960s vision exist in Roszak (1969) and Foss (1972). The postscarcity argument is made by Bookchin (1971) from a "serious" left perspective.

3. We are quite serious about this. Two close activist friends of one of the authors committed suicide within six months of each other in 1973. Judah (1974) notes that many seekers claim that if they hadn't found Krishna Consciousness they would have died. Our own research indicates a similar level of desperation among devotees of Guru Maharaj Ji. Judah also cites a case of a young man who was in and out of the Hari Krishnas and finally committed suicide. During our study of the Divine Light Mission, there were three suicides among ashram residents. The *Statistical Abstract of the United States* (U.S. Department of Commerce, 1975) shows that between 1970 and 1973 the suicide rate for males between the ages of fifteen and twenty-four rose from 13.5 to 17 per 100,000 and that

the rate of increase was double that of the previous decade. Between 1960 and 1970 young male suicides increased at the rate of .49 per year, from 8.6 per 100,000 in 1960 to 13.5 in 1970. The average rate of increase between 1970 and 1973 was 1.2 per year.

4. There is a rare unanimity on this point. All researchers cited in this work adhere to the notion that the groups they studied began in the late 1960s or early 1970s. Those who studied their groups over periods of several years note that the groups they studied stabilized between 1972 and 1973. For observations of Marxist sectarians, see O'Brien (1978) and Foss (1974); for Jesus Freaks, see Mauss and Petersen (1974) and Simmonds, Richardson, and Harder (1974); and for Hari Krishnas, see Judah (1974, p. 183).

5. All observations of the Divine Light Mission, Guru Maharaj Ji, and his devotees come from Foss and Larkin (1975).

6. The freaks evolved during the most radical phase of the white middle-class youth movement in 1968 and 1969. Also called freak radicals and "prairie people" within the Students for a Democratic Society (SDS), they combined a radical critique of American society with cultural dissidence. A synthesis of the New Left and the hippies, they tended to live in communes, use psychedelic drugs, avoid work, and experiment with a wide variety of sexual indulgences while concurrently reading the writings of Mao Tsetung, glorifying the heroics of Ché Guevara, and rooting for the National Liberation Front in Vietnam.

7. Judah (1974, p. 125) notes that most Krishna devotees acknowledge they were against all authority in the late 1960s. Later on, he quotes a devotee as saying (1974, p. 171)—in response to the question, "You have no difficulty at all accepting the fact that (Prabhupada) is the supreme authority? And that he can tell you exactly what to do with your life?"—"No! No question at all! When you accept the spiritual master, it is understood that you will follow perfectly the dictates of the scripture." Judah interprets the willingness of the Krishna devotees to subject themselves to authority as indicative of the possibility that rebellious youth "were actually seeking an authority by which they might live" (Judah, 1974, p. 127). Although he hedges his bets by advising against overgeneralizing, Judah is at pains to explain this particular inversion of 1960s culture. Judah's problem is that he accepts the devotees' redefinitions of their past at face value without analyzing the devotees' purposes in the redefinitions. As was the case in the *premies* of

the DLM, old sins were exaggerated and cultural inversions justified on the basis of new means to old goals; for example, changing the world. Such self-serving redefinitions were, in themselves, attempts to bridge the life construction crisis described here, which Judah overlooked.

8. From this, we do not in the least exclude the Marxist sectarians, for, while the latter claimed to be "materialistic" and "scientific," to use the "dialectical method," to be opposed to "antiintellectualism," and to be striving for a proletarian class revolution on the material plane, they were faced with the undeniable fact that the working class resolutely ignored them. The proletarian revolution would therefore come about through the inevitable working out of the contradictions of capitalism, which for at least the immediate future are outside control of the sect members but which, when they should ripen, will make the working class properly class conscious. For this reason, the Marxist sectarians' proletarian revolution had precisely the same subcultural function as the Jesus Freaks' Second Coming of Christ—since the apocalypse could not be advanced through immediate action in the material world, it was best to preoccupy oneself with the attainment of the Marxist version of spiritual perfection—that is, true consciousness—through thorough assimilation of the sect's version of Marxism, study of the sect newspaper and pamphlets, and rote learning of the writings of Marx, Engels, Lenin, Stalin, Mao, Enver Hoxha, and Kim II Sung. True consciousness divorced from practice and thus became an end in itself.

We might add that the attenuation of conflict has been thoroughly documented in the literature. See Richardson, Harder, and Simmonds (1972), Kopkind (1973), Robbins, Anthony, and Curtis (1975), Adams and Fox (1972), and Howard (1974).

9. Although many sociologists seem to shrink from such a term as *psychic pain,* the term describes quite accurately the subjective experience of ex-movement participants in the early 1970s. The testimony in Judah (1974), Petersen and Mauss (1973), Enroth, Ericson, and Peters (1972), Adams and Fox (1972), and our own work (Foss and Larkin, 1975; Foss, 1974) all attest to the psychic difficulties of youth in the early 1970s. See also Note 3.

10. This is an unavoidable consequence of all social movements, successful or not. For an elaboration, see Foss and Larkin (1978).

11. Evidence for this assertion will be found in Gordon (1974), Petersen and Mauss (1973), Judah (1974), Robbins, Anthony, and Curtis (1975), and Foss and Larkin (1975).

12. Our research indicates that the newer arrivals in post-movement groups tended to be more from working-class backgrounds, have a more rigid and doctrinaire approach to their beliefs, and had little knowledge and awareness of the revolt of the 1960s.

13. Gordon (1974) notes that alternative identities are subsumed (or consolidated) within the newly taken Christian identity. Our position concerns alternative and contradictory *reality systems,* of which personal identity is but a part.

References

Adams, R., and Fox, R. "Mainlining Jesus: The New Trip." *Society,* 1972, *9*, (14), 50–56.

Balswick, J. "The Jesus People Movement: A Generational Interpretation." *Journal of Social Issues,* 1974, *30*, 23–42.

Bookchin, M. *Post-Scarcity Anarchism.* Berkeley, Calif.: Ramparts, 1971.

Cahill, T. "True Believers and the Guises of the Weasel." *Rolling Stone,* 1973, no. 136, 1, 42–50.

Cameron, C. (Ed.). *Who Is Guru Maharaj Ji?* New York: Bantam, 1973.

Enroth, R., Ericson, E., and Peters, C. B. *The Jesus People.* Grand Rapids, Mich.: Erdmans, 1972.

Erikson, E. *Childhood and Society.* New York: Norton, 1950.

Feldon, D. *Mindfuckers.* New York: Straight Arrow Books, 1972.

Festinger, L., Reichen, H., and Schacter, S. *When Prophecy Fails.* New York: Harper & Row, 1956.

Foss, D. *Freak Culture: Life Style and Politics.* New York: New Critics Press, 1972.

Foss, D. "Saving the Soul in the Seventies." Unpublished manuscript, Department of Sociology, Rutgers, the State University, Newark, N.J. 07102, 1974.

Foss, D., and Larkin, R. "The Premies: A Study of the Followers of the Teenage Perfect Master, Guru Maharaj Ji." Unpublished manuscript, Department of Sociology, Rutgers, the State University, Newark, N.J. 07102, 1975.

Foss, D., and Larkin, R. "From 'The Gates of Eden' to 'Day of the Locust': An Analysis of the Dissident Youth Movement of the 1960s and Its Heirs in the 1970s—the Post-Movement Groups." *Theory and Society*, 1976, *3*, 45–64.

Foss, D., and Larkin, R. "Seven Ways of Selling Out: Post-Social Movement Adaptations in a Comparative Historical Perspective." Paper presented at the 73rd annual American Sociological Association meeting, San Francisco, August 1978.

Foss, D., and Larkin, R. "Worshiping the Absurd: The Negation of Social Causality Among Post-Movement Youth." *Sociological Analysis*, 1978, *39*, 157–164.

Freud, S. *Civilization and Its Discontents*. New York: Norton, 1962. (Originally published 1931.)

Friedenberg, E. *The Vanishing Adolescent*. New York: Dell, 1959.

Gillis, J. *Youth and History*. New York: Academic Press, 1974.

Gordon, D. "The Jesus People: An Identity Synthesis." *Urban Life and Culture*, 1974, *3*, 159–178.

Hashimoto, H., and McPherson, W. "Rise and Decline of Sokagakkai: Japan and the United States." *Review of Religious Research*, 1976, *17*, 82–92.

Hendin, H. *The Age of Sensation: A Psychoanalytic Exploration of Youth in the 1970s*. New York: McGraw-Hill, 1975.

Hoffman, A. *Revolution for the Hell of It*. New York: Dial Press, 1968.

Hoffman, A. *Woodstock Nation*. New York: Vintage Books, 1969.

Howard, J. *The Cutting Edge: Social Movements and Social Change in America*. New York: Lippincott, 1974.

Judah, J. S. *Hare Krishna and the Counterculture*. New York: Wiley, 1974.

Kenniston, K. *Young Radicals*. New York: Harcourt Brace Jovanovich, 1968.

Kenniston, K. *Youth and Dissent*. New York: Harcourt Brace Jovanovich, 1970.

Kohn, M. *Class and Conformity*. Homewood, Ill.: Dorsey, 1969.

Kopkind, A. "Mystic Politics: Refugees from the New Left." *Ramparts*, 1973, *12*, 26–35, 56–57.

Levine, F. *The Strange World of the Hari Krishnas.* New York: Fawcett-World, 1974.

Malko, G. *Scientology: The Now Religion.* New York: Delta, 1970.

Mauss, A. and Petersen, D. "Les 'Jesus Freaks' et le Retour à la Respectabilité." *Social Compass,* 1974, *21,* 283–301.

Mehnert, K. *Twilight of the Young: The Radical Movements of the 1960s and Their Legacy.* New York: Holt, Rinehart and Winston, 1976.

Needleman, J. *The New Religions.* New York: Doubleday, 1971.

O'Brien, J. "American Leninism in the 1970s." *Radical America,* 1978, 27–62.

Oh, J. K. "The Nichiren Shoshu in America." *Review of Religious Research,* 1973, *14,* 169–177.

Petersen, D., and Mauss, A. "The Cross and the Commune: An Interpretation of the Jesus People." In C. Glock (Ed.), *Religion in Sociological Perspective.* Belmont, Calif.: Wadsworth, 1973.

Richardson, J., Harder, M., and Simmonds, R. "Thought Reform and the Jesus Movement." *Youth & Society,* 1972, 185–202.

Robbins, T., and Anthony, D. "Getting Straight with Meher Baba: A Study of Mysticism, Drug Rehabilitation and Postadolescent Role Conflict." *Journal for the Scientific Study of Religion,* 1972, *11,* 122–140.

Robbins, T., Anthony, D., and Curtis, T. "Youth Culture Religious Movements: Evaluating the Integrative Hypothesis." *Sociological Quarterly,* 1975, *16,* 48–64.

Roszak, T. *The Making of a Counterculture.* New York: Doubleday, 1969.

Simmonds, R., Richardson, J., and Harder, M. "Organizational Aspects of a Jesus Movement Community." *Social Compass,* 1974, *21,* 269–281.

U.S. Department of Commerce. *Statistical Abstract of the United States.* Washington, D.C.: U.S. Government Printing Office, 1975.

Yankelovich, D. *The New Morality.* New York: McGraw-Hill, 1974.

12   *Steven M. Tipton*

New Religious Movements and the Problem of a Modern Ethic

~~~~~~~~~~~~~~~~~~~~~~~~~~~~~~~~~~~~~~

Religious movements arise and people join them for a number of reasons. One reason 1960s youth have joined alternative religious movements in the 1970s, I will argue, is to make moral sense of their lives. One correlate of their conversion is a change in our collective moral sensibility that has now found political expression. Interpreted in this way, the process of religious conversion begins with problems of right and wrong that an earlier view cannot resolve and a later one can. Such problems are couched in the social situation of those who face them, and their solution turns on changes in that situation. The conflict of values between mainstream American culture and counterculture during the 1960s framed problems that alternative religious movements of the 1970s have resolved by mediating the conflict's two sides and transforming their divergent moral meanings. Contrasting styles of ethical evaluation have shaped this conflict and its mediation. These styles distinctively characterize the romantic tradition of the counter culture and the two traditions that underpin mainstream culture, biblical religion, and utilitarian individualism.[1]

286

Biblical religion conceives of reality in terms of an absolute objective God who is the creator and father of all human beings. God reveals himself to them in sacred scripture and commands them to obey him. Biblical morality embodies an "authoritative" style of ethical evaluation. This means it is oriented toward an authoritative moral source whose will is known by faith, conscience, and scriptual exegesis. The moral question, "What should I do?" is posed by asking, "What does God command?" An act is right because authority commands it. It is to be done in obedience, the cardinal virtue of this ethic.

Besides this revelational aspect, biblical religion includes a rationalist line of development, characterized by a "regular" style of ethical evaluation. It is oriented to rules and principles of right conduct as discerned by dialectical reason. It poses the moral question, "What should I do?" by asking, "What is the relevant rule or principle?" An act is right because it conforms to principles formulated by reason. To do the act, therefore, is a matter of rationality, the virtue of this ethic.

Utilitarian individualism begins with the individual person as an actor seeking to satisfy her own wants and interests. She asks, first, "What do I want?" and, second, "Which act will yield the most of what I want?" Wants are taken as given in a way that suggests such notions as happiness, pleasure, or self-preservation as the good. Good consequences are those that most satisfy wants. Right acts are those that produce the most good consequences, as reckoned by cost-benefit calculation. So functions the "consequential" style of evaluation employed by utilitarian culture. Its virtue is the efficiency of actors in maximizing the satisfaction of their wants.

The 1960s counterculture rose up against and repudiated these two conceptions of reality in America, biblical religion and utilitarian individualism, especially the latter. The counterculture begins with the individual not as an actor rationally pursuing his self-interest but as a personality that experiences, knows, and simply *is:* "The way to do is to be." Self-awareness is the touchstone, not self-preservation. The counterculture lays down a few rather diffuse moral rules, for example, to love everyone and hurt no one, based on the monist premise that all existence is one. To some extent, it advocates acting to maximize consequences that satisfy individual wants ("Do whatever turns you on. . . . Do your own thing"), but it translates wants into universal needs for love and awareness.

Neither a logic of following rules nor of maximizing consequences predominates in the counterculture's ethic. What does is the idea that everyone ought to act in any given situation in a way that fully expresses himself, specifically his inner feelings and his experience of the situation. This "situational-expressive" style of evaluation is oriented to the feelings of the agent, those of others around him and to their situation, as discerned by empathic intuition. The moral question, "What should I do?" is posed by asking, "What's happening?" An act is right because "It feels right," most simply, or because it expresses the inner integrity of the agent and responds most appropriately to the situation. The chief counterculture virtue is sensitivity of feeling.

Biblical, utilitarian, and countercultural views of society diverge sharply. In Protestant Christianity, the individual person becomes individual. She stands alone before God, abstracted from all social relations, and makes moral choices as a sovereign agent. Yet she faces unconditional moral demands revealed as God's will, to be fulfilled by autonomous action within society. Society is understood as a holy community dedicated to building God's kingdom on earth and bound by God's objective moral judgment in doing so. Utilitarian society is a collection of individuals whose relations rest on the mutual advantage of exchange, not on duties given by reason or revelation. The social order is defined by the sum of the individual wants and interests of its constituents, not by fixed moral ends and rules. In the ideal Christian community, social relations exhibit the virtue of charity; in utilitarian society, refereed by the state, social relations exhibit the contingent fact of reciprocity. One gives in order to get, or because one has already gotten. One does not give in order to give. The counterculture sees the ideal society to be an organismic community of persons who "encounter" each other face to face in an intimate confluence of feelings and wills, without the mediation of roles ("role playing"), unequal status ("power tripping"), or abstraction ("head tripping"). Persons are to "be" with each other (à la the "be-in") rather than to do anything in particular together. They relate to one another as ends in themselves, not as reciprocal means to the satisfaction of their own individual ends. All persons are possessed of benignly congruent selves, allowing decisions to be reached collegially without recourse to fixed rules, authority, or cost-benefit calculation.

Biblical morality affirms that there are features of an act itself (being commanded by God or conforming to rules of reason), other than the good or bad consequences it produces, that make it right. Such an ethic is called "deontological." Utilitarianism, on the contrary, is a "teleological" or consequential ethic. It defines right acts solely by their good consequences. This puts it at odds with any ethical system that uses rules and direct imperatives ("Thou shalt not kill") to specify that a particular act is itself right or wrong. For utilitarianism, doing the right thing is a matter of choosing whichever means effect a given end. It does not direct the individual to do or not to do any particular act in itself. In the situational-expressive ethic, the intuited sense of those involved in a given situation suggests the most appropriate feeling about it and the most fitting action in response to it. If an individual persists in feeling otherwise, however, no act-specific commandments or principles can be invoked to sway him against that feeling. Neither can they be invoked to sway the utilitarian who has calculated consequences accurately but defined their goodness by reference to peculiar interests of his own. Insofar as rules and commands prescribing acts and intentions in themselves do, in fact, form and transmit norms in social life, utilitarianism and, to a lesser extent, the situational ethic are disposed inherently toward moral normlessness. The utilitarian's almost exclusive concern with outcomes and the hippie's with inner feelings make for the breakdown of any autonomous regulatory structure (Merton, 1957; Gouldner, 1970).

The counterculture challenged utilitarian culture at the most fundamental level. It asked "What in life possesses intrinsic value?" and "To what end ought we to act." It rejected money, power, and technical knowledge, key elements of "the good life" of middle-class society, as ends good in themselves. Instead, it identified them as means that did not, after all, enable one to experience what is intrinsically valuable—love, self-awareness, and intimacy with others and nature. The divergence between biblical religion and utilitarian culture, and the latter's incapacity to generate prescriptive rules by itself, opened space for the counterculture to emerge. Because the counterculture's ethic, for all its emphasis on intrinsic values, left their realization to unregulated feelings, it offered little basis for the stable institutionalization of its values. The integrity of utilitarian culture with the structural conditions of modern society—technological production, bureaucratic organization, and empirical science—blocked the counterculture's growth and bound its revolutionary impulse to failure. But, in the process, utilitarian culture and the social institutions it rationalized were stripped of moral authority, especially in the eyes of the young. The conflict of values during the 1960s left both sides of the battlefield strewn with ideological wreckage. In this atmosphere of disillusionment, many youths sought out alternative religious and therapeutic movements. Here they have found a way to get along with the demands of conventional American society and their own maturing lives and to sustain countercultural values by reinforcing them with moralities of authority, rules, and utility. Changes in the ethical outlook of 1960s youth who have joined Zen Buddhist communities describe one aspect of this larger transformation.

Zen and Ethics

Youth of the 1960s now living in Zen communities were typically raised in relatively secularized, well-educated, and achievement-oriented upper-middle-class families. They attended elite colleges, often majoring in the liberal arts. They used psychedelic drugs to seek personal meaning, and they took a peripheral part in political protest during the 1960s. After college, few went on to the professional or executive careers their fathers pursued. Most of them "dropped out" and now perform unskilled labor, craft, or service work (housecleaning, carpentry, caring for the aged) between periods of full-time monastic training. Mostly unmarried, they live singly or as stable couples within communal households.[2]

Young Zen students typically look back on their earlier moral views as a patchwork whose confusion helped lead them to Zen. Coming from secularized Jewish, liberal Protestant, and Catholic backgrounds, most felt themselves little influenced by the authoritative ethic of biblical religion. Although possessed of a sense of principled obligation, they saw conventional moral rules in an ambiguous light. Rules apply with welcome force to political issues of distributive justice and civil rights: "Politics was clear-cut—people shouldn't get ripped off." But in interpersonal relationships an ethic of obligation suffocates feelings under the weight of reason. A student complains, "I couldn't tell the difference between how I actually felt relating to people and all the things I *should* feel." Rules also appear "unrealistic" in relation to the actual operation of self-interest, which is thought to be omnipresent, especially in economic life, yet not quite justifiable. "Just going by what I wanted was an easy thing for me to fall into," remembers one student. "But it's destructive because then you don't live life at all. You just deal with it." A situational-expressive ethic, rooted in the counterculture and sometimes in prior exposure to bohemian culture, is identified with experiencing life as it is and ought to be. In this ideal world, says a student, "There's a certain clarity that feels right through all the shit, and that's what you go by." Too often, though, feelings can't be trusted in the actual world, because they are biased: "The problem came from my feeling of being 'special' and feeling the other person as being 'other,' instead of our being together in a situation." As a result, the situational-expressive ideal breaks down into egoism.

American Zen mediates the moral conflict between mainstream and counterculture with an ethic that is at once antinomian and regular. Students of Zen report that it enables them to enact the situational-expressive ethic idealized but unattained in the counterculture. This ethic rests on the assumption that persons have certain feelings that lead spontaneously to appropriate action. Zen students see themselves as having and acting on such feelings more reliably now than in the past. They attribute this new capacity to the "practice" of Zen meditation, first of all, and to the way of life and social relationships generated within the *sangha*, the community of fellow Zen students.

Both Zen meditation and communal life are governed by rules. Instead of the counterculture's largely implicit obligations of love and noninjury, these and other moral obligations are formalized in Zen by explicit rules, which the adherent is obliged to follow. A set of general "precepts" forbids killing, stealing, lying, sexual promiscuity, and use of intoxicants. Numerous "rules of order" and ad hoc regulations govern monastic life and the performance of meditation. These rules are justified in consequential style (by Buddhism's "Four Noble Truths") as instrumental means to releasing the adherent from desire and thus from suffering. More basically, the rules are justified as a true expression of the nature of existence. Release from suffering as the good consequence that makes acts right is translated into release from delusion as the good state of consciousness that arises from acting rightly, that is, in accord with rules that reflect reality. In this respect Zen Buddhism holds a regular ethic analogous to the tradition of natural law in Christianity. This transforms the effects of an otherwise antinomian ethic analogous to the counterculture's situational-expressive ideal. Like the hippie, the ideal Zen student spontaneously expresses himself and directly responds to the situation at hand. Only now, in doing so, he "expresses his Buddha Mind" shaped by meditation and the monastic regimen instead of simply "doing his own thing." Let us look more closely at how felt realization of counterculture ideals comes about in American Zen.

Zen practice reportedly engenders feelings that lead to appropriate action. What sorts of feelings are these? A student replies, "Now I'm more able to feel the situation from a place that allows for the different persons to be there without it breaking the situation down into myself and 'other.' The situation is there, it's happening, and it's happening through me and the other people who are there." Feelings of unity with others and the conditionality of one's individual identity, anchored in the experience of meditation, hold up through events felt to separate oneself from others. The monist inference that fundamentally "All is one" occurs within a paradoxical logic that does not deny the existence of dualistic phenomena.

Zen students see no rational consistency inherent in their moral feelings and responses, because "Everything changes all the time. Each situation is itself." Nor do moral feelings carry any fixed prescriptive content: 'It's more a clear, empty mind state where you simply respond. If the building's on fire, you grab everyone you can, yell 'Fire!' and run out. When things get more complicated, you just look at it carefully, without holding onto any particular idea or desire about it, and you'll naturally feel what the right thing is to do." In this form, Zen students posit a constant state of mind from which appropriate acts "naturally" arise according to situational conditions.

Does such a state of mind bear any resemblance to the Western idea of moral character or virtue? If so, it appears closer to the Aristotelian ideal of the person who knows, feels, and does the right action integrally and naturally than it does to the Kantian ideal person, who self-consciously acts from duty, as distinct from personal inclination. Compassion is identified as the essential characteristic of persons who act rightly. It is embodied by the Bodhisattva, a moral exemplar and personality ideal in the Mahayana Buddhist tradition, whose explicitly impossible aims the adherent vows to achieve: "What we're talking about is actually the Bodhisattva's way. It's a lot to swallow. It's bigger than life. The vows are like a koan:

> Sentient beings are numberless, I vow to save them;
> Desires are inexhaustible, I vow to put an end to
>   them;
> The dharmas are boundless, I vow to master them;
> The Buddha's way is unsurpassable, I vow to attain it.

I can relate to the endlessness of it. Endless compassion and giving without any thought or condition. Without any attachment." Imitation of the Bodhisattva by acting from compassion entails a certain state of consciousness described as "nonattachment" to one's individual self and a "total acceptance" of all existence. This amounts to the felt realization of acosmic monism: "True compassion is attachment to everything instead of to some particular idea of ourselves that we have." Referring to such definitions, the Zen student rejects comparison of nonattachment to either self-denial or altruism, of self-regarding or other-regarding moral motives. Unattached to considerations of self-interest or even perceptions of his own specialness, the Bodhisattva is free to experience the situation directly and respond in a fashion that is both compassionate and

honestly self-expressive. Thus American Zen students have found
a cardinal moral virtue, a personality ideal, and an ideal state of
consciousness, all deeply rooted in the Buddhist tradition, to open
an avenue toward realizing the situational-expressive ethic of the
counterculture.

Attainment of the ideal character, in turn, requires meditating and living according to Zen's moral precepts and monastic regulations. But these are seen to have a purely descriptive as opposed
to prescriptive status. "The precepts aren't there to order us
around," explains a student. "They're there because they *are* there
in reality. If you really understand your relationship with everything, there's no such thing as killing. It's just a 'not.' When we hurt
someone, we are cutting off our own hand." The premise of
monism is necessary to make sense of this view of rules. For the Zen
student, the unity of all existence is axiomatic. Its conscious realization by a given individual is conditional. Therefore, the precepts
are seen to describe the nature of existence unconditionally. And
they describe the "natural" actions of a given individual, as she
herself understands them, *if* she has realized the unity of existence
in her own attitudes and behavior.

Given Zen's monist premise, the precepts and rules of
Buddhism merely offer an ex post facto description of compassionate behavior flowing from the nonattached, all-accepting state
of consciousness idealized by the Bodhisattva. In this sense, these
rules describe the dynamic of the situational-expressive ethic. This
viewpoint, which resembles the Pauline counsel to "Love God and
do what you will," appears to reverse the usual claim of rule
moralities that a good state of consciousness or character results
from the commission of right acts and omission of wrong ones,
which the rules define.

Nonetheless the monastic and meditational practices by
which the Zen student, unlike the hippie, develops the ideal state of
consciousness are in their own way "right" acts defined by rules,
which in Zen make up an orthopraxy more clearly than they do an
orthodoxy. In this form, moral rules find their way back into a
situational-expressive ethic. Zen sustains the counterculture ideal
by regularly reinforcing the otherwise uncertain attitudes and
states of consciousness necessary to enact it reliably.

Moral and Social Responsibility

Zen's synthesis of situational and regular ethical styles breeds striking changes in ideas of moral responsibility, relativism, and freedom held by 1960s youth. A shift from a negative to a positive conception of liberty has occurred, usually attributed to the experience of doing Zen meditation with others in a regularized monastic setting. A student compares the two conceptions: "Freedom used to mean just, 'I get to do what I want to do.' But I know now that it's within the restrictions that we can really be who we are. When we all adopt the same posture in the meditation hall, it's to eliminate the distraction of choice—what do our small, petty minds want to do?—so we can express ourselves most fully." Zen students reject the extremes of popular relativism ("If nothing is absolutely right, then absolutely nothing is wrong") and fundamentalistic moral absolutism. Says one, "You can say 'Everything is relative,' and that's so. But the conclusion that therefore you can do anything you want to is not so. Because the opposite is also true. There are absolutely so's." The existence and need for norms formulated in the regular style are acknowledged, even while the appropriateness of an act as a situational response is held to be its ultimate right-making characteristic.

The Zen student's attitude of moral responsibility reflects the counterculture's ambivalence toward rules yet reconciles its two facets. He recognizes the community's rules as applying to his behavior in the breach as well as the observance and also sees the rules themselves as an object of nonattachment. A student discusses this bifocal view: "When I do something I know is wrong, I accept that I did it. I don't try to cover it over anymore. Sometimes I break the precepts. Now I just watch myself do it. I don't beat myself up about it. I make myself suffer less because of doing something wrong and because of fighting against feeling guilty about it, too. . . . There's less charge when you do what's right, too, because you just experience those things happening, instead of yourself being the cause of it all. Instead of getting off on it, I'm aware now of being uncomfortable with that feeling of being righteous." This attitude consolidates regular and situational elements into a moral psychology that admits feelings of responsibility for complying with moral rules yet fosters self-acceptance in the absence of biblical expiatory rites or pastoral relationships. By espousing nonattachment to feelings of righteousness as well as guilt, this attitude of moral responsibility also implies acceptance of others in a morally pluralistic culture and acceptance of the social world itself as a morally imperfect place. In the latter connection, ideas of *karma* come to bear on explaining the inevitability of evil. "There's some basic flaw or karma, and all I can do about that is practice," says a student. "We're all interconnected and compassion expresses that. But it's also true that we can't take care of everything for people. Some suffering is just inevitable." The danger of withdrawal from social concern may inhere in this attitude. But the student sees it as enabling her to reject normlessness and act on moral concerns, without being impelled by feelings of self-righteous anger into the sort of confrontational posture she discredits from experience of 1960s conflicts.

The question of what to do about social conflict and injustice is answered in part by Zen students' ideas of how to resolve moral disagreements. They espouse the sort of ongoing, diffuse interaction indicated by the situational-expressive ethic. Says one, "Even after a real disagreement with someone, you come back to the situation clear. It happened; then you come back and meet the other person again, and something else is happening. The relation keeps renewing itself." Such a resolution process relies on attitudes tied to Zen practice: a present-oriented, moment-by-moment sense of time; nonattachment to one's feelings and judgments; and the intent to "let go" of them instead of defining and elaborating them. It also relies on a communal setting, in which each person relates to others in many different ways, some of them requiring cooperation in housekeeping tasks necessary to all.

Zen students generally disapprove what they see to be the antagonistic spirit and confrontational style of radical politics in the 1960s. "Radical politics makes sense intellectually," one comments, "It's just that a lot of people who came to that intellectual conclusion hadn't cracked the emotional nut of their own anger and hatred." Social responsibility for Zen students begins with the necessity of a compassionate rather than antagonistic spirit and with a style of exemplary service rather than aggressive confrontation. This stance calls to mind the moral example of the Bodhisattva. It is predicated on the monistic assumption that society is one interdependent whole and that social change, so far as it is possible, begins with self-transformation and spreads outward harmoniously. "Social problems are our own problems of what we can do about society," says a student. "Instead of being outside us, society is just part of that wilderness of mind that we are, that we have to deal with."

What *can* the Zen student do about social problems conceived in this way? His radical religious answer asserts that "sitting *Zazen* [meditation] enlightens the whole world." Faced with particular issues, he is likely to affirm a politics of monist conservatism, holding that "social problems are not necessarily soluble, or even here to be solved. They're here to be worked on." The activist may construe such a reunion of the social world with "the wilderness of mind" as regression toward self-absorption and the acceptance of social ills. But he should note that the Zen student rejects social Darwinism and the reciprocal use of others for one's own self-interest. Against these principles of utilitarian society, he opposes the communal solidarity of the *sangha:* "Practicing [Zen] with your brothers and sisters in the *sangha,* the oneness of everything comes out in a feeling of human solidarity. That's the opposite of 'It's a dog-eat-dog world.' Usually people focus on the institutions, instead of the person's actual feeling or perception. But that's how practice comes into the world, and how it changes things. . . . The *sangha* is a kind of mandala for the whole society." The condition of the larger society, then, continues to appear problematic to the Zen student in a way familiar from the counterculture. But he does not diagnose this condition as susceptible to direct change, whether political or psychedelic, and he rejects either such role for the Zen community. Still, that community is perceived to be an exemplar for the society. Like a mandala, it embodies some image or principle of universal order. Its members seek by their everyday activity to extend this order harmoniously into the society as a whole, holding out some promise, however hedged, of social institutional change to come.

This point of view reflects developments in the lives of its proponents and in American society since the 1960s. Youthful expectations of dramatic social change by radical political means have faded along with psychedelic hopes for similar changes of consciousness. The ensuing focus on slower, more evolutionary changes anchored in the daily activity of work and householding has been reinforced by the longer-term, more conservative projects and concerns intrinsic to adulthood as a stage of life in comparison to youth. The social issues that dominated the 1960s—Vietnam, civil rights, social inequality, political power and its corruption—emphasized two-sided conflict between sharply opposed interest groups—black and white, rich and poor, draft resister and military. The ecological and economic issues generally perceived to dominate the 1970s imply social conflict, to be sure, but they lend themselves to more monistic interpretations of the social world. They appear more directly rooted in the mode and style of life pursued by the society as a whole, oriented toward material consumption and production, toward individualistic competition for goods, status, and power.

Ecology, in particular, has offered a monistic interpretation of societal conditions that is powerfully convincing to Zen students and congruent with their religious vision. The millennialism implicit in the Zen community's understanding of itself as an exemplary elite comes to light most clearly in an ecological context. A student warns, "There's no more time to keep on going like we have, tramping over every other species. The environment can't take it. The cornucopia is running out. The truth is that we need everything else that's alive in order to survive. It's all interdependent. That's straight Buddhism!" In a world headed toward ecological catastrophe, some Zen students see themselves exemplifying necessary personal attitudes and patterns of interpersonal behavior. Moreover, they see their communities exemplifying the cooperative life-style, social structure, and economy needed by the larger society if it is to survive. Ideally, these communities feature small-scale, low-consumption, and no-waste economies, which are labor-intensive and based on farming, trades, and crafts occupations aimed at self-support. They are localized communities with co-residential core groups whose social structures combine communal intimacy with monastic self-control. Ascetic labor in its classic monastic form gives rigor to the economic activity of self-support and the spiritual activity of self-realization.

The social ethic of the Zen community assumes its greatest political and institutional definition within this vision of "Ecotopia" (Callenbach, 1975). Even at this extreme, it is an exemplary ethic, not an aggressively activistic one. It consistently sees institutional change as arising from self-transformation. The Zen student may transform herself by practicing within a specially structured community, but that community is itself taken to be the result of the master's and his disciples' state of consciousness. A student summarizes the contrast between Zen's social ethic and that of 1960s activism by reference to the figures of Buddha and Moses: "[Activists] were trying to transform the external social thing, and that's going to transform individuals. Here we work on ourselves, and in some way the world changes. That's very much the difference between Moses and Buddha. Buddha was a prince, and what put him on the path was seeing sickness, old age, and death—and the way to salvation. Desire is the big problem. What started Moses off was seeing a Hebrew slave being beaten by an Egyptian. What he discovered in his *samadhi* [state of awareness] is that you have to get in there and right social wrongs, create some social situation where there's justice. Well, they were both enlightened. It's a matter of how it expresses itself in history. . . . When I first began sitting, I felt more like socialism wasn't where it was at, and Zen was. Now it's like Zen doesn't exclude anything." The activist prophet identifies himself with an oppressed people and seeks to alter their social situation to fulfill their ultimate destiny. The exemplary prophet identifies himself with the unalterable predicament of humankind and seeks to alter his own consciousness to transcend it. (He does so, significantly enough, in a politically precarious era undergoing disjointed social and cultural change.) The Zen student espouses a notion of social responsibility grounded in a radically psychological critique of human existence that proposes an exemplary *mode* of personal and social activity in daily life, not a social program with some specific content.

The daily life of the youthful resident in certain Zen communities has an implicit social content that gives some bite to her exemplary ethic. A communal life-style, social structure, and form of property ownership predominate over the autonomous household or individual. Families and children are accommodated but kept subordinate to the requisites of monastic life. Communal businesses are in operation, some of them vertically integrated. Bureaucratic and professional work in the larger society has been left behind. Ascetic labor has been divorced from the ethic of individual success and consumption. The consequences of downward occupational mobility have apparently been accepted by many youths from upper-middle-class backgrounds. The Zen community sees itself as giving rise to a more satisfying kind of awareness, work, and love than its members found in the larger society and as doing so in a way that may become ecologically necessary for the entire society in the future. Moral ideals and social arrangements compatible with the 1960s counterculture have developed within the doctrinal tradition and monastic structure of Zen Buddhism to enable 1960s youth to live with American society in the 1970s even as they seek to live out an alternative to it.

Cultural Change in a Modernized Society

Zen's ethic of antinomian rules relies on the collectively disciplined practice of meditation for the experience of nonattachment and compassion that leads to appropriate action. Zen's moral example comes across in face-to-face relationships among students and between student and master. The regimen of a monastic community generates rules to order the whole of everyday life, rites to establish its attitudinal texture, and social boundaries to exclude deviant behavior. The monastic regimen underwrites Zen's ethical assumption that humans continually face obligatory moral choices and responsibilities for others that reflect their objective needs, not their subjective wants. Negative liberty from restraint on attempts to satisfy individual wants turns into positive liberty to do the right act through the experience of meditating and living according to set rules. The monastery's housekeeping interdependence and its diffuse relationships allow for situational-expressive resolution of disagreements.

In these various respects, the full impact of American Zen's ethic requires a monastic organization built around daily meditation and relationship to a master. As such, it is likely to remain the province of relatively small numbers of monks, now little more than a thousand nationwide. But larger numbers meditate regularly in nonresidential groups or by themselves. They may meet with a master or hear a lecture on occasion, and they are usually familiar with Zen literature in English. The institutional location of these persons (in the arts, education, ecology, psychotherapy and the human potential movement, government, liberal denominations and the Catholic religious orders) will continue to give them a part in spreading Zen's ethic. To whom? To a larger and looser third circle of upper-middle-class urbanites for whom Zen's ethic stands as a personal ideal more thought about than ritually practiced and so is more situational and less regular in effect than it is for the monastic. For meditation-based religious movements such as Zen Buddhism, the greater the influence of monastic core groups on their wider circle of lay members, the greater ethical emphasis orthopractical rules will receive in relation to antinomian intuition.

Similar concentric circles of influence characterize other neo-Oriental religious groups, oriented either to meditation (for example, Tibetan Buddhism) or to devotion to a guru (for example, Meher Baba). Many of these other groups rely less on monastic organization and seem more suited to developing a mass lay membership than does Zen (Anthony and Robbins, 1977). How effectively they do develop as lay religions will be a key factor in the spread of neo-Oriental ethics.

A second factor in spreading neo-Oriental ethics lies with movements like Transcendental Meditation (TM) that teach meditation or "train" human potential without direct reference to Oriental religion. They usually imply a monist view of the world that may carry over into intentions toward harmonious cooperation with others and service to them. But it may also be subsumed into a consequential ethic that makes cooperation with others and compliance with rules into means to satisfy one's own wants. This is particularly the case for the clientele (versus the staff) of such movements who respond to explicit advertising or implicit promises that the training or meditation will enable them to control stress and tension symptoms, and to increase ego performance in bureaucratic work, education, and interpersonal settings.

As long as the structure of American society continues to revolve around technological production, bureaucratic organization, and a massed urban population, outright rejections of the instrumental behavior rationalized by utilitarian culture are likely to flourish only within small subcultures or for short periods in the life cycle of their adherents. Otherwise, Americans must respond to the practical demands exerted on adults by the modernized society in which they live. Yet they must also respond to the integrity of meaning exerted by the different moral traditions with which they think. In this double-edged process, members of alternative religious movements carry nonutilitarian perceptions, assumptions, loyalties, and styles of evaluation out into a utilitarian culture. It absorbs these contrary elements even as it dilutes and makes them over. "Awareness," too, becomes a commodity to be merchandised for consumption. The good becomes still another "goodie." Yet in the process the goodness of experience becomes less identified with the good *things* of life. The possession of happiness and the unrestrained freedom to pursue it become more elusive not only in fact but also in meaning. This process of reciprocal cultural change will go on for as long as utilitarian culture cannot justify by itself the dedicated work, cooperative behavior, and distributive justice that its political and social structure requires. It will continue, too, for as long as utilitarian culture cannot symbolize the enchantment the human mind finds in the world around and within itself (Weber, [1904–1905] 1958a, [1919] 1958b). Alternative cultural views will rise up against the current of the utilitarian mainstream. They will be swept up in it and will influence its course in turn.

If the external conditions necessary to support the production and consumption cycle of modern society (for example, only moderate scarcity of energy, resources, and middle-class employment) should sharply deteriorate, whether for ecological, geopolitical, or economic reasons, then the utopian visions of alternative religions may inform deep changes in America's social structure as well as its culture. For the present, however, alternative religious movements influence the culture more directly than they influence the society's structure. They reintegrate the meaning of social life for 1960s youth more directly than they reintegrate 1960s youth to society. The cultural changes carried by alternative religions have an ambiguous social effect on 1960s youth. They adapt them to adulthood in conventional society, and they enable their alternative visions of that society to endure within it.

In some regards, these movements find alternative grounds to motivate and rationalize conventional patterns of response to existing structures of opportunity: Work diligently as an expression of meditation in everyday life; leave off political conflict, because you are one with your opponent. But in other regards these movements back unconventional patterns of response to conventional job, education, housing, and other opportunities: Live alone or coupled in a communal setting, serve people instead of a career, work on and off to buy time instead of things, learn from a master instead of a professor.

In contemporary society at large, unconventional "life-style" patterns have begun to stake their claims to normalcy. The stable, home-owning nuclear family with a working husband and a homemaker wife is no longer the model household unit (Hirschhorn, 1976). Singles, working women, and women with children and without husbands have all increased. More importantly, the average individual is now likely to spend substantially less of her life within a nuclear family than she was in generations past and she is likely to undergo more changes in residence, income, job, and marital status with less linearity than before. From a base among urban 1960s youth, how far will such changes in life-style and household formation spread? Let us grant that they will exert pressure for budgetary shifts away from durables and toward market and social services and for urban planning to save time as well as space. Beyond this, how much difference will they make in the structure of utilitarian society? The answers to these questions remain to be seen.

For those outside of alternative religious movements, even more than for those inside, the importance of these movements at present lies chiefly in the ideas they carry, not in the social models they embody. Chances are it will be an unforeseeable length of time before American society turns into a fundamentalist theocracy, a monastic ecotopia, or one vast encounter group. But the ideological upsurge of conservative Christianity, ecological monism, and human potential psychologism throughout American culture is already unmistakable. So is the weakening of liberalism, that synthesis of rational religion and humanism with utilitarian views that has long held sway over the center of American culture. This weakening has created a vacuum of meaning these other three ideologies are expanding to fill. We are witnessing the beginning of a postliberal culture, rooted in personal life-style but reaching through social values into the polity.

Whatever direction this nascent culture eventually takes and whichever ideology comes to dominate it, the initial lines between the would-be successors to liberalism have been drawn. Each of them already has a constituency, and each also has a spokesman in American public life. The civil religious rhetoric of President Jimmy Carter reflects the resurgence of a relatively conservative Christianity. That of "Self-Determination," a statewide "political-personal network" anchored by California legislator John Vasconcellos, applies human potential psychology to politics. California Governor Jerry Brown states an ecological monism influenced by Zen teaching. What does Brown have to say about morality and the shape of society? How has his distinctive ethic entered into the conventional climate of political opinion?

Governor Brown and the Eco-Monist Ethic

Jerry Brown is hardly a Zen Buddhist in the self-proclaimed sense that Jimmy Carter is a born-again Christian. Brown is perhaps even less a Buddhist than he is a lawyer raised a Roman Catholic and educated by Jesuits. Formal status aside, his working position as an eco-monist relies on a regular ethic whose natural-law premises characterize these two rationalized religions. This ethic clashes with the utilitarian view that each individual should act to satisfy his own wants. Asked whether American values need reform, Brown asserts the need for deontological principles opposed both to utilitarian individualism and to the counterculture's ethic: "I think American values need reassertion in terms of fundamental roots. I think there has been an overemphasis on the ability of material comfort, on the ability of our economic machinery to provide human happiness. The growthmanship of the 1960s, which equated growth in GNP with human happiness, I think, is far from the founding fathers. . . . Every civilization that has gone through a sensate, sensual culture has fallen, and I think that is a real possibility; and to that extent I would like to see an austerer, leaner commitment on the part of the people of this country" (in Peters, 1976, pp. 51–52).[3] The means of utilitarian culture do not lead to its end; a growing GNP does not provide human happiness. Neither do self-expression and surrender to the senses, those hip alternatives to utilitarian accumulation. Why not? Human nature is "weak." It is "brought down by its own instincts," not elevated and set free by them. Against the counterculture's Pelagian view that human nature is good in itself and corrupted only by its environment and against the mainstream utilitarian view that it is a mutable mixture of good and bad, Brown counterposes an Augustinian view of the evil inherent in our nature: "Can we alter the human condition? No. We can't make saints out of sinners. St. Augustine had something to say about that. . . . We have to take the darker side into account in all that we do" (in Peters, 1976, p. 52).

Given Brown's view of human nature, which resembles Carter's evangelical conviction that we are sinful yet we can be saved, Brown, too, arrives at the need for a deontological ethic that prescribes and proscribes particular acts as right or wrong in themselves. Brown calls for "fundamental principles" of right and wrong to regulate human behavior and an "austere" commitment by Americans to follow these principles. Brown also calls for "a type of government" and culture that can curb our instinctive "self-indulgence." He dismisses the life of utilitarian or expressive satisfaction of wants as a contemplative might, characterizing it as a vain chase after "every impulse that floats through your consciousness." He does not accept such wants as given, as would a utilitarian. Instead, he opens them to evaluation ("I don't think that's what people want, anyway"), as would a natural-law rationalist (Brown, 1976, p. 72).

Against individual satisfaction of wants, Brown counterposes the possibility of "a life of service and common purpose," and he talks with approval of a regular ethic that can encourage civic duty and social responsibility: "In this culture, wherever we are, we have to find ways of resurrecting that sense of obligation and civic duty that appears to me to be diminishing through the society" (Brown, 1977b, p. 10). He sees self-interested individuals in a mobile urban society convinced by utilitarian culture that they have the right to "go and come wherever they want" while dumping social obligations into the lap of a welfare state. But people can take care of each other better than the state can, Brown argues. And the state can no longer afford to pay the rising costs of trying to care for people, because the economic growth that once fattened its coffers has now declined into "an era of limits." Thus regular ethical assumptions underpin Brown's critical diagnosis of government spending and social services.

Traditionally conservative criticism of big government echoes here, but Brown isn't simply attacking the welfare state on behalf of the laissez faire individual once again. He is calling for a localized, communal cooperation among persons in terms that sound familiar to eco-monist and hip critics of bureaucratic society: "We have centralized too much power, and we have to get back to neighborhoods and communities where people in face-to-face relationships can deal with the fundamental issues of justice, of education, of jobs, of birth, of death, of healing, of compassion, and of bearing one another's burdens that is done at the local level" (Brown, 1977b, p. 8). Face-to-face relationships in a communal context promote mutual aid, justice, and compassion. As in the Zen monastery or *sangha*, such situational-expressive support for right action is now reinforced by an ethic of rules and obligation. The kind of compassionate service Zen calls for in work and everyday life Brown calls for in order to sustain society (Peters, 1976, p. 18).

In describing his administration, Brown rejects a liberal approach based on legislative programs aimed at preset welfare goals: "I don't have any goals; they will evolve as we go along" (in Peters, 1976, p. 15).

The situational-expressive style of this evolution seems unmistakable at times. "To be a leader, you have to be at one with the people you lead. You have to feel it," Brown reports (in Peters, 1976, p. 14). He affirms the situational-expressive truth that "Life just is. You have to flow with it. Give yourself to the moment. Let it happen" (in Peters, 1976, p. 14). But for all its gradual, fluid unfolding, the political process in Brown's view is not entirely free of regularity. In a line that recalls the beginning of Carter's inaugural speech, Brown remarks, "What we need is a flexible plan for an ever-changing world" (in Peters, 1976, p. 12). That plan rests on the assumption that human nature never changes. It is governed by a natural law that extends to social life, where it guides positive law and the dialectical process of making and enacting legislation. Brown explains how this dialectic functions (in Peters, 1976, pp. 11–12):

> I think by asking people [questions], that's a way of slowing things down. If you ask something in a way that really seeks out the meaning of the situation or the assumptions on which a statement was made, that requires a pause and requires a reflection that would be missed. . . . That's the traditional *satyagraha*. Isn't that what Gandhi talked about?—"expose the truth in the situation, and then the people by recognizing it are moved by it." That's the power of unarmed truth. I think it works in a situation where there's all this confusion, that truth has a power that it normally might not have. By truth, I mean something that arises out of a situation, and people open their eyes, given the asssumptions they all share, they'll perceive it to be the case. And oftentimes it's just there if you focus on it, and you get people to focus on it . . . by discussing it, by confronting some of the confusion, by pulling together concepts that are contradictory that people haven't perceived as contradictory.

Brown names Gandhi as the patron saint of this dialectical method, not Socrates or St. Ignatius, but the latter figures can claim some credit for it, too. The truth "arises out of a situation," and people will perceive it if they "open their eyes." But to do so they must dialectically question the meaning of situations and discuss their assumptions about them, teasing out and resolving contradictory concepts along the way. Only then will the truth take casuistic form and move people in one direction.

Brown's regular ethic stresses the need for rule of law in a pluralistic society. Faced with criticism of the U.S. Supreme Court's claim to "moral authority" to intervene in issues like busing and abortion, Brown replies, "We are now in a society where it is very hard to find a consensus. We are fragmenting, we're proliferating

at every level of economics and morality and politics. The Court is a
unifying mechanism and a beacon of light if it acts wisely. I think by
and large, given the complexity of our country, the heterogeneity
of our people, they're doing an excellent job [of finding] this balance between the momentary perception of what needs to be done
and the more elementary articulation of what the principles are by
which we all live" (Brown, 1975, p. 6).

Such confidence that situationally specific prescriptions can
be generalized to consistent first principles "by which we all live"
distinguishes the regular ethic. Formal rules of the sort that government must legislate, enforce, and interpret grow more critical as
a society's informal consensus over moral values and norms grows
looser and less effective. Muses Brown, "If there was a social compact that basically threads everybody together, then [formal] rules
would occupy a smaller part of the whole network by which people
relate. Now, as this social compact appears to be breaking down a
bit, then more and more rules are needed to glue everybody together. . . . I think you need more [formal] rules as the informal
and internalized rules become less effective" (Brown, 1977b, p. 25).
Like Carter, Brown recognizes the importance of Durkheim's central problem: How does a differentiated society achieve normative
integration? Neither Carter nor Brown is satisfied with reciprocal
self-interest and "law-and-order" authority as sufficient grounds
for answering this problem.

As a political speechmaker, Brown's opening line states that
"We are entering an era of limits," where we will have to lessen our
expectations and tighten our belts (in Peters, 1976, p. 7). Here the
recognition of scarcity, that there are not enough resources for
each self-interested individual to get her own satisfactory share,
leads not to increased competition or to self-serving contracts, as it
would for utilitarians, but rather to common sharing according to
regular principles. This occurs because eco-monists ideally recognize that all persons are "part of a species or wider community."
Brown merges Carter's biblical theme of humility and mercy in the
face of human weakness into the eco-monist theme of individual
and technological limits in the face of all life's interdependence
(Peters, 1976, p. 47). The eco-monist ethic justifies protecting the
environment and sharing its resources according to regular princi-

ples. These derive from the planet's ecological limits and the needs of its inhabitants as a community, not from the subjective wants of individuals. Despite Brown's nonprogrammatic "case study" approach to particular policy issues and the apparent mixture of liberal and conservative elements in his policy decisions, Brown's general views consistently reject utilitarian individualism in favor of a regular ethic with an eco-monist content.

Moral meanings carried by conservative Christianity, eco-monism, and the human potential movement have already found their way into the polity. There each has begun to build its own image of a more coherent and cohesive society over against utilitarian individualism, or inside its psyche. Within the symbolic integrity of these images, trustworthy moral authority, rational principles, or authentic feelings will lead us as citizens to give up our individual interests for the common good, or at least to rediscover them there in enlightened form. In this translation from alternative religious movements into civil religious rhetoric, the process of getting saved from the 1960s becomes part of a larger cultural effort to save ourselves from utilitarian society and to save society from our self-interested selves.

Neither recent civil religious rhetoric nor alternative religious movements have overturned tradition and replaced it with something entirely new. Rather, they have drawn out strands from traditional moralities and rewoven them into a fabric that ties into American culture as a whole yet differs in pattern from any one of its traditions. As a romantic successor to modernism, the hip counterculture carried on the iconoclastic injunction to "Make it new!" in more radical form. The attempt to make life new in day-by-day experience and action, not just in art, poses problems for that side of the human condition that calls for order and regularity, for a measure that lasts. This call grows stronger as youth turns toward adulthood, and alternative religious movements of the 1970s have answered it as the 1960s counterculture could not. In doing so, these movements have carried on situational-expressive ideals by recombining them with moralities of authority, rules, or utility. Neo-Oriental groups, like Zen Buddhism, recombine the situational-expressive ethic with the regular ethic of rationalized religion. Neo-Christian groups recombine the situational-

expressive ethic of the hip counterculture with the authoritative
ethic of revealed biblical religion. The human potential movement
recombines the situational-expressive ethic with the consequential
ethic of utilitarian individualism. Alternative religious movements
of the 1970s are not rehearsing a new version of 1960s iconoclasm,
aimed at knocking over their predecessor along with its targets.
Instead, these movements draw from the old targets of biblical
religion, rationalism, and utilitarian culture itself, as well as from
non-Western traditions, in order to synthesize their ethics. In this,
they are "religious," in the literal sense that they "bind together"
heretofore disparate cultural elements, revitalizing tradition as
they change it.

Notes

1. This interpretation rests on Robert N. Bellah's argument
in Glock and Bellah (1976, pp. 333–352). I have developed its
specifically normative aspect, using a taxonomy of styles of ethical
evaluation taken from Potter (1965, pp. 363–398). The discussion
of utilitarian and counter culture also draws on Gouldner (1970,
pp. 61–87). Utilitarian culture, not utilitarian philosophical theory
is the object of analysis here. I have interpreted it as closest in
practice to the philosophical position of general impersonal ethical
egoism ("Everyone ought to act so as to produce the greatest balance of good over bad consequences for him or her, and any choice
that doesn't affect him or her is morally indifferent").

2. These data come from formal interviews averaging four
hours each with ten Zen students, done in the San Francisco Bay
area in 1976, and earlier informal interviews with twenty or so
others done over several years of participant observation. The
average age of formal interviewees was 30.6 years. They averaged
6.3 years experience in Zen groups. Six were males, four females.
Three were married, three single, and four living with someone.
Five were WASP, three Jewish, and two Catholic in religious or
ethnic background. Cmpared to other Zen students in this age
group, these interviewees were among the most highly educated,
verbally articulate, and politically active. Six had been active in
political protest. Four held advanced degrees (3 MAs, 1 JD),
another three had BAs, and three had two or more years of college.
At the time they were interviewed, five were employed in unskilled

blue-collar jobs (gardeners, housecleaners), two in skilled blue-collar jobs (a carpenter and a mechanic), two were schoolteachers, and one a lawyer. All but one had used marijuana and psychedelic drugs, several of them steadily. For corroborating social composition data, see Wise (1971).

3. *Thoughts: Edmund G. Brown, Jr.* (N. J. Peters, Ed., 1976) is a collection of excerpts from Brown's speeches, interviews, and press conferences that has circulated widely in California. Although it leaves the original context of quoted remarks unspecified, it alphabetizes them under such headings as "Human Nature and Values." This arrangement, for better or worse, has become the context that remains visible to the public eye.

References

Anthony, D., and Robbins, T. "A Typology of Non-Traditional Religious Movements in Modern America." Paper presented at the annual meeting of the American Association for the Advancement of Science, Denver, Colo., February 1977.

Brown, E. G. PBS "Firing Line" interview. October 11, 1975. Mimeo transcript. Charleston, S.C.: Southern Educational Communications Association.

Brown E. G. "Playboy Interview: Jerry Brown." *Playboy,* 1976, *23,* (3), 69–187.

Brown, E. G. PBS "Agronsky At Large" interview. April 1, 1977a. Mimeo transcript. Washington, D.C.: WETA/26.

Brown, E. G. "The New Class." *CoEvolution Quarterly,* 1977b, *1* (13), 8–39.

Brown, E. G. "Speech to the Commonwealth Club." April 15, 1977c. Mimeo transcript. Sacramento, Calif.: Governor's Press Office.

Callenbach, E. *Ecotopia.* Berkeley, Calif.: Banyan Tree Books, 1975.

Glock, C. Y., and Bellah, R. N. *The New Religious Consciousness.* Berkeley: University of California, 1976.

Gouldner, A. W. *The Coming Crisis of Western Sociology.* New York: Avon, 1970.

Hirschhorn, L. "Urban Development and Social Change: The Demographic Dimension." Working Paper No. 3. Childhood and Government Project, Earl Warren Legal Institute, School of Law, University of California, Berkeley, 1976.

Merton, R. K. *Social Theory and Social Structure.* New York: Free Press, 1957.

Peters, N. J. (Ed.). *Thoughts: Edmund G. Brown, Jr.* San Francisco: City Lights, 1976.

Potter, R. B. "The Structure of Certain Christian Responses to the Nuclear Dilemma, 1959–1963." Unpublished doctoral thesis, Harvard Divinity School, 1965.

Weber, M. *The Protestant Ethic and The Spirit of Capitalism.* New York: Scribner's, 1958a. (Originally published 1904–1905.)

Weber, M. "Science as a Vocation." In H. H. Gerth and C. Wright Mills (Eds.), *From Max Weber.* New York: Oxford University Press-Galaxy Books, 1958b. (Originally published 1919.)

Wise, D. "Dharma West: A Social-Psychological Inquiry into Zen in San Francisco." Unpublished doctoral thesis, Department of Sociology, University of California at Berkeley, 1971.

13   *Harry M. Johnson*

Religion in Social Change and Social Evolution

It is now time to try to pull together some of the themes and questions raised by the contributors to this book. My comments are not intended to settle controversies but merely to offer one more or less coherent opinion. My purpose is to help some readers to see the book as a whole. Other readers will need no help and may find my comments either wrong or nearly self-evident.

The Nature of Religion

At the very least, a religion is a quasi-cognitive, affective, and evaluative symbol system that serves to some extent as a basis for making meaningful evaluative choices, not only in the active goal-directed sense of choice but also in the more reactive sense in which one "chooses" affective responses to events one has perhaps had no discernible part in bringing about. Modern sociologists, anthropologists, and even some theologians stress the point that a religion is a kind of code, model, or paradigm that shapes or patterns a more or less "total" way of life: inner experience, action, and judgment. It provides ultimate meaning to human life and death, beyond the meaning that can be provided by the most rigorous empirical investigation and the resultant knowledge. This conception of religion is similar, I think, to the one expressed by Parsons and by Neal in Chapters One and Nine.

Because of its tendency to be comprehensive and cultural (rather than utterly unique to individuals), religion must have implications for social life; an important aspect of its code is moral. Speaking of Greek and Roman religion, H. J. Rose says (1959, p. ix) that "neither was attached to any system of ethics," but his whole treatise shows that both Greek and Roman religion was profoundly concerned with the welfare of communities and with individuals' loyalty to them; while these religions were not attached to a *universalistic* system of ethics, they did foster particularistic social values and practices.

Further, the fundamental aspect of common commitment, strengthened and renewed by dint of private and cooperative study, ritual, and personal histories of decisions in "living," means that a religion is to some degree institutionalized. This in turn means that religion is necessarily "conservative." It legitimates certain interests, quite possibly including the interests of political leaders in maintaining their authority. Religion is also necessarily "integrative" to some extent, at least for those who, in accepting it and living by it, form, as Durkheim wrote, a moral community. There is a conservative, integrative implication in Santayana's very definition of piety ([1905–1906] no date, p. 181): "a sentiment of gratitude and duty" based on the "consciousness that the human spirit is derived and responsible." Taking as his example "pious Aeneas" (as Virgil constantly calls him), Santayana says, "In truth, Aeneas's piety . . . lay . . . in his function and vocation. He was bearing the Palladium of his country to a new land, to found another Troy, so that the blood and traditions of his ancestors might not perish. . . . His tenderness, like Virgil's own, was ennobled and made heroic by its magnificent and impersonal object."

The "conservative" and integrative aspects of all religion, however, do not necessarily preclude, and are in no way necessarily incompatible with, social conflict over religion or social change guided and motivated, in part, by religious symbols. These statements, of course, are in line with well-known historical facts and with the theoretical formulations of Durkheim, Weber, and

Parsons. Because different religions may be incompatible, their adherents may well come into conflict. Moreover, if religious symbols are to mobilize motivation for significant social change (change in the structure of society, for example, in authority or property or kinship and the family), then these religious symbols must first integrate those who are committed to them to the extent that these co-adherents are able to cooperate with one another and support one another effectively. Thus, if religion can ever have any "revolutionary" influence, it can have it only by first having an integrative influence. Further, a "revolutionary" movement is itself an effort to integrate a society in terms of a new symbol system. The effort requires that the existing structure be disrupted, but the goal and the measure of success is later reintegration. (Since an inchoate religion must change in the processes of becoming in-stitutionalized and spreading, some adherents, of course, will be dissatisfied with the results of the revolution and will regard the "success" as a betrayal. In any case, all "religious" successes are almost by definition approximations.)

Political leaders can crush an incipient or weak religious movement or foster it for their own purposes. But once a religious "program" is institutionalized it tends to "have a life of its own." David Little (1969) is convincing on the point that the inner logic (the symbolic logic, to use Parsons' playful but felicitous expression) of Calvin's theology moved toward individual autonomy and democratic institutions; even the prestigious religious and political founders and leaders could not long, against these tendencies, maintain a closed, repressive system (see also Parsons, 1968d). This point may be subsumed under something more general that many writers have stressed; namely, that ascetic Protestantism had, and perhaps every religious code has, unanticipated consequences.

Once a religious code is institutionalized, we might say that people high and low have it almost as if it were their destiny. Not only the untouchables but also the Brahmans were locked in Hin-duism until cultural codes that were developed elsewhere called into radical question the legitimacy of the system. Even now, of course, the old system is still very much alive, although it is chang-ing (Dumont, 1970). Patrimonial rulers have a great deal of power, but they cannot change at will the religiously based value systems

and motivational tendencies of their subjects. It should be noted
also that, even when rulers who combine political and religious
authority do consciously or unconsciously manipulate religious
symbols, their motive is not necessarily selfish (to enhance their
own power at others' expense). The rulers in the Byzantine tradition had a wide throne to accommodate God himself sitting invisible beside them. This fusion of political and religious authority had
a (selective) scriptural basis in part, but it was at least strengthened
by the emperors' pressing need to defend their realm, including
their subjects, against Islam, which was a constant menace on their
borders. Garsoïan suggests that the pattern of fusion may have
been influenced by Islam itself, one of whose basic ideals is the
fusion of political and religious authority. Ironically, the Islamic
rulers of the Ottoman Empire were "stuck" with this same pattern,
for it certainly contributed to the weakness and long-drawn-out
decay and dismemberment of the empire, in which non-Muslim
minorities, kept from full participation in the polity and societal
community, withheld complete loyalty and eventually collaborated
with foreign powers for their liberation. (On the Byzantine and
Ottoman empires, see Garsoïan, 1972.)

The belief that one's religion is based on science is one variety of "scientism." This is pseudo-science (in the modern sense) or a
reversion to an older, looser meaning of "science"; but of course it
may be genuine religion. Zen Buddhism, for example, provides its
adherents with a program of training designed (in this case,
explicitly) to create a solidary moral community, composed of
people who can more or less successfully harmonize their feelings
and their actions with varying unique situations, in such a way as to
maintain "freedom," composure, and mystical contact with the
postulated inner harmony of all things. Although this religious
orientation (this code for action and feelings, to which converts
commit themselves) is not contrary to science, one cannot maintain
that harmony with science *requires* this particular orientation. The
high valuation of "extreme" states of feeling found in some other
religions; the possibility of embracing and cultivating deep attachments, with all their risks; the principled drive to master the conditions for achieving greater and greater cultural, social, and personal control over more and more problems and aspects of the

human condition—all these orientations are equally in harmony with science—and equally nonrational. (It is perhaps worth mentioning even at this late date that Parsons in *The Structure of Social Action*, 1937, following Pareto's explicit and Durkheim's and Weber's implicit example, makes an important distinction between nonrationality and irrationality. Irrationality involves ignorance or error. Nonrationality does not, even though it is not logical and experimental.)

Religion is misconceived, misclassified, and misunderstood if it is taken as *primarily* cognitive, as science in the modern sense is. Attempts have indeed been made to rest religious faith and "belief" on evidence and logic; but social scientists, I think, are pretty much agreed that faith and belief do not actually rest on evidence and logic in the same way that science does. Few people, if any, have chosen their religion after a careful study of all the available religious orientations, and probably few have given up their religion because of questions concerning the historical accuracy of its myths.

"[A] belief," says Northrop Frye (1971, p. 36, my emphasis), "so far as a belief is verbalized, is a statement of willingness to *participate* in a myth of concern." "To believe in God," says Miguel de Unamuno (epigraph to Kaufman, 1972), "is to long for his existence, and, further, it is to act as if he existed; it is to live by this longing and to make it the inner spring of our action." In a thoughtful and courteous review of Hans Küng's *On Being a Christian* (1976), the Jewish scholar Samuel Sandmel (1978, p. 101) makes the following significant comment concerning something "characteristic of those who utilize philosophy or scholarship in the study of the particular religion of which they are communicants": "There are orthodox Jews who in their scholarship deny the Mosaic authorship of the Pentateuch and the divine origin of the laws, and yet observe all the Mosaic and rabbinic laws with utmost punctiliousness. . . . In his analyses, Küng [a Swiss Catholic theologian] is repeatedly a denier. Ultimately, though, he is a staunch affirmer of Christian beliefs and Christian theology. Some Christians seem not to have seen this. To me, it seems crystal clear." In *The Life of Reason* ([1905–1906] no date, pp. 178, 180), George Santayana stressed the same point and also indicated in a more positive way what religion *is* about: "Do we marshal arguments against the miraculous birth of Buddha or the story of Cronos devouring his children? We seek rather to honor the piety and to understand the poetry embodied in those fables. . . . Piety, in its nobler and Roman sense, may be said to mean man's reverent attachment to the sources of his being and the steadying of his life by that attachment. . . . This consciousness that the human spirit is derived and responsible, that all its functions are heritages and trusts, involves a sentiment of gratitude and duty which we may call piety."

Religious beliefs, then, are not to be understood primarily as apprehensions of a preexisting reality; rather, they are cultural and personal symbolic codes, models, or paradigms that, insofar as people are committed to living by them, actually *create* and *sustain* aspects of social and personal reality apart from the codes themselves. (That is, religion does not simply sustain religion; it also helps to sustain a certain patterning and tone in social relations and in personality.) The evaluative, direction-giving, choice-guiding, meaning-creating, reality-making aspects of a religion that living people are committed to live by also make it quite clear that religion is not simply an illusion or a delusion, or just a matter of wish-fulfilling or reality-denying fantasy. It has to do with an extremely important level of reality. In the term that Parsons, following Durkheim's insight, has used, a religion is *constitutive* symbolism; that is to say, not only does it "represent" a *transcendent* reality (not fully realized) but, in doing so, it also circumscribes and organizes (in part, of course) the *empirical* entities we call *social systems* and, reciprocally with them, the personalities who participate in these social systems.

American Zen Buddhism shows us that a "religion" need not involve reference to personal gods. Another example is communism. Parsons' analysis of the religious background and essentially religious character of communism is one of the most interesting sections of his chapter.

Religious Evolution

Some social scientists are skeptical about the whole subject of cultural and social evolution; or, although they are perhaps willing to regard literate societies as superior in some important way to nonliterate societies and to regard modern science as superior to that of central Brazilian tribes, they may feel it necessary to stop short of comparing religions invidiously. It may seem to be unscientific to think that one religion is "better" than another. Although, as Parsons reminds us, Max Weber's study of the Protestant Reformation in comparative perspective led Weber to attribute to it worldwide sociocultural significance ([1920] 1958), he remained reluctant to regard Western civilization as *generally* superior to other great civilizations.

If the "advanced" civilizations are somehow superior to the "primitive," however, then it certainly is at least logically possible that one advanced civilization may be more advanced than another. Nevertheless, only an ethnocentric ignoramus would lightly make any sweeping judgment. Parsons seems to be appropriately cautious and scientifically "within bounds" in thinking of sociocultural evolutionary directionality (toward greater adaptive capacity of organized society) as a scientific working assumption to be developed for ordering complex facts of history. The value of the assumption, if any, lies in its scientific utility. As far as the evolutionary significance of the Reformation is concerned, Parsons (1968a, pp. 693–694) is far from dogmatic: "[Awareness of non-Western cultures] inevitably raises in an acute form the question of how far Weber was right . . . that the social and cultural developments of the modern West were of *universal* significance. . . . Weber may in this context be accused of 'ethnocentrism'. . . . Quite clearly, it is a crucial problem, but I very much doubt whether anything approaching a definitive position on it will be attainable in our time. At least, I do not think the 'Weberians,' of whom in this sense I count myself one, can yet be ruled out of court on this issue."

An evolutionary advance is some kind of sociocultural innovation that takes root and grows strong (becomes actually institutionalized) in a particular society. Its very "superiority," however, tends to result in its being copied by or creatively adapted to other societies. Thus the adaptive superiority of the innovating society may be short-lived. The greater adaptive capacity tends, therefore, not necessarily toward the longer survival of the innovating *society,* but toward the survival of the *innovation* (in some society or societies and perhaps in modified forms). Indeed, as Parsons emphasizes, "inferior" societies (like "inferior" species) may survive for an extremely long time if they are well adapted to environments that are stable although perhaps narrow. Thus, if the Reformation introduced or made possible certain "advances," these have already been taken over, at least to a large extent, in many non-Protestant societies and among non-Protestants in predominantly Protestant ones.

In the two complex events analyzed by Cheng, the Meiji restoration and the Chinese revolution of 1911, we find examples of evolutionary pressure, one successful, the other not. Evolutionary pressure is the felt need to do something new and adaptive in the face of a challenge from abroad, the challenge of an alien system or systems that have *already achieved* a higher level of adaptive capacity, so that the challenged society must either catch up or run the risk of losing autonomy or at least remaining "backward." In these cases, the "superior" system has achieved superiority by complex processes in which religion has probably been involved. As for the challenged societies, their (relatively) "indigenous" religion—plus, of course, related social structure at lower levels —becomes important for its being *either* relatively flexible and adaptable, perhaps even facilitating the "needed" change, *or* relatively rigid, standing much more as an obstacle.

In the Japanese case, the indigenous religion was "conservative" relative to the challenging society, but it was flexible enough to participate in "revolutionary" social change. As for China, only after the Communist Revolution—which, as Parsons remarks, was (very roughly) equivalent to the Protestant Reformation—only then was China able to make marked progress in "modernization." It is striking that Communist China has given high priority to "correct" attitudes and ideas (that is, to the quasi-religious aspects of the Revolution) (see Young and Ford, 1977; MacInnis, 1969).

In dealing with secularization, Victor Lidz is implicitly dealing also with an aspect of religious evolution. The earliest evolutionary stage of "secularization" (in a sense used by Bellah, 1970b) is desacralization of social structure, which occurs most clearly in what Bellah calls the "historic" stage. In the "primitive" stage especially, and to a lesser extent in the "archaic" stage, (both stages earlier than the historic), "the world" is accepted, even taken for granted; but the social structure of society is treated as "sacred" (in principle, as eternal and fundamentally "good"). The result is a basis for societal identity and solidarity that is stable but that has low flexibility (adaptive capacity). In the "historic" stage, the vision of a clearly transcendent order desacralizes the social structure, making possible and meaningful a fairly radical "rejection" of "the world" (or withdrawal from it), at least as an ideal. Then, in due time, comes the fourth stage (in Bellah's scheme), occupied solely by the Protestant Reformation; in this stage, we have "secularization" in a sense used by Parsons; namely, a new religious interest in "secular" society, which is conceived to be in drastic need of reformation but to be also worth reforming, a more critical and conditional acceptance of the world, legitimated by the fundamentally religious ultimate goal of building the kingdom of God on earth.

"Secularization," in the sense in which Lidz uses the term, is a still later stage, essentially Bellah's fifth (and latest, not necessarily the last). With the Enlightenment, as Lidz explains, there came sources of legitimation that are not directly tied to religion.

In what sense is secularization in this form an evolutionary advance? Two points seem to be especially important.

First, legitimating societal values (conceptions of the ideal society) have become extremely *generalized*, thus capable of legitimating an indefinite series of social and structural changes at the institutional, organizational, and role levels. This generalization is obviously an ingredient in a high degree of adaptive capacity. Such a generalized value system is likely to be more secure, of course, the more extensively it is in fact spelled out (or specified, to use Parsons' precise word) at "lower" levels (social institutions, specialized collectivities, and social roles); in particular, a system of universalistic law must eventually be securely institutionalized (see Parsons, 1971; Parsons, 1977; Fuller, 1977).

Second, the at least partial emancipation of the value system from religion is another step in the "emancipation from ascriptive ties" (see Parsons, 1969). However universalistic a religion may be in a relative sense (for example, Christianity is said to involve the "emancipation" of Judaism from a relatively small ethnic base), nevertheless any religion is ascriptive in practice to the extent that, in the course of generations, many or most of its adherents are born into it. (We noted earlier that few people choose their religion after a careful comparison of existing possibilities.) This apparently unavoidable "ascriptive" aspect of religion means that the legitimating system will in effect be discriminatory if it is strictly religious; adherents of any religion other than the legitimating one will be to some extent "second-class citizens." From this point of view, "secularization" in the sense of separation of church and state is an evolutionary advance because, other things being equal, it makes possible a more inclusive society, hence a more secure solidarity, hence a more dependable basis for all kinds of more specific "adaptive" efforts in the societal polity and economy.

It should be noted, however, as Lidz does note, that secularization in his sense does not mean that religion is dying out, as a certain kind of rationalist is likely to think. The two following points seem to be especially important.

First, societal identity and purposefulness require that there be a civil religion (Bellah, 1970a). Although the civil religion may well depend to some extent for its vitality on underlying traditional religions (as, for example, the civil religion of the United States is derived, in part, from Judaism and Christianity), the fifth-stage civil religion is nevertheless obviously much more inclusive and open than were and are the civil religions, say, of ancient Israel, modern Israel, Pakistan, or Iran.

Lidz emphasizes the second reason that secularization does not necessarily mean the death of religion. This is the need for meaning and emotional adjustment in connection with the great private crises of life, such as birth, death, marriage, divorce, and personal suffering. Two "needs," then—that for a civil religion and that for private orientation—give life to religion despite all the forms of secularization we have discussed. These needs give point to Lidz's comparative treatment of the effects of the Enlightenment in various countries. The United States is relatively lucky, because Enlightenment values are fundamentally congruent with the prevailing so-called Protestant ethic (faith in progress through active implementation of certain universalistic innerworldly values). As

Lidz notes, France for a long time suffered from the conflict between militant anticlericalism and traditional Catholic conservatism.

The Protestant Reformation

Max Weber's complex ideas about the Protestant Reformation and its effects ([1904–1905] 1958) have been resisted for several reasons. Yet, after the immense scholarship has been sifted, his basic thesis does not fall through (see especially Little, 1969; also Eisenstadt, 1968, 1973; Nelson, 1973). The basic thesis, broadly stated and somewhat expanded, is that under favorable conditions ascetic Protestantism did in fact have a strong independent influence in activating and organizing important changes in law, political institutions, economic activity, science, and education. Several comments may help to qualify, amplify, or interrelate some of the chapters in this book.

1. The "Reformation" brought about by ascetic Protestantism involved significant *changes* in individuals' motivation. It did not simply release or increase economic greed, which has always been extremely common. Moreover, ascetic Protestantism, as it worked out in history, changed the motivation of many people who did not consider themselves Protestants, and, of course, for these and others Protestantism helped to change significantly the social milieu in which all personality drives and capacities worked themselves out. Indeed, one might say that its "ultimate" effects had to be enjoyed or suffered in the lives of individuals, not only in their average motivation, self-esteem, opportunities, educational level, and participation in the polity and societal community but also in their life conditions—their material welfare, safety, health, and longevity. In a broad sense, as a result of the Protestant Reformation individuals have more freedom and greater autonomy (see Bourricaud, 1977; Alexander, 1978).

2. Because in his chapter Sagan insists so strongly on his contention that sociocultural evolution is somehow given direction by the development of the psyche, I should like to reenforce another of his points, which he perhaps takes too much for granted to insist on; namely, that it would be drastically wrong to attempt to

reduce sociocultural evolution to psychological development. Insofar as individuals' psyches (cognitive and motivational systems) had been involved in the origination of new cultural symbolism and in the institutionalization of social and structural change, those psyches had, of course, been shaped by socialization in the broadest sense; that is, had themselves emerged from interpersonal experiences informed and controlled, to a large extent, by culture and more or less organized social systems. Culture, social systems, and personal cognition and motivation are all interdependent in processes of change.

The rationality of the Calvinists, for instance, was of a specific kind, not just an expression of psychological maturity in general. In the historical background lay Greek philosophy and science and the achievements of the Renaissance. Robert K. Merton (1938) points out that Puritan scientists regarded the study of nature as the study of God's work, and they could be sure of its lawfulness because he had created it. As Petersen's account (see also Nikiprowetzky, 1975) shows, the concept of ethical monotheism itself was the product of a long history; the one god of Israel had to emerge as the one God of the whole universe and of all history and therefore the basis of the ultimate unity of all things. David Little (1969) is very clear on the point, finally, that "rational" capitalism (and one might say rational science or rational adjudication) depended on structural differentiation. That is to say, the Puritans and their successors, by virtue of the legitimating sacred vision of the future kingdom of God on earth, were freed from any necessary allegiance to traditional methods, organizations, and institutions; and, being engaged (if they happened to be) in business, *as a completely legitimate calling,* they were not only free to organize it according to universalistic and functionally specific—that is to say, rational—standards but also, and even more, it was their duty to do so if they were to take building that kingdom seriously.

One of the sticking points in Calvinist doctrine was the predestination of souls. Parsons argues that *this* aspect of predestination (there was more to it) had to be abandoned. The conception of building the kingdom of God as a source of societal legitimation could have no meaning if nothing that men and women might strive to do could really change anything. Elimination of the doctrine of predestination insofar as it applied to human conduct, was necessary to give consistency to the theological system as a whole.

3. A third comment can be very brief. Ascetic Protestantism as a cultural program, code, or paradigm could not work out automatically. Neither Weber nor Parsons is an idealist in the sense of a cultural determinist.[1] In achieving enough institutionalization to become effective, ascetic Protestantism had to overcome obstacles, and in this it had variable success in different places. Moreover, even when it was institutionalized, its precise effects depended on social and environmental conditions. Political opposition, as in France; prolonged struggle against powerful alien peoples, as in South Africa (see Loubser, 1968); or relative lack of natural resources, as in Scotland—none of these prevented ascetic Protestantism from having identifiable characteristic effects. But these obstacles did mean that effort had significantly different results also. Even more, religious ideas themselves were changed in the processes of interaction with nonreligious variables.

The Industrial Revolution

From a book I have already referred to several times (Little, 1969), we learn that Puritan theology had some influence on the common law, specifically shaping the law of corporations against monopolies and in the direction of greater freedom from interference by the state. Parsons' thesis in this book, that the separation of workplace from the home had religious significance, is strongly implicit in Little's book. Parsons adds the extremely interesting point that the differentiation between workplace and residence, accompanied by an extension of universalism (a theme several times stressed by Little), *paralleled* the much earlier Christian movement from its original relatively particularistic basis in the ethnic Jewish community to the more universalistic basis of belief and commitment regardless of ethnicity.

The parallelism extends also to the fact that both changes were the occasion of considerable conflict, with strong feelings for and against. The Jewish Christians in Jerusalem, under pressure from non-Christian Jews there, being anxious to demonstrate their loyalty as Jews, eventually repudiated Paul, although they had earlier accepted his ideas reluctantly. At the time of Paul's conversion, there already existed Gentile Christian communities. Paul's innovation was to declare, as dogma, that faith in Christ's redemption of humankind superseded the Jewish law (made it unnecessary for Christians to be circumcised or to observe other ritual requirements of the old order). Further, Paul's missionary activity on this basis was so successful that at his death Gentile Christians far outnumbered Jewish Christians. The conflict over Paul's mission to the Gentiles, somewhat muffled and confusingly reported in the book of Acts (Bornkamm, 1973), is seen clearly in the authentic letters of Paul, which were not known to the author of Acts. As for the much later disruption caused by the creation of factories, one gets a good idea of it from Smelser (1959), to whose book Parsons refers.

Religion and Inequality of the Sexes

Broadly speaking, the feminist movement is another aspect of what Parsons calls emancipation from ascriptive ties—an aspect emphasized in the popular term "women's lib." The problems raised by Marie Augusta Neal can hardly be understood unless we distinguish clearly between the functioning of mythological symbols on the one hand, and the carefully inferred, elaborated, and integrated theology of experts on the other. At the strict theological level, it has been recognized for a long time that divinity need not be thought of as literally male. What bothers the Christian and Jewish feminists of whom Neal writes is that the symbolic imagery in which doctrine is indirectly expressed seems to work powerfully at an unexamined level of consciousness. Inevitably myths reflect some of the taken-for-granted things in the culture and social systems in which they arose. Indeed, if they had not, they could not have communicated anything at the time. In this sense, there is a built-in unconscious conservative bias even in profoundly "revolutionary" myths such as the Christ story.

Christ happened to be a man. In the Hebrew tradition, it could hardly have been otherwise. Many passages in the New Testament make clear, however, that Christ's maleness is an accident; his role as a model for the perfect servant of God is obviously meant as much for women as for men. The church is "the body of

Christ" but it is also "the bride of Christ," although the church referred to in both cases obviously includes both men and women. The church is also "the salt of the earth," "the ark," "the table of the Lord," "Israel," "God's planting," "branches of the vine," and many other things (see Minear, 1960). It should be obvious that the New Testament writers did not expect all these symbols to be reconciled with one another on the literal, denotational, "imagist" level.

It seems undeniable, however, that the broad tendency of basic Judeo-Christian imagery strongly suggests the superiority of men over women. Further, it seems likely that, whatever the deep *central* analogies might have been, this peripheral level of operation of the symbols was also in some sense intended. The feminists are undoubtedly right in asserting that, in relatively unsophisticated minds and in many learned ones as well, the peripheral connotations of the specific images continue to be effective, all the more powerfully perhaps in that their inner current tends to be taken for granted. Even if this inner current is recognized, the problem remains, for the myths with their specific imagery tend to resist change. They constitute a relatively fixed framework, which gives them a particularly important boundary-maintaining function. In a way, and to some extent, adherents of the faith are "stuck" with the undesirable peripheral connotations of the imagery.

I believe that Neal is correct in asserting that the women's liberation movement is very important for the future. She is also correct, of course, in saying that there is a good deal of opposition to change. Liberal theologians and other leaders who perceive the need for broader interpretations must always keep in mind the more conservative strict constructionists, called by Parsons "fundamentalists" and by some religious writers "legalists."

It might be said that one task of creative theologians and church leaders is to deal with legalism as imaginatively and tactfully as possible, broadening interpretation without breaching the religious "code" itself. At the same time, of course, theologians and other religious leaders must be sensitive to the legitimate grievances of groups seeking cultural and social and structural change. The urgency of the need for change is revealed in the presence in the feminist movement of "dedifferentiation," a rather common phenomenon in movements for change (Parsons, 1968c, 1977). As

Parsons notes, an important aspect of dedifferentiation is absolutism. That is to say, concern about a particular injustice is often so strong that it becomes exclusive; other important values are lost to sight; perspective becomes distorted. Some feminists are declaring that God is a woman. Compare them with certain black theologians, who declare that God is black. It would be difficult to find purer cases of dedifferentiation.

We should recognize, however, that this kind of rhetoric is often intended to wake people up. Dedifferentiation not only *symbolizes* dissatisfaction and alienation but also *signalizes* the actual presence and intensity of negative feelings. It may, therefore, alert others to existing weaknesses in solidarity and dangers to the continuity of pattern maintenance (and change). Being alerted, these others may bestir themselves to do something constructive about these weaknesses and dangers. In this sense symbolic or cultural "extremism," has, at a much more articulate level, a positive function somewhat resembling the positive function of what the insensitive call "senseless" violence: Both are "demonstrations" (Johnson, 1971, p. 350).

Nevertheless, the crisis in Christian symbolism may be less drastic than some feminists believe. It is remarkable how a religious tradition can adapt itself (although slowly) to challenges. For instance, it is a long way from the relatively passive expectant waiting of the early Christian church to the active innerworldly asceticism of the Reformation and later. Once the broad drift of the feminist movement becomes more widely accepted, we may definitely expect changes to occur in Judeo-Christian symbolism and interpretation:

1. There will be a greater emphasis on sexually equalitarian theology, with explicit rejection of "accidental" sexist overtones.

2. Scriptural passages in which the "central" theology is clear will be selectively emphasized and expounded.

3. The now-offensive aspects of mythology will be, quite honestly, explained away by being put in historical context.

4. As far as possible, without counterproductive obtrusiveness, the imagery itself will be treated in such a way as to emphasize central rather than peripheral meaning. For example, a spokesperson for the Church of Christ Scientist (the Christian Scientists)—a

man, by the way—in expounding Christian Science doctrine for outsiders, quite casually says, "Man is created in the image and the likeness of his divine father-mother, as the first chapter of Genesis makes clear" (see Stokes 1975, p. 70). This interpretation perhaps came the more easily because the founder of Christian Science was a woman.

5. The new consciousness will express itself in new stories, involving women as well as men in prominent positions, symbolizing new values as far as sexual differences are concerned; and some of these nonsacred stories (like the nonfeminist *The Christmas Carol* by Dickens) will acquire quasi-mythological influence (see the suggestive review article by Carol P. Christ, 1977).

6. Long before symbolism itself becomes radically changed, it will be possible (against opposition, to be sure) to install women as priests and ministers and church officials at all levels. Symbolism may have unconscious effectiveness, but it is not an invincible tyrant. Changes in the actual status of women will, in turn, have a tendency to highlight the "central" meaning of theology and make it increasingly clear that the apparently "sexist" aspects of mythology are "accidental."

The Ecumenical Movement

The problems raised by Shepherd's chapter on conversion and adhesion are rather complicated. "Adhesion" (or adhering to several religions at the same time) was quite natural in the archaic polytheistic world (Nock, 1933). The tendency toward adhesion today that Shepherd thinks he perceives has to be carefully scrutinized before one could interpret it securely.

We should attend to what Shepherd actually says. The main drift seems to be that people, being either anxious about the danger of nuclear war or eager to escape temporarily from the so-called iron cage of bureaucracy, care little about the intellectual aspects of religion and just want a distracting polysymbolic bath, a psychedelic, kaleidoscopic variety of religious symbolism, which they do not take very seriously. But, if we look more closely, we see several ambiguities. First, one should distinguish between mixing several religions at the same time and running through a succession of trials. Shepherd mentions that some of the religious attachments he is writing about are brief affairs, almost flirtations. Foss and Larkin give us some examples. Second, one should also distinguish carefully between (1) random assortments whose collectors seem to care nothing about overall integration and (2) other mixtures that *are* more or less integrated. Syncretism and eclecticism do not necessarily imply total lack of coherence. The Jesus and evangelical movements, however selective they may or may not be in their involvement in the Christian tradition, would hardly fit the category of adhesion unless their adherents were, say, Hari Krishna followers or Zen Buddhists at the same time. Third, Shepherd also mentions, in passing, that self-improvement techniques are also flourishing today, along with his polymorphous religions. All these varying points, it seems to me, are uncomfortably subsumed under the headings of adhesion and inclusivism. Several comments suggest themselves.

One, undoubtedly some magic is involved, as in the widespread use of astrology and other scientistic beliefs. Magic is probably not felt to be inconsistent with "religion" in the sense of a symbolic system having to do with ultimate meaning and the grounding of values. As Sagan notes, the combination of religion and magic is almost certainly universal. One might seek to reduce uncertainty and bad fortune within a very wide range of religious perspectives.

To be sure, magic has declined since the seventeenth century (see Thomas, 1971, chaps. 21, 22). For one thing, the growth of the scientific outlook has made more people aware that magic is a closed system (since anything that happens can be "explained"). The scientific outlook has also increased the drive to develop rational technology, which in turn, by reducing uncertainty, has reduced the "need" for magic. For these reasons, magic once accepted with little question, has tended to lose prestige and is widely regarded as superstition. One suspects, therefore, that resort to magic today is more common among the poorly educated than among the well educated, just as it is far more common among the nonliterate peoples than among the more advanced.

Yet one has to qualify these fairly obvious points. As Keith Thomas notes, anthropologists have long recognized that magic is expressive as well as quasi-instrumental. What Sagan calls "the feeling of omnipotence" may actually be a strong wish that something were so or might be so. Magic often expresses solidarity with others, and it always expresses concern and hope; but, precisely because it is a closed system, it never actually eliminates uncertainty: For various reasons within the system, it may *not* work. It may be that children at some point have the illusion of being omnipotent and may in a loose sense practice "magic," but the normal adult does not think him- or herself omnipotent, at least when he or she is in reasonably good shape. Anthropologists have observed that primitive magicians do not try to bring down the rain when rain will not come; they perform the rain rituals toward the end of the dry season, when the rain might come anyway.

Magic seems to be similar to a certain kind of prayer—the request or petition. Every worshiper knows that God may or may not fulfill such prayers, since his infinite wisdom may have a better plan. The difference, of course, as Sagan points out, is that the "theory" or conceptual system underlying magic is different from that underlying the religious prayer for this or that event. (I should imagine, also, that since prayer is connected with the sacred and magic often is not, prayer is probably less often associated with petty, immoral, or questionable wishes.)

It would not be very surprising, then, to find that magic is on the increase if anxiety, especially over personal problems, is increasing. Furthermore, a good deal of magic can slip through if it is called science, for, as Keith Thomas correctly observes, the prestige of science extends far beyond the circles in which the nature of science is at all clearly understood.

Two, insofar as modern "adhesion" involves dabbling *at the same time* or in close succession in several incompatible religions, properly speaking, then, if this dabbling is not simply harmless curiosity, one has to wonder whether it may not be a sign of a personal identity problem. In this age (as in New Testament times), many people may well be searching for meaning and a basis for integrity.

There are phenomena, however, superficially resembling malintegration or unstable identity, that are actually something else—something like an ecumenical impulse. Several deliberately syncretizing religions, such as Universalism, Baha'ism, and many "community churches," are based on the assumption that all religions are fundamentally alike or at least that all have elements of truth. These syncretizing or eclectic movements do not qualify as true cases of adhesion, however, because the integration of the different religions thus brought together is achieved through careful interpretation and selective emphasis. It is quite possible that some individuals do the same thing privately, "mixing their own," so to speak, as Shepherd suggests. All this, of course, would be quite compatible with the maintenance of a vigorous civil religion in Bellah's sense.

Ecumenism in Christian circles, more often than not, is a desire to unify or orchestrate the different branches of Christianity (Brown, 1969; Van der Bent, 1978), but it does also, at least at times, extend to sympathetic dialogue with other religious traditions.

Three, Tipton notes that Zen meditation can be used to gain self-control, which may then be used for a variety of purposes (and, one may add, within a variety of religious systems). As a religion, Zen has a cognitive or quasi-cognitive framework and a value system; but some of its practices can be treated as purely instrumental. However, as Max Weber observed, one should distinguish between more or less effective *techniques*, on the one hand, and religious rituals, on the other.

It seems to me, then, that ecumenicalism and fairly rigid exclusivism, both more or less combined with self-improvement and "magic," are more characteristic of the modern United States than is either amorphous religious eclecticism or true adhesion. The United States is religiously "inclusive" in the sense that it has institutionalized religious freedom and equality. This institutionalized inclusiveness, however, must be distinguished from indiscriminate inclusivism on the part of individuals.

"Materialism" and "Individualism" Under Attack

The Zen Buddhists of whom Steven Tipton writes feel that certain things in the modern world are unacceptable and that their new religious code, attitudes, and practices will gradually from small centers spread out, like Paul's little Christian communities, and eventually, perhaps, eliminate or transform these unacceptable things, among which, apparently, are a rigid ethic, a selfish individualism or utilitarianism, concern for social status, waste and spoiling of the environment, and large-scale organizations in which human relationships are squeezed into the instrumental requirements of production. The new ideal is spontaneous self-expression that is at the same time disciplined and oriented to others.

The Zen Buddhists who live in "ideal" communities are perhaps only the "dedifferentiating" extremists. Tipton himself here and there calls attention to continuity as well as discontinuity with traditional American values. Further, like Foss and Larkin, he notes that generational experience must be taken into account in our interpretations of new religious movements; thus Zen Buddhism and similar Eastern movements may or may not give us a clue to what the religious orientation of the fairly distant future will look like.

It is by now almost a commonplace that there is going on in American society a shift of emphasis from the instrumental to the expressive (to use the terms Parsons has made familiar). But this is probably not an absolute shift (see Parsons and Platt, 1973; Parsons, 1975); that is, it is not likely that the expressive will push the instrumental out or even become dominant. There is perhaps some irony in the fact that the very success of Western civilization in raising the material conditions of life has made it possible now to give more attention to spiritual and high cultural concerns (see White, 1961). It is significant that the disaffection from "materialism" is strongest in the broadly middle-class college population, who tend to take it for granted that they will have shelter and enough to eat. At the lower end of the stratificational system, many jobs hold no prospect of anything but a routine future as far as the possibility of creative contributions is concerned: People in these dead-end jobs relax and get whatever fulfillment they can from their leisure. In keeping with this emphasis, it is notable that there is (quite understandably) absolutely no discernible diminution of interest in "materialistic" matters such as higher pay and better working conditions. Marie Augusta Neal takes it for granted that complete equality of opportunity for women would mean that some women, as well as some men, would take superior status as a goal, a reward, and an opportunity for achievement, that is, for contributing to human welfare.

As Parsons's chapter in this book should make clear, utilitarianism and individualism are very ambiguous (see also Parsons, 1977). Utilitarianism as an ideological movement did indeed stress the rational pursuit of self-interest, but the utilitarians tended to take for granted (without reflection) the operation of social institutions that are not rational at all in the sense that suggests expedient pursuit of self-interest. Radical opposition to all individualism is another case of dedifferentiation. It is true, as Parsons shows in his chapter, that an ideological bias he calls the "economic approach" or "establishment economism" still assumes that almost all social good comes from the individual pursuit of self-interest. It is also true, however, that this distorted ideology tends to ignore or play down the actual importance of such nonrational factors as social values and institutional norms. Pure selfishness is not so rampant as this ideology may lead us to suppose. Utilitarian ideology does, of course, continue to exist and need correction, as much from social science as from religion.

Related to the tendency to take utilitarianism at face value is the tendency to think of "individualism" as something necessarily selfish and antisocial. The analysis of ascetic Protestantism, however, should make us skeptical. A debated question, to be sure, is whether the values of ascetic Protestantism have died out. It is unlikely that they have, however, if we consider that in this supposedly cynical and materialistic society people are still intensely interested in *how* they and others make money and achieve "success."

To take up another theme, the ideal of harmony between duty and inclination is not new. It is strong in the whole Judeo-Christian tradition. The aim of the American Zen Buddhists as described by Tipton is not entirely different from the aim of Christians as prescribed by Calvin and his successors (see Little, 1969). The chief difference is that Zen Buddhism is perhaps less active and optimistic. It seems to be close to the goal of adjusting to the world, whereas Western Christianity, especially since the Reformation, has been closer to the goal of mastery over the world. It seems to me, in any case, that we ought to have a healthy skepticism concerning attempts in the modern world to suppress the self. Concern for self-esteem may be regarded as universal: What must be weighed, judged, and possibly criticized is the culturally dominant standard or standards for self-esteem. Here again, the Judeo-Christian cultural tradition has always pressed toward service to others and toward humility in self-estimation. This ideal is presumably just about as difficult for Zen Buddhism to achieve on a wide scale as it has been for Christianity.

What social scientists should avoid, it seems to me, is the dedifferentiation, at both extremes, that Parsons analyzes so well: *either* establishment economism *or* revulsion against all forms of individualism and all calculation of self-interest. In another article, which should be better known, Parsons emphasizes that there are *four* kinds of formal organization, not just bureaucracy and the market, and that it is doctrinaire to assert in general for all situations that just one of the four—say, the democratic association— should prevail, rather than a variable mix of the four types (see Parsons, 1968b, 1957).

In any case, it is unlikely that Western societies will sink or rise into mystical devaluation of "the world" in the sense that would involve rejecting "materialism," status seeking, and effective organization. Any kind of ambitious goal attainment requires the coordination of differentiated contributions. It is inconceivable that the difficult problems of avoiding nuclear war, protecting the environment, and developing alternative sources of energy might be solved without sophisticated technology and extensive formal organization. Responsible, public-spirited men and women will continue to regard these problems as challenges to be overcome, as people in the West have worked for centuries to overcome disease, illiteracy, religious bigotry, racism, drought, and poor yields of grain.

We are already moving toward important changes; my impression is that there is a growing tendency to become aware of the social and "human" costs of economic activities (to demand a more realistic societal accounting), a tendency to shift the balance between productivity and enjoyable work toward the latter (where there is a conflict), a tendency to see that eventually we might be better off if we did not depend on fossil fuels. But all these tendencies and others will not do away with planning and organization. Planning and organization, with differential authority, will be required indefinitely if only for the basic problems of achieving and maintaining high general levels of education, health care, justice through law, and world peace.

Further, it seems unlikely that the West will quietly retrogress while Asia and Africa are in general struggling to develop effective "materialistic" organizations. Cheng's chapter in this book is a reminder of the more general tendency in the world at large. Religion itself will tend to be judged relative to its consonance or dissonance with such broad goals as the ones I have mentioned.

Notes

1. At least two commentators have cited Parsons (1966, p. 113) as warrant for calling him a cultural determinist. Only extreme superficiality or carelessness, however, would leave such a statement unqualified. The very sentence these commentators quote (in part) and, even more, the context as a whole (pp. 109–115) make it absolutely clear that Parsons, like Max Weber, recognizes that culture and conditions interact and are both important and that, under certain conditions and after perhaps severe conflicts, cultural values may gain a kind of cybernetic control in social systems. This control is quite different, however, from determination. The passage in question is well worth careful study.

References

Alexander, J. C. "Formal and Substantive Voluntarism in the Work of Talcott Parsons: A Theoretical and Ideological Reinterpretation." *American Sociological Review,* 1978, *43,* 177–98.

Bellah, R. N. "Civil Religion in America." In *Beyond Belief.* New York: Harper & Row, 1970a.

Bellah, R. N. "Religious Evolution." In *Beyond Belief.* New York: Harper & Row, 1970b.

Bornkamm, G. *The New Testament: A Guide to Its Writings.* (R. H. Fuller and I. Fuller, Trans.) Philadelphia: Fortress, 1973.

Bourricaud, F. *L'individualisme institutionnel: essai sur la sociologie de Talcott Parsons.* Paris: Presses Universitaires de France, 1977.

Brown, R. M. " 'Secular Ecumenism': The Direction of the Future." In D. R. Cutler (Ed.), *The Religious Situation: 1969*. Boston: Beacon Press, 1969.

Christ, C. P. "The New Feminist Theology: A Review of the Literature." *Religious Studies Review*, 1977, *3* (4), 203–212.

Dumont, L. *Homo Hierarchicus: The Caste System and Its Implications*. (M. Sainsbury, Trans.) Chicago: University of Chicago Press, 1970.

Eisenstadt, S. N. "The Protestant Ethic Thesis in an Analytical and Comparative Framework." In S. N. Eisenstadt (Ed.), *The Protestant Ethic and Modernization: A Comparative View*. New York: Basic Books, 1968.

Eisenstadt, S. N. "The Implications of Weber's Sociology of Religion for Understanding Processes of Change in Contemporary Non-European Societies and Civilizations." In C. Y. Glock and P. E. Hammond (Eds.), *Beyond the Classics? Essays in the Scientific Study of Religion*. New York: Harper & Row, 1973.

Frye, N. *The Critical Path: An Essay on the Social Context of Literary Criticism*. Bloomington: Indiana University Press, 1971.

Fuller, L. L. "Law and Human Interaction." In H. M. Johnson (Ed.), *Social System and Legal Process*. San Francisco: Jossey-Bass, 1978. Also in *Sociological Inquiry*, 1977, *47* (3–4), 59–89.

Garsoïan, N. G. "Early Byzantium," "Later Byzantium," and "The Ottoman Empire." In J. A. Garraty and P. Gay (Eds.), *The Columbia History of the World*. New York: Harper & Row, 1972.

Johnson, H. M. "Stability and Change in Ethnic-Group Relations." In B. Barber and A. Inkeles (Eds.), *Stability and Social Change*. Boston: Little, Brown, 1971.

Kaufman, G. D. *God the Problem*. Cambridge, Mass.: Harvard University Press, 1972.

Küng, H. *On Being a Christian*. (E. Quinn, Trans.) New York: Doubleday, 1976.

Little, D. *Religion, Order, and Law: A Study in Pre-Revolutionary England*. New York: Harper & Row, 1969.

Loubser, J. J. "Calvinism, Equality, and Inclusion: The Case of Afrikaner Calvinism." In S. N. Eisenstadt (Ed.), *The Protestant Ethic and Modernization: A Comparative View*. New York: Basic Books, 1968.

MacInnis, D. E. "Maoism and Religion in China Today." In D. R. Cutler (Ed.), *The Religious Situation: 1969*. Boston: Beacon Press, 1969.

Merton, R. K. "Science, Technology and Society in Seventeenth-Century England." *Osiris*, 1938, *4* (2), 360–362.

Minear, P. S. *Images of the Church in the New Testament*. Phildelphia: Westminster Press, 1960.

Nelson, B. "Weber's Protestant Ethic: Its Origins, Wanderings, and Foreseeable Futures." In C. Y. Glock and P. E. Hammond (Eds.), *Beyond the Classics? Essays in the Scientific Study of Religion*. New York: Harper & Row, 1973.

Nikiprowetzky, V. "Ethical Monotheism." *Daedalus*, 1975, *104* (2), 69–89.

Nock, A. D. *Conversion*. New York: Oxford University Press, 1933.

Parsons, T. *The Structure of Social Action*. New York: McGraw-Hill, 1937.

Parsons, T. "The Distribution of Power in American Society." *World Politics*, 1957, *10*, 123–143. Reprinted in *Structure and Process in Modern Society* (New York: Free Press, 1960) and in *Politics and Social Structure* (New York: Free Press, 1969).

Parsons, T. *Societies: Evolutionary and Comparative Perspectives*. Englewood Cliffs, N.J.: Prentice-Hall, 1966.

Parsons, T. "Commentary" [on Clifford Geertz, "Religion as a Cultural System"]. In D. R. Cutler (Ed.), *The Religious Situation: 1968*. Boston: Beacon Press, 1968a.

Parsons, T. "Components and Types of Formal Organization." In P. P. LeBreton (Ed.), *Comparative Administration Theory*. Seattle: University of Washington Press, 1968b.

Parsons, T. "On the Concept of Value Commitments." *Sociological Inquiry*, 1968c, *38* (2), 135–160. Reprinted in T. Parsons, *Politics and Social Structure*. New York: Free Press, 1969.

Parsons, T. "The Problem of Polarization on the Axis of Color." In J. H. Franklin (Ed.), *Color and Race*. Boston: Beacon Press, 1968d.

Parsons, T. "Full Citizenship for the Negro American?" In *Politics and Social Structure*. New York: Free Press, 1969.

Parsons, T. *The System of Modern Societies*. Englewood Cliffs, N.J.: Prentice-Hall, 1971.

Parsons, T. "Interview with Talcott Parsons." *Revue Européenne des Sciences Sociales et Cahiers Vilfredo Pareto,* 1975, *13* (34), 81–90.

Parsons, T. "Law as an Intellectual Stepchild." *Sociological Inquiry,* 1977, *47* (3–4), 11–58. Also in H. M. Johnson (Ed.), *Social System and Legal Process* (San Francisco, Jossey-Bass, 1977).

Parsons, T. and Platt, G. M. *The American University.* Cambridge, Mass.: Harvard University Press, 1973.

Rose, H. J. *Religion in Greece and Rome.* New York: Harper & Row, 1959.

Sandmel, S. "Review of Hans Küng, *On Being a Christian.*" *Religious Studies Review,* 1978, *4* (2), 99–101.

Santayana, G. *The Life of Reason.* In I. Edman (Ed.), *The Philosophy of Santayana.* New York: Random House, no date. (Originally published 1905–1906.)

Smelser, N. J. *Social Change in the Industrial Revolution: An Application of Theory to the British Cotton Industry.* Chicago: University of Chicago Press, 1959.

Stokes, J. B. "What Is a Christian Scientist?" In L. Rosten (Ed.), *Religions of America.* New York: Simon & Schuster, 1975.

Thomas, K. *Religion and the Decline of Magic: Studies in Popular Beliefs in Sixteenth- and Seventeenth-Century England.* London: Weidenfeld and Nicolson, 1971.

Van der Bent, A. J. *What in the World is the World Council of Churches?* Geneva: World Council of Churches, 1978.

Weber, M. *The Protestant Ethic and the Spirit of Capitalism.* (T. Parsons, Trans.) New York: Scribner's, 1958. (Originally published 1904–1905.)

Weber, M. "Author's Introduction." In M. Weber, *The Protestant Ethic and the Spirit of Capitalism.* (T. Parsons, Trans.) New York: Scribner's, 1958. (Originally published 1920.)

White, W. *Beyond Conformity.* New York: Free Press, 1961.

Young L. C., and Ford, S. R. "God Is Society: The Religious Dimension of Maoism." *Sociological Inquiry,* 1977, *47* (2), 89–97.

Index

Women (Continued)
tionship, 238–241; as missionaries, 230, 232; movement by, characteristics of, 220–221; as nuns and sisters, 232–233; ordination of, 234–238, 242; in religious symbolism, 225–230, 326–329; and social movements, 233–234; subordination of, 218–221; as witches, 231–232
Wood, G. S., 206, 217
World Christian Liberation Front, as postmovement group, 264
World Council of Churches, 230–231
Worship, objective and subjective types of, 56–57
Wright, A. F., 170, 189–190
Wright, G. E., 139, 149
Wright, M. C., 176, 190
Wu, J. C. H., 170, 190

Y

Yahweh, 95, 113, 114, 123, 125–126, 128, 129, 130, 131–132, 134
Yahwism: characteristics of, 123–126; and end of Judahite state, 129–131; and monarchy, 127–129; sociological context of, 120–123

Yang, C. K., 170, 190
Yankelovich, D., 265, 285
Young, L. C., 320, 339
Youth Against War and Fascism, as postmovement group, 266
Yuan Shih-k'ai, 175, 178, 181, 184
Yuhaus, G. J., 247

Z

Zalman, S., 154, 156–157, 158, 163
Zaddiks: analysis of, 150–167; diversity of, 155–158; and divine coitus, 161–165; hereditary nature of, 151, 164; history of, 151; Lurianic creation myth related to, 160–165; and magic, 152, 155, 157; nature of authority of, 152–154; problems of, 163–164; structural strains and charisma of, 154–158
Zborowski, M., 161, 167
Zen Buddhism: and antinomianism, 291, 292, 300; and ecology, 298–300, 303, 304–310; and ethics, 290–294; moral and social responsibility in, 295–300; and social change, 316, 318, 332–333, 334–335
Zusya of Hanipol, 154